WORLD CITIES

YESTERDAY AND TODAY

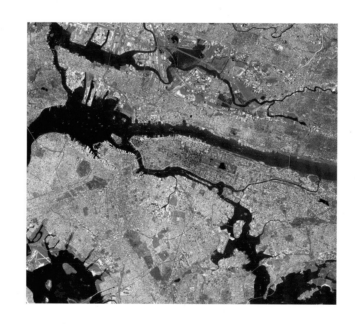

PALA
PRAGAE QVO

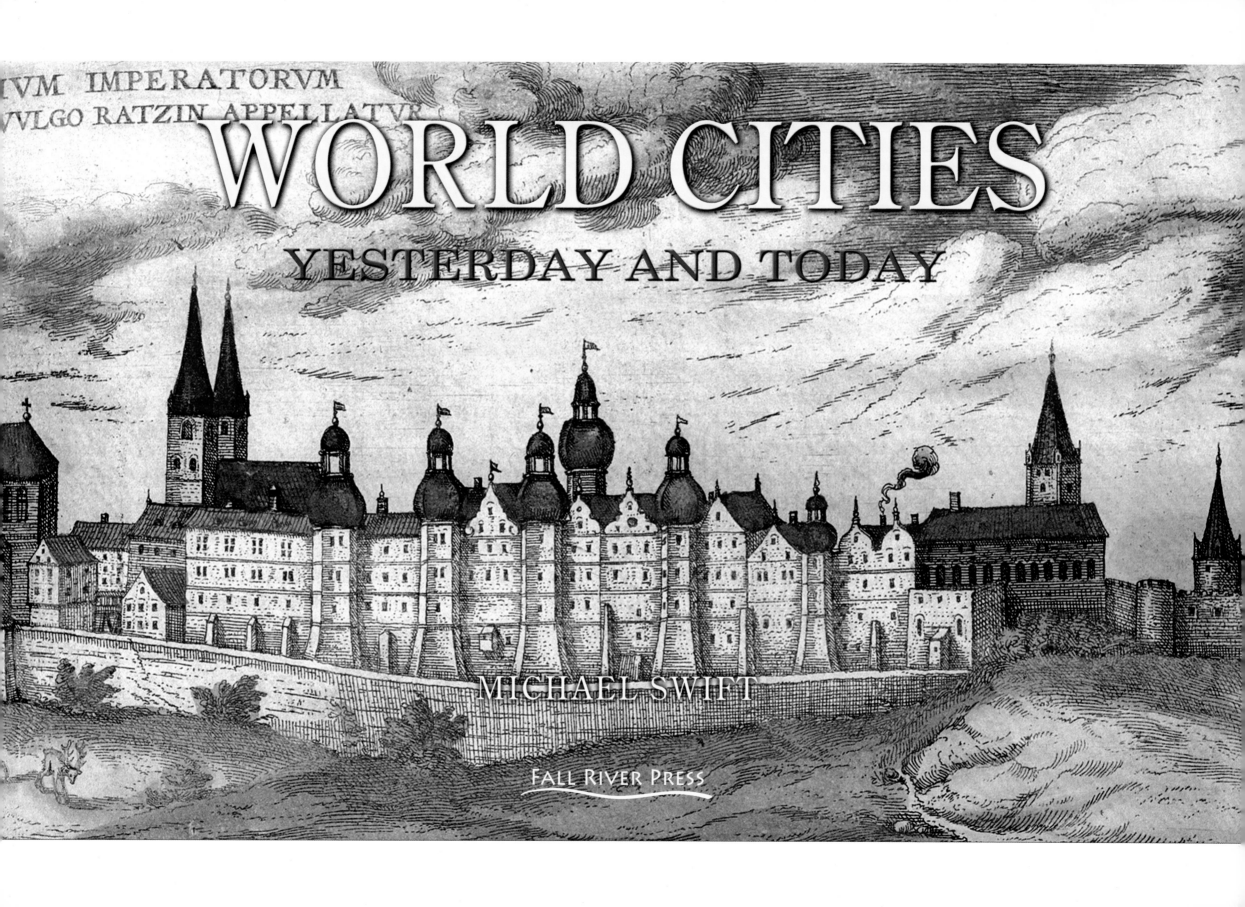

IVM IMPERATORVM
VVLGO RATZIN APPELLATVR

WORLD CITIES

YESTERDAY AND TODAY

MICHAEL SWIFT

Fall River Press

This 2009 edition published by Fall River Press, by arrangement with Compendium Publishing Ltd.

Editor: Rebecca Snelling
Designer: Compendium Design/Danny Gillespie

Fall River Press
122 Fifth Avenue
New York, NY 10011

ISBN: 978-1-4351-1435-7

Printed in China through Printworks Int. Ltd.

1 3 5 7 9 10 8 6 4 2

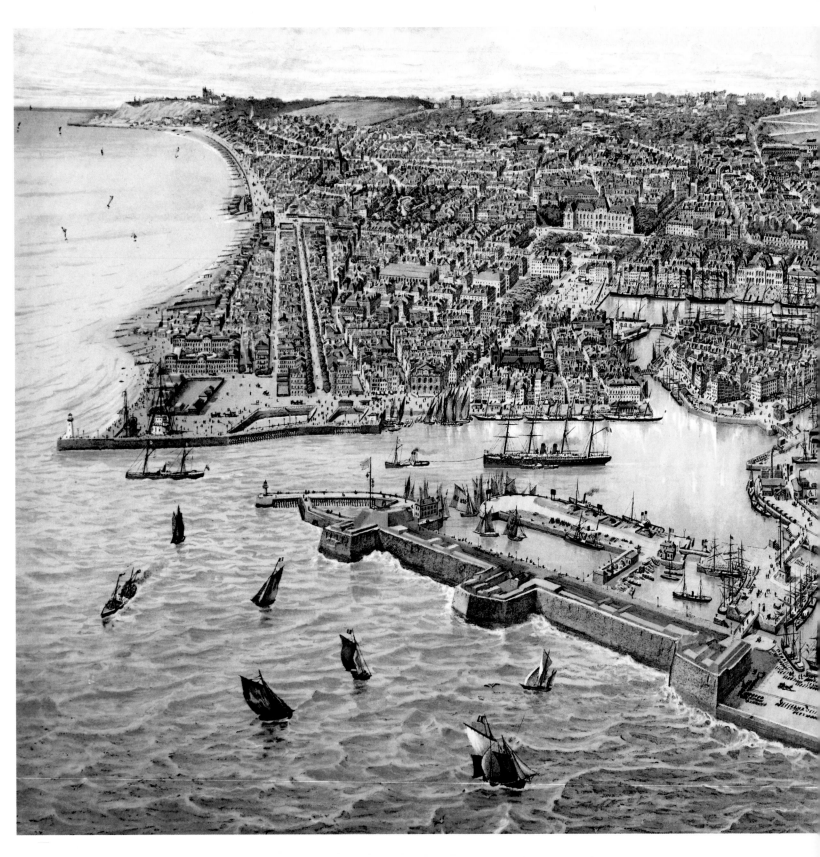

PAGE 1: Satellite image of Manhattan and the other four boroughs of New York City. *See page 174*

PAGES 2-3: Prague. *See page 202*

RIGHT: Le Havre. *See page 119*

CONTENTS

INTRODUCTION

In the history of mankind the growth of cities is a relatively recent phenomenon. The concentration of large numbers of people in a single area could not be sustained until human society developed in such a way as to permit commerce and the construction of structures, such as drainage, without which such a concentration could not operate. In 1950 the Australian philologist and archaeologist Gordon Childe posited the theory that it was possible to define an ancient city based upon ten basic precepts. These included: the fact that not all residents produced their own food and that this led, therefore, to the development of specialist trades; that there were monumental public buildings; that there was trade in raw materials; and that there was a system of taxation.

All of the great ancient civilizations developed urban centers. In the western world, the first were those based in Mesopotamia—modern-day Iraq—such as Eridu, Ur, and Uruk, which date back some 7,500 years; while in the east the Indus Valley civilization, in the northern part of the Indian subcontinent, has settlements dating back some 5,000 years. As the great ancient empires grew, so the importance of urban settlement—for defense, trading, and the demonstration of power—grew ever more significant. In Greece, Asia Minor, Italy, and North Africa, the final millennium of the era before the birth of Christ was to witness massive urbanization with cities such as Athens and Rome becoming prominent.

By the end of the 1st century B.C. it has been estimated that Rome housed a population of some one million residents; such was the scale of the city as it continued to grow through the next centuries that it was not until the 19th century that modern cities started to achieve a population level similar to Rome before its decline in the 5th century A.D.

In the development of cities there were a number of factors that were crucial. A city could only survive if food and other goods could be easily transported to it; thus the city's location adjacent to trading routes was essential. The supply of fresh water was often crucial, and so proximity to a river or a supply of water was a prerequisite. It is no coincidence that the earliest settlements in Mesopotamia were located within the verdant lands supported by the rivers Tigris and Euphrates. A third consideration—and hugely significant in an age when life was undoubtedly nasty, brutish, and short—was defense. Cities, with their concentration of wealth and population—the latter ideal for trading as slaves if captured—were ready targets. Most of the cities featured in this book had their initial boundaries set by the construction of city walls or other fortifications, and many were to suffer severely during war. It was only in the late 18th and early 19th centuries, as military techniques and equipment improved, that the traditional walls proved inadequate and were swept away.

Many of the cities grew up from relatively small trading posts; there was little or no pre-planning of the street layouts and the facilities, such as water supply or drainage, were often inadequate, leading to disease and other social problems. Historically, however, some cities were more rigorously planned. Many of the Roman settlements grew up out of erstwhile military fortifications and had a grid pattern of streets linked to the main gates; even today, it is possible to recognize the historic Roman street pattern underlying major centers with Roman origins. The pre-planning of cities was considerably easier when the settlements were "new build"—such as many of those built in North America after the European settlement. The grid pattern of cities such as New York arose as a result of defined building plots being carved from undeveloped land.

Although the number of cities grew after the decline of Rome, they were relatively small, with their populations numbered in the low thousands. Trade remained an essential driving force for further urbanization with organizations such as the Hanseatic League encouraging commerce. However, it would not be until the late 18th and early 19th centuries that factors evolved that would see the massive growth in the urban population of the world. In many respects the cities of the post-Renaissance World were not greatly different in scale to those that preceded the Renaissance, although perhaps having grander public buildings and private residences, but most of this development had taken place within the cities' existing boundaries. Three primary factors were to result in the massive growth of the great cities over the past 200 years.

These three factors were the Industrial Revolution, the Transport Revolution, and huge population growth. The first of these resulted in the growth of great industrial works—from iron works to textile mills, from potteries to car factories—that required the huge concentration of people. Initially much of this new industry was water-powered and so ribbon development along fast-flowing rivers and streams occurred; once steam power was harnessed, however, industry could be based anywhere and this led to the concentration of trades into certain areas, such as the cotton industry around Manchester and, a century later, to the car industry around Detroit. It was, however, all very well to be able to produce vast amounts of industrial goods but without the means of moving the raw materials and finished goods to and from the market, the Industrial Revolution would have failed. The late 18th century, with the construction of canals, and the 19th, with the development of railways, ensured that the Transport Revolution was able to support this massive growth in industrial production. The improvement in

The greatest city of ancient times, Rome would not be surpassed until the Industrial Revolution swelled European urban populations to over a million souls. This is Ancient Rome from *Civitates Orbis Terrarum*, the first systematic depiction of cities from throughout the known world, published in six volumes between 1572 and 1617. It contained mainly contemporary views of cities from the New World to India with the occasional historic survey. Printed in Cologne, the atlas eventually contained a total of 546 engravings of cities; some of the illustrations were maps, others were oblique prospects. The series was edited principally by Georg Braun (1541–1622), a cleric from Cologne who was dean at the city's cathedral, with the majority of the engravings—some 363 in total—undertaken by Franz Hogenberg (1535–1590). Following Hogenberg's death, the fifth and sixth volumes—published in 1598 and 1617 respectively—were completed by Simon van den Neuwel (Novellanus). *The Stapleton Collection/Bridgeman*

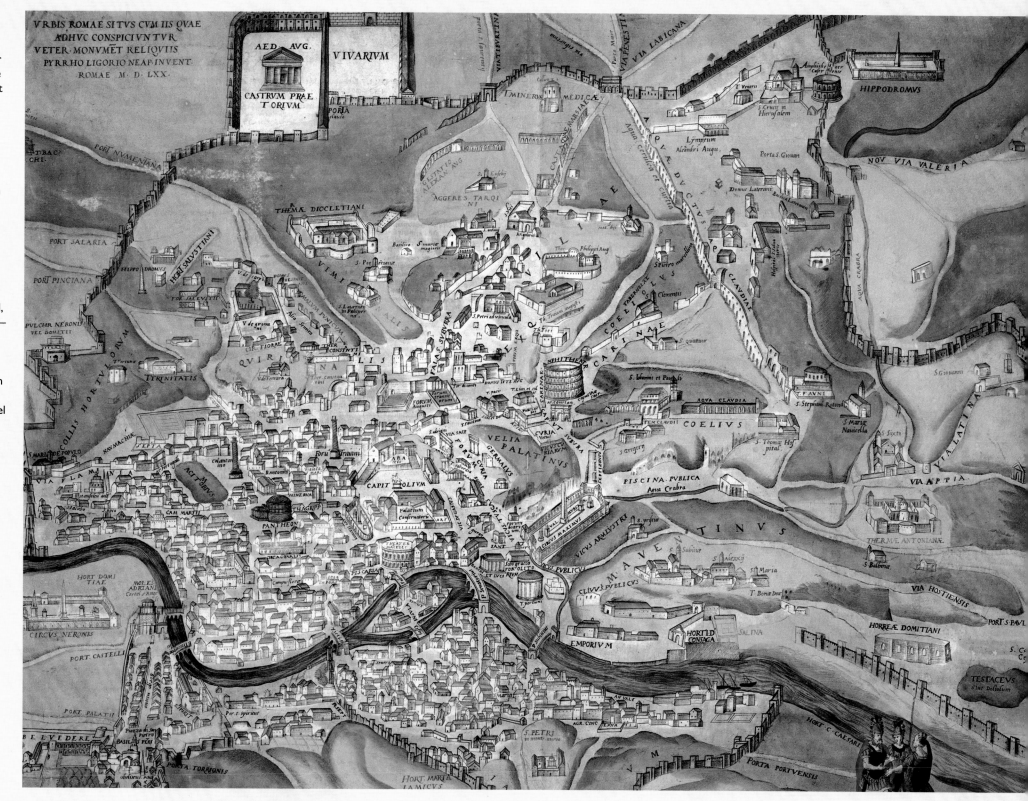

RIGHT: The maps produced by Braun and Hogenberg relied upon the work of earlier cartographers or upon the researches of the Antwerp artist Joris (Georg) Hoefnagal (1542–1600), who travelled widely through western Europe drawing maps for the *Civitates*. After Hoefnagal's death, his son Jakob (1575–1630) continued to undertake research for the project. For northern Europe, Braun and Hogenberg relied largely upon the work of the Danish cartographer Heinrich van Rantzau (1526–1599), better known to cartographers as Rantzovius. Other sources included the maps of Sebastian Munster (1489–1552), produced in the middle of the 16th century and the unpublished works of Jacob van Deventer (also known as Jacob Roelofsz; 1505–1575). In all, *Civitates* drew upon the work of over 100 other artists and cartographers. This is Jerusalem. Note Golgotha at upper left.

BELOW: Frontispiece of the Fifth Volume of *Civitates Orbis Terrarum. Archivo Iconografico, S.A./Corbis*

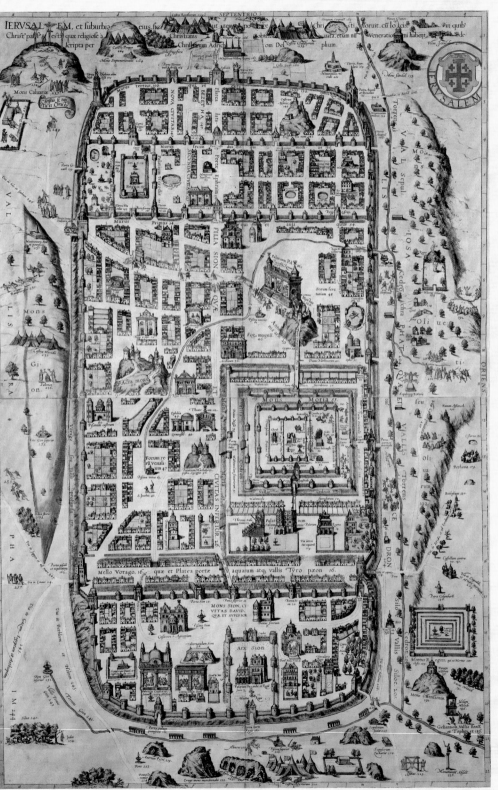

transport provision was also essential for the growth of cities in that it allowed for the efficient and rapid movement of foodstuffs from the agricultural centers. The third and final factor was the huge growth in the population in those societies undergoing industrialization. Such was the scale of the population growth that traditional agriculture could no longer support it; this led to significant migration from countryside to city and from country to country—a process that continues today.

Cartography is a graphic way to explore how cities have evolved. Maps record the physical nature of a city and its changes. Originally they were surveyed by physically recording the street plans and buildings. However, as with other arts, the skills of the cartographers have improved immeasurably over the years as has their equipment. This improvement will be evident by comparing the maps in this book. The earliest date back to the 16th century, when the impact of the Renaissance first led to renewed practice of cartography. The factors behind the production of the maps varied—from a desire purely to record the physical nature of a city for commercial gain, through to the desire of the military to gain detailed knowledge—and these factors continue to pertain through the period of the book. It is perhaps no coincidence that the United Kingdom's primary cartographic business—the Ordnance Survey—started its career as a branch of the military.

The earliest cartographers had little more than the most basic equipment to assist them; as technology has improved, so too have the tools available to them. From the early 20th century aircraft were used for the gathering of information, a process that continues to this day with the latest software for example, permitting the development of three-dimensional imagery. However, the most significant change over the past fifty years has been the ability to obtain images from space. These dramatic images show in great detail how far the world is now dominated by great urban centers and how far these cities have developed since their origins at the dawn of human civilization.

HOW TO USE THIS BOOK

Brief history of city

Color boxes show the area covered by maps.

Modern satellite image showing all or significant portion of city.

Color key around maps links back to boxes on satellite view

Locator globe showing city's position

ALEXANDRIA

egypt

Now the second largest city in Egypt with a population in excess of four million, Alexandria (once known as the "Pearl of the Mediterranean") is the country's most important sea port—a role that it has been fulfilling for more than 2,000 years. Its name derives from its founder, Alexander the Great, who established the city in 332 B.C. Alexandria was the center of Hellenistic rule in the Nile delta and provided a link between the Greek and Egyptian cultures. During the pre-Christian era it was renowned as the home of one of the great libraries of the world and of one of the Seven Wonders of the Ancient World—the Pharos (lighthouse).

By the 2nd century B.C. the city was coming under Roman influence and it was in Alexandria that the great love story of Cleopatra , Julius Caesar, and Mark Antony was played out to its tragic conclusion.

Following the gradual decline in the power of Rome, Alexandria became part of the Byzantine Empire centered on Constantinople. Under Arab rule the capital of Egypt was transferred to Al-Fustat—see Cairo on page 50—and Alexandria's political and economic importance declined. However, the city was still a place of grandeur with—according to the victorious Arab general—some 4,000 palaces, 4,000 baths, 12,000 gardeners, and 4,000 places of amusement, although its library had been destroyed.

During the Arab rule several mosques were constructed, but there was also a spirit of religious toleration that permitted the city's Christian minority to practise their faith and new churches were built during the 12th and 13th centuries. However, the medieval period saw further decline of the city as a commercial center, and by the 13th century the canal linking the city to the Nile had silted up.

On July 2, 1798, Emperor Napoleon seized the city as part of his campaign in Egypt. The city remained in French hands until it was captured by the British. Alexandria (with the rest of Egypt) was restored to Ottoman rule in 1802, but the country was effectively self-governing thereafter.

In July 1882, the British Royal Navy bombarded the city in support of a nationalist uprising led by Arabi Pasha (1839–1911). British interest in the region had been fostered by the construction of the Suez Canal between 1859 and 1866, and in 1914 Egypt became a British Protectorate, a status it held until 1922 when the British established a constitutional monarchy. This survived until a coup in 1952, when Gamal Abdel Nasser (1918–70) came to power.

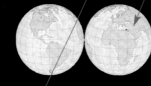

BELOW: This image of Alexandria was taken by astronauts on board the International Space Station in December 2002 using an Electronic Still Camera.

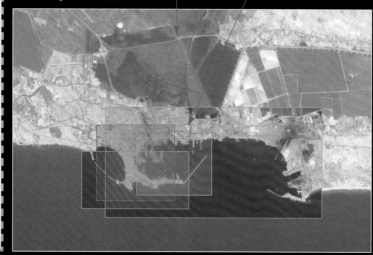

10

LEFT: This view from the north shows the city shortly after Egypt had been conquered by the Ottoman Empire. In the foreground can be seen the old harbor; this had fallen into disuse by the 16th century to be replaced by a new one to the east. Prominent to the east of the harbor is the Pharos, the 3rd-century B.C. lighthouse that was one of the Seven Wonders of the Ancient World. It had been destroyed in an earthquake in the early 16th century and replaced by a fortress by the time this map was drawn. In the center is the Abbu El-Abbas Mosque; this had been rebuilt in the late 15th century and was again to be rebuilt in the 18th. In the 1st century B.C. Queen Cleopatra arranged for three ancient obelisks to be moved to the city—two of these can be seen adjacent to the city walls on the east. These were relocated in the 19th century to London, New York, and Paris. In the southeast corner of the map is the Nile Gate. By the 16th century the canal, which linked the city to the River Nile, had become largely silted up and food and other material was brought to the city by camel train.

11

ALEXANDRIA

EGYPT

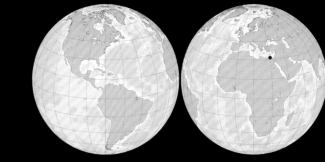

Now the second largest city in Egypt with a population in excess of four million, Alexandria (once known as the "Pearl of the Mediterranean") is the country's most important sea port—a role that it has been fulfilling for more than 2,000 years. Its name derives from its founder, Alexander the Great, who established the city in 332B.C. Alexandria was the center of Hellenistic rule in the Nile delta and provided a link between the Greek and Egyptian cultures. During the pre-Christian era it was renowned as the home of one of the great libraries of the world and of one of the Seven Wonders of the Ancient World—the Pharos (lighthouse).

By the 2nd century B.C. the city was coming under Roman influence and it was in Alexandria that the great love story of Cleopatra, Julius Caesar, and Mark Antony was played out to its tragic conclusion.

Following the gradual decline in the power of Rome, Alexandria became part of the Byzantine Empire centered on Constantinople. Under Arab rule the capital of Egypt was transferred to Al-Fustat—see Cairo on page 50—and Alexandria's political and economic importance declined. However, the city was still a place of grandeur with—according to the victorious Arab general—some 4,000 palaces, 4,000 baths, 12,000 gardeners, and 4,000 places of amusement, although its library had been destroyed.

During the Arab rule several mosques were constructed, but there was also a spirit of religious toleration that permitted the city's Christian minority to practise their faith and new churches were built during the 12th and 13th centuries. However, the medieval period saw further decline of the city as a commercial center, and by the 13th century the canal linking the city to the Nile had silted up.

On July 2, 1798, Emperor Napoleon seized the city as part of his campaign in Egypt. The city remained in French hands until it was captured by the British. Alexandria (with the rest of Egypt) was restored to Ottoman rule in 1802, but the country was effectively self-governing thereafter.

In July 1882, the British Royal Navy bombarded the city in support of a nationalist uprising led by Arabi Pasha (1839–1911). British interest in the region had been fostered by the construction of the Suez Canal between 1859 and 1866, and in 1914 Egypt became a British Protectorate, a status it held until 1922 when the British established a constitutional monarchy. This survived until a coup in 1952, when Gamal Abdel Nasser (1918–70) came to power.

BELOW: This image of Alexandria was taken by astronauts on board the International Space Station in December 2002 using an Electronic Still Camera.

ALEXANDRIA, vetuftiffimum Ægypti emporium, Amplifsima ciuitas, ab Alexandro Magno condita, muris, turri- et propugnaculis ea forma, qua heic depicta videtur, ante Cirifti aduentum, Annis CCC.XX. conftructa fuit, magnifica olim, et nunc quoque bene munita confpicitur, fed intra moenia ruinis, et ruderis plena, Magnitudine Lutetia Parifiorum respondet.

ALEXA   NDR   IA.

LEFT: This view from the north shows the city shortly after Egypt had been conquered by the Ottoman Empire. In the foreground can be seen the old harbor; this had fallen into disuse by the 16th century to be replaced by a new one to the east (left). Prominent to the east of the harbor is the Pharos, the 3rd-century B.C. lighthouse that was one of the Seven Wonders of the Ancient World. It had been destroyed in an earthquake in the early 16th century and replaced by a fortress by the time this map was drawn. In the center is the Abbu El-Abbas Mosque; this had been rebuilt in the late 15th century and was again to be rebuilt in the 18th. In the 1st century B.C. Queen Cleopatra arranged for three ancient obelisks to be moved to the city—two of these can be seen adjacent to the city walls on the east. These were relocated in the 19th century to London, New York, and Paris. In the southeast corner of the map is the Nile Gate. By the 16th century the canal, which linked the city to the River Nile, had become largely silted up and food and other material was brought to the city by camel train.

MEDITERR   ANEVM   MARE

PLAN-GUIDE

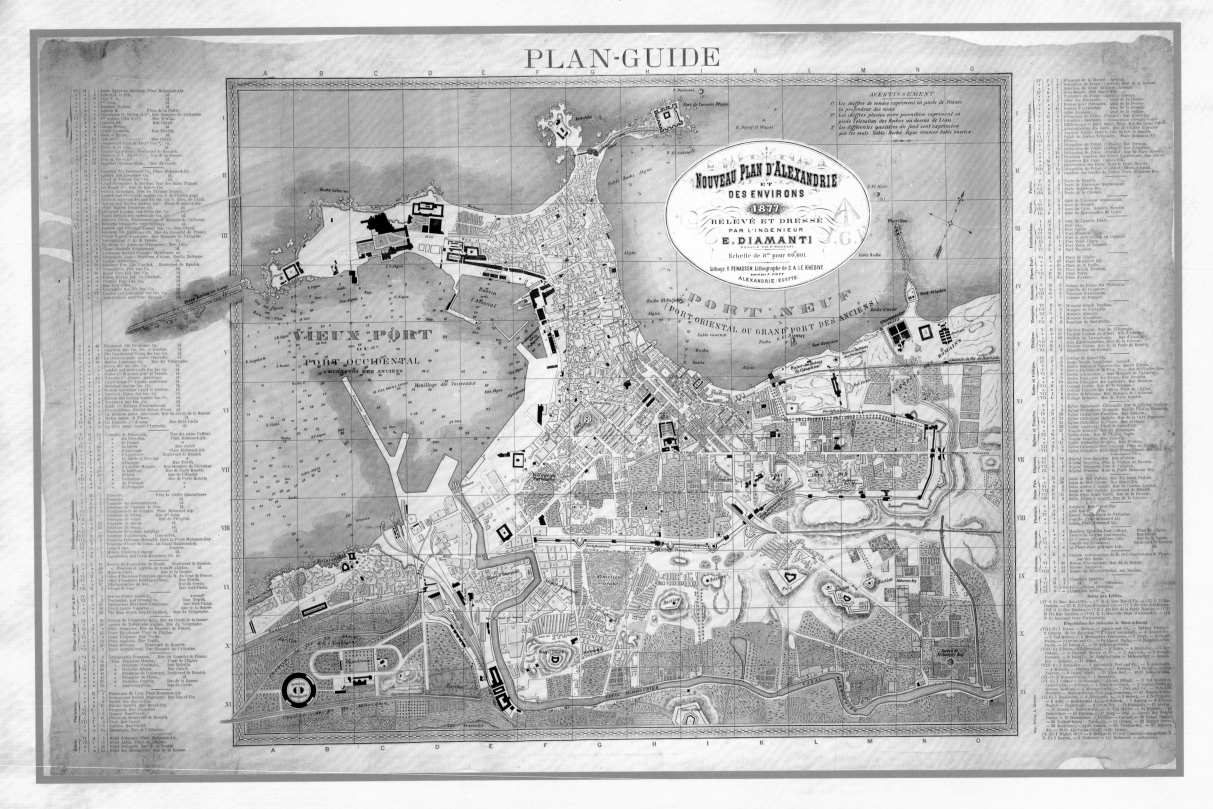

LEFT: Described as the "Nouveau plan d'Alexandrie et des Environs" (New plan of Alexandria and its Environs), this French-language map of the city was produced in 1877 by E. Diamanti. The French, like the British, had cause to increase their interest in Egypt as a result of the opening of the Suez Canal, and the final decades of the 19th century witnessed some regional rivalry between Britain and France as both sought to take advantage of the declining power of the Ottoman Empire. In Egypt, it was the British that ultimately triumphed, although the British Agent Sir Evelyn Baring tried to ensure that the rivalry did not lead to conflict between the two powers. He was one of the influential figures who laid the foundations for the Entente Cordiale of 1904, which set the seal on vastly improved Anglo-French relations.

RIGHT: Labeled "Alexandria, the City, Bay and adjacent Coast. Capt. D'Arcy 1801," this is a chart of the Old Port, showing channels, anchorage, and buoyage, with, above, a map of the coast from Alexandria to Port Said. This is probably a copy made by d'Arcy from a French original. The date of the map is significant in that it was in 1798 that the French forces under Napoleon Bonaparte invaded Egypt, and the map is contemporaneous with the British efforts to force Napoleon's retreat. Although the French assault was primarily military, alongside the army came a significant number of scholars who were among the first to try and make a systematic study of the surviving structures of Ancient Egypt.

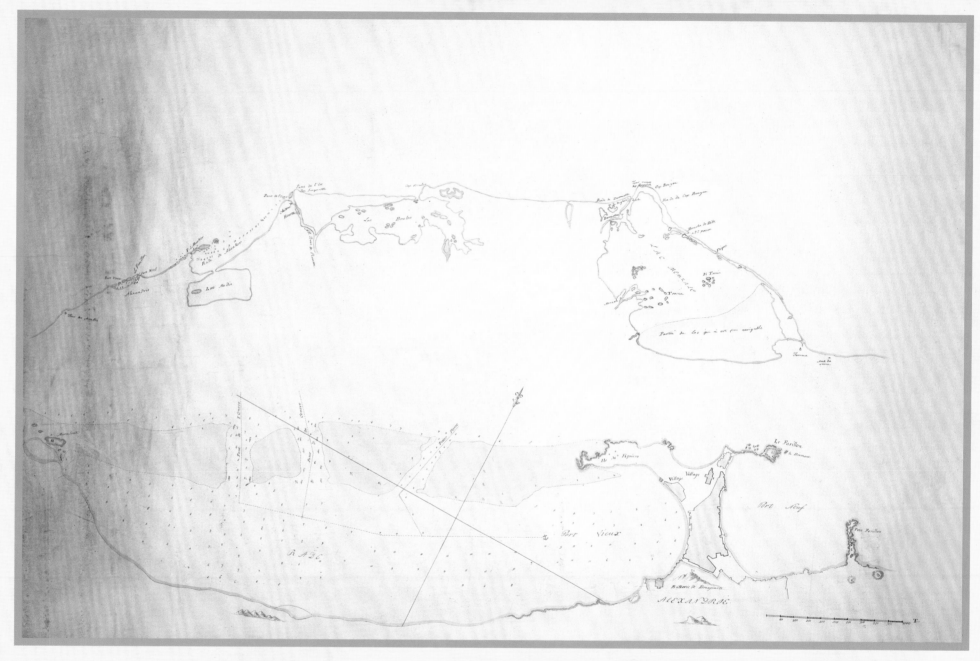

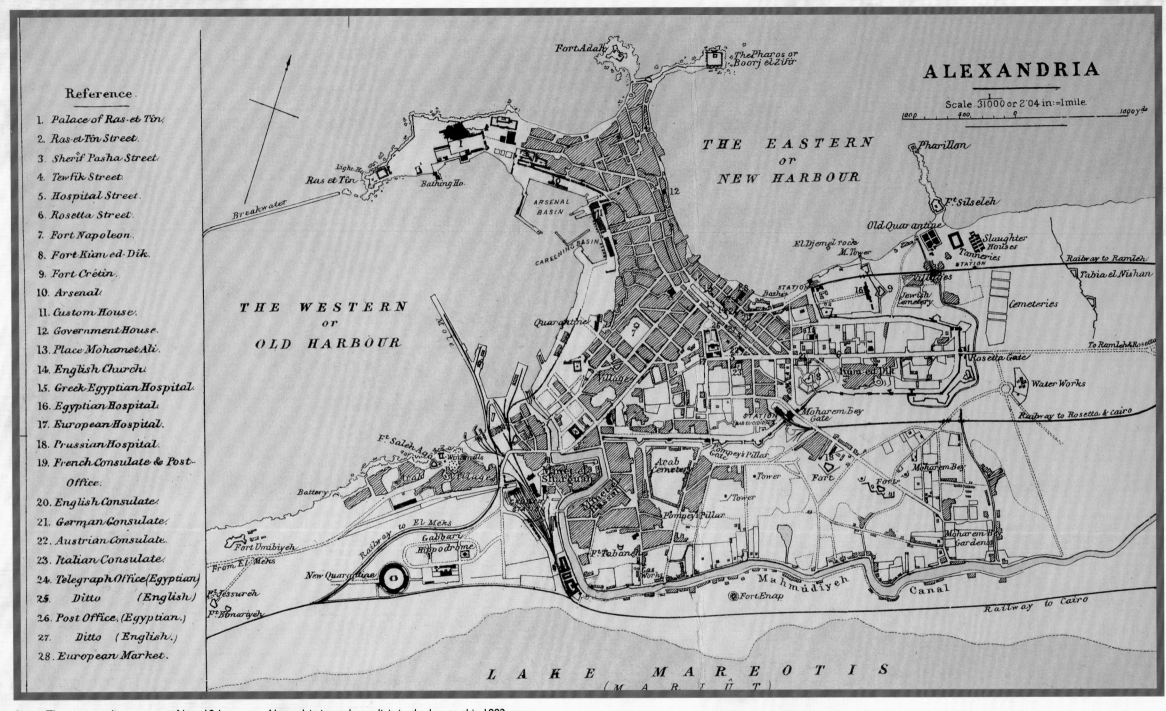

ALEXANDRIA

Scale $\frac{1}{31000}$ or 2.04 in:=1mile

Reference.

1. Palace of Ras-et-Tin.
2. Ras-et-Tin Street.
3. Sherif Pasha Street.
4. Tewfik Street.
5. Hospital Street.
6. Rosetta Street.
7. Fort Napoleon.
8. Fort Kûm ed-Dik.
9. Fort Crétin.
10. Arsenal.
11. Custom House.
12. Government House.
13. Place Mohamet Ali.
14. English Church.
15. Greek-Egyptian Hospital.
16. Egyptian Hospital.
17. European Hospital.
18. Prussian Hospital.
19. French Consulate & Post-Office.
20. English Consulate.
21. German Consulate.
22. Austrian Consulate.
23. Italian Consulate.
24. Telegraph Office (Egyptian)
25. Ditto (English)
26. Post Office (Egyptian.)
27. Ditto (English.)
28. European Market.

THE EASTERN or NEW HARBOUR

THE WESTERN or OLD HARBOUR

LAKE MAREOTIS (MARIÛT)

ABOVE: The cosmopolitan nature of late 19th-century Alexandria is made explicit in the key to this 1882 map. Produced to a scale of 1:31,000, it records the city at the time that the British had renewed their interest in Egypt as a result of the completion of the Suez Canal. In July 1882 British forces, in support of the nationalist uprising of Arabi Pasha against the country's Ottoman rulers, had bombarded the city and, following this, Egypt was effectively to be ruled by Sir Evelyn Baring from 1883 until his retirement in 1907. The remains of the city's walls are visible but the modern age—in the guise of railway lines—is also now present. The British recognized the strategic importance of the harbors at Alexandria and used them as a base for the Royal Navy.

AMSTERDAM
NETHERLANDS

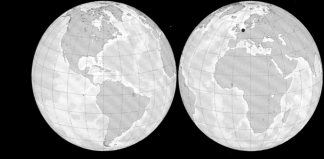

D escribed as the "Venice of the North" and possessing more miles of canal than its Italian counterpart, Amsterdam is the capital of The Netherlands and the official residence of the Dutch monarch. The country's government, however, is sited at The Hague (Den Haag). The city, with a population of more than 700,000, is located on the Amstel, which flows, via a series of floodgates, into the IJsselmeer (IJ). A center of the diamond trade, Amsterdam is also a popular tourist destination, with more than two million visitors drawn to the city annually.

The city's origins date back to the 13th century and the establishment of Amstelledamme, a settlement built on dykes on both banks of the Amstel. By the start of the 16th century Amsterdam was a vitally important trading center, but the stability that had brought this prosperity was threatened by the religious disputes of the Reformation era and by the revolt against the Spanish rulers of the Low Countries.

After 1578 the city became one Europe's most important trading ports and received large number of religious refugees from elsewhere in Europe, drawn by its religious toleration. The 17th century was Amsterdam's golden age; it was at the heart of an expanding commercial empire that stretched from North America to the Far East, and the port was the most important in the world. However, not all was positive; in the 1660s the city suffered severely from plague, whilst there was also growing rivalry with Britain over international trade.

A new instability came at the end of the 18th century following the French Revolution of 1789, and in 1806 The Netherlands became the kingdom of The Netherlands under Louis Napoleon, brother of the French emperor, with Amsterdam as its capital. In 1810 this state became part of France and thus subject to the blockade of European trade imposed by the Royal Navy during the Napoleonic Wars. In 1814, a new kingdom of The Netherlands, formed by the union of Belgium, Luxembourg, and The Netherlands, was established; this survived until the 1830s, when the modern state emerged following Belgian independence.

In World War I The Netherlands remained neutral but, in May 1940, it was occupied by German forces. Some 100,000 of Amsterdam's Jewish population—including the famous diarist Anne Frank (whose house is now a museum)—were deported during the occupation, which ended with liberation by Canadian forces on May 5, 1945.

BELOW: Satellite image of Amsterdam and its surroundings from NASA.

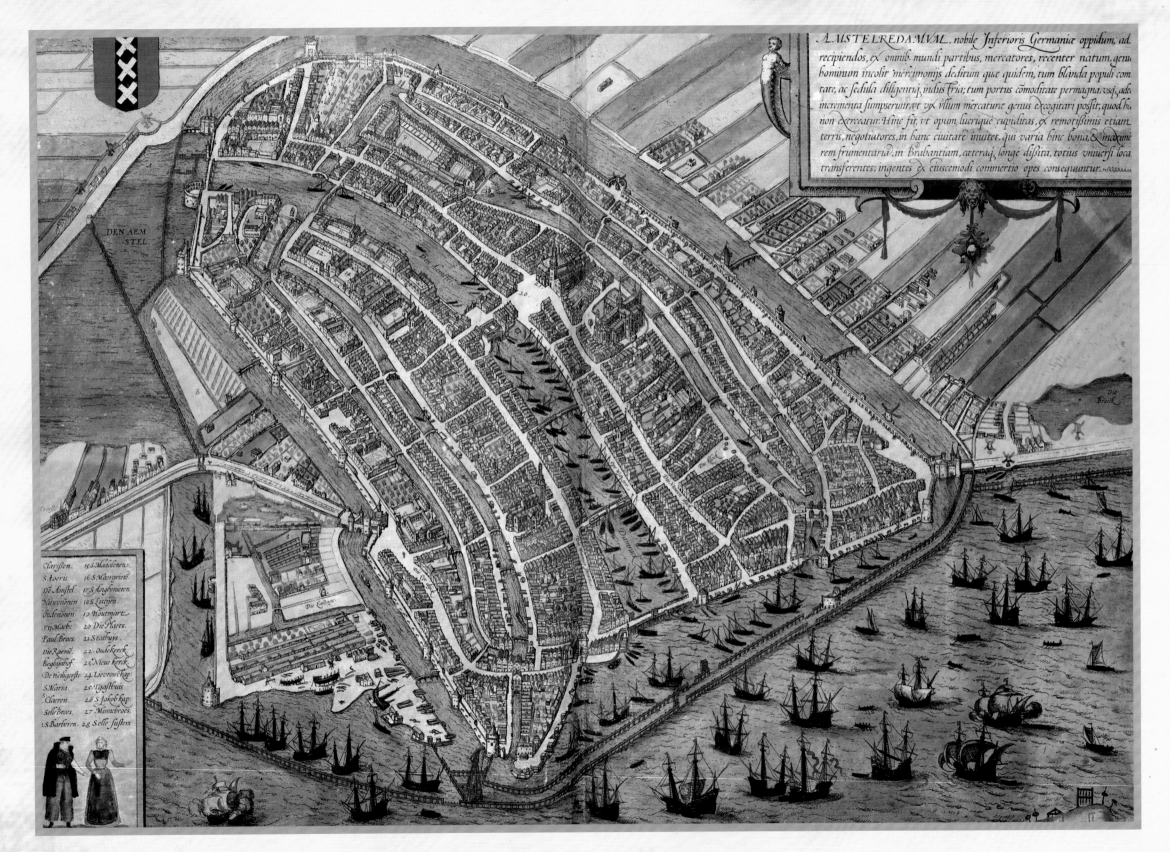

AMSTELREDAMVM, nobile Inferioris Germaniæ oppidum, ad. recipiendos, ex omnib. mundi partibus, mercatores, recenter natum, genu. hominum incolit mercimonijs deditum quæ quidem, tum blanda populi com. tate, ac sedula diligentiaq, indus Fria; tum portus comoditate permagna, vsq, ad. incrementa sumpserunt, vt vix vllum mercaturæ genus excogitari possit, quod ha. non exerceatur. Hinc fit, vt opum, lucrique cupiditas, ex remotissimis etiam terris, negotiatores, in hanc ciuitate inuitet, qui varia hinc bona, & maxime rem frumentaria, in Brabantiam, æteraq, longe dissita, totius vniuersi loca transferentes; ingentes ex eiuscemodi commertio opes consequuntur.

DEN AEM STEL

Die Brack

Clariffen.
S. Anerii.
Di Amftel
Nieuwonnen
Oudenonnen
vi Mach.
Paul Broes.
Die Raemie.
Beghijnhof.
De Heiligheifte.
S. Maria.
S. Claeren.
Selle Broes.
S. Barberen.

15 S. Madalenen.
16 S. Margrieten.
17 S. Anghenieten.
18 S. Liscijen.
19 Houtmart.
20 Die Plaers.
21 Stathuys.
22 Oudekerck.
23 Nieue kerck.
24 Lievronekap.
25 Tjafthuis.
26 S. Jakob kap.
27 Minnebroes.
28 Selle fufters.

LEFT: The relationship between the concentric canals and the areas of human habitation at this time is evident in this view of the city. In the foreground can be seen the IJ, the bay leading off the Zuiderzee, which was the route by which shipping reached the city. Between the 15th and 18th centuries the city was protected from attack by a crude wooden barrier that can be seen clearly. The major channel running through the city of the city was the River Amstel with, at its northern end, the Damrak (or Dam Reach), which represented a sheltered harbor within the city. This area was subsequently drained and is now one of the city's main roads. The outermost waterway—The Singel— was originally part of the city's defenses, but by the late 16th century the city was starting to expand beyond this defensive line. Also visible are two of the city's churches: the Oude Kerk (Old Church), which dated originally from the 14th century and the city's foundation, and the Nieuwe Kerk (New Church), which was built in the 15th century.

RIGHT: Produced by Cornelis Danckerts (c.1603–56), this map of Amsterdam portrays the city during its golden age. Earlier in the century, as the city expanded out from its original core, new canals—the Herengracht, Keizersgracht, and Prinsengracht—had been completed and by the end of the 17th century the city's population reached about 100,000. Fourteen years prior to the date of this map the city's commercial position had been enhanced as a result of the Treaty of Westphalia, which had settled the Thirty Years' War and effectively closed Antwerp as a port.

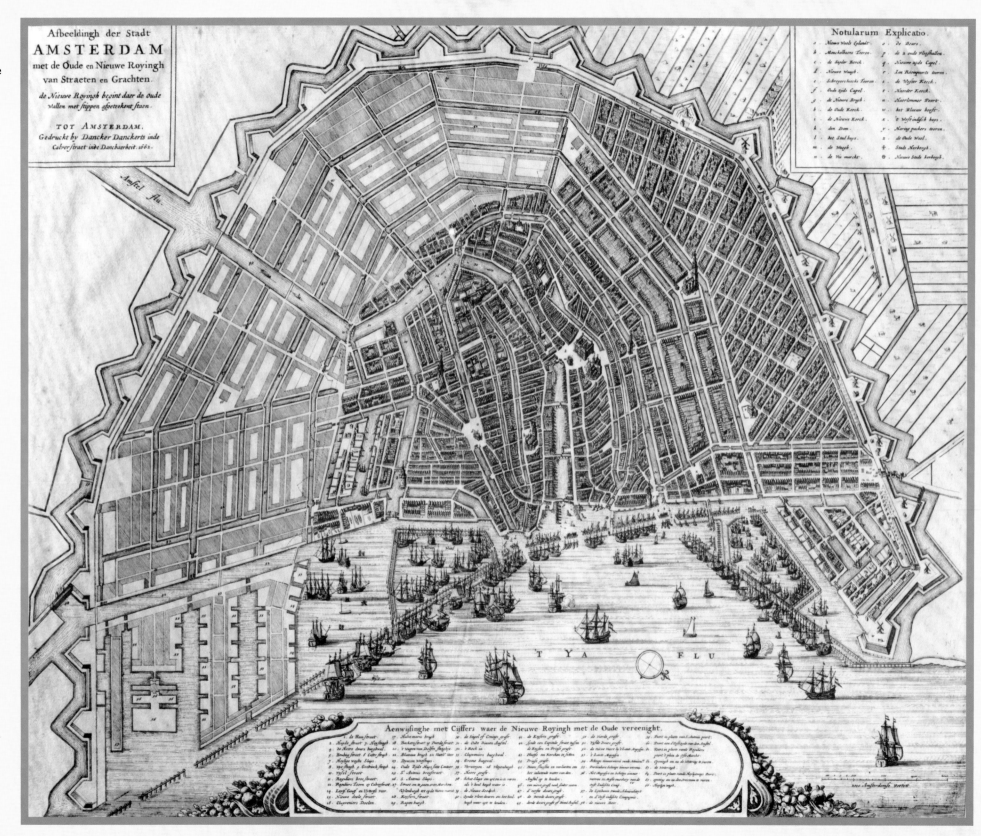

AMSTELODAMI VETERIS ET NOVISSIMI DELINEATIO PER JOANNEM DE RAM.

LEFT: Produced by Nic Visscher, this map of the city of Amsterdam is undated but portrays the city as it existed in the late 17th or early 18th centuries. The key provides an index of street names and important buildings. The city's crest—a shield with three vertical crosses of St Andrew—is designed to reflect the three great dangers faced by the city: fire, flood, and plague. This symbol was flown by ships registered to the port of Amsterdam and can still be seen throughout the city.

RIGHT: Published in Nuremberg, Germany, in 1727 by the company Homann Erben, this map of Amsterdam is oriented with north toward the lower right and was drawn to a scale of about 1:9,000. The index, which is in Dutch, describes points of interest and the city's ramparts. In addition to the map itself, there is a panoramic view of the city seen from the IJ.

ANTWERP

BELGIUM

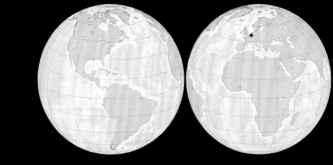

The second largest sea port in Europe, Antwerp—Antwerpen in Flemish and Anvers in French—is situated on the eastern bank of the tidal River Scheldt, 55 miles inland from the river's estuary in the North Sea. According to legend, the city's name derives from the Flemish *Handwerpen*—literally tossed hands—which refers to the story of a giant, Druon Antigonus, who occupied a castle on the site during the period of Roman occupation. He is alleged to have severed the hands of any trader who refused to pay duties to him.

During the Middle Ages Antwerp prospered and became the North Sea's most important trading port for wool. It continued to thrive in the 15th and 16th centuries: foreign trading houses were established, the port expanded, and banks were founded, making the city the busiest and wealthiest in Europe.

However, this prosperity suffered significantly during the late 16th century as a result of religious conflict. Following the Protestant revolt in the Low Countries, the Eight Years' War broke out between Spain and its erstwhile territories in the Low Countries. After the city was taken by Spanish forces in 1585, its Protestant population was expelled and the great trading houses and banks moved to Amsterdam.

Antwerp suffered further when, following the creation of the United Provinces, the Dutch gained control of maritime traffic on the Scheldt; this was compounded in 1648 when the Treaty of Westphalia, which settled the Thirty Years' War, closed the Scheldt to shipping. Under Dutch rule, some measure of prosperity returned to the city as it was now able to handle traffic to and from the extensive Dutch overseas empire. In 1830 the city was captured by those favoring Belgian independence, and it suffered significant damage as a result of bombardment from the citadel. Belgium achieved its independence in 1831.

In World War I the invading German forces lay siege to the city in September 1914; liberation would not come until 1918. Again in World War II the city was occupied by the Germans and devastated by bombing. Since 1945 the city has grown significantly as a major trading port once more and most of its fortifications have been dismantled.

BELOW: Antwerp is on the right bank of the River Scheldt, which is linked to the North Sea by the Westerschelde estuary. Second only to Rotterdam in Europe, its modern port facilities are obvious from the air. Image obtained on 23 May 2001, by the ETM+ sensor on the Landsat 7 satellite.

LEFT: The city and port of Antwerp owe their existence to the River Scheldt and the importance of the river is evident in this late Renaissance view, with shipping occupying the city's entire river frontage. The city's defensive walls had been strengthened in the early 16th century and were to be put to the test in 1584 when the city was besieged by the Spanish forces led by the Duke of Parma. The city fell after 13 months and became part of the Spanish Netherlands. In the center of the harbor area is the fortress of Het Steen (The Stone): this had originally been constructed in the early 13th century but was rebuilt in the 1520s, when it became known by its present name. With the city's defenses much modified, Het Steen had no military purpose and from the mid-16th century was used as a prison. The most dominant ecclesiastical structure shown on this map is the Onze-Lieve-Vrouwekathedraal (Cathedral of Our Lady); this church, the largest Gothic structure in the Low Countries, dated originally to the late 14th century but was not completed until the 16th century. The church became a cathedral in 1559.

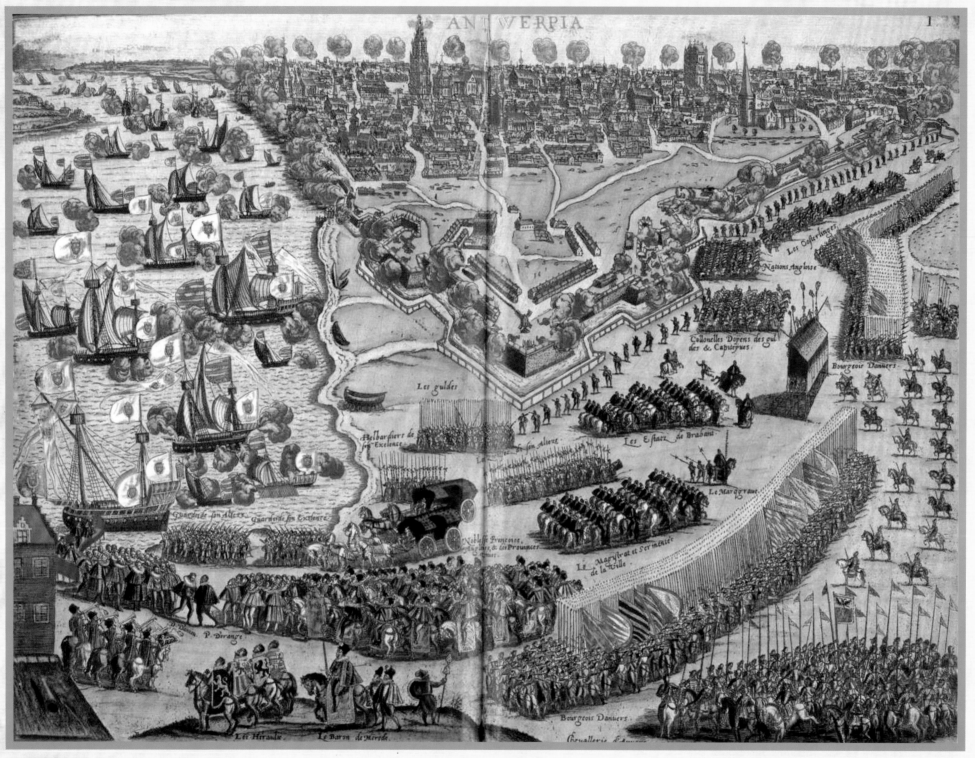

ANTWERPIA

LEFT: The city of Antwerp suffered severely during the religious wars that led to the struggle for independence from Spain for the Low Countries. Although Catholic, the French were seen by the Dutch as allies against the Spanish and in 1582 Prince François of France (1555–84), Duke of Anjou and Alençon, landed with his army and fleet at Antwerp in support of the Dutch rebels. This map, printed by Christophe Plantin (c.1520–89), a printer based in Antwerp from 1549, records the arrival of Prince François at the city. François had been created Duke of Brabant and Count of Flanders, but was not with the Dutch and his attempted entry into the city resulted in a military disaster when, having been allowed entrance, the French troops found the gates closed behind them and about 1,500 eventually perished in a massacre. This was the end of François's military career and he died prematurely the following year of malaria.

RIGHT: This is a plan of the city showing its defenses. Churches are shown as blue crosses and there are notes on length, breadth, and area of the city. The map was drawn to an original scale of 3 inches to 100 Antwerp perches.

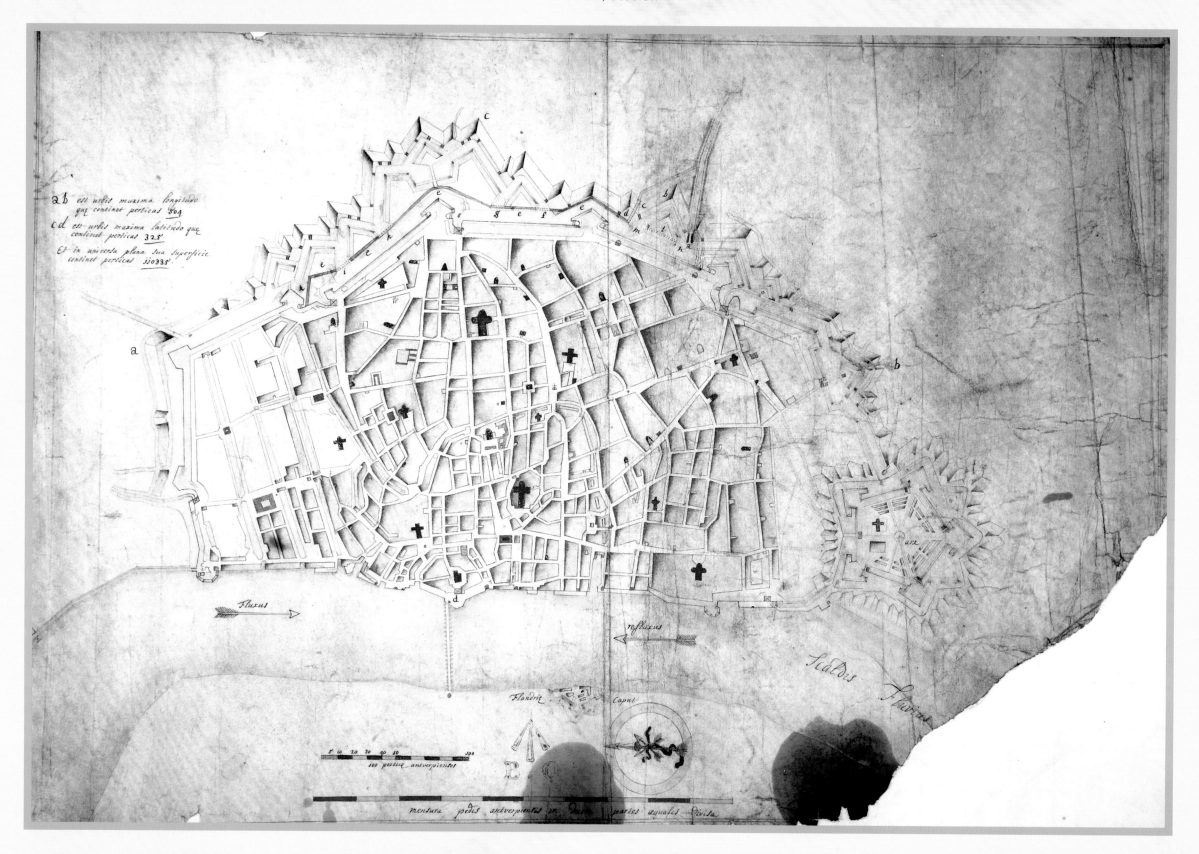

Pag. 172

SCALDIS ANTVERPIA

LOCORVM INSIGNIVM
AC
VIÆ TRIVMPHALIS
Quæ Ser. Princeps. FERDINANDVS AVSTRIACVS, Hispaniar. Infans. etc.
ANTVERPIAM est ingressus.
DESIGNATIO.

1. Castrum.
2. Porta CÆSAREA apud quam LÆVIA
   Ser. Principi oblata.
3. Templum S. Georgij et b. PEGMA I.
   ADVENTVS. GRATVLATIO.
4. Templum et Coenob. virginum III. Reg.
   S. Francisci ubi ARCVS LVSITANORVM.
5. Crux Aerea in Monte prope quam
   ARCVS PHILIPPEVS.
6. Mons in quo PORTICVS XII. CÆSARM.
   AVSTRIACORVM.
7. Templum S. Iacobi prope quod PEGMA II.
   APOTHEOSIS D.ISABELLÆ CLARÆ EVGENIÆ.
8. ARCVS FERDINANDEVS.
9. Basilica Neapoleitanorum vulgo Burgi.
10. PEGMA III Templum Lusi repræsentans.
11. Forum Marius.
12. Curia, siue Domus Cusos.
13. Templum D.VIRGINIS Cathedrale.
14. PEGMA IV. MERCVRIVS ANTVERPIENS.
15. Officina Monetæ Regiæ apud quam
    ARCVS MONETALIS.
16. Templum et Coenob. D.Michaelis Ord.
    Præmonstrat. Hospitium Ser.Principis.
    prope qua Arcus horum PELICANORVM.
17. Templum S. Walburgis.
18. Templum S. Andreæ.
19. Templ. et Domus Profess Societ. IESV.
20. Collegium Societ. IESV.
21. Templ. et Coenob. Praemonst. S.S.Saluatoris.
22. Templ et Coenob. Carthusianorum.
23. Templ. et Coenob. Dominicanorum.
24. Templ. et Coenob. Franciscanorum.
25. Templ. et Coenob. Carmelitarum.
26. Templ. et Coenob. Augustinianorum.
27. Templ et Coenob. Capucinorum.
28. Templ. et Coenob. Discalceatorum Carmel.
29. Templ. et Coenob. Minimorum.
30. Templ. et Coenob. Mariemorum.
31. Templ. et Coenob. Alexandrinorum.
32. Hospitale Magnu.
33. Templ. et Coenob.Virginum Leprosis
    minus tam remotum Ex Tri SMICKEN.
34. Templ. et Coenob. Faventinorum.
35. Templ. et
    Coenob. Nouissimis.
36. Templ. et Coenob.
    Nicranum. Sororum.
37. Templ. et Coenob.
    Albarum Sororum.
38. Templ. et Coenob. Claricarum.
39. Templ. et Coenob. Annuntiatarum.
40. Templ. et Coenob. Carmelitarum
    Discalceatarum.
41. Barrium.num.
42. Porta Kipdorpij.
43. Porta Rubra.
44. Porta Lutea.
45. Propugnaculum S. Laurentij.
46. Porta ad Wenum.
47. Porta Præa ad Scaldim.
48. Porta Crenelorum.
49. Domus Occidentium.
50. Domus Helenorum.
51. Domus Petri Pauli Rubens.
52. Officina Aromatum.
54. Officina
    Vitrarum.
55. Forum Equinum.
56. Forum Boarium.
57. Forum Piscium.
58. Macellum.
59. Mons Pietatis.

IVL. CÆSARIS SCALIGERI.
In Laudem ANTVERPIÆ Epigramma.

RIGHT: Described as a "Plan of the Town, Fortifications and Citadel of Antwerp," this map, which is aligned with north toward the left, records the city as it existed immediately prior to the dawn of the railway age. The harbor facilities are already extensive but, emphasizing the volatile nature of contemporary Europe, so too are the city's defenses. The date is significant: on August 25, 1830, revolution broke out in Belgium against the country's Dutch rulers and, on October 4, 1830, the Belgians declared their independence. The Dutch responded by sending troops into Belgium, defeating the Belgian army at Leuven before being forced to retreat by the threat of the French army. The kingdom of Belgium was established with the first king, Leopold I, being crowned on July 21, 1831. Britain was one of the guarantors of Belgian independence, a position that lead to Britain's initial involvement in World War I in 1914 when Germany invaded Belgium as part of its assault on France.

ABOVE: This Dutch map records the city of Antwerp during the period when, after the Treaty of Westphalia (1648), the River Scheldt was closed for shipping. It was during these years that the city's commercial prosperity declined in favor of Amsterdam.

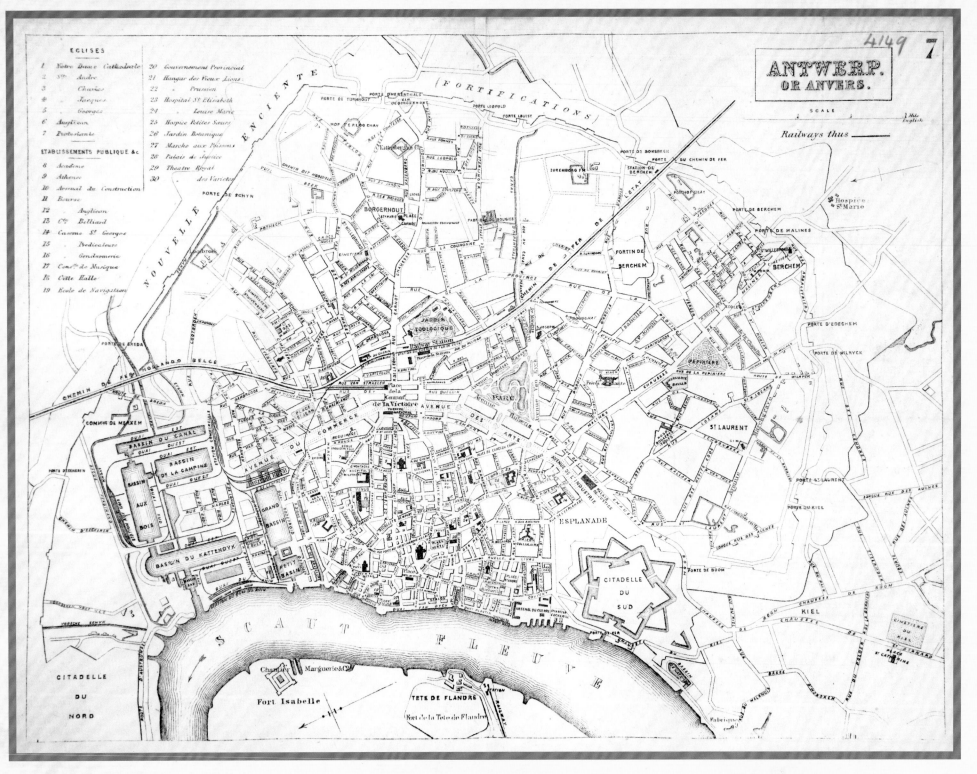

Produced by Bradshaw & Blacklock of Manchester, England, this map records the city of Antwerp toward the end of the period when commercial shipping on the Scheldt was severely restricted. The city was to expand considerably during the last decades of the 19th century as the city became the main port serving Belgium. The map is aligned with north toward the left. The extensive harbor facilities and the growing railway network are clearly delineated.

AUGSBURG
GERMANY

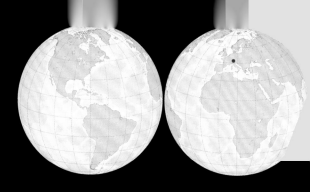

Now the third largest city in the German state of Bavaria with a population approaching 300,000, Augsburg's origins date back to the pre-Roman era, when it was occupied by the Licatii tribe. When the Roman Empire suffered from the barbarian advance, Augsburg was captured by the Ostrogoths in the 4th century and destroyed by the Huns early in the next. The name Augbsburg—city of Augustus—was given to the settlement by the Franks following its rebuilding.

Under Frankish rule the city started to prosper as a commercial center, aided by its location on a number of the major trading routes of Europe. The Via Claudia led south across the Alps toward Italy, whilst the River Lech provided access to the River Danube, linking eastern and western Europe.

Even more significantly, Augsburg developed into a major center of the banking industry during the 14th century. Partly due to the wealth generated by this, but also as a result of the flourishing trade in salt and silver extracted from the surrounding district, by the Renaissance it became one of the richest cities in Germany. During this period it also became one of the major centers for the manufacture of armor and one of the leading locations for foundries used in the casting of cannon.

As elsewhere in Germany, Augsburg suffered strife as a result of the Reformation in the early 16th century, but whilst religion was important, fiscal profit and mercantile freedom reigned supreme in Augsburg. Religious peace in the city was largely maintained, despite increasing confessional tensions, until the Thirty Years' War (1618–48). In 1629, Ferdinand II issued the Edict of Restitution resulting in the installation of an entirely Catholic city government that radically curtailed the rights of local Protestants. This persisted until April 1632, when the Swedish army of Gustavus Adolphus took the city without resistance. Just over two years later, the Swedish army was routed at nearby Nördlingen, and by October 1634 Catholic troops had surrounded Augsburg. The Swedish garrison refused to surrender and a disastrous siege ensued before the city was again in Catholic hands. For the next 150 years the city was effectively ruled by the bishop.

In 1871 Bavaria became a kingdom within the German Empire and was to maintain its own monarchy until after World War I. During the 19th century the city grew as an industrial center with large cotton and woolen mills, and plants manufacturing acetylene gas, paper, chemicals, jewelry, and leather goods.

BELOW: Satellite image of the city of Augsburg (centre) and its surrounding area in Bavaria, southern Germany. North is at top. Forested areas are dark green, agricultural fields are lighter shades of green and brown, urban areas are grey and water is black. Image created using NaturalVue data obtained from the Landsat 7 satellite.

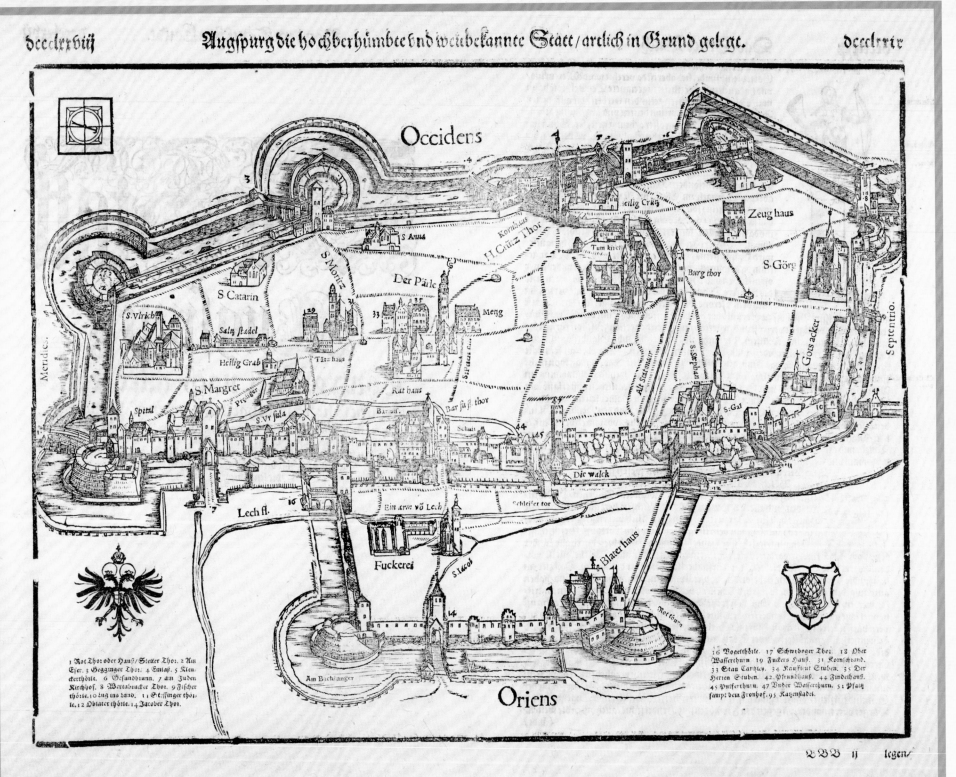

Augspurg die hochberhümbte vnd weitbekannte Statt / artlich in Grund gelegt.

Occidens

Oriens

LEFT: Produced originally by Sebastian Munster (1489–1552) and reproduced as a woodcut in the book *Cosmographia* in 1544, this map of Augsburg is aligned with north toward the right of the map with east (oriens) toward the bottom. Prominent as part of the defenses of the walled area to the east of the River Lech are the three towers—from north to south; the Oblatterwallturm, the Fünfgratturm and the Jakoberwallturm, with the Jaker-Tor (gate) situated between the latter two. These are among the city's defenses that remain extant.

RIGHT: By the 16th century Augsburg had become one of the most important financial centers of the Holy Roman Empire and, through this, one of the wealthiest cities in Germany. The city was surrounded by two sets of walls, one on either side of the River Lech. To the east of the river, in the smaller of the two enclosed areas, was the Fuggerei; this was the world's first social housing complex when built in 1516 and was financed by public donation. The main—western—part of the city was dominated by the Perlachturm (Perlach Tower), which had originally been built in 1182 as a watchtower and enlarged in both 1410 and 1527 when a belfry was added, and by Dom St Maria (Cathedral of the Holy Virgin). The cathedral, built upon the site of a Roman temple, was largely constructed in the 11th century, though remodeled between 1331 and 1431.

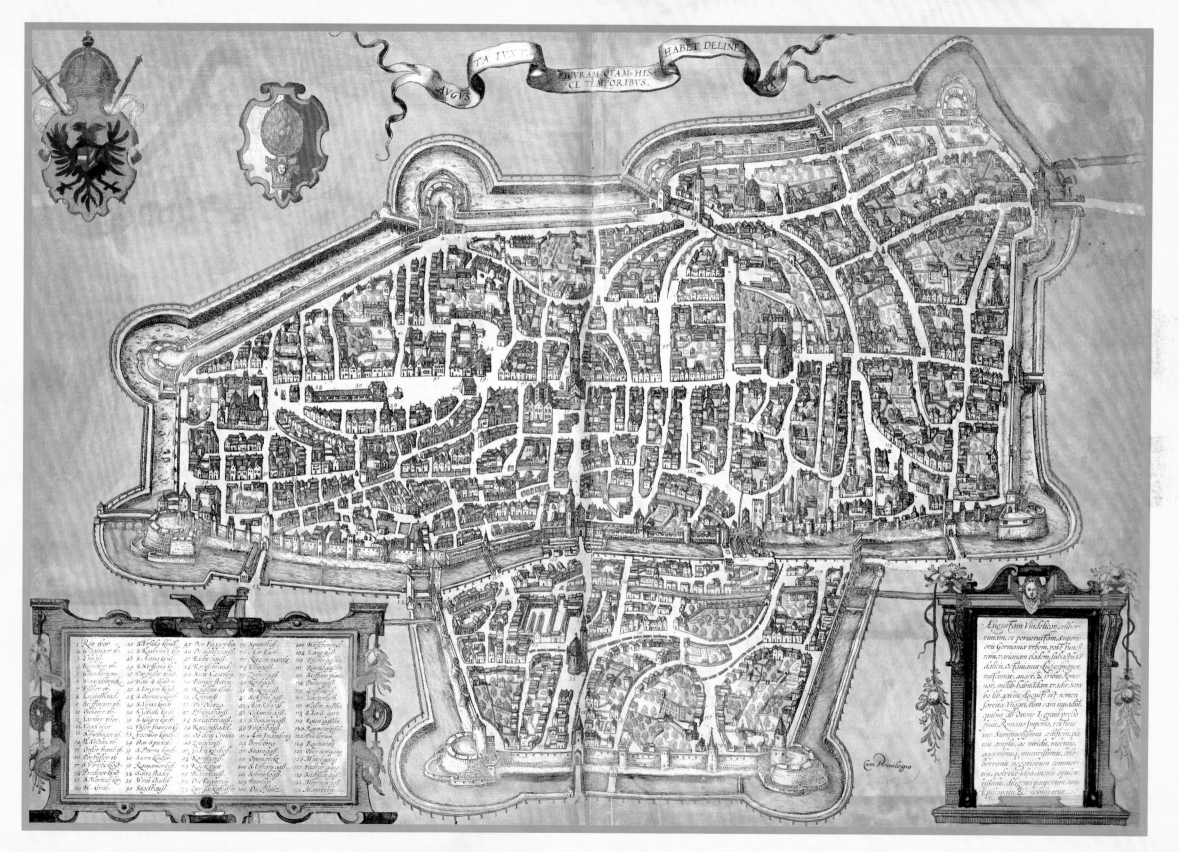

ABOVE: Drawn originally by Johann Thomas Kraus
(c.1696–1775), this etching of Augsburg provides
a panoramic view of the city from the southeast
across the River Lech. Note the title incorporates
the Roman name of the city in Latin (Augusta
Vindelicorum) and the more modern Augsburg,
here spelled "Augspurg."

BARCELONA

SPAIN

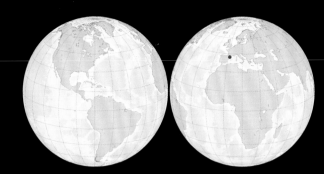

Situated on the Mediterranean coast of Spain between the estuaries of the rivers Llobregat and Besòs, Barcelona is the capital of the autonomous region of Catalonia. It has a population of almost 1.7 million, making it the second largest city in the country.

The city's origins are obscure, but it undeniable that a settlement was established by the 1st century B.C. and that in 15B.C. the Romans founded Barcino in the area following their conquest of the Iberian peninsula.

Roman rule lasted until the early 5th century B.C., when the Visigoths crossed the Pyrenees from southern Gaul and established court at Barcino. They held it until the early 8th century B.C., before surrendering to Moorish invaders from Africa.

Unlike the rest of Iberia, Moorish domination in northern Spain was destined to be relatively short-lived. In 801A.D. Louis the Pious (778–840), the son of the Emperor Charlemagne, recaptured the city and the region was ruled by the Carolingian Counts of Barcelona and their successors until 1258, when the king of France, Louis IX (1214–70), renounced his claims in northern Spain to King James I of Aragon (1208–76) in return for James's claims on territory in southern France.

The city remained part of the kingdom of Aragon until 1469 when, with the marriage of Ferdinand II of Aragon to Isabella of Castille, the kingdom of Spain was united. During the late 18th and 19th centuries the city gained importance as one of the country's most important industrial centers. In 1897 the city was further expanded by the incorporation of six neighboring districts and the laying out of the Eixample (Extension). It was during the second half of the 19th century and the first decades of the 20th that the noted Catalan architect Antoni Gaudí (1852–1926) undertook much work in the city, designing buildings that have now been designated as UNESCO World Heritage Sites.

As with the rest of Spain, Barcelona was severely affected by the Spanish Civil War. The city was bombed for three days in March 1938 by Italian aircraft based on Majorca. Many buildings, including the medieval Cathedral of Santa Eulalia (in which 1,000 were killed), were damaged. The city ultimately fell to the Nationalist army on January 26, 1939, and, along with the rest of Spain, was under the rule of General Franco until his death in 1975. Aided by events such as the 1992 Summer Olympics and by growing numbers of tourists, the city has developed markedly in the two decades since Spain became a member of the European Union.

BELOW: Barcelona, as photographed in 2003 by NASA's Landsat 7 satellite.

LEFT: Detail from the *Civitates Orbis Terrarum* image above showing the cathedral. Construction began in 1298 on the site of an earlier structure; it was not completed until the 19th century, when the main façade was finished.

ABOVE: Reproduced in *Civitates Orbis Terrarum* by Georg Braun and Franz Hogenberg, this records the city as it existed toward the end of the 16th century—viewed from the south with the Mediterranean Sea to the east. The city at this date effectively covered the Gothic Quarter (Barri Gòtic).

ABOVE: In 1715, following a 13-month long siege of the city, work commenced during the reign of King Felipe V on the construction of a massive, star-shaped citadel. The building was completed five years later and this Spanish map of 1726 shows the citadel as completed. The building was designed to house soldiers for the maintenance of public order, but in reality it was converted into a prison and achieved notoriety during the period of French occupation in the early 19th century. It was demolished in 1878 and a park—the Parc de la Ciutadella—created in its place.

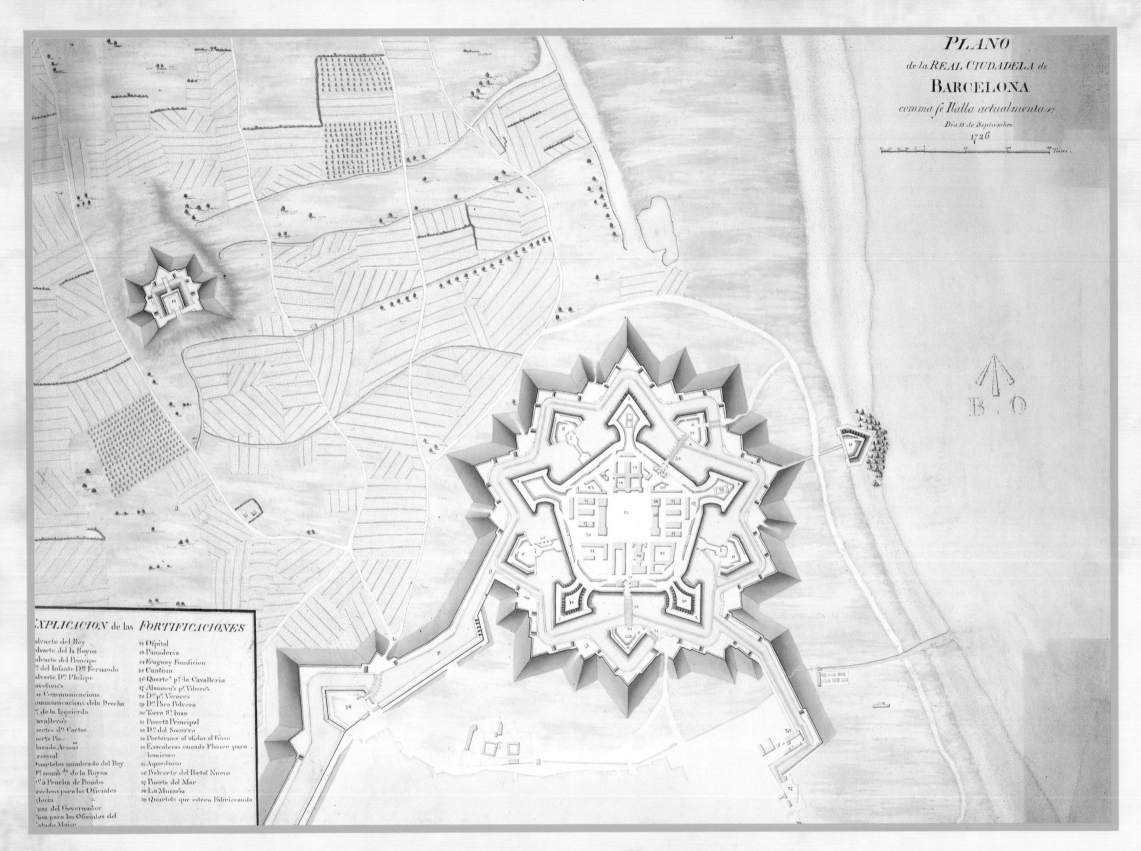

PLANO
de la REAL CIUDADELA de
BARCELONA
comma se halla actualmente
Dia 13 de Septiembre
1726

EXPLICACION de las FORTIFICACIONES

...lvarte del Rey
...lvarte de la Reyna
...lvarte del Principe
...º del Infante Dº Fernando
...lvarte Dº Philipe
...avelien's
...² Communicacions
...ommunicacions dela Brecha
...º de la Esquierda
...cavallero's
...ertes dº Carlos
...erto Pio
...lasade Armas
...rcenal
...Quarteles numbrado del Rey
...º numbº de la Reyna
...º à Prueba para Bomba
...avelons para los Officiales
...lecia
...asa del Governador
...asa para los Officiales del
...Estado Maior

19 Ospital
23 Panaderia
24 Fragua y Fundicion
25 Cantina
26 Quarteº pª la Cavalleria
47 Almazen's pª Viberes
28 Dº pª Viveres
29 Dº Pra Polvora
30 Torra Sª Juan
31 Puerta Principal
32 Dº del Socorro
33 Porteros ofidos al Fosso
34 Escaleras encado Flanco para
    lomismo
35 Aquedusto
36 Balvarte del Portal Nuevo
37 Puerta del Mar
38 La Muralla
39 Quartels que esteen Fabricando

LEFT: Another Spanish map from the late 18th century shows to good effect the inter-relationship between the district of Montjuic, as yet largely undeveloped, on the west (left-hand side of the map) with the Old Town in the center and the early 18th-century citadel toward the east. Montjuic itself is dominated by the Castell de Montjuïcon the bluff in the extreme southwest of the district. This was originally constructed in 1640, but was rebuilt by King Felipe V after 1705 and again by the Bourbons later in the century. Following a period as a prison, the building is now a military museum. The central part of the Old Town—Ciutat Vella—is dominated by the cathedral.

RIGHT: Signed by Major Duncan Macgregor of the 78th Highlanders, Assistant Quarter Master General, and produced to a scale of 1 inch to 256 yards, the military provenance of this map shows it to have been produced by the British army during the Peninsular War. At this time British forces, largely led by Arthur Wellesley (later the Duke of Wellington), in alliance with the Portuguese and Spanish, sought to drive the French occupiers out of the Iberian peninsula.

BERGEN

NORWAY

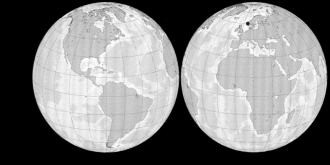

Situated in the southwest of Norway, in the county of Hordaland, Bergen is believed to have been founded in 1070 by King Olav Kyrre, the son of Harald Hardråda. The original Norse version of the name is either "Bergvin" or "Bjørgvin," which is derived from two words—"berg" or "bjørg," meaning "mountain," and "vin," meaning a "meadow." Thus the literal translation of the place-name is the "meadow among the mountains," and the city's location on the shore surrounded by the seven mountains (*de syv fjell*) is evident on this map.

Between 1217, when it replaced Trondheim, and 1299, when it was supplanted by Oslo, Bergen was effectively the capital of Norway and the city remained the largest in the country until the mid-19th century. The city's prosperity owed much to its proximity to the sea and the trade in dried cod from further north. By the end of the 13th century Bergen was one of the most important bureau cities of the Hanseatic League, as well as a center of trade for Frisian merchants from the Low Countries. Both these groups of traders occupied a separate quarter close to the harbor where Frisian or Low German was spoken rather than Norse. It was not until 1536 that the king was able to make the foreign traders use Norse. As one of the Hanseatic ports, Bergen was attacked by the Victual Brothers—privateers who operated in the Baltic in the late 14th century—and sacked by them in 1393.

In 1349 the Black Death reached Bergen via a ship from England, and almost half the Norwegian population died in the ensuing plague. The economy of the country was weakened as a result and, with the death of the last monarch in the Fairhair dynasty, Norway was united with Sweden and Denmark in 1380 under the Danish Queen Margrethe (Margaret) I. Whilst Sweden ceased to be part of the Kalmar Union in 1521, in 1536 Denmark declared Norway to be a Danish province and the country remained part of the enlarged Danish kingdom until the Treaty of Kiel in 1814, when Denmark was forced to cede control of Norway to Sweden. The union under the Swedish crown survived until 1905, when Norway again achieved independence.

BELOW: Satellite image of the city of Bergen and its surrounding fjords (narrow sea inlets) on the southwestern coast of Norway. North is at right. Forested areas are dark green, agricultural fields are lighter shades of green and brown, urban areas are grey and water is black. Image created using NaturalVue data obtained from Landsat 7.

LEFT: Drawn originally by Hieronymous Scholeus, this map was reproduced in *Civitates Orbis Terrarum* by Georg Braun and Franz Hogenberg and records the city as it existed toward the end of the 16th century. The shield with the three blue lions is the Danish coat of arms; at the date that the map was prepared, Norway was a Danish province. Next to the Danish arms is the seal of Bergen—a fortified structure on a red background—whilst further to the right can be seen Norway's arms (a single gold lion on a red background). On the hillside below, the Norwegian arms rope walks are visible; in an era when shipping was powered exclusively by wind, rope-making was a vitally important industry. Among notable structures illustrated are the fortress of Bergenhus (Bergenhus festning), which dated originally to the 11th century, the wharf (Bryggen or Tyskebruggen [German Wharf]), which was declared a UNESCO World Heritage Site in 1979, and the cathedral (Domkirken), which was largely rebuilt in the 13th century.

BILBAO
SPAIN

S ituated on the River Nervión on the north coast of Spain, Bilbao (Bilbo in Basque) is the most important city of the Basque region, with a population of over 350,000.

The city was founded on August 15, 1300, by Don Diego López de Haro V, the Lord of Biscay, across the river from an existing fishing village, now known as Old Bilbao. The origins of the name are uncertain. In Spanish the derivation is believed to be from *bel vado*, which could be translated as good river crossing, whilst the Basque alternative is *bi albo*, meaning two river banks.

The original city, like other Basque settlements, consisted of just three parallel streets—Somera (Upper), Artekale (Middle), and Tendería (Shopkeepers)— but the city soon expanded to the seven streets that form the basis of the historic center.

Economic and urban growth continued, albeit more slowly, during the late 16th and early 17th centuries. It was during this period that the streets linking the historic center with Arenal (Bidebarrieta and Correo), which later became the hub of the city's social life, were first developed. Population growth continued in the 18th century and the city was further enhanced by the discovery later of iron ore in the surrounding hills. Following the Industrial Revolution, Bilbao became one of the industrial centers of Spain, with shipbuilding and the iron and steel industries growing rapidly.

In 1808 the French captured the city and caused major damage. Later, during the Carlist civil wars of 1833–76, the city was besieged on no fewer than four occasions, although it was never to fall. During the final quarter of the 19th century Bilbao more than doubled in size as a result of the extension project of 1876 proposed by Ernesto Hoffmeyer and Severino Achúcarro y Alzola. The expansion continued into the 20th century with the absorption of outlying districts, such as Deusto, and the development of existing districts within the city, such as Basurto and Begoña. During the Spanish Civil War Bilbao supported the Republican side but was captured by the Nationalist forces of General Franco on June 19, 1937. Despite destruction wrought elsewhere in the war, the buildings of Bilbao escaped relatively lightly.

Bilbao, like much of industrial Europe, has witnessed a decline in its heavy industries in recent decades. However, this has been countered by the development of other sectors of the economy, such as the construction of a branch of the Guggenheim Museum, which was designed by Frank Gehry and opened in 1997.

BELOW: Bilbao from NASA's Landsat 7.

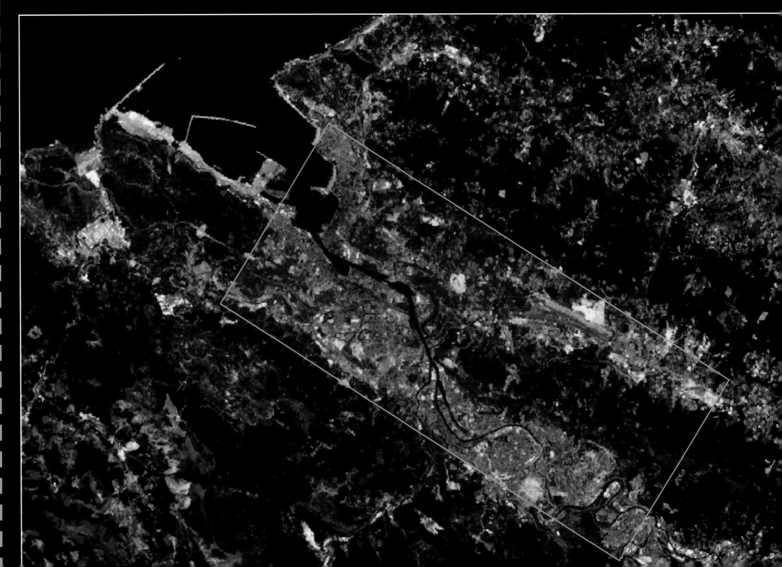

BELOW: Founded in the early 14th century, the importance of the city as a trading center grew significantly in the early 16th century as a result of the granting of several commercial privileges, in particular control over the export of Merino wool. This map records the city at the end of the 16th century when it had expanded well beyond the small three-street settlement. Adjacent to the Church of St Anthony (Iglesia de San Antón) can be seen San Antón Bridge spanning the River Nervión. This was a medieval structure that was rebuilt, slightly upstream of the original, in the 1870s.

BOSTON
UNITED STATES

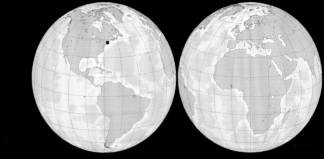

Boston is the capital of Massachusetts. With a population of around 600,000, the city is also the largest in New England. The deep natural harbor enabled Boston ultimately to become the most important port city in New England and, prior to the Revolution, it was one of the main centers of British influence in North America. The original settlement grew up on a peninsula between the Charles River and an arm of the sea called Boston Harbor.

European settlement began in the early 17th century. With its predominant Puritan ethos of moral rectitude, education, and hard work, it grew rapidly. In 1635 the first European school in North America, the Boston Latin school, was established, to be followed the next year by the foundation of the first university—Harvard. In 1673 the town's first shipyard was completed and, by the middle of the 18th century, the settlement had become the most important European city in North America with a population of 25,000. However, the city was to be rocked by two disasters: in 1755 Boston was hit by an earthquake, estimated at up to 6.3 on the Richter Scale, and in 1760 the first "Great Fire" of the city destroyed some 349 buildings.

The fire occurred during the Seven Years' War; this conflict had profound consequences for the development of the city. Although Britain and its allies had proved victorious, the costs of the victory and those needed to defend the newly enlarged British Empire in North America resulted in the imposition of taxes that proved hugely unpopular among those who lived in the colonies. During the late 1770s, Boston became the epicenter of revolt against the British and saw the Boston Massacre.

After the War of Independence (1775–83) Boston continued to grow, becoming a major port dealing in commodities such as salt and tobacco. Industrialization in the 19th century was a further boost to the city's growth, and its population was stimulated when poverty and famine in Europe drove large numbers of immigrants to seek new opportunities in the New World.

A further great fire, started on November 9, 1872, destroyed some 776 buildings in the city's central financial district. But this did not cause any great disruption to the city's continued growth during the late 19th and early 20th centuries. As with other major cities in the US, however, immediately post-World War II Boston suffered decline, although recent decades have seen it once again prosper as a tourist, cultural, and financial center.

BELOW: Boston taken by Landsat 5 in 2008. Launched in 1984 the satellite collects data for the U.S. Geological Survey and, in celebrating its 25th anniversary in 2009, has far exceeded its life expectancy.

ABOVE: "Boston, its environs and harbour, with the rebels works raised against that town in 1775, from the observations of Lieut. Page of His Majesty's Corps of Engineers, and from the plans of Capt. Montresor." Boston was first settled in the mid-17th century and was named after Boston, in Lincolnshire, England, from where the early Puritan settlers had come. It became the capital of Massachusetts Bay province and, by the start of the 18th century, was the largest English-speaking settlement in North America. During the 18th century, however, it was to be overtaken in population terms by both New York and Philadelphia.

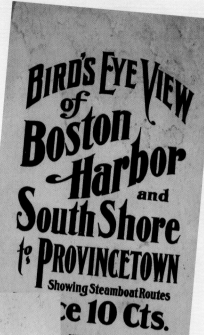

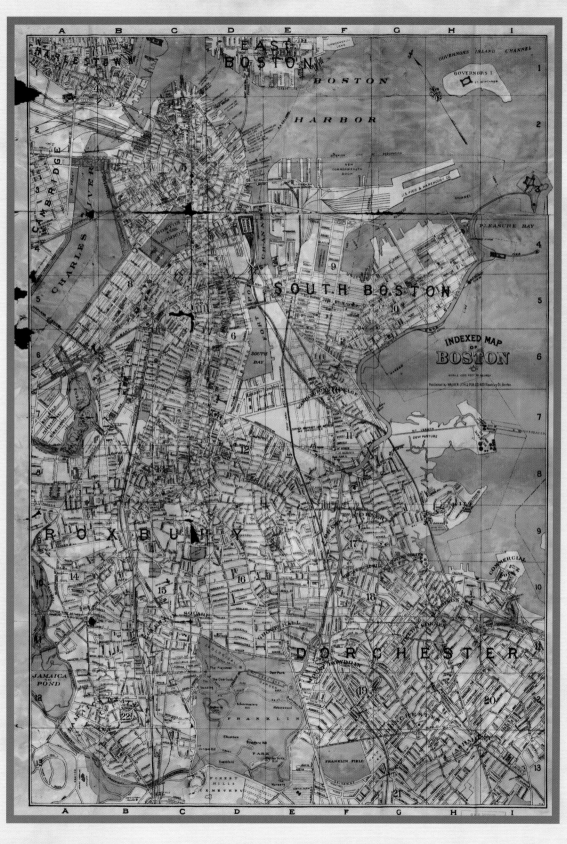

OPPOSITE PAGE, LEFT: This is a plan of Boston, Massachusetts, and its environs, showing in detail the military works undertaken in 1775 and 1776. The map is dedicated to Lord George Germain, Secretary of State, by the author/publisher Henry Pelham. It was engraved in aquatint by Francis Jukes and published in London on June 2, 1777.

OPPOSITE PAGE, RIGHT: Bird's eye view of Boston Habor and South Shore to Provincetown showing steamboat routes. Published by John F. Murphy, c.1905. Oriented with north to the left, it is not drawn to scale.

FAR LEFT: The cover of John F. Murphy's steamboat route map with key.

LEFT: Drawn to a scale of around 1:14,400, this map was published in the late 19th century by the Walker Lith. & Pub. Co of Boston.

ABOVE: Published by Currier & Ives of New York in 1873, this panoramic view of Boston shows the city toward the end of the 19th century.

BRUSSELS

BELGIUM

Now the capital city of Belgium and one of the main centers for the European Union and NATO, Brussels (Bruxelles in French and Brussel in Flemish) lies in the valley of the River Senne, a tributary of the Scheldt. It has a population of one million, of which 80 percent are French-speaking. The city's name derives from an old Dutch phrase meaning "village in the marsh" (broec—marsh, and sele—village).

In the 12th century Brussels benefited as an intermediate staging post between the important commercial hubs of Bruges and Ghent in the west and Cologne in the east. The growth of the city continued, and at the end of the 14th century Brussels became the capital of Brabant and thus, consequent upon the marriage of Philip the Bold (Duke of Burgundy) to Margaret III (Countess of Flanders) in, 1369, whose son Antoine inherited the title of Duke of Brabant, fell under the influence of the Burgundians.

In 1477, Charles I, Duke of Burgundy, was killed whilst attempting to conquer Lorraine. Both the French king, Louis XI, and Maximilian of Habsburg claimed the title. The resulting settlement saw the title of the Duchy of Burgundy pass to the French, although the territory in the Low Countries, including Brussels, and Franche-Comté was to pass to Habsburg rule.

The arrival of the Habsburgs, most notably following the accession of Charles V (who inherited the remnants of the Duchy of Burgundy in 1506 and became King of Spain from 1516 and Holy Roman Emperor from 1519), boosted the prestige of the city of Brussels further.

In 1695, still ruled by Spain, the city was attacked by the French forces under Marshal de Villeroy, with some 4,000 houses destroyed by fire along with many of the medieval buildings surrounding the Grote Markt. Following the War of Spanish Succession, fought between 1701 and 1714, the former Spanish territory in the region, including the city of Brussels, passed to Austrian rule.

In 1794, following the French Revolution, the area was occupied by the French; it was to remain under French rule until 1814. As part of the Congress of Vienna, Belgium passed to Dutch rule; this was, however, to be relatively short-lived and, on August 25, 1830, revolt broke out in Brussels, resulting in the creation of an independent kingdom of Belgium with Brussels as its capital.

BELOW: The center of Brussels as photographed by the French Spot-5 satellite.

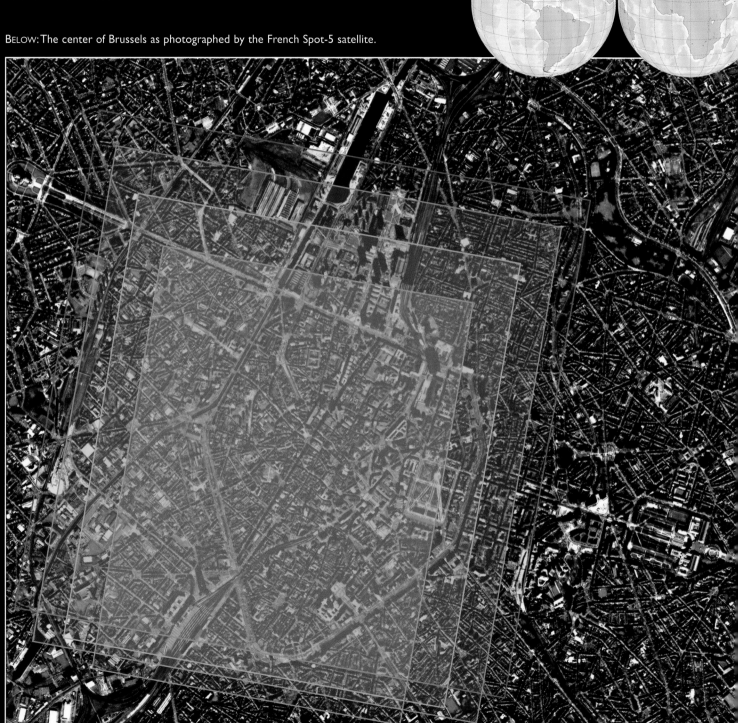

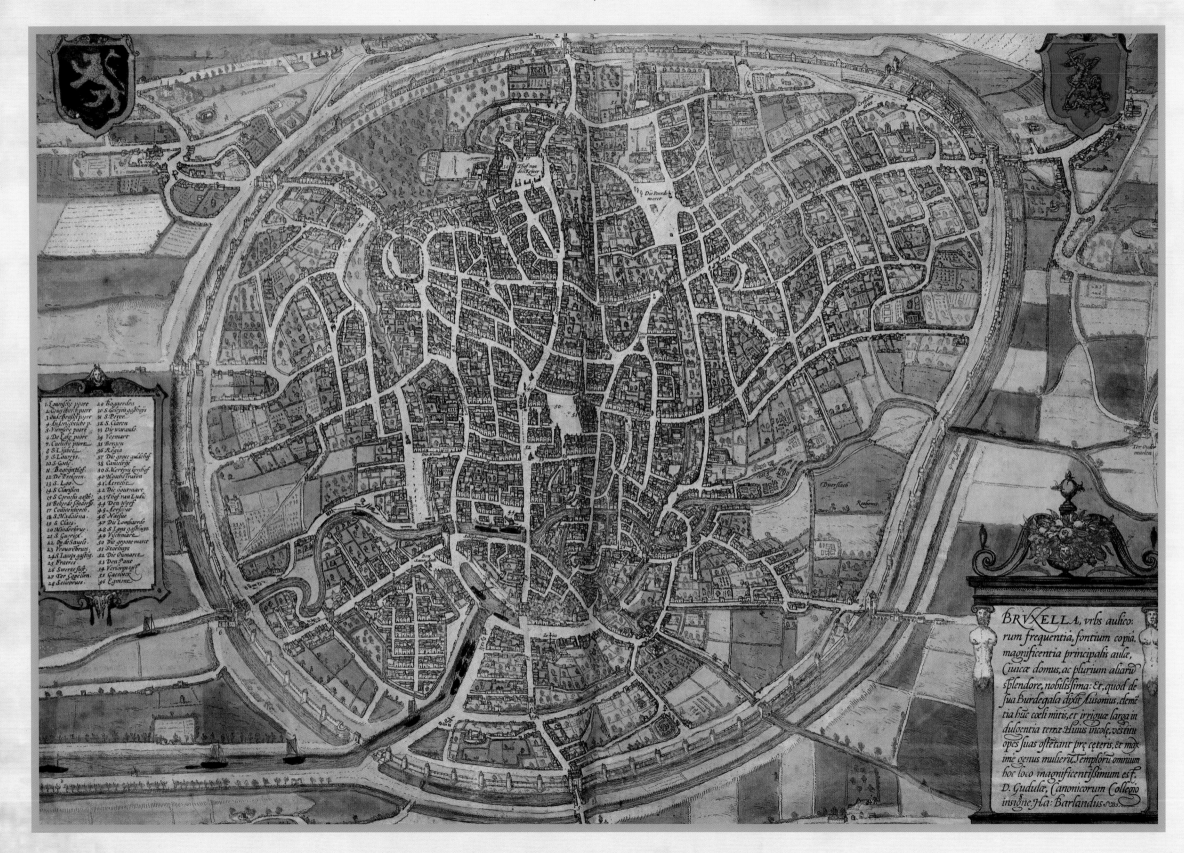

LEFT: During the Middle Ages the city of Brussels had expanded beyond the original city walls and in the 14th century a new set of walls was built. By the time this map was drawn the city was the capital of the Spanish Netherlands and a number of its significant buildings were in place. These included the 16th-century Egmont Place, the Coudenberg (or Koudenberg) Palace, which dated originally to the 12th century but which had been considerably enlarged in the 15th, and the Hôtel de Ville (or Stadhuis), which also dated from the 15th century.

RIGHT: Described as a "Plan de la Ville de Bruxelles" (a plan of the city of Brussels), this map was drawn to a scale of 4 inches to 300 toises and printed by Sieur, Le Rouge, Paris. The map is aligned with north toward the left. Toward the right of the map—on the south of the city—can be seen the Fort de Monterey. In 1670, following orders from the Spanish government, the Count of Monterey built a fort in Obbrussel to protect the city of Brussels against possible attacks. Erected in 1675, this fort was dismantled in the following century to give way to several important toll roads and urban development. The key indicates the location of the principal buildings of the city. At this date, Brussels was notionally part of Austrian-ruled Brabant; however, the War of Austrian Succession had broken out in 1740 and most of the Austrian territory in the Low Countries, including Brussels, had been seized by the French. The city and territory were restored to Austrian rule in 1748.

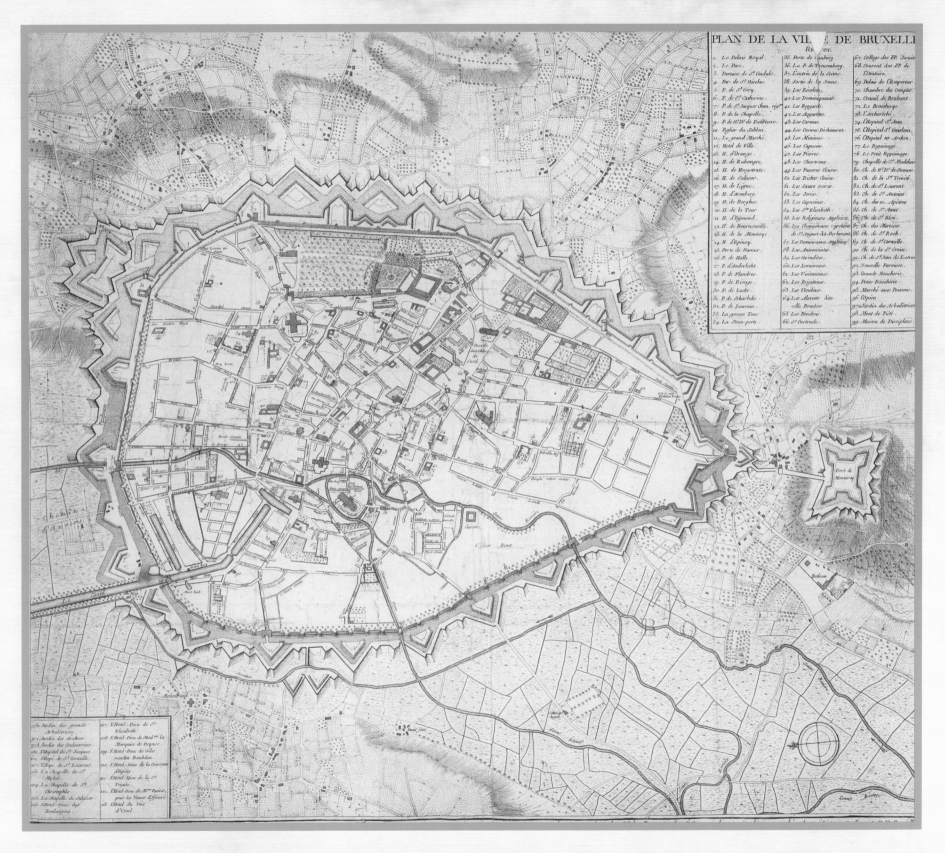

PLAN
TOPOGRAPHIQUE
DE LA VILLE
DE
BRUXELLES
et de ses Environs
Echelle de 150 Toises de France

ABOVE: Engraved by L. A. Dupuis, this map of Brussels records the city as it existed toward the end of the 18th century. At this date the city was still under Austrian rule—a position restored following the War of Austrian Succession (1740–48), which was settled by the Treaty of Aix-La-Chapelle (October 18, 1848)—but this was not to last much longer. In 1794 the city was seized by the French as a result of the war that broke out in 1792 following the French Revolution of 1789 and the subsequent execution of the French king, Louis XVI, and his Austrian-born queen, Marie Antoinette.

RIGHT: Produced by Bradshaw & Blacklock of Manchester, England, this map records the city of Brussels in the mid-19th century. The map, which is aligned with north toward the right, records the growth of the city during the first half of the 19th century, in particular the creation of the wide boulevards built upon the site of the former city walls and the arrival of the railway. The first railway, linking Brussels with Mechelen, opened in 1835; this was also the first main line railway to open in continental Europe.

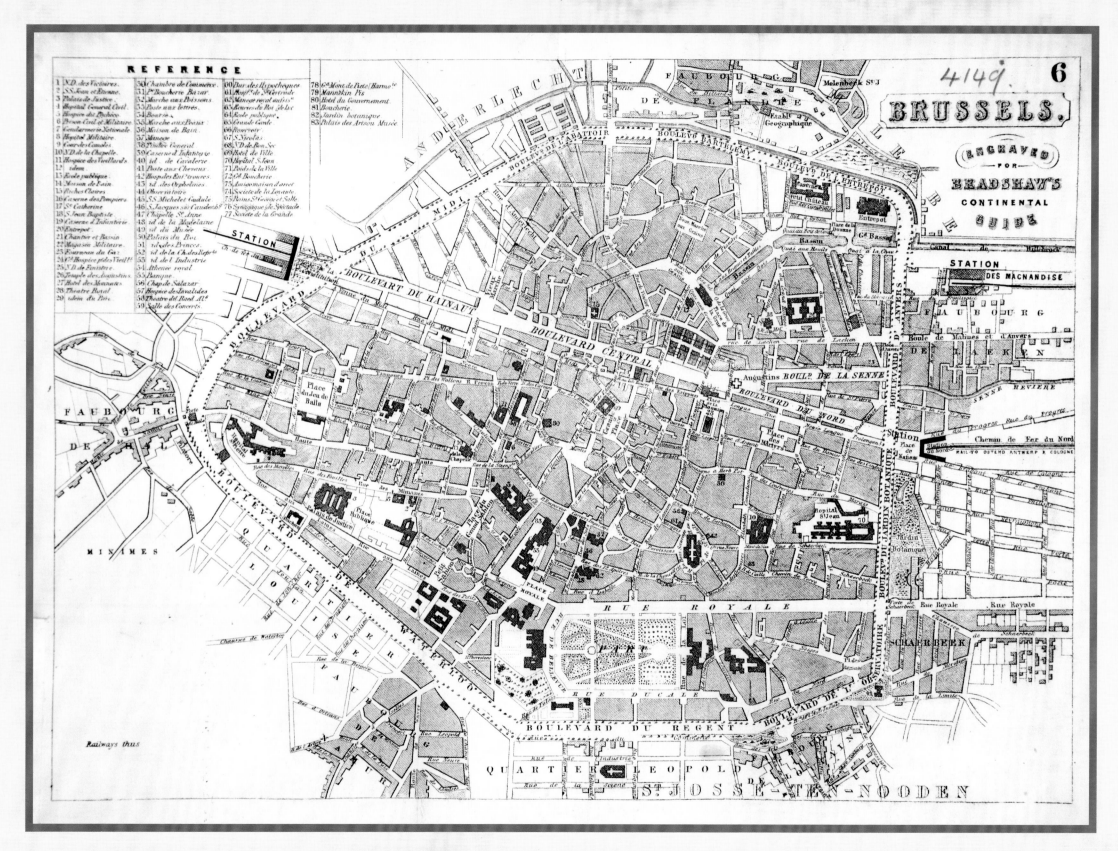

CAIRO

EGYPT

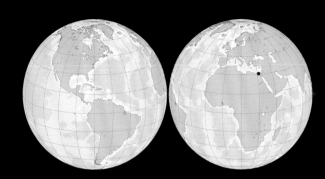

With a population of around 11 million, Cairo is the capital city of Egypt, located on the River Nile about 100 miles inland from the Mediterranean.

In 640A.D., following a siege of the fortress of Babylon, the Byzantine governor of Egypt surrendered to a Muslim army led by Amr ibn al-A'as, who became the first Arab ruler of the country. The new rulers sought to move the country's capital from Alexandria to a new city, Al-Fustat, founded in 751 on the east bank of the Nile across from the fortress of Babylon (south of modern Cairo).

For three centuries Al-Fustat and Egypt belonged to a series of dynasties, including the Umayyads (with their capital at Damascus), who were the first rulers of the Muslim Caliphate from 660–750A.D., and the Abbasides (with their capital at Baghdad), who controlled Egypt until the late 10th century.

By that time a new threat had emerged—this time from the west, where Ubayd Allah al-Mahdi Billah, the founder of the Fatimid dynasty, had established a military base in Tunisia in 909. One of his successors, Ma'ad al-Muizz Li-Deenillah, sent an army under Gawhar al-Siqilli to capture Egypt and it was Gawhar who founded the city now known as Cairo in 969A.D. The new settlement was designed to be the residence of the Fatimid Caliphs, with the administration and economic center remaining at Al-Fustat. The Fatimids were to rule Egypt for two centuries.

By the late 12th century Egypt had become a battleground between the Crusaders and the Seljuk Turks and, in 1168, Cairo fell to Asad ad-Din Shirkuh bin Shadhi, who was named governor of the city by the Sultan of Damascus. Much of the Seljuk army was comprised of slaves and former slaves known as Mamluks.

The Mamluks were to rule Cairo until 1517 when Egypt was captured by the Ottoman Empire, although the Mamluks continued to exercise power locally thereafter under the control of a Turkish governor, or Pasha. The Ottoman Empire continued to rule Egypt until the end of the 18th century when, following a French landing in 1798, Cairo was occupied by Napoleon for three years. The French were succeeded by the dynasty established by Sultan Muhammad Ali-Pasha al-Mas'ud ibn Agha, which was to rule the revolution of 1952, although for much of that period, from 1882 onward, the country was occupied by British troops and thus a de facto British Protectorate.

BELOW: Cairo and the pyramids taken in 2001 by NASA's ASTER (Advanced Spaceborne Thermal Emission and Reflection Radiometer) aboard the Terra satellite. The pyramids, almost subsumed by Cairo's relentless growth, are obscured by patchy cloud cover at top center.

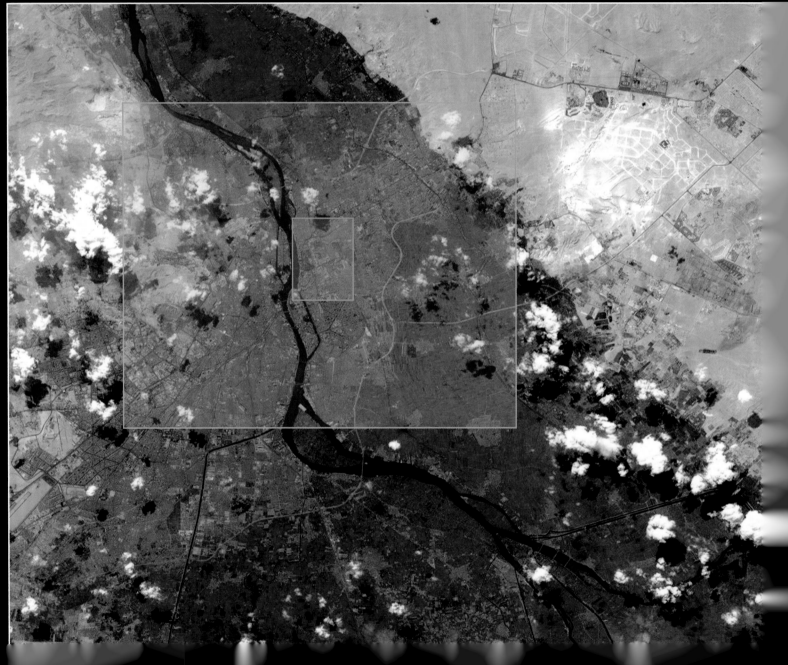

LEFT: The city of Cairo was under the rule of the Mamluks until Egypt was captured by the Ottoman Empire and this map, drafted during the first century of Ottoman rule, shows the city as it then existed. Many of the fortifications in and around Cairo dated from the 12th and 13th centuries and reflected the fact that northern Egypt was fought over by the Christian and Moslem armies during the period of the Crusades. Also visible, across the Nile, is the Giza plateau with its pyramids and the sphinx. At this date there was a considerable distance between the city and these ancient ruins; however, as Cairo has expanded so these archaeological remains have become subsumed within the area of the city.

RIGHT: This late 19th-century map of Cairo, at a scale of 1:18,000, was produced at the same time as renewed British interest in Egypt—a result of the opening of the Suez Canal in 1866. In 1882 British forces had acted in support of a nationalist rising led by Arabi Pasha against the country's Ottoman rulers. After the British intervention, the country was effectively ruled by the British Agent and Consul General Sir Evelyn Baring, from Alexandria, between 1883 and 1907. By the date of this map the first railways had arrived to serve the city, with stations both to the north and south.

CALAIS

FRANCE

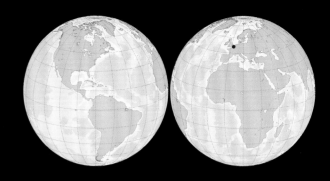

Located on the French side of the English Channel at its narrowest point, about 22 miles across, Calais, with a population of some 77,000, is the largest town in the *département* of Pas-de-Calais. The oldest part of the town, Calais-Nord (which was severely damaged during World War II), is situated on an artificial island surrounded by canals and harbors, whilst the newer section of the city, St-Pierre, lies toward the south.

The city's origins are uncertain, although a port had certainly developed by the 10th century, when it was improved by the Count of Flanders, and it gained its first walls courtesy of the Count of Boulogne in 1224. However, as a result of its pivotal location, the city's importance grew significantly in the years when England and France were at war over the succession to the French throne, after the death of the French king, Charles IV.

The end of English rule over Calais, the last part of France to remain under English domination, came on January 1, 1558, when the French under Francis, Duke of Guise, attacked. Thereafter the history of Calais was to parallel the rest of France. During the 19th century, with the growth of the railway network and the rise of steam-powered ferries, the city's importance grew as a result of the cross-channel shipping traffic.

However, the 20th century witnessed the final great battle for Calais during World War II. As the war progressed the Germans believed that the route through Calais would be that adopted by the Allied forces in any future invasion of France. As a result, the area around Calais was heavily fortified as well as being used as a site for the launch of flying bombs against targets in England. The city and surrounding districts were heavily bombed, sustaining serious damage, with the old town, Calais Nord, effectively demolished. The actual invasion—D-Day of June 6, 1944—occurred further west in Normandy, and it was not until October 1944 that Calais was finally liberated.

After the war the city was rebuilt and it resumed its role as a major port handling ferry traffic to and from England; although this continues, much of the traffic now goes through the Channel Tunnel, a long-cherished dream that was finally opened in 1994.

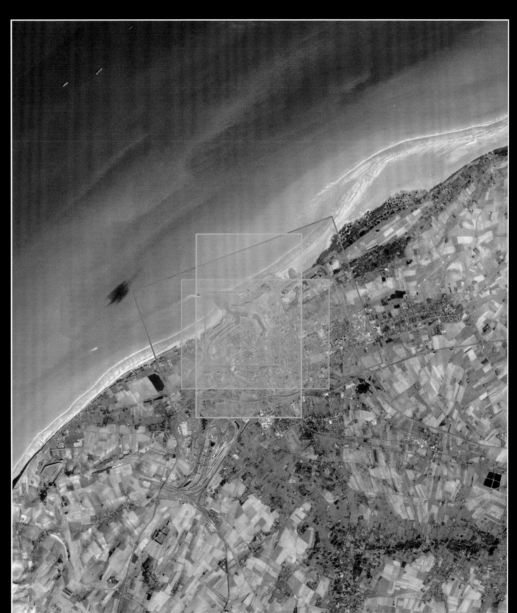

LEFT: Calais taken by the taken by ASTER in 2002.

BELOW: Calais' proximity to England, some 22 miles opposite Dover is obvious from this ASTER image.

Dover

Calais

CALARIS, *Sardiniæ primaria ciuitas, quatuor in partes diuiditur, media quæ fortissimo septa est muro, propriè Calaris, ea verò, quæ orientem spectat, nouum oppidum dicitur: Ea verò pars, quæ meridiem respicit, atque mediterraneū mare, vocatur La Gliapola, seu, la Marina, et quæ ad occidentem vergit, Stampax nominatur, suntq́ hæ tres partes, suburbia quædam, et appendices Calaritanæ vrbis.*

LEFT: For some 400 years subsequent to the successful Norman conquest of England in 1066, England and France had fought for control of much of northern and western France; in 1558, however, England's last territorial possession in France—Calais—was finally to be lost and this late 16th-century map, one of the maps published in *Civitates Orbis Terrarum* by Georg Braun (1541–1622) and Frans Hogenberg (1535–90), shows the city contemporaneously with the English loss.

RIGHT: Calais 1596. A rough plan of Calais showing the citadel, gun batteries, gates, and churches. No scale shown. Some forty years after its loss to the English, in 1596–1598 Calais was occupied by the Spanish. Once it was returned Jean Errard (1554–1610) strengthened the citadel but it was master fortifier Sébastien Le Prestre de Vauban (1633–1707) who transformed the defenses in 1690.

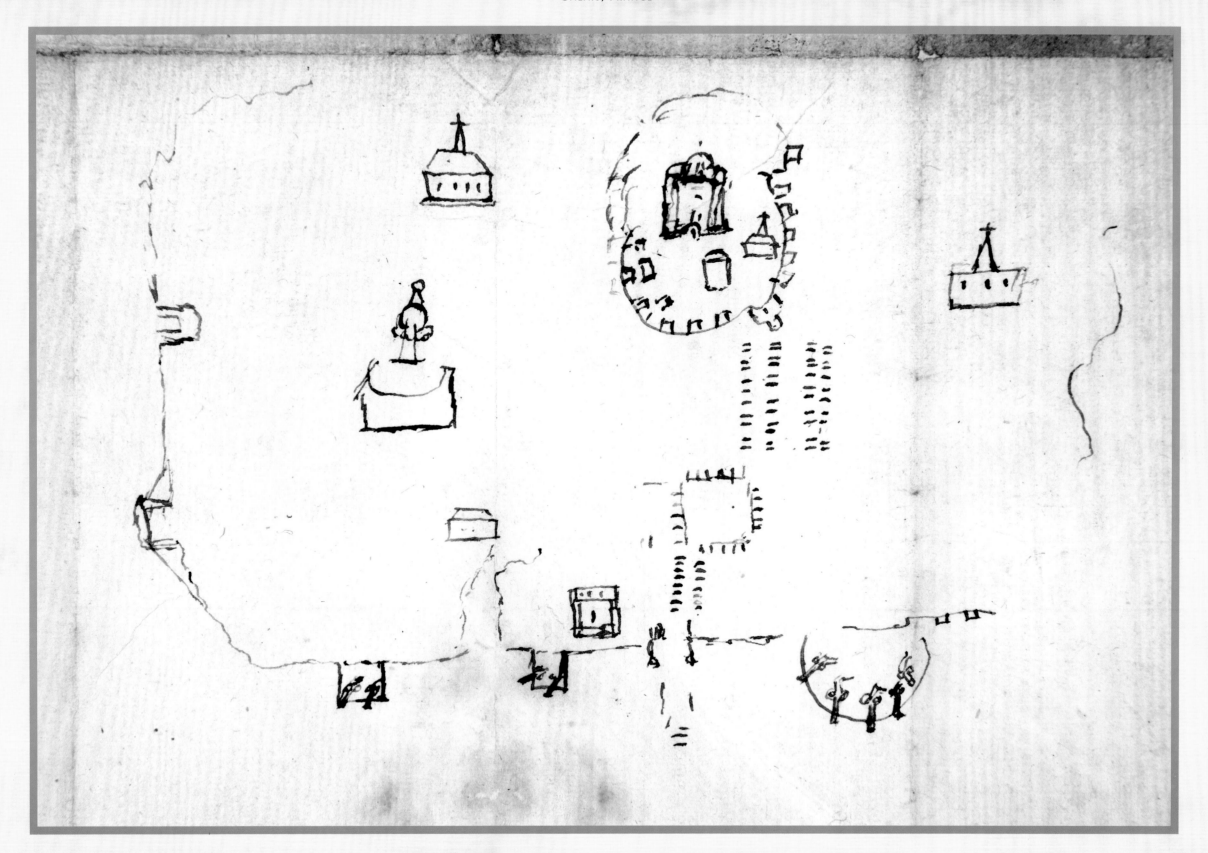

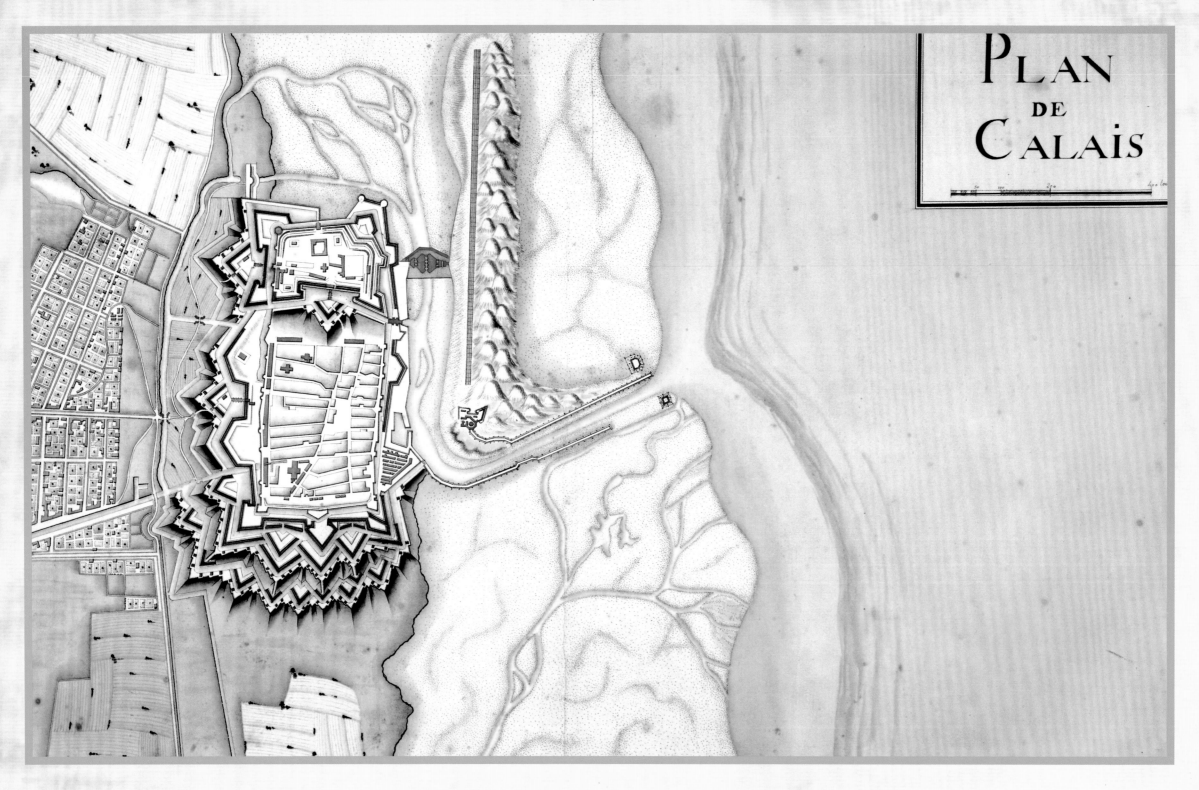

PLAN DE CALAIS

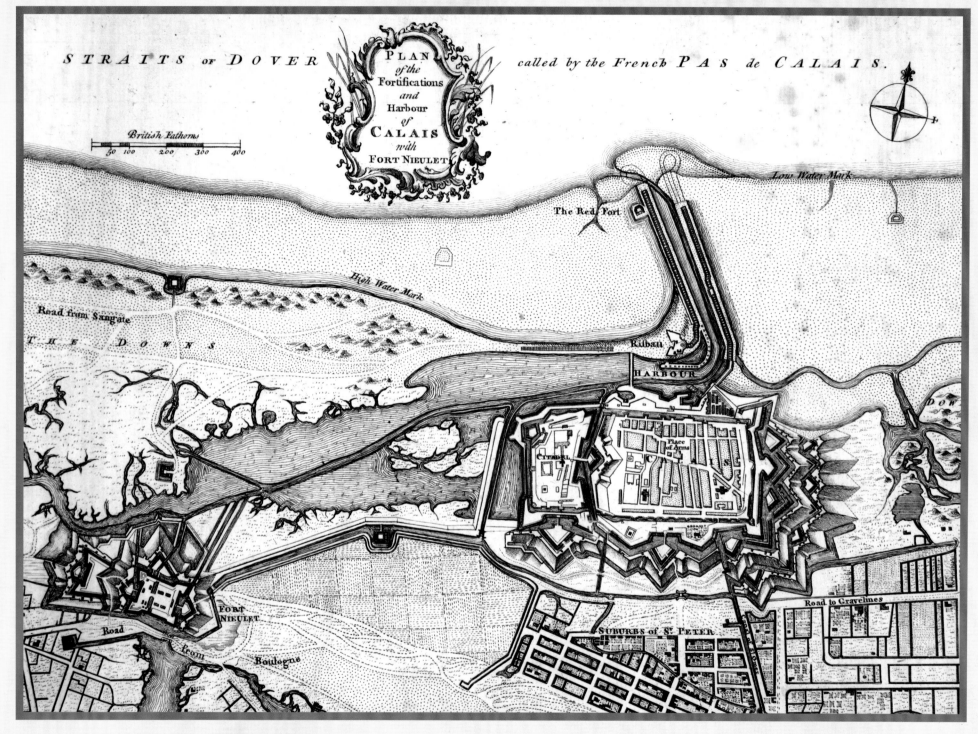

CHICAGO
UNITED STATES

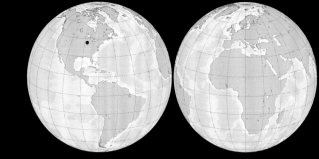

Popularly known as the Windy City, Chicago is the third largest city in the US in terms of population and a major center of trade, industry, and commerce. Situated on the western shore of Lake Michigan, its importance initially was as a transport hub, as it provided a link, courtesy of the canalized Chicago River and the Illinois Waterway, between the Great Lakes and the Mississippi.

Prior to European settlement the region was occupied by a number of Native American tribes, primarily the Potawatomis. A woman from this tribe married the first European settler, Jean Baptiste Pointe du Sable, who reached the area in the 1770s and established a trading post. Twenty years later land was ceded by the Native Americans to the US.

The town of Chicago, with a population of 350, was granted a city charter on March 4, 1837. By the end of the 1830s the city's population had reached 4,000 and, during the next decade, growth was significant, aided by the completion of a number of major transportation projects.

However, in 1871, disaster struck when fire destroyed much of the city. Due to the availability of lumber, much of it had been constructed in timber and destruction was widespread. New regulations were brought in that restricted the use of timber, but the swampy ground on which the city was sited was unsuitable for the erection of tall masonry buildings. This led to the use of steel-framed structures and the development of the skyscraper.

The end of the 19th century and the early 20th century saw the city's population grow to 1.7 million, much of it the result of inward migration from Europe. Like a number of other US cities, Chicago suffered major race riots. In the 1920s Chicago was also notorious as the home of gangsterism, with figures such as Al Capone involved in major criminal activity.

Since the 1930s the city has continued to develop; iconic buildings such as the Sears Tower (the world's tallest building when completed in 1974) and the John Hancock Center dominate the skyline. Post World War II, the city witnessed a decline as the suburbs grew and the wealthy abandoned the inner-city areas, but this trend was reversed by schemes designed to encourage revitalization and regeneration of some of these inner-city areas, and this process is continuing into the 21st century.

BELOW: Chicago taken by Landsat in 2003.

BELOW: Drawn originally by James T. Pamatry and published by Braunhold & Sonne of Chicago in 1857, this panoramic view of the city of Chicago records the city from the east. During the 1840s the city's growth had been great, and by 1860 the population had reached 90,000.

THE CITY OF CHICAGO.

NEW YORK. PUBLISHED BY CURRIER & IVES, 115 NASSAU ST.

LEFT: Produced by Currier & Ives, New York in the late 19th century, this panoramic view of the city, portrayed from the east, shows the extent of the its growth by this date.

RIGHT: Described as "All elevated trains in Chicago stop at the Chicago Rock Island and Pacific Railway Station, only one on the Loop," this map was prepared for the Chicago, Rock Island & Pacific Railway by Poole Bros of Chicago. It provides a bird's-eye view of the elevated railway system and Loop. It also includes indexes to points of interest and a color illustration of "Elevated station at the "Rock Island Van Buren Street station." The first "L"—the Chicago & South Side Rapid Transit Railroad—opened on June 6, 1892, when a small steam locomotive pulling four wooden coaches with 30 passengers departed the 39th Street Station and arrived at Congress Street 14 minutes later. Over the next year the service was extended to 63rd Street and Stony Island Avenue, then the entrance to the World's Columbian Exposition in Jackson Park. The network grew rapidly, and other railroads soon opened. In 1895 the Metropolitan West Side Elevated was the first to use electric traction. A drawback of the early, elevated services was that none of the lines entered the central business district. Instead, trains dropped passengers at stub terminals on the periphery. This was due to a state law requiring approval by neighboring property owners for tracks to be built over public streets, something not easily obtained in the central area. The first section to enter the business district was the Union Loop, which opened in 1897 through the influence and power of Charles Tyson Yerkes.

FOLLOWING PAGE: "The City of Chicago, showing the burnt district." Published in *Harpers Weekly*, August 1, 1874, from a colored print published by Currier & Ives, it shows part of the area that burned from Sunday October 8 to early Tuesday October 10, 1871, killing hundreds and destroying about four square miles of city.

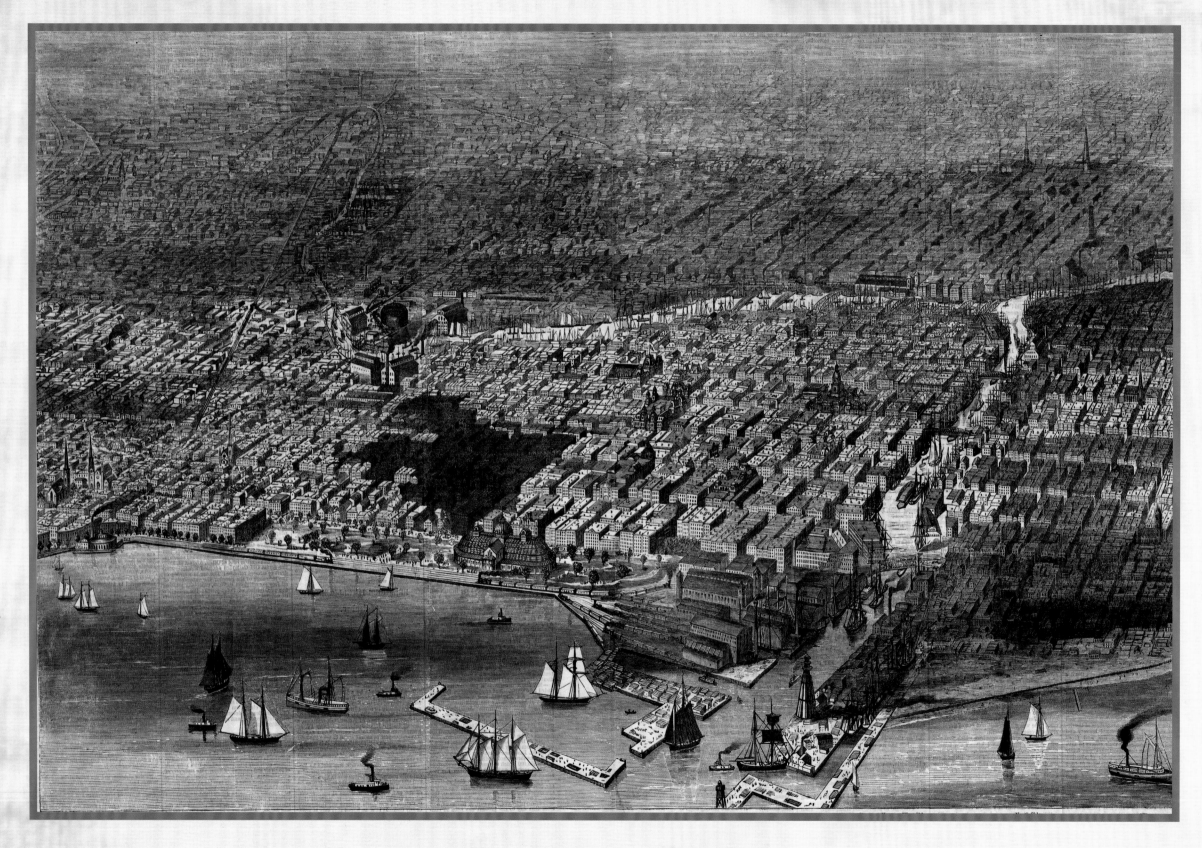

COLOGNE
GERMANY

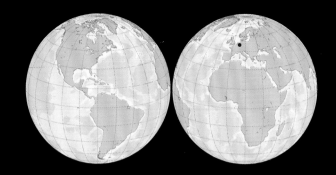

Situated on the River Rhine in the German Land of North Rhine-Westphalia, Cologne (Köln) has a population of just over one million and, with eight bridges crossing the river within its city boundaries, is a major transport and commercial center. Cologne possesses the largest university in Germany and is also an important manufacturing city, with companies such as Ford having major plants in the district.

The city's origins date back to the 1st century B.C. when the Ubii tribe settled on the west bank of the Rhine. Their initial settlement was called Oppidum Ubiorum (city of the Urbii) and a Roman military base was also established at the site.

As the Roman Empire declined the position of Cologne came under threat from the Germanic tribes. In 355A.D. the city was besieged and briefly captured by the Alemanni. A century later it was seized by the Salian Franks and became their capital. The city was raised to the status of an archbishopric in 785A.D.

In 1798 the French army occupied Cologne and, following the Treaty of Lunéville, the city became part of the French Département de la Roer (named after the River Ruhr). The French closed the university following their occupation and it was not restored until after World War I. In 1801 the city's residents were granted French citizenship and the French legal system—the Code Napoleon—was introduced; it was in use in the region until 1900. In 1814, however, French occupation ceased as the city was captured by the Prussian army and, following the Congress of Vienna, Cologne and the surrounding area became part of Prussia.

During the 19th century Cologne grew rapidly, reaching a population of 700,000 by 1914. Following the Armistice of 1918 and the Treaty of Versailles in 1919, the British occupied Cologne until 1926. In 1936 it was reoccupied by the Germans in one of the first aggressive moves undertaken by Nazi Germany.

Cologne suffered severely during World War II, enduring more than 260 raids, including the first 1,000-bomber raid undertaken by the Royal Air force—Operation Millennium—on May 31, 1942. In all some 20,000 civilians were killed by Allied raids during the war and much of the central area of the city was completely destroyed. Many of the historic buildings have since been rebuilt or restored.

LEFT: Satellite image of northern Germany. Water is blue, vegetation is green, urban areas are grey. Cologne (Köln) is Germany's fourth largest city after Berlin, Hamburg, and Munich, and one of the oldest.

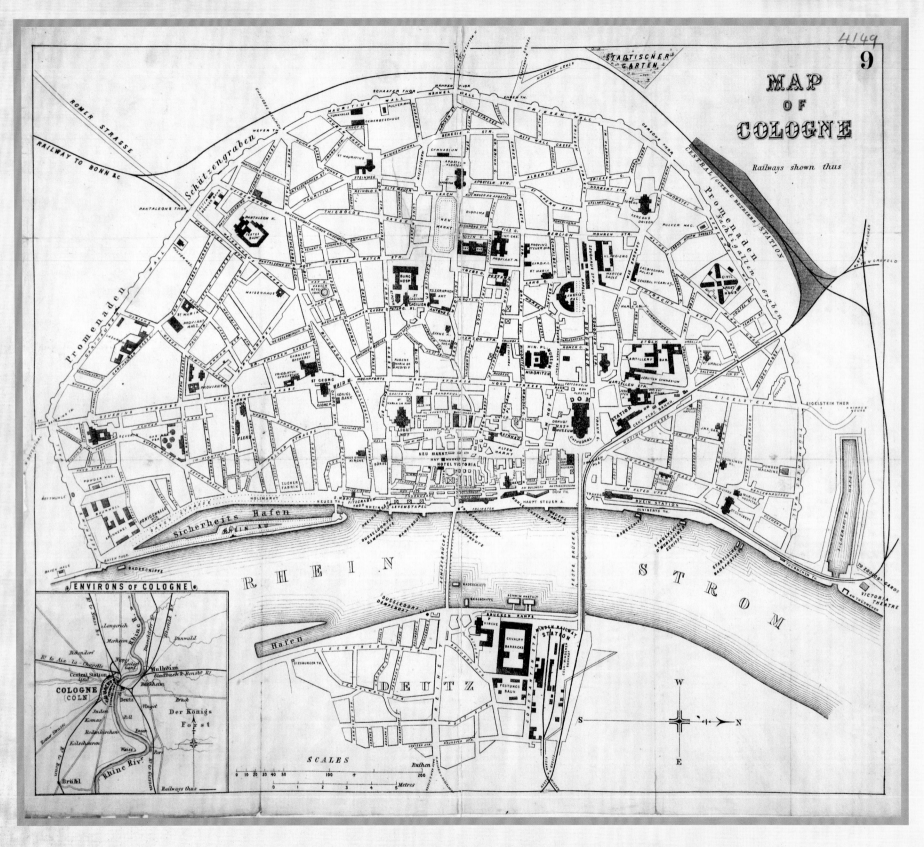

MAP
OF
COLOGNE

Railways shown thus

COPENHAGEN

DENMARK

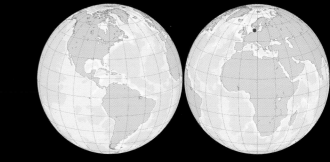

Copenhagen, the capital of Denmark, sits on the eastern side of the island of Sjaelland (Zealand), the largest of the 480 islands that, along with the Jylland (Jutland) peninsula, form the kingdom of Denmark—known in Danish as København. The name is derived from Køpmandenes Havn or "the harbor of merchants."

In 1167 the area was bestowed by Valdemar the Great to Bishop Absalon of Roskilde, who built the fortress of Slotsholmen as a defense against Wendish pirates. A settlement grew up around the fortress and, in 1254, the city was granted its municipal charter. By the start of the 15th century Copenhagen had a population of around 4,000 and had become an important naval and commercial base. The wealth of the city was enhanced by the imposition of tolls in 1426 on shipping passing through the sound between Sjaelland and southern Sweden. During the latter half of the 15th century the city's walls were extended and its university was founded in 1479.

By 1700, the city's population had expanded to 60,000, but almost a third died in 1712 following an outbreak of plague, and, in 1728, much of the old city was destroyed by fire. The city suffered a second major conflagration in 1795. Impressive buildings such as the palace of Christianborg Palace and the Marble Church (Frederiks Kirke) were completed in the 18th century.

In 1801 the Battle of Copenhagen was fought as the British fleet sought to prevent the Danish fleet help lift the blockade of France; it was during this engagement that Admiral Nelson famously put his telescope to his blind eye to ignore an order from the fleet's commander. Six years later, with Denmark supporting Napoleon, a British force landed at Vidbaek and bombarded the city; causing serious damage, the British also seized the Danish fleet.

Following the Napoleonic era Copenhagen entered a period of relative decline and it was not until the second half of the 19th century that the city started to grow again. In 1867 the city walls were demolished and a number of parks—most notably the famous Tivoli Gardens—were constructed. The city's commercial position was strengthened, following the ending of the shipping tolls in 1857, by the creation of a free port in 1894.

During World War II, despite its claimed neutrality, Denmark was occupied by the Germans until May 4, 1945. Copenhagen today is by far the most important commercial and industrial city in the country, and plays host both to the country's parliament, as well as to its monarch.

BELOW: This Landsat Thematic Mapper image shows Copenhagen in 2004. The island of Saltholm is at right and just below it the artificial island (Pepparholmen) that is part of the five-mile long Øresund Bridge, which opened up for traffic in July 2000, joining Denmark and Sweden.

COPPEN-HAGEN.

LEFT: Aligned with north toward the right, this map of Copenhagen was produced at the height of the Napoleonic Wars and records the British siege of the city undertaken between August 23 and September 6, 1807. At this stage the Danes were supporting Napoleon and the British army landed at Vidbaek in order to attack the city. The map records the location of the British artillery at this time. The city, within its defensive ramparts, is clearly delineated with the northern part of the city defended by the Citadel of Frederickhaven (sic). The island of Amager to the city's east lies between Copenhagen and Malmo in southern Sweden.

FAR LEFT: Viewed from the east, this panoramic view of the city of Copenhagen was produced by the Dutch artist Rombout van den Hoeye (born 1622) and records the city during the second half of the 17th century when, following the reign of King Christian IV, the city had undergone a considerable transformation with the construction of such notable buildings as the Rosenborg Palace, Holmens Church and the Trinitatis Church with the Round Tower. The city considerably expanded during this period, with the development of the Christianshavn district, and its fortifications were improved. These proved their worth in 1658–9 when the city withstood a siege by Swedish forces led by Charles X Gustavus.

KJOBENHAVN.

LEFT: This map records the Danish capital city and its environs in the early 1860s. The central core of the city with its original fortifications can be seen clearly, as can the island of Amager to the east. Further to the east is the coast of southern Sweden; the relatively narrow passage between the island of Sjaelland and southern Sweden was one reason for Copenhagen's strategic importance, particularly when the Danish crown ruled both sides of the strait. Although the city walls were still intact at this date, they were to be dismantled later in the 1860s. The scale of this map allows for the outlying villages and towns situated around Copenhagen to be clearly shown; as the city expanded during the late 19th and 20th centuries, many of these were formally incorporated within the greater Copenhagen area. From the mid-20th century onward, the city's planners conceived the "five-finger" plan, with the city expanding along five corridors radiating from the central core into the suburbs. This version of the map, held in Britain's National Archives, incorporates manuscript additions from the early 1880s that show works proposed.

CORK

IRELAND

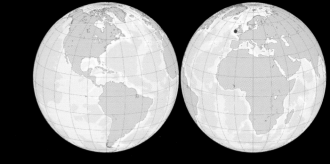

Now the Republic of Ireland's second city, with a population in excess of 119,000, Cork—or "Corcaigh" (marshy place)—lies on the estuary of the River Lee on the south coast. The city originated as a monastic settlement established by St Finbar in the 6th century, but its development as an urban center started in the 9th century when the Vikings established a trading post in 846A.D. The Vikings remained the dominant force locally until 1177, when the settlement was besieged and captured by the Anglo-Normans.

The city grew during the Anglo-Norman period, although it suffered heavily as a result of the Black Death in 1349 when more than half its population of 2,000 died. During these years, Cork remained very much an outpost of English power in this part of Ireland. The surrounding countryside remained mostly in the hands of the native lords, many of whom were antipathetic to English rule. As with other Anglo-Norman settlements, Cork was a prosperous trading center during this period. In 1491, following the overthrow of King Richard III and his replacement by Henry VII in the Wars of the Roses, one of the many Yorkist pretenders to the throne, Perkin Warbeck, landed at Cork hoping to foment rebellion; he failed, however, and a number of Cork's prominent citizens were executed for treason as a result. During the 16th century, following the Reformation, the English endeavored to change the nature of the Irish population by encouraging the migration of Protestants from Wales and Scotland—the so-called "Plantations"—and this led to significant religious turmoil and rebellion toward the end of the century and into the 17th century.

In 1641, Ireland was beset by a Catholic rebellion, and Limerick became a haven for the Protestant refugees, withstanding a siege from the Catholic rebels. As a result of this, Murrough O'Brien, the Ear of Inchiquinn, who commanded the English forces in the city, expelled any resident Catholics from within the city walls. Although O'Brien briefly backed the Confederation of Kilkenny, the city quickly surrendered to Cromwell's forces in 1649.

In the 18th century Cork took in further refugees, this time Huguenot Protestants from France, and this influx resulted in considerable redevelopment of the city, with the result that most of the buildings visible in the map of the late 16th century were swept away.

BELOW: Satellite image of the city of Cork (center) and its surrounding area on the southern coast of Ireland. North is at top. Forested areas are dark green, agricultural fields are lighter shades of green and brown, urban areas are grey, water is black and clouds are white. The sea at bottom right is the Celtic Sea. Image created using NaturalVue data obtained from the Landsat 7 satellite.

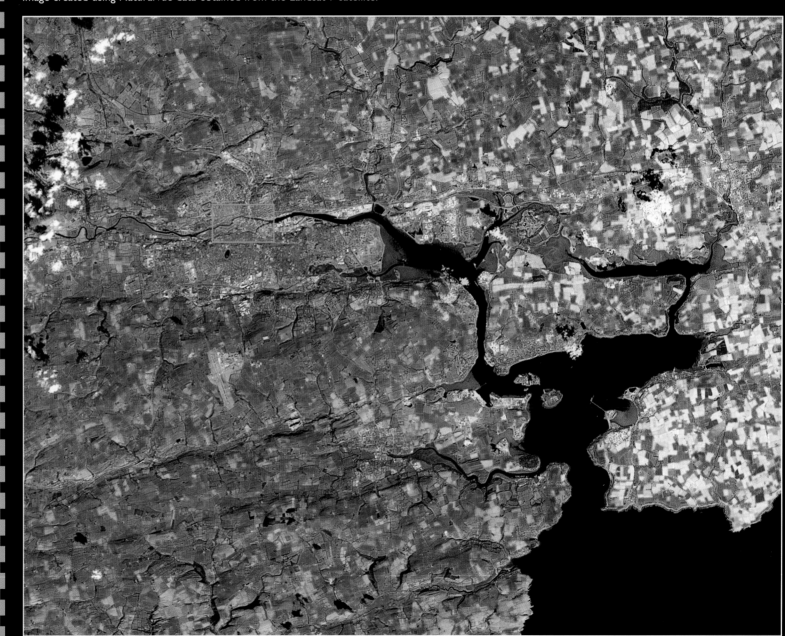

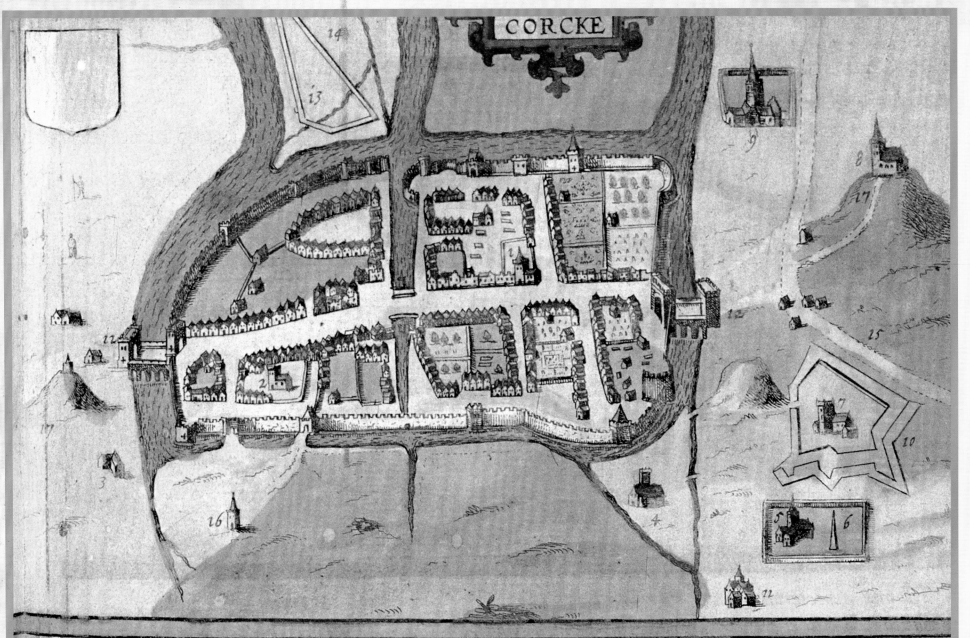

CORCKE

LEFT: This map, which is aligned with the south toward the top, portrays the city of Cork at a time when the English rulers in Ireland were actively seeking to increase the Protestant population of the country by encouraging migration from England and later from Scotland. The city walls shown were finally to be demolished in 1690. Of the medieval buildings illustrated little now survive, as the city was to suffer severely during the war of the 1640s when it was captured by insurgents.

1. Chrifts Church.	6. The Spyre.	11 The Bifhops houfe	16. Shandon Caftle.
2. S. Peters Church.	7. Holly Rode.	12 The Ports.	17. The Hills commanding
3. S. Franis Abbey.	8. S. Steuens Church.	13 The Entrance Fort.	the Town.
4. Abbey ofey Ifle.	9. S. Augustines.	14 The Walke about	
5. S. Barries Church.	10 The new Fort	15 The Way to Kinfale	

CRACOW
POLAND

Now the third largest city in Poland, Cracow (Krakow), situated on the Vistula River in the south of the country, is the capital of the Lesser Poland region. Between 1038 and 1596 it was the capital of Poland, and it is widely regarded today as the country's spiritual home. The city was designated a World Heritage Site by UNESCO in 1978, and later the same year the Archbishop of Cracow, Józef Wojtyla, became the first non-Italian pope for 455 years when he was elevated to the papacy as John Paul II.

The city's golden age began in 1364 when King Kazimierz (Casimir) III the Great, who ruled Poland from 1333 to 1370, founded the University of Cracow; this was only the second university to be established in Central Europe. Cracow witnessed the construction of many superb buildings and attracted many prominent scientists, thinkers, and artists. It also became a member of the Hanseatic League in the 15th century. This network of traders linked the Baltic with the Low Countries and with England, developing commerce and aiding the growth of prosperity.

The late 15th and early 16th centuries witnessed a massive growth in learning in the city and several prominent writers and artists were based there. These included Hans Dürer, the younger brother of Albrecht, who was the court artist in the early 16th century. However, the city's golden age was drawing to a close; in 1572 King Sigismund II, the last of the Jagiellon line, died childless and the throne ultimately passed to Sigismund III of the Swedish royal house of Vasa.

Sigismund III's rule was marked by war in which Swedish troops pillaged the city, by plague (which cost some 20,000 lives), and by the decision in 1596 to make Warsaw the new capital of Poland. By the 18th century Poland was in relative decline, bounded by the three more powerful states of Austria, Russia, and Prussia. These arranged for Poland to be partitioned in three phases and Cracow eventually became part of the Austrian province of Galicia. Poland as a country had ceased to exist.

Poland again gained independence after World War I, but was once more partitioned in 1939 following the invasion of the country by German and Russian forces. Polish independence, albeit with redrawn borders, was yet again achieved in 1945, although Cracow remained a Soviet client state until the fall of the Berlin Wall in 1989.

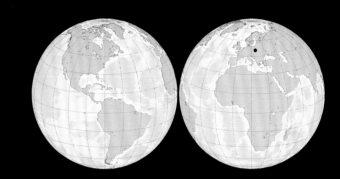

BELOW: Satellite image of the city of Crakow (center) and its surrounding area in southern Poland. North is at top. Forested areas are dark green, agricultural fields are lighter shades of green and brown, urban areas are grey and water is black. Image created using NaturalVue data obtained from the Landsat 7 satellite.

CRACOVIA
MINORIS POLONIAE METROPOLIS.

A. Aula Regia.
B. T. S.ti Stanislai.
C. T. S.ti Georgij.
D. T. Corporis Christi.
E. Monast. Bernardinorum.
F. Praetorium.
G. T. S.ti Trinitatis.
H. T. S.te Mariae.
I. Porta Vielizka.
K. Porta Bognizki.
L. Porta Sceuinski.
M. T. S.ti Leonardi.
N. T. S.ti Andreae.
O. T. S.ti Iacobi.

Depictum ab Egidio vander Rye,
communic. Georgius Houfnaglius.

ABOVE: By the late 16th century Cracow was a center of learning, with numerous colleges, as well being the capital of the Polish-Lithuanian kingdom. Its prominence, however, was to decline when Warsaw became the country's new capital in 1596. Behind the city walls, rebuilt in the 13th century following the city's destruction by the Mongol army of Batu Khan, can be seen Wawel castle and cathedral. The former, which had its origins in the 10th and 11th centuries, was largely destroyed by fire in 1499 but had been rebuilt. Located slightly outside the city walls was the Jewish quarter of Kazimierz; this had been established in 1494 when King Jan Albrecht expelled any Jewish people resident within the city walls. It ultimately became one of the most prosperous Jewish communities in Europe.

RIGHT: This map, part of a larger map covering the Austro-Hungarian Empire, was originally published by the Militärisch-geografisches Insititut, Vienna, in 1880 and distributed by R. Lechner. It was revised in 1887. The colored manuscript additions show the positions of forts around the city. The map originally illustrated a report submitted by Major A. M. Murray, Royal Artillery, in September 1890 to the British War Office.

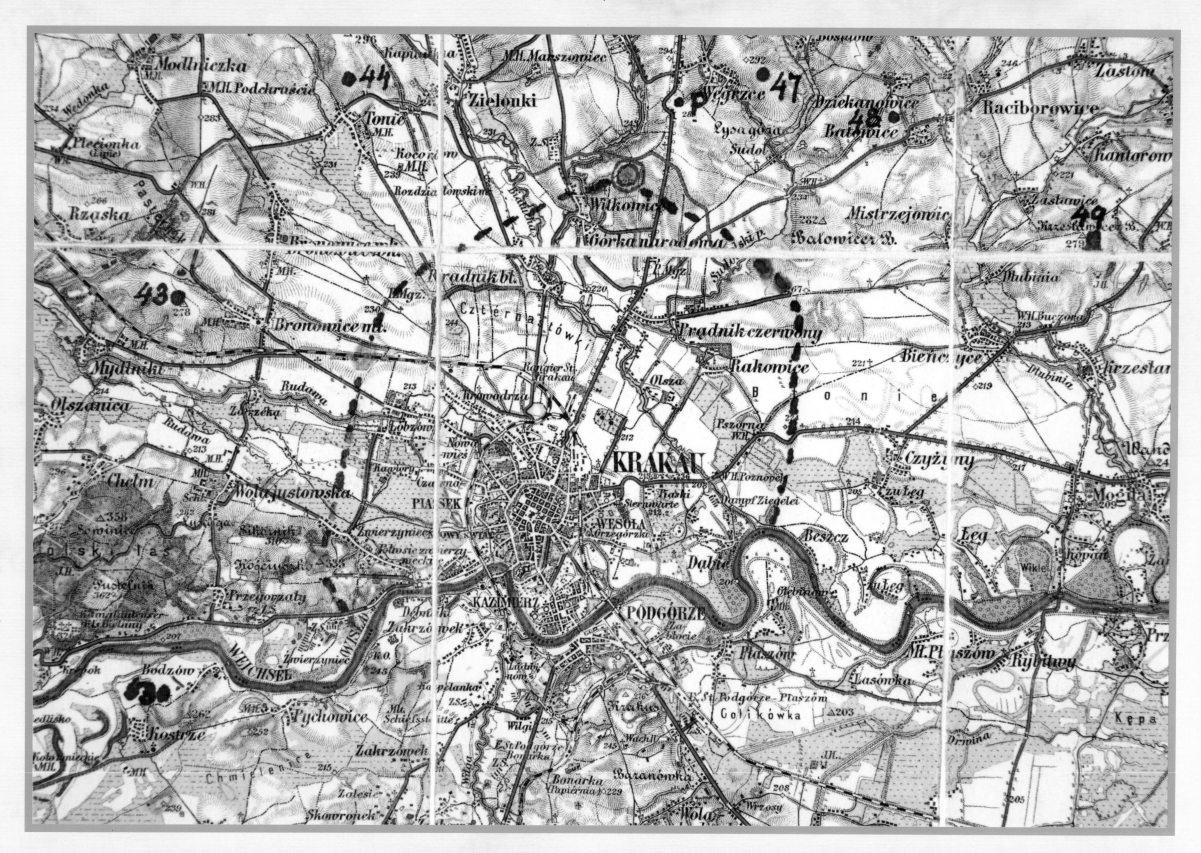

DUBLIN

IRELAND

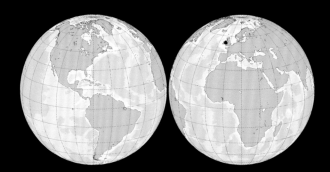

Dublin, located on the River Liffey, is the capital of the Irish Republic. Known in Irish as either Baile Atha Cliath (town of the hurdle ford), the older of the two, or Dubhlinn (dark pool), the city and its suburbs has a population in excess of one million.

The city's original Irish name refers to a ford across the Liffey over which St Patrick, Ireland's patron saint, is believed to have crossed in 448A.D. during his mission to convert the Irish to Christianity. However, the city's rise to pre-eminence began with the first Viking raids in the second half of the 8th century. They were driven out in 902, only to return again in 917 under Ivar the Boneless, and a new settlement was established—"Dyfflin." Viking influence gradually declined as a result of inter-marriage with the local population and with the conversion to Christianity, and this power was further eroded in 1014 when the Irish High King, Brian Boru, defeated a Viking army at the Battle of Clontarf.

For the next century and a half Dublin came under Irish rule but, following the Anglo-Norman invasion of 1169 at Wexford, the city was captured in 1170. Under the Anglo-Normans, Henry II ordered the construction of Dublin Castle in the early 13th century and the city walls were extended to the north in 1312. The Anglo-Norman defenses of the city were further strengthened by the creation of the "Pale," a heavily defended territory intended to keep the native Irish away. In 1316, Edward and Robert Bruce led an army toward Dublin but failed to take the city.

Following the Reformation and the dissolution of the monasteries, much land in and around the city was released and a considerable amount of building work took place. During the 17th century further work was also undertaken, but it was during the 18th century that many of the city's finest surviving buildings were built. Although Ireland shared a monarch with the rest of the British Isles, the country retained its own parliament until they 1801 Act of Union, and as a capital city during the Age of Enlightenment the city benefited from an influx of foreign craftsmen. It was only when the aristocratic patronage that had aided Dublin's development transferred to London that Dublin's role as a leading-edge city gradually diminished, although it continued to expand during the 19th century as a result of industrialization and the migration from the rural to urban areas.

BELOW: This Spot image of Dublin shows 2008's fifth-richest city in the world—a far cry from its 1960s' persona as "the last 19th Century City of Europe."

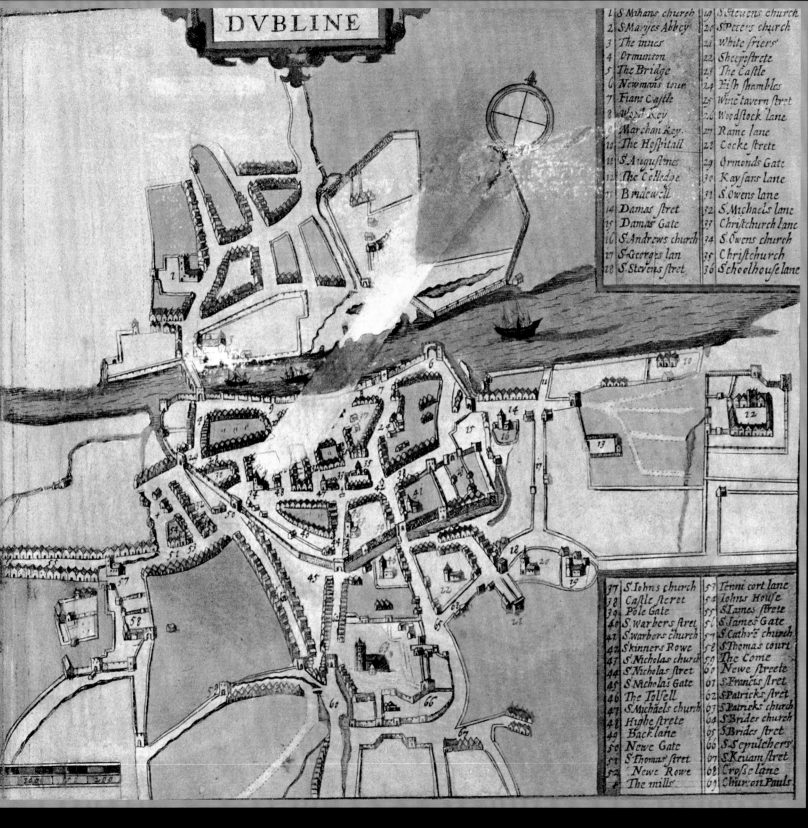

DVBLINE

1	S. Mihans church	19	S. Steuens church
2	S. Maryes Abbey	20	S. Peters church
3	The innes	21	White friers
4	Ormunton	22	Sheepestrete
5	The Bridge	23	The Castle
6	Newmans tour	24	Fish shambles
7	Fians Castle	25	Wine tavern stret
8	Wood Key	26	Woodstock lane
9	Marchan Key	27	Rame lane
10	The Hospitall	28	Cocke strete
11	S. Augustines	29	Ormonds Gate
12	The Colledge	30	Kaysars lane
13	Bridewell	31	S. Owens lane
14	Damas stret	32	S. Michaels lane
15	Damas Gate	33	Christchurch lane
16	S. Andrews church	34	S. Owens church
17	S. Georges lan	35	Christchurch
18	S. Steuens stret	36	Schoolhouse lane

37	S. Iohns church	53	Tennis cort lane
38	Castle steret	54	Iohns House
39	Pole Gate	55	S. Iames strete
40	S. warbers stret	56	S. Iames Gate
41	S. warbers church	57	S. Cathr̄ church
42	Skinners Rowe	58	S. Thomas court
43	S. Nicholas church	59	The Come
44	S. Nicholas stret	60	Newe streete
45	S. Nicholas Gate	61	S. Francis stret
46	The Tolsell	62	S. Patricks stret
47	S. Michaels church	63	S. Patricks church
48	Highe strete	64	S. Brides church
49	Back lane	65	S. Brides stret
50	Newe Gate	66	S. Sepulchers
51	S. Thomas stret	67	S. Keuam stret
52	Newe Rowe	68	Crosse lane
	The mills	69	Churcon Pauls

LEFT: At this time, the late 16th century, Dublin was still a relatively small city, but prominent buildings on the south side of the River Liffey—such as the castle, which dated originally to the 13th century and the earliest period of English occupation of Ireland, Christ Church Cathedral, which was originally a monastery until it was dissolved in 1539, and Trinity College, founded in 1592—are all visible in this map.

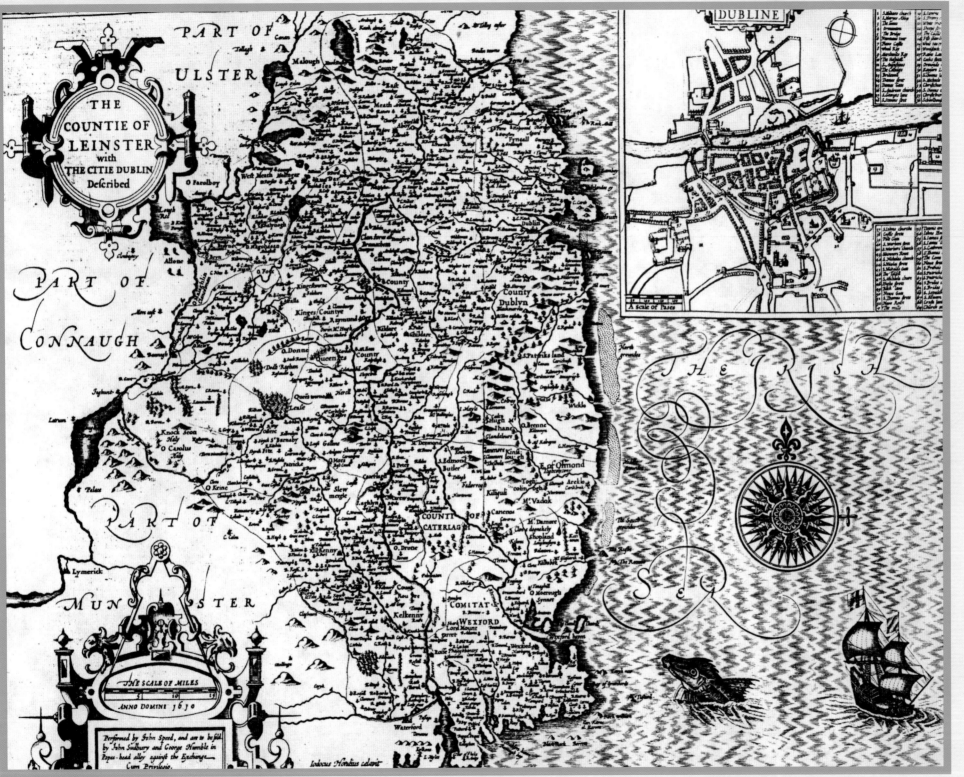

LEFT: Dublin is shown as an inset to a map of the county of Leinster, drawn and engraved by Jodocus Hondius (1563–1612). It was published in *Theatre of the Empire of Great Britain* by John Sudbury and George Humble.

RIGHT: This is a sketch map of the city of Dublin and its environs produced in 1803, two years after the Act of Union, which had seen parliamentary responsibility for Ireland transferred from Dublin to London. The key identifies those buildings in red as belonging to the king (ie King George III); those in black as public buildings; and those in gray as private property. Also identified are those buildings used for the potential defense of the city. The map was produced at the height of the Napoleonic Wars and the threat of military invasion of Ireland by the French was real; in 1798 a rebellion in Ireland had seen French landings in County Mayo and County Donegal in support of the rebels. The Grand Canal, seen heading southwestward from the Liffey, circled the south side of Dublin and turned inland, providing access for water-borne traffic to the island's interior. The Grand Canal, with a length of 80 miles and 52 locks along its route, provided a link between Dublin Bay and the River Shannon. Construction of the canal began in 1756; it was completed in 1804. Apart from its use for transport, the canal also improved the water supply to the ever-growing city. Its importance declined with the rise of the railways from the mid-19th century. Today the canal is used primarily by leisure craft.

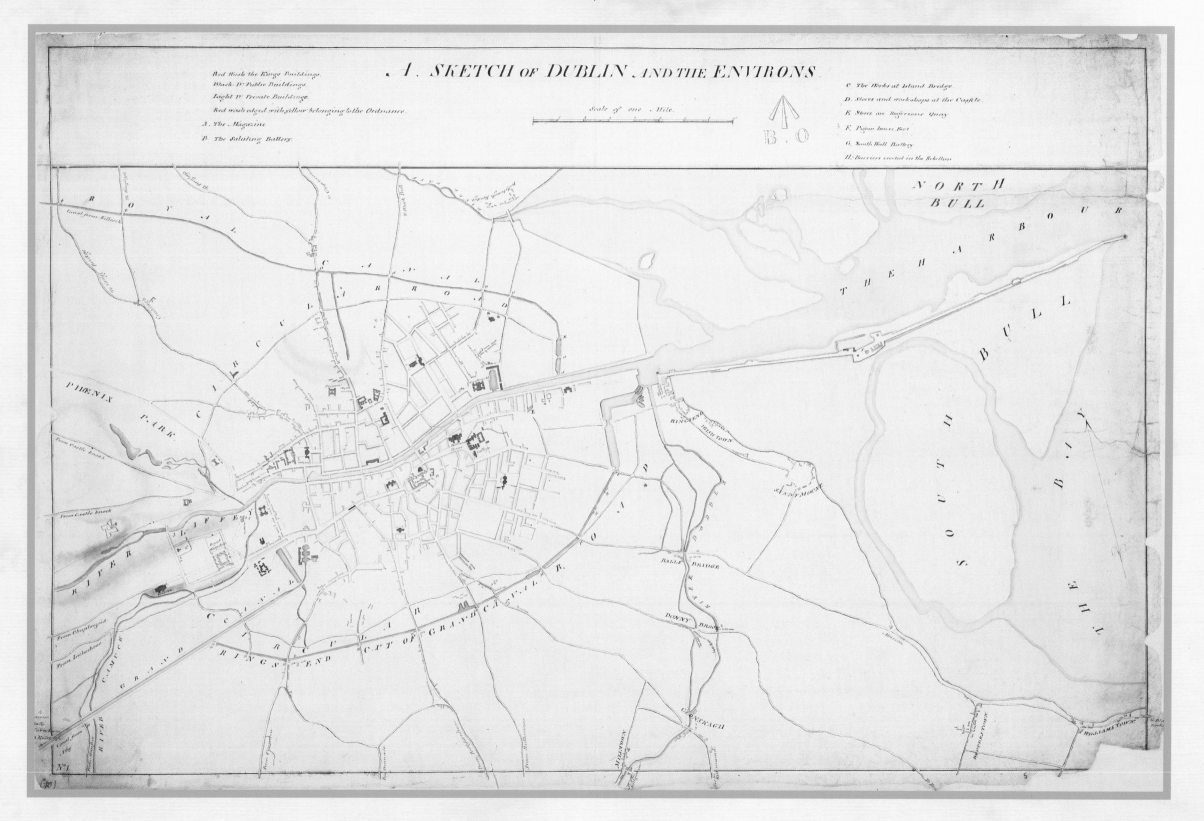

A SKETCH OF DUBLIN AND THE ENVIRONS.

Red Wash the Kings Buildings.
Black D.° Public Buildings.
Light D.° Private Buildings.
Red wash edged with yellow belonging to the Ordnance.
A. The Magazine
B. The Saluting Battery.

Scale of one Mile.

C. The Works at Island Bridge.
D. Stores and workshops at the Castle.
E. Stores on Rogerson's Quay.
F. Pigeon house Fort
G. South Wall Battery
H. Barriers erected in the Rebellion

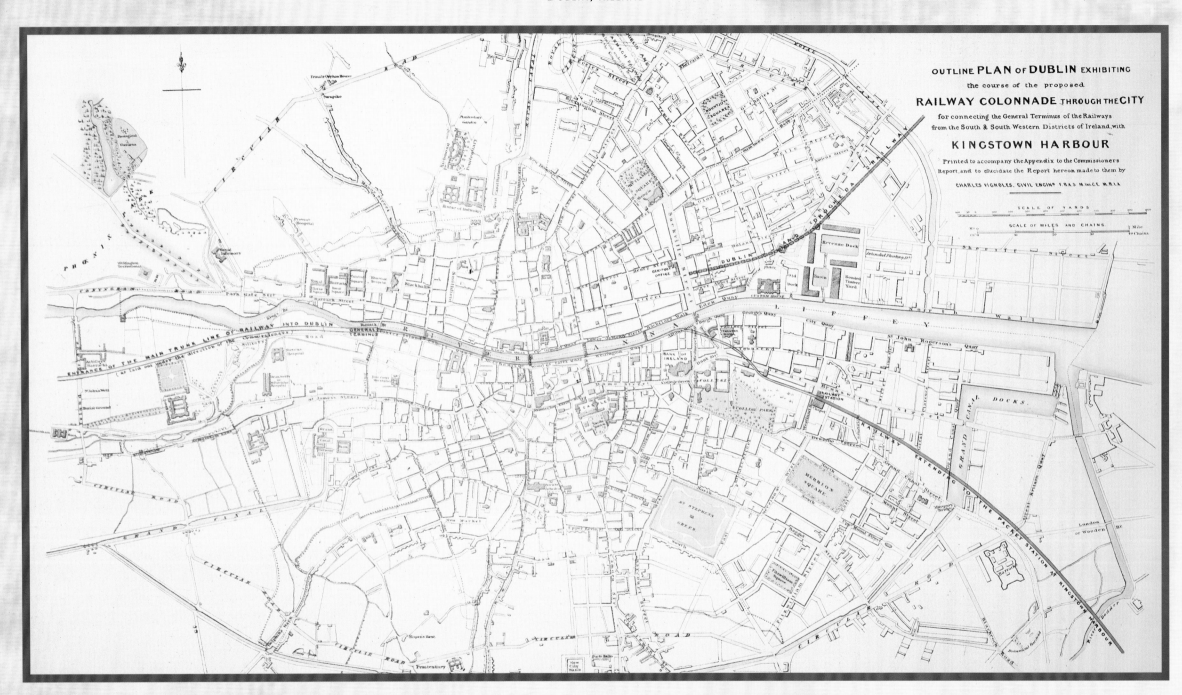

OUTLINE PLAN of DUBLIN EXHIBITING
the course of the proposed
RAILWAY COLONNADE THROUGH THE CITY
for connecting the General Terminus of the Railways
from the South & South Western Districts of Ireland, with
KINGSTOWN HARBOUR

Printed to accompany the Appendix to the Commissioners
Report, and to elucidate the Report hereon made to them by
CHARLES VIGNOLES, CIVIL ENGINᴿ F R A S M ᴵⁿᶜ E M R I A

ABOVE: This is a map from the survey undertaken by the Irish Railway Commissioners, which was presented to parliament in 1837. It shows the proposed construction of railways in Dublin. By the date of this map, the first railway in Ireland—the Dublin & Kingstown Railway—had opened; this is the line shown in blue heading southeastward. The railway station mentioned is Westland Row. The D&KR was originally built to the British standard gauge of 4 feet 8.5 inches, but was converted to the Irish standard gauge of 5 feet 3 inches in 1855. North of the River Liffey is the Dublin & Drogheda Railway; this was opened from a temporary station to Drogheda on May 26, 1844; this was replaced by Amiens Street (Connolly) station on November 29, 1844. The D&DR and D&KR were eventually connected with a viaduct over the Liffey. To the west of the center is the future line from Kingsbridge (renamed Heuston in 1966) toward Cork; the first section of this line was opened by the Great South Western Railway on August 4, 1846.

EDINBURGH

SCOTLAND

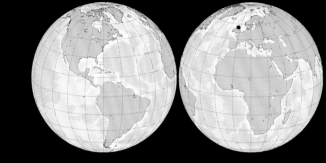

Known as the "Athens of the North," Edinburgh—Dùn Èideann in Gaelic—sits on the south bank of the Firth of Forth and is the capital of Scotland, one of the constituent nations of the United Kingdom of Great Britain and Northern Ireland. With a population approaching 500,000, the city, nicknamed "Auld Reekie," houses the new Scottish parliament and the official royal Scottish residence—the Palace of Holyroodhouse—of the monarch. Whilst Glasgow to the west is the industrial hub of Scotland, Edinburgh, with its museums and galleries, has always been the cultural heart of the country, a fact emphasized by the annual arts festival held in the city each August.

Archaeological evidence shows that the Romans occupied the area from the 1st century, and forts were established to the east and west of the future city during the 2nd century. Land south of the Antonine Wall, which marked the northernmost boundary of the Roman Empire during the second half of the century, remained under Roman rule for a relatively short period.

The initial expansion of the city took place in the 12th century. King David I first established the burgh in the 1120s and founded the Abbey of Holyrood; a royal guesthouse was subsequently added adjacent to the abbey, and this ultimately became a royal palace.

During the 13th to 16th centuries, whilst the city grew in importance, periodic warfare between England and Scotland saw the castle and city change hands on several occasions. By 1360, the city has a population of some 4,000 and was de facto capital of the country, with the castle as the primary royal residence. In 1437 the city became the official capital of Scotland.

The union of the English and Scottish crowns under James VI of Scotland in 1603 saw military threat to the city much reduced, although following the English Civil War and the execution of King Charles I, the castle was surrendered to the Lord Protector's English army. In 1707, the Act of Union resulted in the closure of the Scottish parliament—it would not sit again until devolution saw it reinstated in 1999—but the 18th century witnessed the rapid growth of the city and its importance. The original city—the Old Town—was centered in the area between the castle and Holyrood but, in 1767, construction started on the New Town, with it sweeping Georgian terraces and grand squares. It was during these years that Edinburgh became a center of economic and political theory, with figures such as economist Adam Smith becoming highly influential.

BELOW: Satellite image of the city of Edinburgh, Scotland. North is at the top, water is blue, urban areas are grey, vegetation is green and agricultural areas are brown. Edinburgh is the capital of Scotland and is located in eastern Scotland. It is on the bank of the Firth of Forth, an estuary of the river Forth, which flows into the North Sea. Photographed on July 17, 2000.

EDENBVRG.

Castrum puellarum

EDENBVRGVM.
SCOTIAE
METROPOLIS.

LEFT: By now the undisputed capital of Scotland, Edinburgh was a rapidly growing city at the center of a country in religious turmoil. The reformist John Knox had been appointed minister of St Giles in 1599, whilst the Catholic monarch, Queen Mary, was on the throne surrounded by Protestant advisers. In this late 16th century view the castle can be seen on top of Castle Hill, with the Royal Mile linking it with the site of the Palace and Abbey of Holyrood (although, curiously, neither of these structures is actually illustrated). On the south side of the city can be seen the Flodden Walls; these were constructed in the 16th century following the defeat of the Scottish army at the Battle of Flodden in 1513.

RIGHT: Dedicated to George Lockhart, Member of Parliament for Edinburgh, this map was published in the early 18th century by John Smith (c.1652–1742) and shows the city as it existed immediately prior to the start of the development of the New Town later in the 18th century. Until 1707 Edinburgh had housed the Scottish parliament; this was, however, abolished following the Act of Union with England.

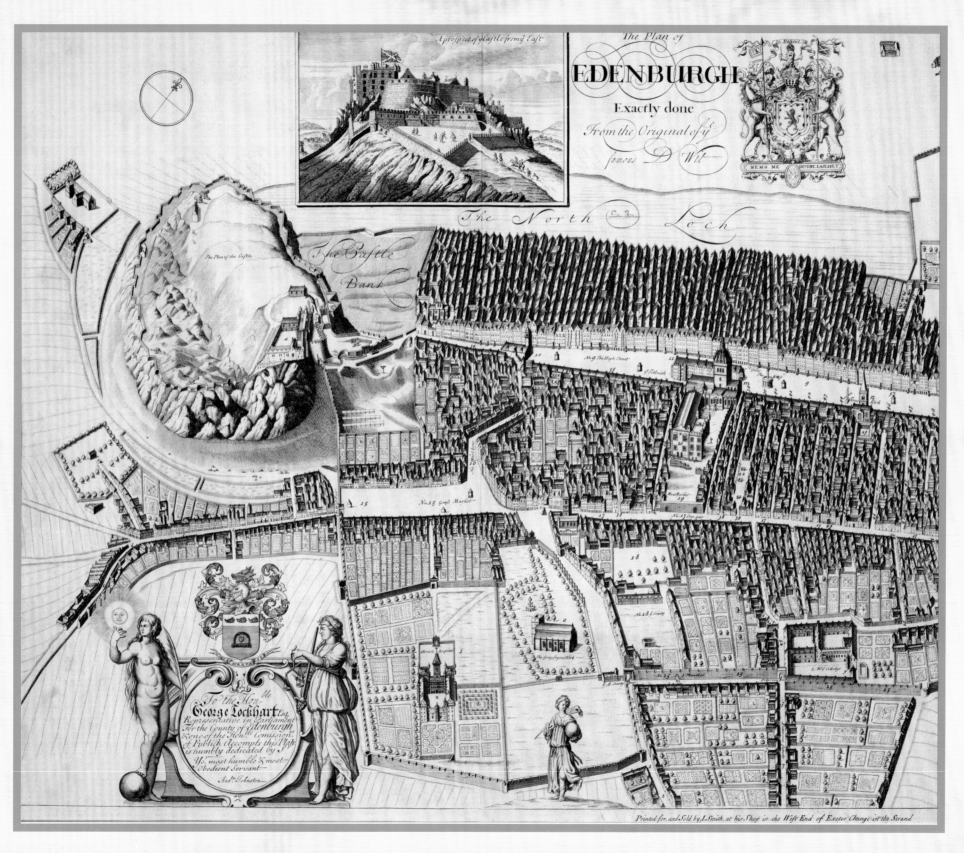

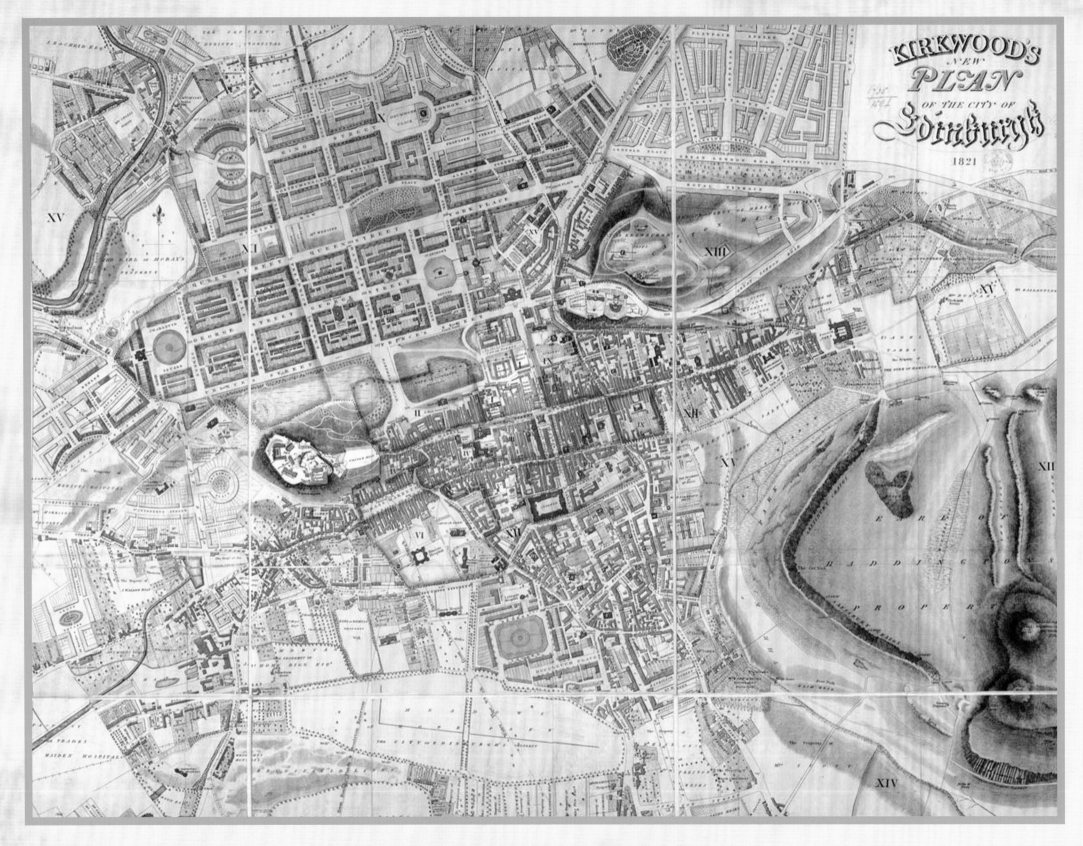

LEFT: Taken from Kirkwood's *New Plan of the City of Edinburgh*, this map records the massive growth of the city during the 18th century. North of the castle, which is located to the left of the map, can be seen the squares and rigid grid of the New Town with Princes Street, now one of the most famous shopping streets in the world, running east–west immediately to the north of the castle. The New Town was built in stages between 1765 and 1850 and it, along with the Old Town—the district between the castle and the Palace of Holyroodhouse—was declared a UNESCO World Heritage Site in 1995. The first phase of the New Town was completed in 1800 with the building of Charlotte Square; this is the square illustrated here at the western end of Princes Street. The construction of the New Town coincided with Edinburgh's emergence as one of the most important centers of learning.

RIGHT: Taken from a book which was published in London by Chapman & Hall in 1844, this map records Edinburgh with the New Town virtually completed. This era marked the dawn of the railway age in Scotland; the Edinburgh & Dalkeith Railway opened from a station at St Leonards, on the south side of the city, in 1831 (with passenger services commencing the following year). The Edinburgh & Glasgow Railway opened from Haymarket station on the east of the city in 1842. However, the major impact of the railways was to occur in 1846 with the opening of North Bridge—now Waverley—station in the valley between the castle and Princes Street.

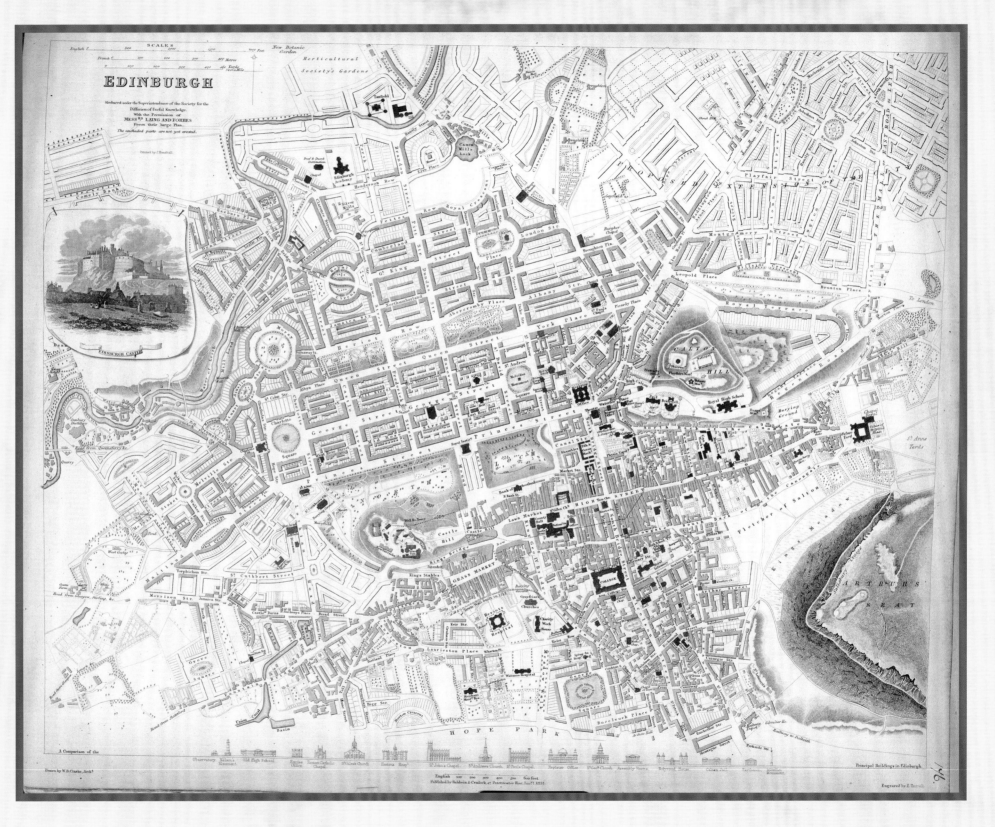

EXETER

ENGLAND

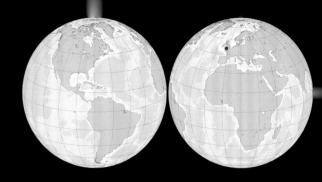

The county town of Devon sits slightly inland from the estuary of the River Exe, with a population of just under 120,000. It was established on the east bank of the river above the wide flood plain by the Dumnonii, the Celtic tribe who dominated southwest England prior to the arrival of the Romans. Traces of the original Roman walls can be found in the surviving sections of the city's walls today. The city was also the destination of the Fosse Way, the Roman road that stretched through the Midlands to Lincoln (Lindum Colonia) via Bath, Cirencester, and Leicester.

Following the Roman withdrawal from the British Isles in the early 5th century, Exeter, along with the rest of Devon, became part of the Anglo-Saxon kingdom of Wessex to the east. Later it was captured by the Normans, who constructed a new fortress, Rougemont Castle.

During the Middle Ages, Exeter, with the River Exe navigable up to the city's quay, was a prosperous trading center. However, in the 13th century the Countess of Devon sought to restrict trade to the city by constructing the Countess Weir. This blow was compounded early in the 14th century when the Earl of Devon built a quay at Topsham, seeking to claim duties on all goods passing to and from Exeter. It was only in the 16th century, with the construction of the Exeter Canal, that these restrictions on the city's trade were lifted.

In 1537 the city became a County Corporate, which gave it certain rights of self-government outside the control of the county of Devon. Twelve years later it withstood a month-long siege by the Prayer Books Rebels (a rebellion in Devon and Cornwall led by those opposed to the introduction of the Book of Common Prayer); the latter event is recorded on a plaque at St Mary Steps, a church situated next to the now demolished West Gate.

During the 17th century Exeter prospered from the wool trade, but when this declined and the Industrial Revolution arrived, the city was too distant from the major coalfields to develop as a major industrial center. As a result it avoided the massive redevelopment and growth that occurred elsewhere and much of the city's early architecture survived until the 20th century. However, bombing during World War II and post-war redevelopment has meant that much of the historic heart has now been lost.

BELOW: Satellite image of the city of Exeter (center) and its surrounding area near the southwestern coast of England. North is at top. Forested areas are dark green, agricultural fields are lighter shades of green and brown, urban areas are grey and water is black. Image created using NaturalVue data obtained from the Landsat 7 satellite.

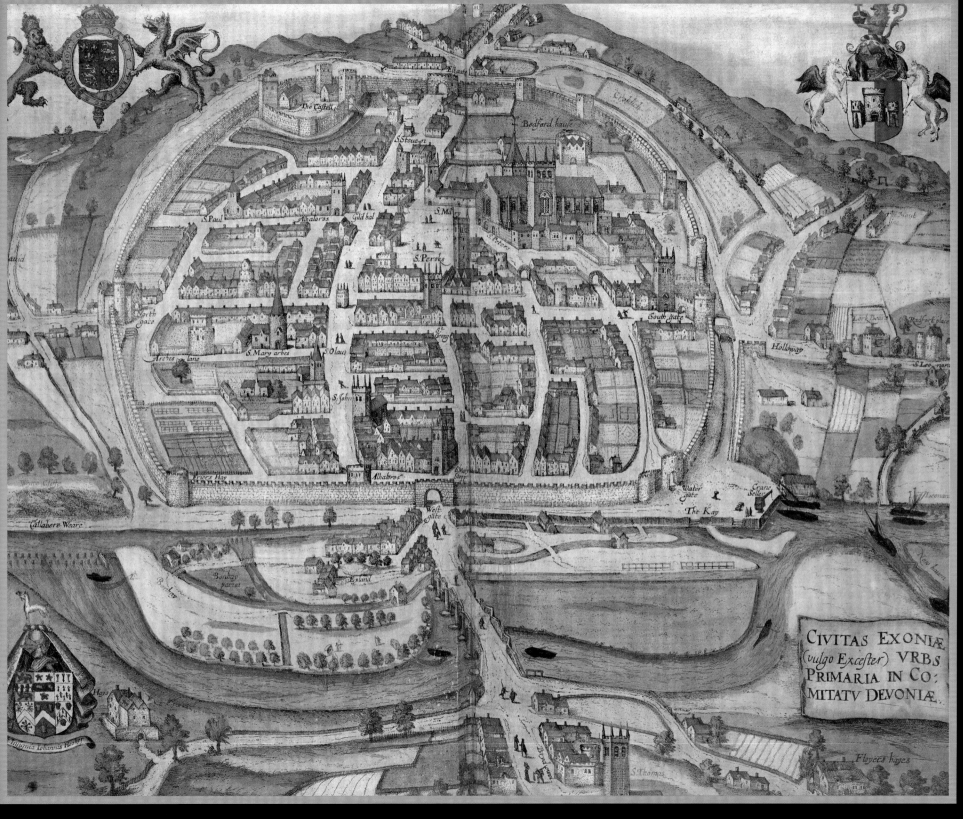

LEFT: This late 16th-century map shows the city of Exeter with its city walls intact. Toward the top of the map can be seen Rougemont Castle; this was first constructed by the Normans in 1068 following their invasion of England in 1066. The medieval castle was to be significantly rebuilt in the 18th century. Dominating the city center is the cathedral of St Mary and St Peter; Exeter became a cathedral city in 1050 when the see covering Devon and Cornwall was transferred from Crediton. Although there was an older church on the site, work started on the construction of the new Norman cathedral in the early 12th century. The lack of a crossing tower means that the cathedral can lay claim to the longest ribbed fan vaulted ceiling in Britain. Outside the Water Gate, toward the bottom right of the map, can be seen the Quay. Although the River Exe was navigable, during the 13th century the construction of a weir prevented ships reaching the city and this severely affected Exeter's prosperity. Fortunes were reversed in the middle of the 16th century when a canal—the first to be built in England—was constructed to bypass the weir, and so avoid the payment of tolls for using the river.

RIGHT: This map was originally produced by John Speed (1552–1629), one of the first makers of county and town maps in England and Wales. This version dates from 1680 and is an inset into his larger map covering the entire county of Devon. It is aligned with north toward the top of the page. The key covers the buildings of interest.

FAR RIGHT: Surveyed and drawn by John Rocque, this map is dedicated to the mayor, alderman and common council of the city. In the surrounding insets illustrations portray a number of notable buildings. These include the cathedral, the bridge across the River Exe, the castle, and the guildhall. The guildhall building illustrated here dates from between 1466 and 1484, with a portico added in 1592. Exeter suffered severe damage during World War II following the so-called Baedeker Blitz of 1942, during which much of the medieval core of the city was destroyed; the guildhall was one of the few non-religious buildings from this period to survive both the bombing and the subsequent post-war redevelopment.

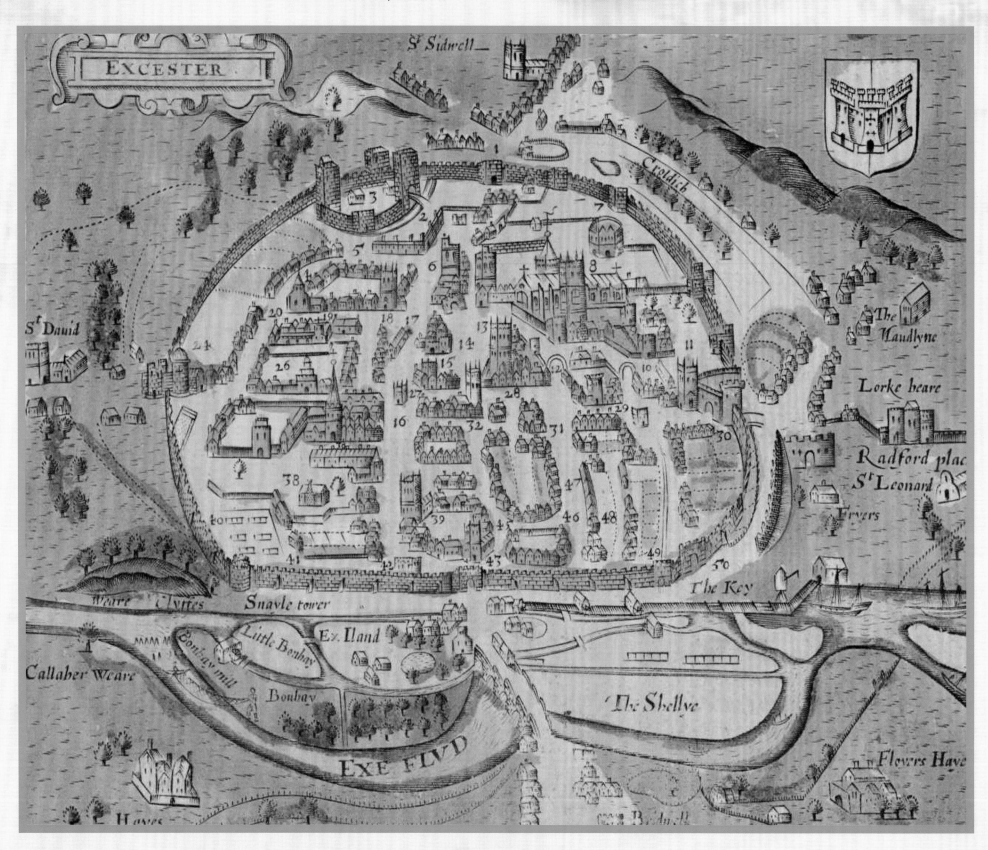

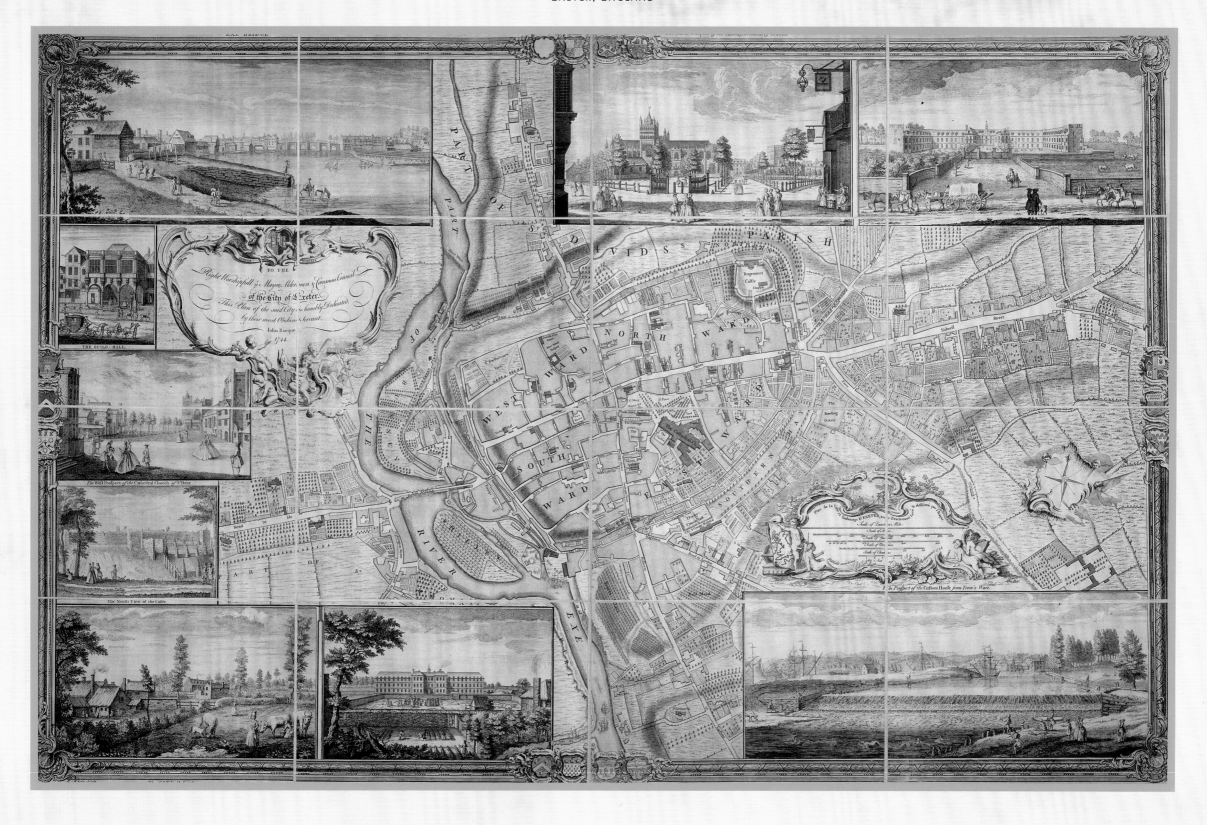

FLORENCE
ITALY

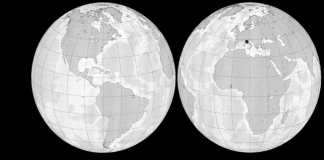

Florence—Firenze—is the principal city of the Italian region of Tuscany, with a population approaching 400,000. Situated on the Arno River, it is widely regarded as the birthplace of the Renaissance and its historic center was declared a World Heritage Site by UNESCO in 1982. As well as being one of the most important cities in the cultural history of western civilization, Florence has long been a major commercial and banking center, and is now one of the country's prime tourist destination.

From the early 13th century the city was riven by factional strife between the Ghibellines, who were pro-Holy Roman Empire, and the Guelphs, who were pro-Papal. Despite this internecine strife, the 13th century witnessed the rise of the city as both a cultural and economic center. One of the Guelphs later exiled was the poet Dante (Durante degli Alighieri; 1265–1321) and one of the leading painters of the period—Giotto (Giotto di Bondone; 1267–1337)—was another native of the city. In terms of economic development, the city became a major center of banking and the wool industry, both of which were essential to medieval trade. However, not all developments were positive; in 1339, for example, King Edward III of England refused to honor his enormous debts, with the result that two of the cities largest banks—the Bardi and Peruzzi—collapsed, and a decade later more than 60 percent of the city's population was to die as a result of the Black Death.

Between 1382 and 1434 the city was under the control of the Albizzi family, but it was their rivals, led initially by Cosimo de' Medici (1389–1464), that were to become the dominant force during the city's golden age of the Renaissance. When Gian Gastone de' Medici died in 1737 the titles passed to Francis I (1708–65), the Holy Roman Emperor and husband of Maria Theresa of Austria, and in 1859, along with the remainder of Tuscany, Florence became part of the unified kingdom of Italy.

During the 19th century the population doubled, and it was to treble over the next 100 years. Although occupied by the Germans in 1943–44, following the Italian surrender the city was declared open and thus spared the damage wrought on many other important cities in Europe during World War II.

BELOW: A Landsat image of Flo.rence taken in 2005. The River Arno is clearly visible.

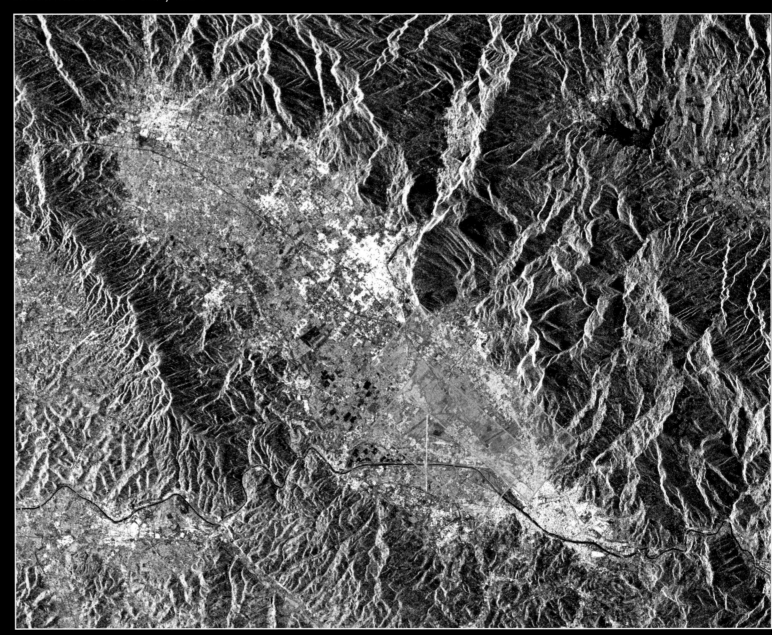

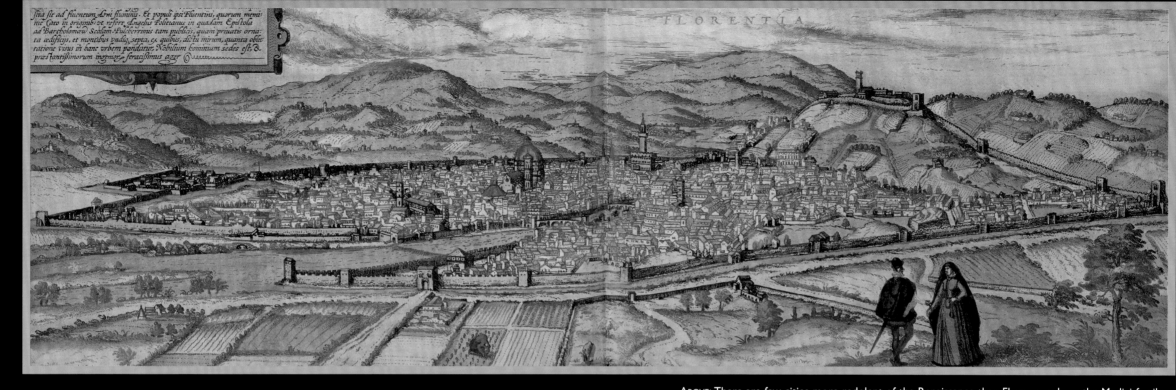

sita sit ad fluentem Arni fluminis. Et populi ipsi Fluentini, quorum menti-
nit Cato in originib: vt refert Angelus Politianus in quadam Epistola
ad Bartholomeu Scalam Pulcherrimus tam publicis, quam priuatis orna-
ta aedificys, et montibus vndiq, septa, ex quibus, dictu mirum, quanta oble-
ctatione visus in hanc urbem pondatur. Nobilium hominum sedes est. &
praestantissimorum ingenior. feracissimus ager

ABOVE: There are few cities more redolent of the Renaissance than Florence, where the Medici family, rulers of the city from the 15th century, proved to be amongst the greatest benefactors of art and architecture in late medieval Italy. Figures such as Brunelleschi, whose cathedral dome dominates the skyline in this late Renaissance map of the city, Michelangelo, Raphael, Leonardo di Vinci, and Giotto dominated the artistic life of Italy and were to have an impact on all European culture. Apart from the cathedral, the map portrays the small neighboring town of Fiesole, which although originally independent of Florence had, by the 16th century, become a wealthy suburb occupied by the city's elite.

FOLLOWING PAGE: Produced by Bradshaw & Blacklock of Manchester, England, this map records the city in the mid-19th century. The map is aligned with north toward the top of the page. By this date the railway revolution had reached Florence. Its first railway station, Leopolda (now known as Stazione di Santa Maria Novella following rebuilding in the 1930s), built in 1844, was designed by Robert Stephenson, son of the railway pioneer George.

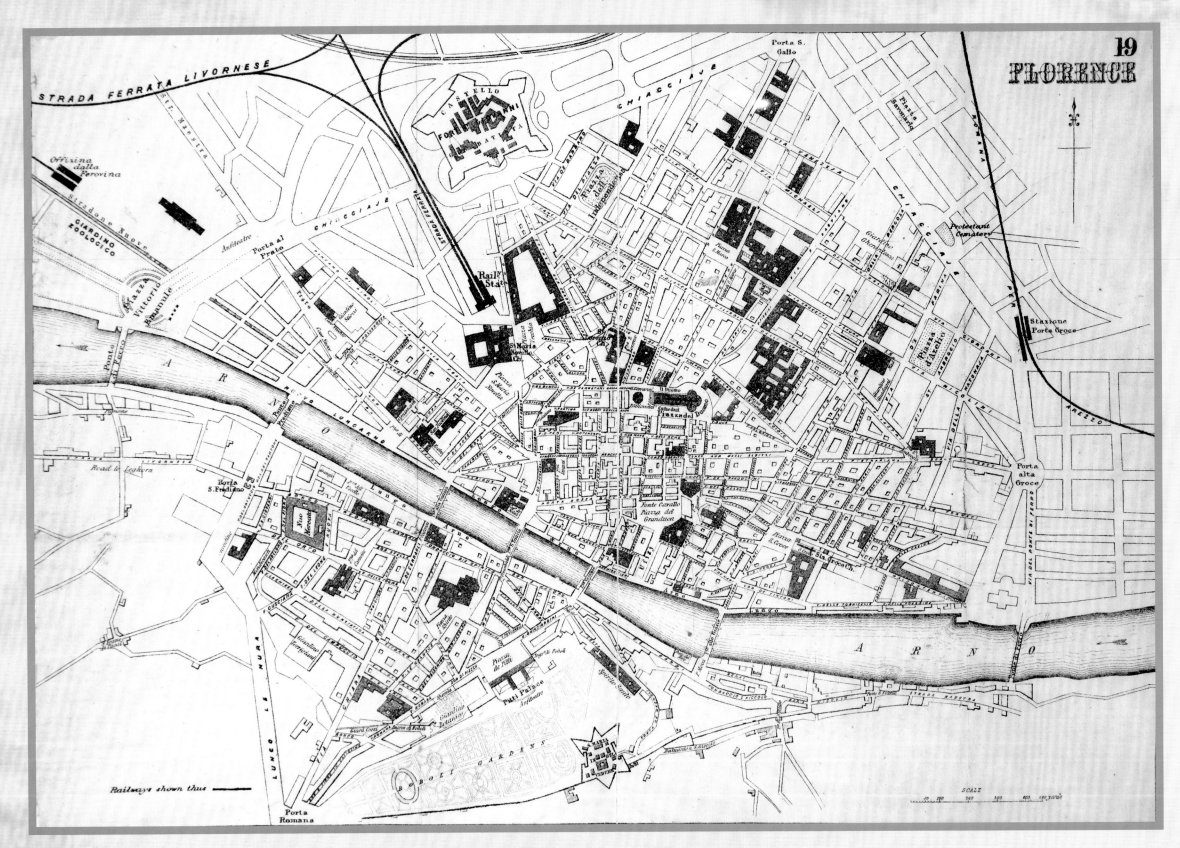

FRANKFURT

GERMANY

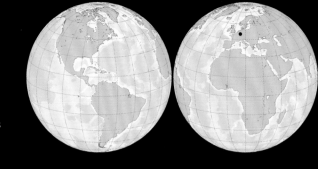

With a population of more than 650,000, Frankfurt am Main is the fifth largest city in the Federal Republic of Germany. It is the home of Germany's main stock exchange, the German Federal Bank, and the European Central Bank. The city's name is derived from *Franconoford*—ford of the Franks—reflecting the city's situation on low-level marshy land in the valley of the River Main.

There is evidence of Roman settlement from the 1st century onward. This lasted until 259/260 A.D., when the Roman Empire contracted westward in Germany, establishing a new border along the River Rhine. Archaeological finds show the continuing occupation of the site after the departure of the Romans and, in the late 8th century, the Emperor Charlemagne (742–814) built a palace and convened a major church council there. This was the beginning of a long association between the city and the Holy Roman Empire. Charlemagne's son and successor, Louis the Pious (770–840), selected Frankfurt as his seat, extending the existing palace and erecting defensive wooden walls and ditches.

In 843, following the Treaty of Verdun, Frankfurt was named the principal city—effectively the capital—of East Francia and was used regularly to host church councils and Imperial Diets (Reichstags). The role of the city in Imperial politics encouraged its growth from the 13th century onward. In 1372 the city was declared an Imperial Free City (Reichsstadt); this effectively made Frankfurt an autonomous city-state answerable only to the emperor.

In 1618 religious war broke out through much of Europe; the Thirty Years' War was, however, to see Frankfurt maintain its neutrality and its status as an Imperial Free City was confirmed by the 1648 Peace of Westphalia. This status remained unchanged until the French Revolutionary and the Napoleonic Wars, when the city became part of the territories that ultimately formed the Grand Duchy of Frankfurt in 1810. Following Austrian defeat in the war, Frankfurt was annexed by Prussia, becoming part of the province of Hesse-Nassau—or Hesse post 1946—and thus ultimately part of Germany.

In the 20th century, the city's history paralleled that of the rest of Germany and Frankfurt suffered massive destruction during World War II. Post-war, it was considered as a possible site for the capital of West Germany. Although Bonn was ultimately selected, Frankfurt's position as a commercial and financial center grew predominant within the new country, a role that it has retained since the reunification of the country following the fall of communism in the east.

BELOW: North is at top. Urbanised areas are pink and grey, vegetation is green and pale areas are bare ground. The major river (blue) seen from left to lower right is the River Main. Frankfurt international Airport is at lower left. Today it vies with London as the business capital of Europe, although its huge exhibition grounds make it unrivaled for such events as the annual Frankfurt Book Fair.

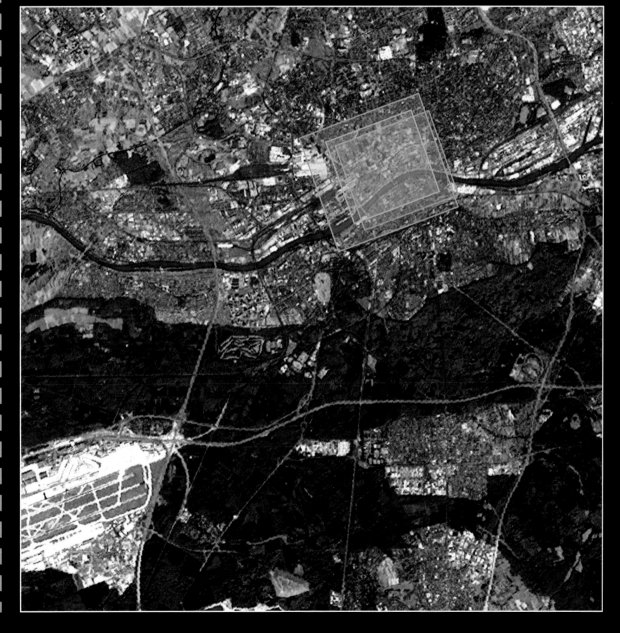

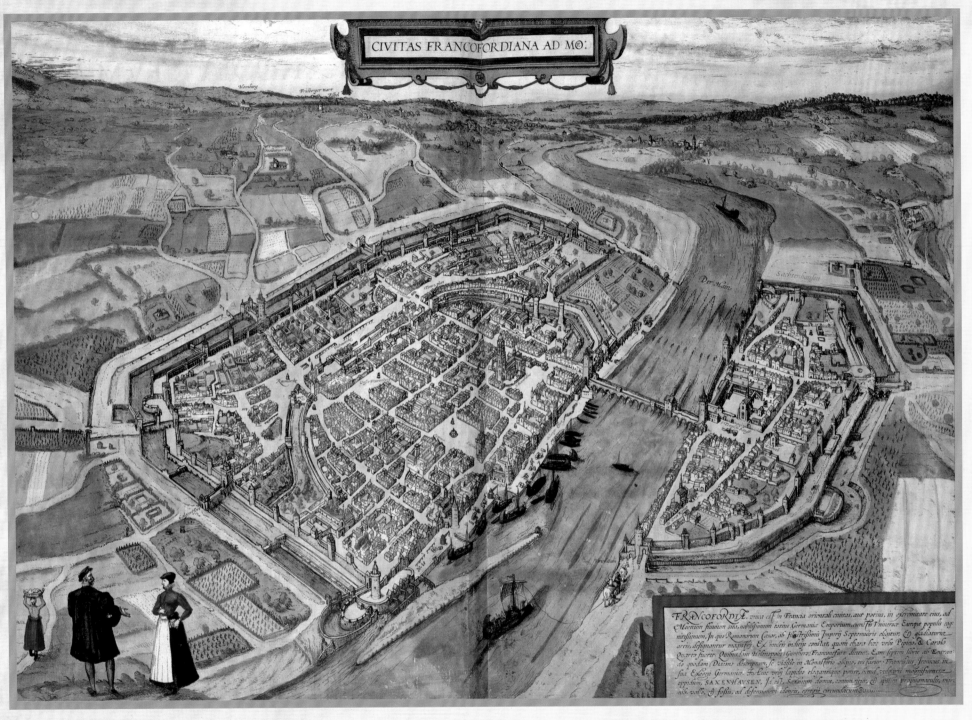

CIVITAS FRANCOFORDIANA AD MO:

RIGHT: Described in Latin as "Francofurti ad Moenum, urbis imperialis, electioni Rom: regum atq. imperatorum consecratae, emporiique tam Germaniae quam totius Europae celeberrimi, accurata delineatio" (Frankfurt am Main, imperial city for the election and coronation of Roman emperors and kings and renowned trading center of Germany and all Europe), this bird's-eye pictorial map shows the river, bridge, quays, streets, and principal buildings. The map was produced by Matthaeus Merian. A dedication to the city and its coat of arms are included as an inset.

ABOVE: The position of Frankfurt on the north bank of the River Main, and the low-lying land on which much of the city was built, are evident in this late 16th century map, which also portrays the suburb of Sachsenhausen on the south bank. This community had grown up during the Middle Ages and was a center of beer-brewing and cider-fermentation. Crossing the river can be seen the Alte Brücke (Old Bridge), which had replaced the original ford in the 13th century. The towers guarding each end of the bridge were rebuilt at the end of the 14th century by Madern Gerthener. Dominating the middle of Frankfurt is the Cathedral of St Bartholomew (also known as the Kaiserdom or Imperial Cathedral); this was built between the 13th and 15th centuries. From 1356 the cathedral was the site of the election ceremony for the Holy Roman Emperor and, after 1562 when the post became hereditary, it was used for the emperor's coronation. The cathedral is dominated by the octagonal Westturm, which was built between 1415 and 1514.

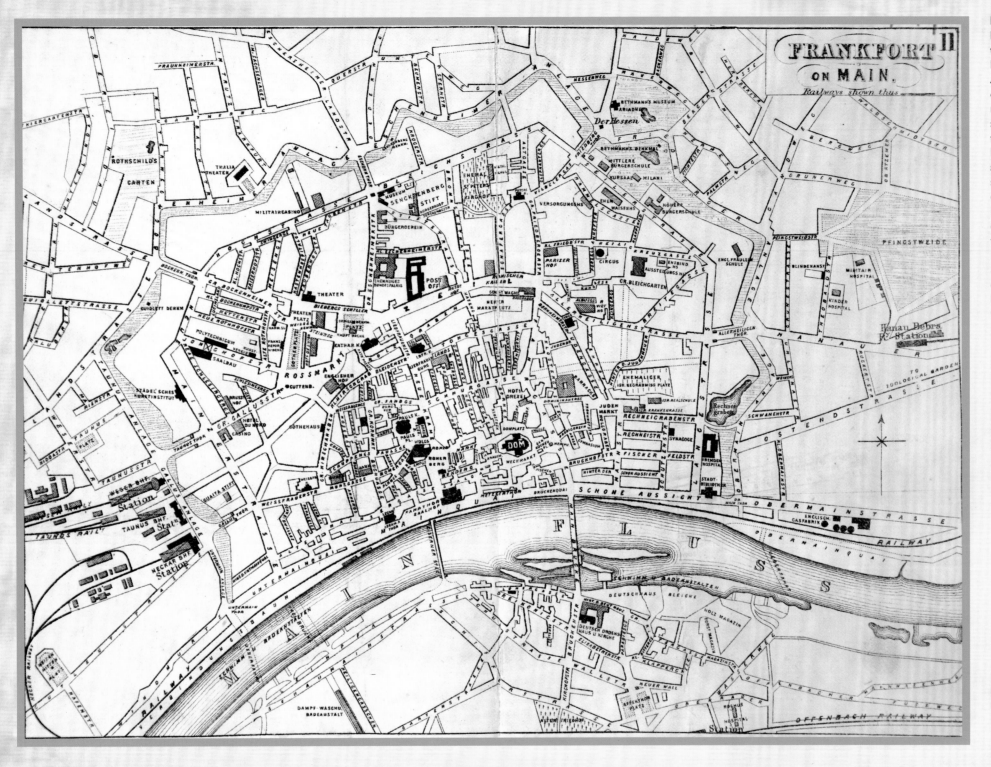

LEFT: Produced by Bradshaw & Blacklock of Manchester, England, this map records the city of Frankfurt in the mid-19th century. Aligned with north toward the top of the page, it shows the first railways to operate in the city. The stations located toward the west of the city now form the site of the Frankfurt Hauptbahnhof, with the area to the north and west of the station now occupied by the massive exhibition halls of the Messe (Trade Fair). Much of central Frankfurt was destroyed by Allied bombing during the war and the area around the Romer was subsequently restored. Much else of the city was completely rebuilt as Frankfurt became the financial center of West Germany prior to the country's reunification.

GENOA

ITALY

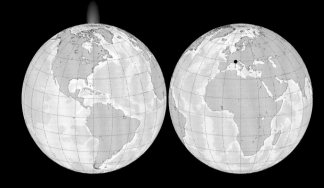

With a current population of over 600,000, Genoa—or Genova as it's known to the Italians—is an important sea port in the northwest of the country. It is the capital of the province of Genoa and the region of Liguria. The name probably derived from the Ligurian word *Genua*, meaning "angle" or "knee."

The oldest known inhabitants of the area were the Ligurians and by the 6th century B.C. the settlement was already an important trading post with evidence of Greek occupation, although both the Etruscans and Phoenicians may well have had settlements in the area as well.

By 1100 the city had emerged as one of the Repubbliche Marinare (Maritime Republics), alongside erstwhile commercial rivals such as Amalfi. Although nominally still under the rule of the Holy Roman Empire, Genoa was now effectively an independent city-state.

The zenith of Genoa's power came toward the end of the 13th century with victories over Pisa at the Battle of Meloria in 1294 and over Venice four years later at the Battle of the Cuzonali Islands. Gradually, however, the Genoese Empire declined: in 1421 the Banco di San Giorgio sold Livorno to Florence to help pay off a debt; Sardinia was lost to Aragon; Corsica to rebellion in 1768 (it was subsequently sold to France); and the colonies in the Middle East to the Ottoman Empire and to the Arabs. The city itself was to fall briefly, between 1394 and 1409, under French control.

In the 15th and early 16th centuries the city was increasingly dominated by Milan and Florence, becoming a pawn in the power politics of Renaissance Italy. In 1528 the pivotal figure in Genoese history of this period—Andrea Doria (1468–1560)—established a new constitution that effectively made Genoa a satellite of the Spanish Empire, but which also helped the city acquire new commercial wealth during the remainder of the 16th century.

Under Spanish overlordship the city suffered from a French siege in 1668 and from a brief Austrian occupation in 1746. However, in 1797, under pressure from Napoleon, Genoa became ` a French Protectorate under the name of the Ligurian Republic, before being formally annexed by France eight years later. Genoa later became one of the centers for the campaign for Italian unification, and it was from there that Giuseppe Garibaldi (1807–82) set out with his 1,000 volunteers in May 1860 to invade the kingdom of the Two Sicilies in the name of a united Italy.

BELOW: Satellite image of the city of Genoa (centre) and its surrounding area in northern Italy. North is at top. Forested areas are dark green, agricultural fields are lighter shades of green and brown, urban areas are grey, and water is black. Image created using NaturalVue data obtained from the Landsat 7 satellite.

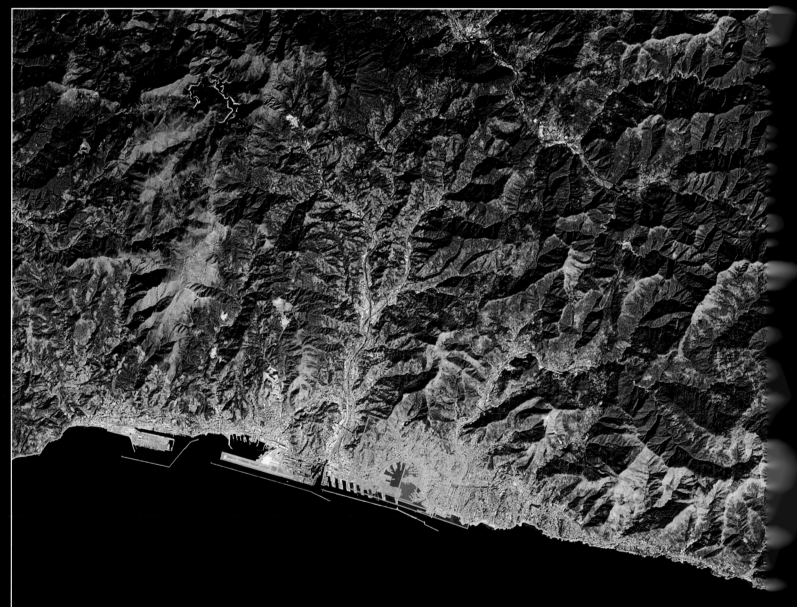

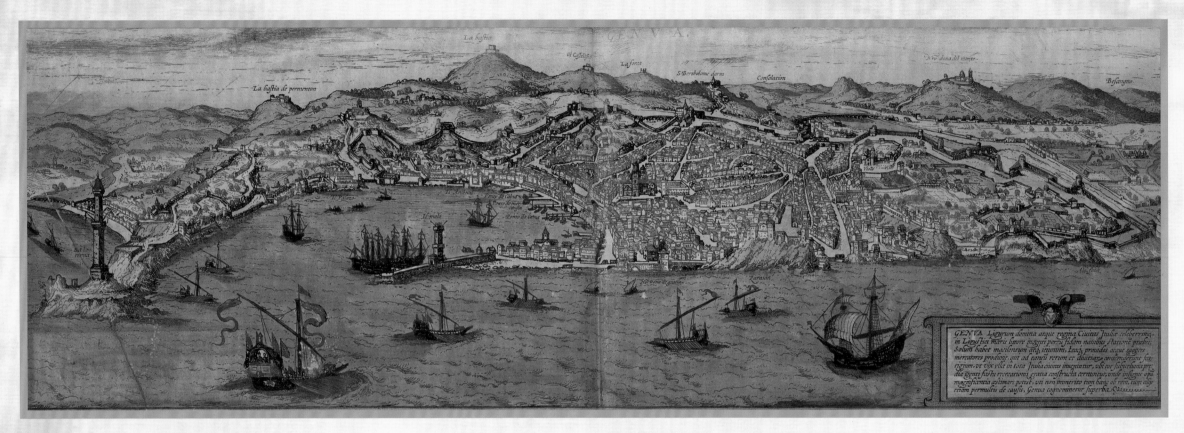

ABOVE: This late 16th century view of Genoa, one of Italy's most important ports, shows the city as it existed in the late Renaissance period. The most conspicuous feature is the Lanterna—or lighthouse. This was built in 1543 to replace an earlier structure that had been destroyed by accident in 1506. The lighthouse is 253 feet in height and a spiral staircase of 375 steps takes visitors to the top. Apart from its use as a trading post, Genoa was also a naval port and the fleet was supplied from the city's arsenal, which was situated alongside the harbor. Also prominent in this view are the Cathedral of St Lawrence, which was begun in the 11th century and which received a new Romanesque façade in the 14th century and a new dome in the 16th, and the city defenses. Genoa, like many other cities in Europe, suffered massive population loss in the 14th century as a result of the Black Death.

RIGHT: Produced by Charles Wylde and incorporated in his work covering a voyage to Constantinople, this map records the city and harbor of Genoa at the end of the 17th century.

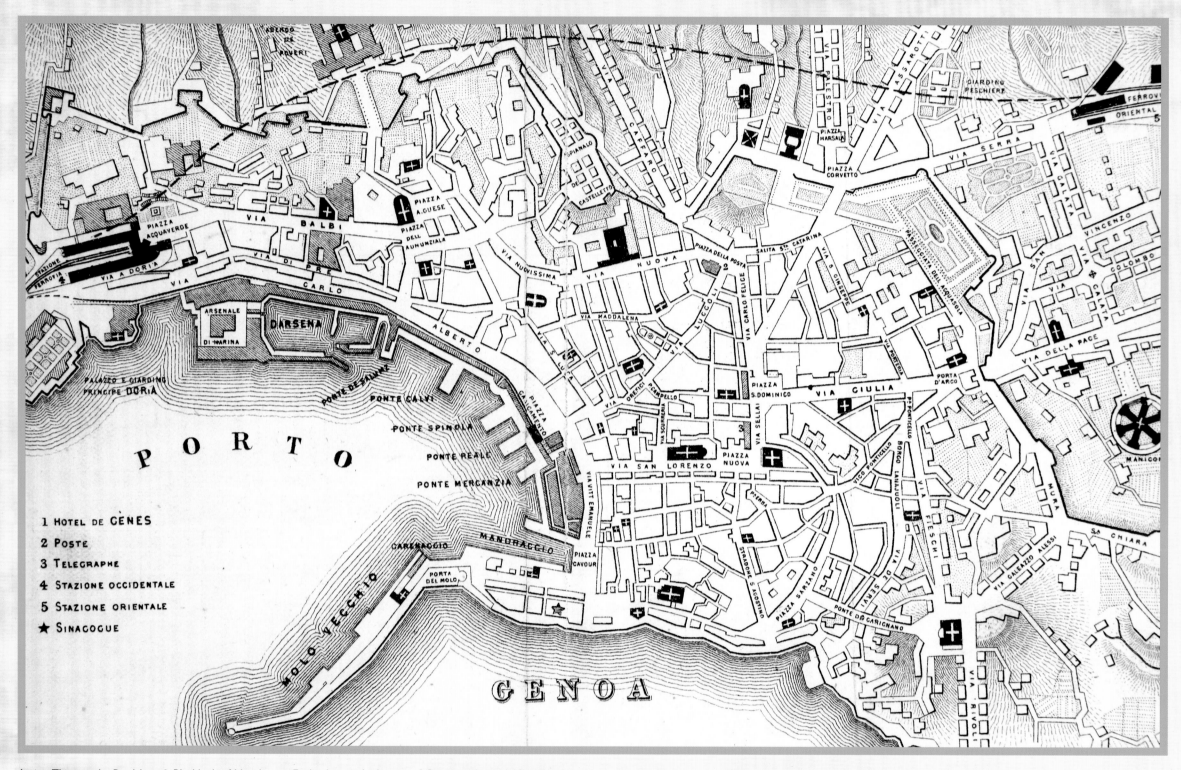

1 HOTEL DE GENES
2 POSTE
3 TELEGRAPHE
4 STAZIONE OCCIDENTALE
5 STAZIONE ORIENTALE
★ SINAGOGUE

ABOVE: This map by Bradshaw & Blacklock of Manchester, England records the city of Genoa in the mid-19th century.
It is aligned with north toward the top of the page and records the expansion of the city and the arrival of the
railway. The city's main station—Stazione Principe—can be seen to the west, as can the route of the tunnel that links
the lines to the west of the city with those to the east. The railway came to Genoa in 1854.

HAMBURG
GERMANY

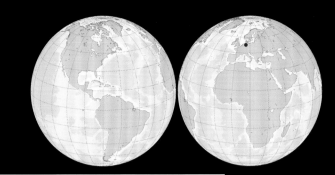

The second largest city in Germany after Berlin, with a population approaching two million, Hamburg is the country's most important port. Its correct title is Freie und Hansestadt Hamburg (the Free and Hanseatic City of Hamburg), a reminder that the city is both a city-state within Federal Germany and of its former importance within the Hanseatic League. It is situated at the southern end of the Jutland peninsula at the confluence of the rivers Elbe, Alster, and Bille.

The city's origins date back to the 9th century when the Emperor Charlemagne ordered the construction of a castle on ground between the rivers Elbe and Alster as a defense against invasion from the east. Following the construction of the castle, a settlement quickly grew up around it and by 834 the city was sufficiently important to be created a bishopric.

In 1189 the Emperor Frederick Barbarossa made Hamburg an Imperial Free City; this, combined with its proximity to the North Sea, quickly saw the port develop, a process aided by its alliance with Lübeck in 1241. This alliance was to the cornerstone of the Hanseatic League, a network of trading ports in northern Europe linking the Baltic countries to Germany, Britain, and the Low Countries that was to dominate mercantile trade throughout the region until the 17th century, when the League was reduced to just three cities—Bremen, Hamburg, and Lübeck. (Its final dissolution was in the 19th century.) During this late medieval period Hamburg experienced great prosperity, and churches, civic buildings, and private residences were all evidence of the wealth generated by the Hanseatic League.

During the Napoleonic Wars, Hamburg was briefly occupied by the French. On May 4, 1842 the city suffered a further devastating fire when a quarter of the city—including three churches and the town hall—were destroyed. Reconstruction work was not completed until the late 1870s. By the end of the 19th century the population of the city had reached 800,000, quadrupling over the course of a century as the port continued to grow in importance.

During the 20th century Hamburg mirrored suffered severely after World War I when the loss of Germany's colonial possessions had an impact on trade through the port and, during World War II, the city suffered devastating fire storms as a result of Allied bombing. More than 40,000 people were killed during these raids, which also left much of the historic city destroyed. Post-war, the city was rebuilt and the port remains one of the most important serving northern Europe.

BELOW: Spot 5 image of Northern Germany showing the mouth of the mighty River Elbe on which Hamburg, Germany's second city, stands.

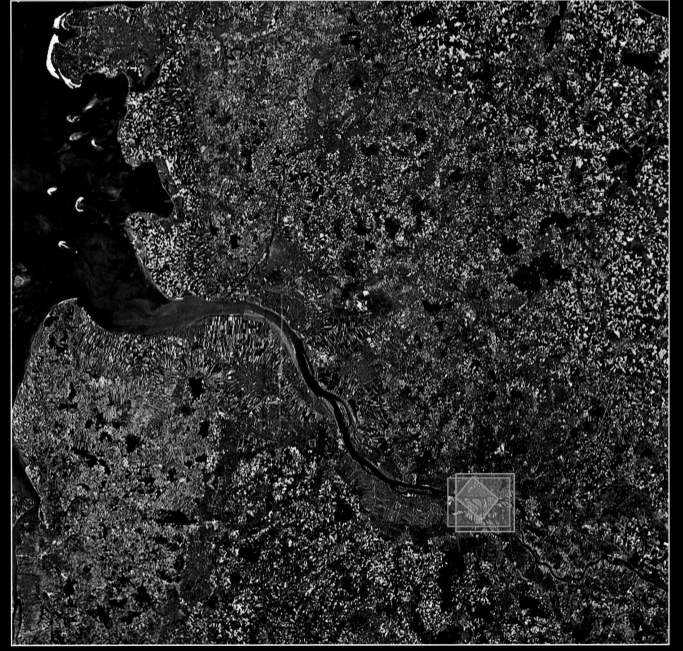

HAMBVRCH EIN VORNĒLICHE HA

S. Nicolaus
Der Heilig Geist
Müller dorff
Die Schaer kirch
Die Nieder bruck
S. Maria Magdalena
S. Katarina
S. Joannes
Der T huem
Sanct Peter
S. Iacob
S. Gerdrut
Der Winser Port
Das Stein Tor

Hamburga, Florentissimum inferioris Saxoni æ emporium, Anglorum frequētatione hoc tē pore celeberrimum Ao Dñi: M. D. LXXII.

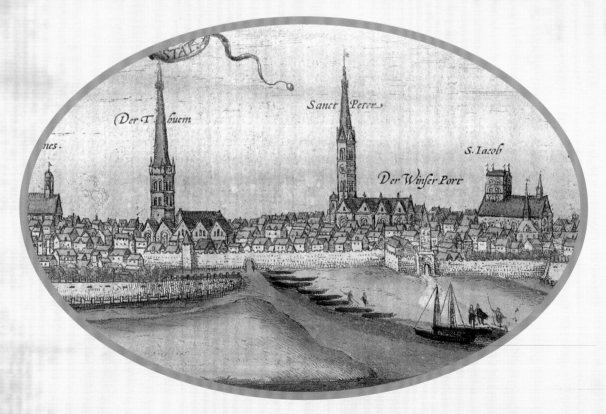

Der T huem
Sanct Peter
S. Iacob
Der Winser Port
nes.

ABOVE AND LEFT: During the late Middle Ages, the city of Hamburg enjoyed a period of immense wealth as a result of its key role within the Hanseatic League of northern European trading cities, and this was reflected in the churches and other buildings constructed during these years. However, by the mid-15th century, the rise of English and Dutch merchants had resulted in a relative decline. From the early 16th century, the city was one of the centers of the Reformation and offered a haven for many religious refugees. At this date the River Elbe was navigable for ships of all sizes and Hamburg, despite being some 70 miles from the sea, was a hugely important port. Upstream of Hamburg, goods were shipped by barge as far as Magdeburg and Dresden. The city's skyline was dominated by the Hauptkirchen (or High Churches) with their green copper spires. The number and scale of the churches built, such St Nicholas on the far left, were indicative of the wealth of the city during the late Middle Ages and Renaissance.

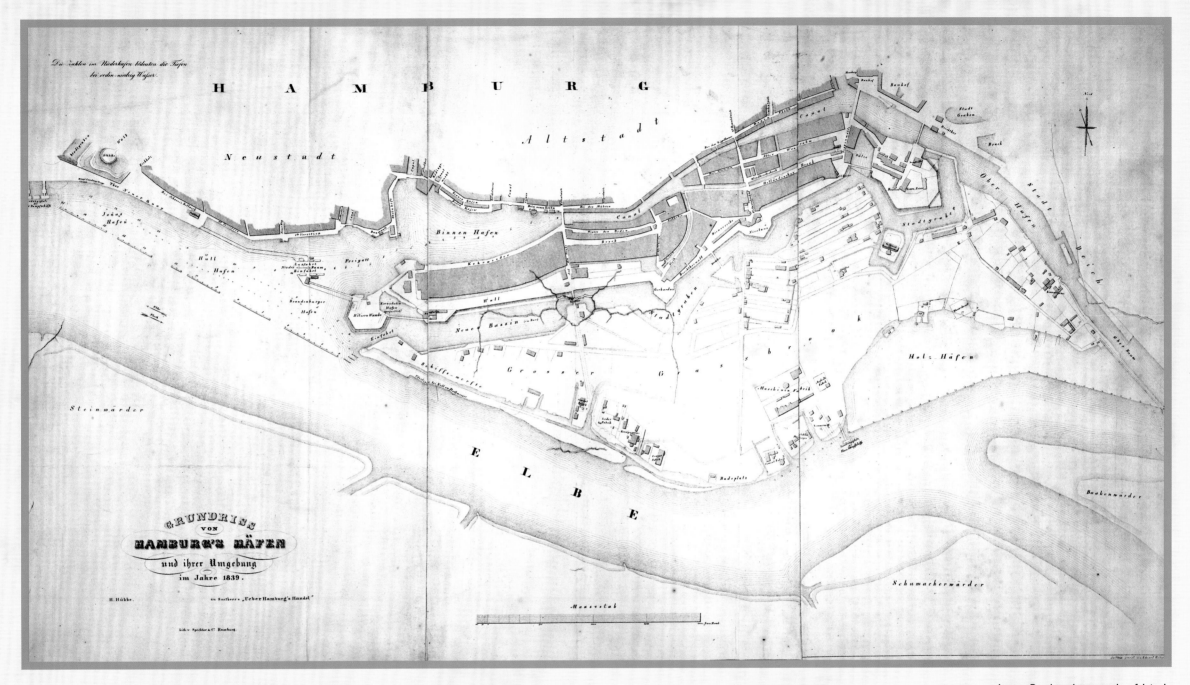

ABOVE: Produced to a scale of 1 inch to 330 Hamburg feet, this lithographed map of the city of Hamburg was published by the local company of Speckter & Co. It records the Elbe and the harbor three years before the devastating fire of May 4, 1842, which destroyed a quarter of the city, including the town hall and three churches.

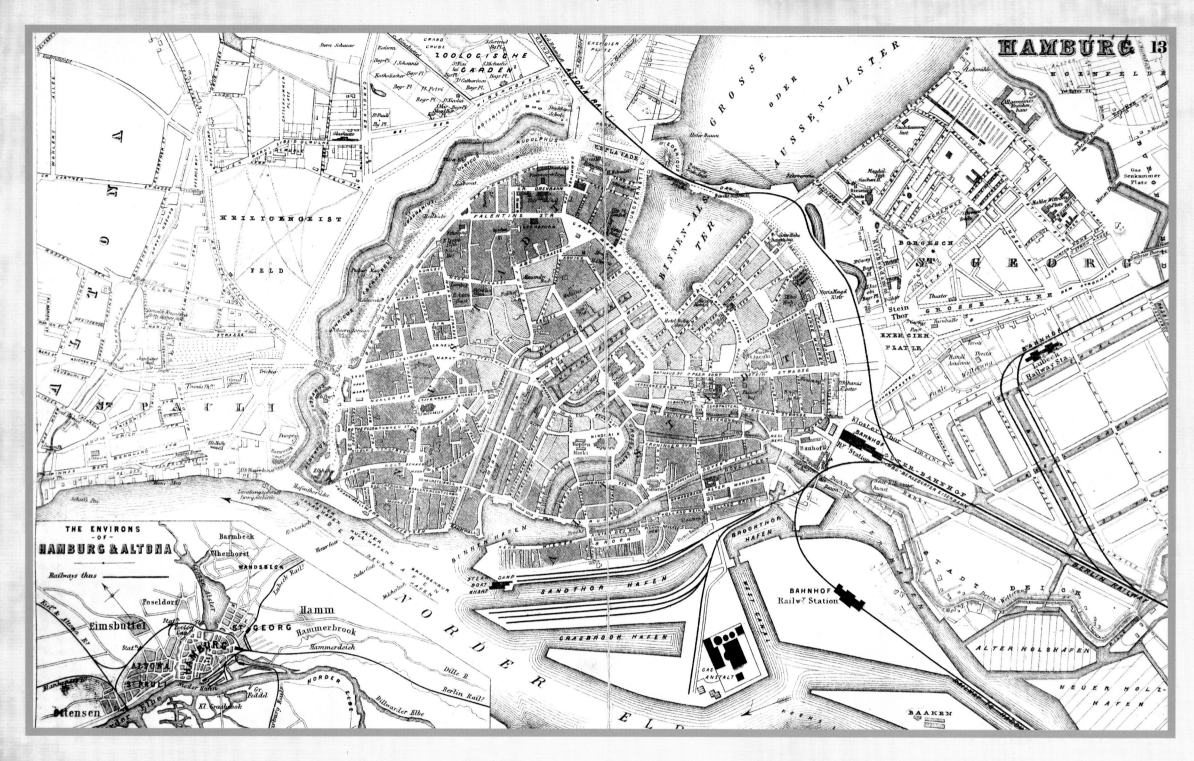

ABOVE: Produced by Bradshaw & Blacklock of Manchester, England, in the mid-19th century after the arrival of the first railways this map records the city of Hamburg after the rebuilding caused by the fire of 1842. It is aligned with north toward the top of the page. The city's extensive harbor facilities and railway network are evident.

ISTANBUL

TURKEY

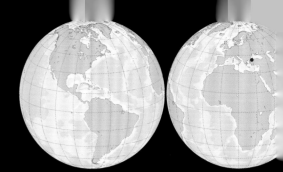

As capital of the Roman and later the Byzantine empires before falling to the Ottoman Turks in the mid-15th century, Istanbul was one of the pivotal cities of Europe for more than 1,500 years. Originally named Byzantium, it was renamed Constantinople before being known as Istanbul.

Little is known of the city until the 7th century B.C., when King Byzas established his Greek colony, Byzantium, on the European side of the Bosphorus. Ideally located, the city's importance as a trading center rapidly grew, and it remained largely independent until becoming part of the Roman province of Asia in 129B.C.

During the 3rd century, the Roman Empire was increasingly fractious and it was decided to create the eastern and western empires. This led to civil war with Constantine, the emperor in the west, vying with Licinius, the emperor in the east, for ultimate control. In 324A.D. Constantine defeated Licinius in battle and Byzantium surrendered to him. Constantine made Byzantium the capital of the whole Roman Empire and the city was renamed Constantinople.

Following the First Crusade at the end of the 11th century, there was a succession of weak emperors in Constantinople. The Crusaders finally breached its walls in 1204 and the city was divided between the Venetian doge and Count Baldwin of Flanders, who was crowned king of Rumania, the first of the Latin emperors.

Later, as the kingdom of Rumania weakened, so the surviving Byzantine states sought to restore power and it was the Empire of Nicaea that ultimately regained control of Constantinople in 1261. The recovery of the city was to launch a renaissance of learning and art, the final flowering of the Byzantine Empire. However, whilst the Christian forces had been fighting each other, a much more ominous threat was coming from the east in the form of the Ottoman Turks. On May 29, 1453, the Ottoman forces finally breached the city's walls and it fell later that day. The successful Ottoman leader, Mehmet II, made the city his capital and from the late 15th century it became known as Istanbul.

The decline of the Ottoman Empire was long drawn out, as the "Sick Man of Europe" struggled to maintain control over territory that stretched over much of the Middle East and southeastern Europe. The final death-knell came with defeat in World War I; on October 29, 1923, the Turkish Republic was announced and, at the same time, the decision was made to transfer the new country's capital to Ankara.

BELOW: Istanbul and the Bosphorus that joins the Mediterranean (below) with the Black Sea (above) taken from the international space station 2004.

BYZANTIVM NVNC CONSTANTINOPOLIS

LEFT: Known as Constantinople until the middle of the 15th century, when the capital of the erstwhile Byzantine Empire was finally captured by the Turks, this map reflects the changes wrought over the previous century. Although a number of older buildings survive—such as the Yediküle and the Golden Gate on the extreme left, and Haghia Sophia, one of the city's main churches that had been converted to a mosque on the orders of Mehmet II—much new construction work had occurred. Most notable amongst the new buildings of the late 15th and 16th centuries were Fatih Camii, a mosque complex that ultimately became the largest in the Ottoman Empire, but which was destroyed in an earthquake in 1766 and subsequently rebuilt, and the Topkapi Sarayi, the imperial residence of the Ottoman Sultan built at the point where the rivers Alibey and Kagithane enter the Bosphorus.

RIGHT: Published in France in 1836, this map of Constantinople is part of a French work described as the "Nouvel Atlas, physique, politique et historique de l'Empire Ottoman et de ses Etats limitophes en Europe, en Asie et en Afrique" (New Physical, Political and Historic Atlas of the Ottoman Empire and its Territories in Europe, Asia and Africa). It was published by Bellizand, Dufour and Company of Paris.

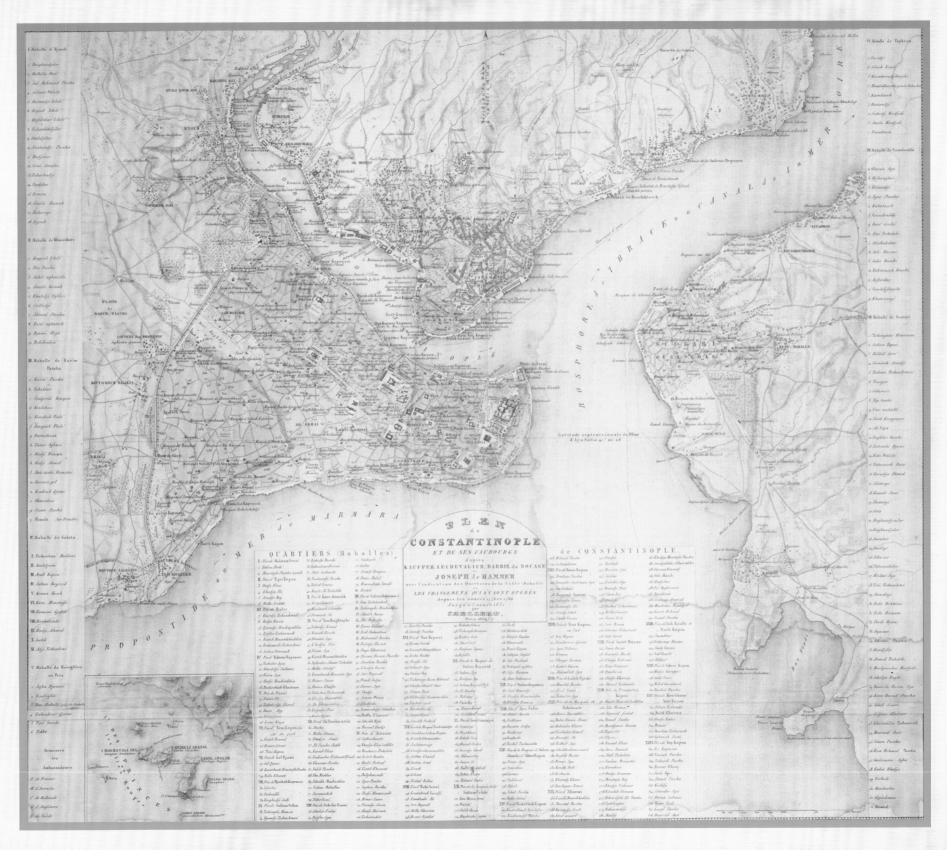

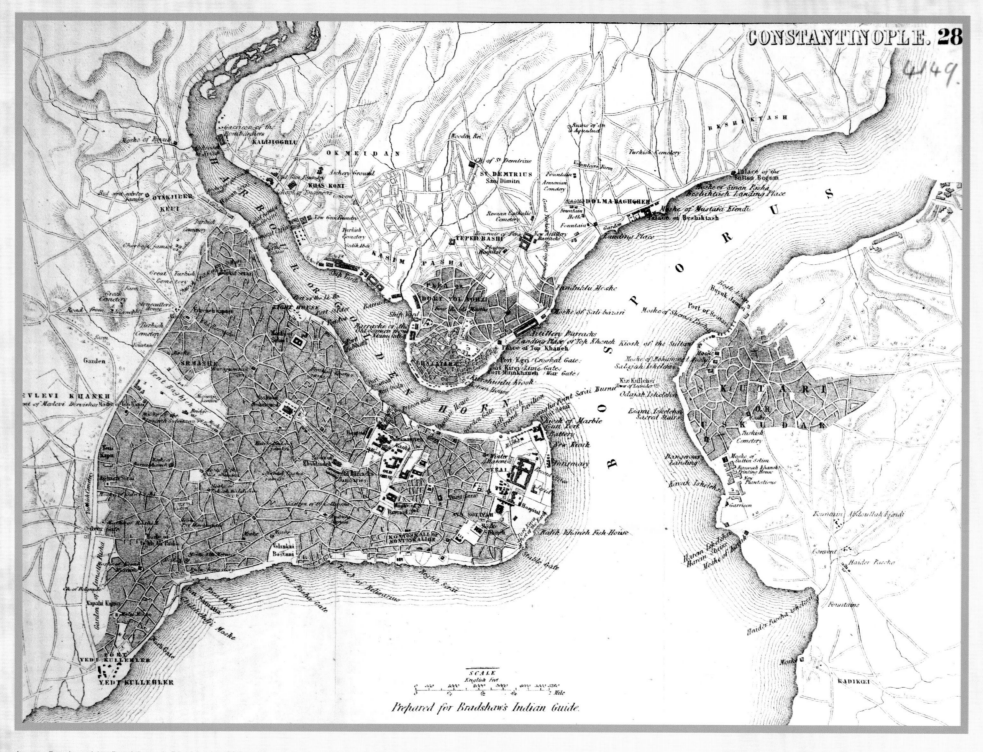

CONSTANTINOPLE. 28

Prepared for Bradshaw's Indian Guide.

RIGHT: By the late 19th century the Ottoman Empire was widely considered to be the "Sick Man of Europe," as its power and prestige gradually declined. In Europe, most of its territorial possessions in the Balkans, with the exception of the eastern Thrace, had achieved independence, and nations such as Romania, Bulgaria, and Serbia had been created, whilst its influence in North Africa was also loosening. This map records the city of Istanbul shortly before the outbreak of World War I. The Ottoman Empire was to fight with Germany and Austria-Hungary against Britain, France, and Russia.

ABOVE: Produced by Bradshaw & Blacklock of Manchester, England, this map records the city of Istanbul in the mid-19th century. Although much of Europe was already undergoing the railway revolution, Turkey was a relative late-comer to the industry and, while the city has expanded considerably during the course of the first half of the 19th century, it was not until 1873 that the first railway to serve the city, linking it with Anatolia, was opened.

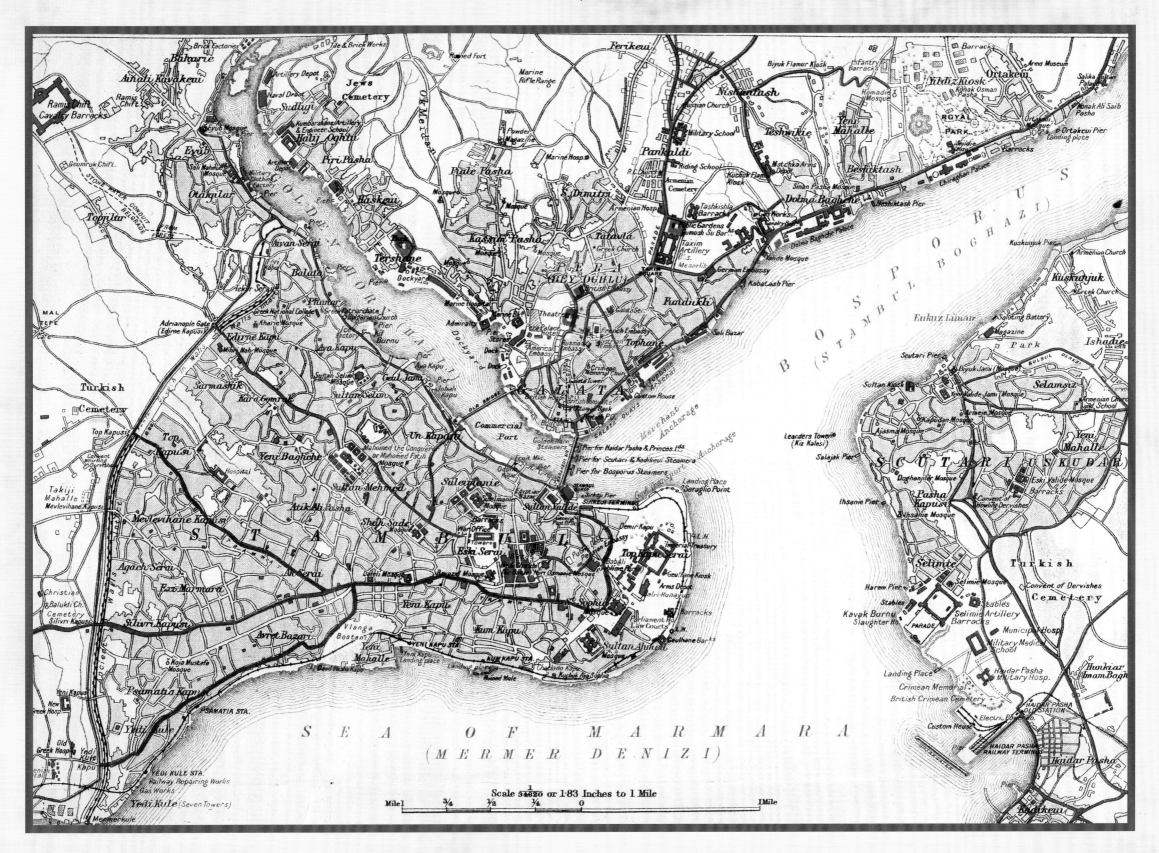

Scale $\frac{1}{54620}$ or 1·83 Inches to 1 Mile

Mile1   ¾   ½   ¼   0   1Mile

JERUSALEM
ISRAEL

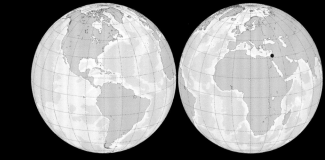

Jerusalem occupies an important position in the history of cartography. The Bible tells us that the city was first mapped in response to a divine command to the Prophet Ezekiel: "Thou also, son of man, take thee a tile and lay it before thee, and portray upon it the city, even Jerusalem" [Ezekiel 4:1]. Furthermore, the late medieval practice of placing Jerusalem at the center of world maps arose from a literal interpretation of Ezekiel 5:5: "This city of Jerusalem I have set in the midst of nations, with other countries round about her."

Jerusalem was proclaimed Israel's capital by King David 3,000 years ago and is one of the world's most ancient cities. Situated nearly 2,700 feet above sea level, the spectacular hill scenery forms the perfect backdrop to the colorful street scenes.

In 63B.C., the region, after passing through the hands of various invading armies, was conquered by Rome, and Herod the Great was established as King of Judea. As a client state of the Roman Empire, Jerusalem was ruled by a local procurator; the most famous of which is Pontius Pilate, who ordered the crucifixion of Jesus Christ.

In 66A.D. came the first of the Jewish revolts. Finally, in 132A.D., Emperor Hadrian ordered the city be razed to the ground and the Jewish population dispersed. Following this destruction, a new city—Aelia Capitolina—was built on the site, and this is the basis of the Old Town.

With the collapse of the Roman Empire Jerusalem passed to the rule of the Byzantine emperors from Constantinople. However, in 638 the city was captured by the forces of Islam, leading eventually to the launch of the first of the Crusades by the Christains, intent on recapturing the Holy Land. For the next two centuries, Islamic and Christian forces fought a bitter war for supremacy in the region, with power going backward and forward. In 1260, Jerusalem was captured by the Mamluk Sultanate, based in Egypt, who maintained control over Jerusalem until 1517 when it was conquered by the Ottoman Empire.

The city remained under Turkish occupation until the British army captured it 1917. British control continued until after World War II when the new United Nations adopted a plan for the partition of Palestine and of the city of Jerusalem. However, the Arab-Israel War of 1948 resulted in the division of the city, a situation that was to persist until 1967 and the Six-Day War, when Israel captured the whole of the city and the West Bank area. The status of Jerusalem since 1967 has remained highly controversial.

BELOW: Jerusalem taken from Ikonos 2003. There is only one box on this image because all of the following maps cover an area wider than this image.

Ezechielis. v.

Hæc est Ierusalem, Ego eam in medio Gentium posui, et in eius circuitu terras.

HIEROSOLYMA VRBS SANC
TA, IVDEAE, TOTIVSQVE
ORIENTIS LONGE CLARIS
SIMA, QVA AMPLITVDINE AC
MAGNIFICENTIA HOC NOS
TRO ÆVO CONSPICVA EST.

LEFT: The 16th century was to witness a change of rulers for the city of Jerusalem: in 1517, following the defeat of the Mamluk sultanate, the city became part of the Ottoman Empire. For the next 400 years it was to remain under Turkish rule. Reflecting the Muslim rule of the city in the 16th century, the Church of St John the Baptist, the oldest surviving church in the city, was in use as a mosque at this time; it would not be restored for Christian worship until the mid-17th century. The citadel, one of the key fortifications of the city, had been rebuilt between 1537 and 1541 by the Turks following their conquest of the city. Also prominent are the Temple Mount with its mosque and the Western (Wailing) Wall; the latter is the sole remaining fragment of the Temple constructed on the mount. Its name derives from the sorrow of the Jews following the destruction of the Temple in the 1st century A.D. Reflecting the fact that the city was and remains a center for three religions, also visible is the Church of the Holy Sepulchre; this was the heart of the Christian quarter of the city and marked the point where Jesus was crucified, buried, and resurrected.

RIGHT: Enclosed with Consul Young's dispatch of September 1, 1845, this map of the city of Jerusalem was produced to a scale of 1 inch to 800 feet. It was drawn originally by architect F. Catherwood in July 1835 and engraved by S. Bellin. The keys refer to places of interest and events referred to in the Bible.

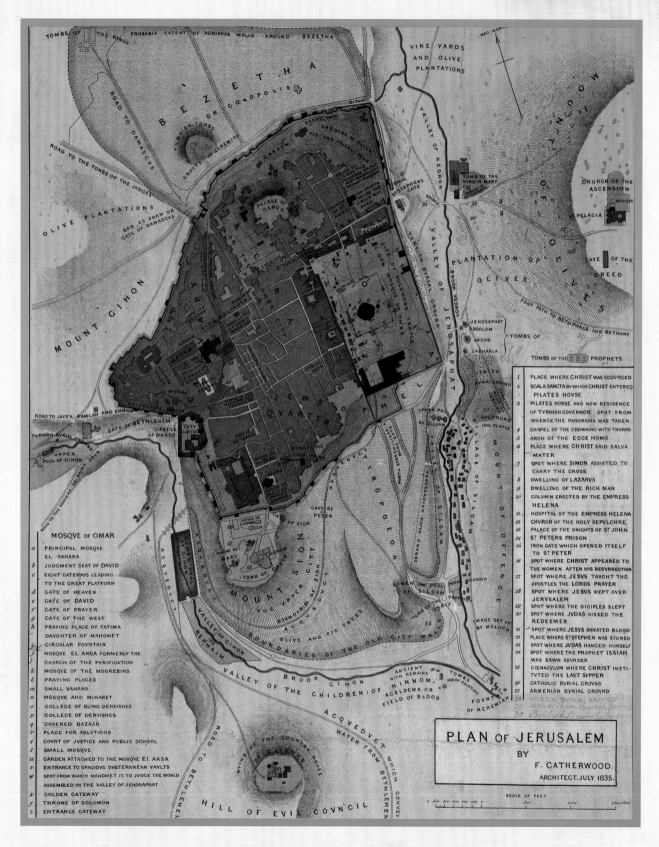

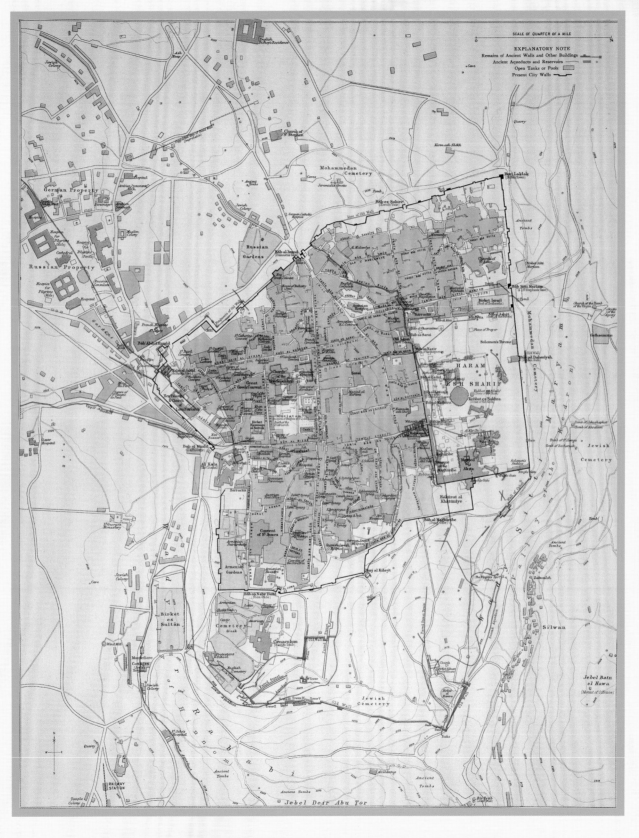

LEFT: Published in 1915 by cartographic publishers J. G. Bartholomew, this map is derived from a book—*Atlas of the Historical Geography of the Holy Land*—designed and edited by George Adam Smith. The book was published during the first full year of World War I when Jerusalem was still under the rule of the Ottoman Empire. As part of the Allied attack upon the Ottoman Empire during the war, Jerusalem was captured by a British force led by Sir Edmund Allenby in December 1917. Following this, Palestine became a League of Nations' mandated territory under the control of the British; it was to retain this status until the late 1940s.

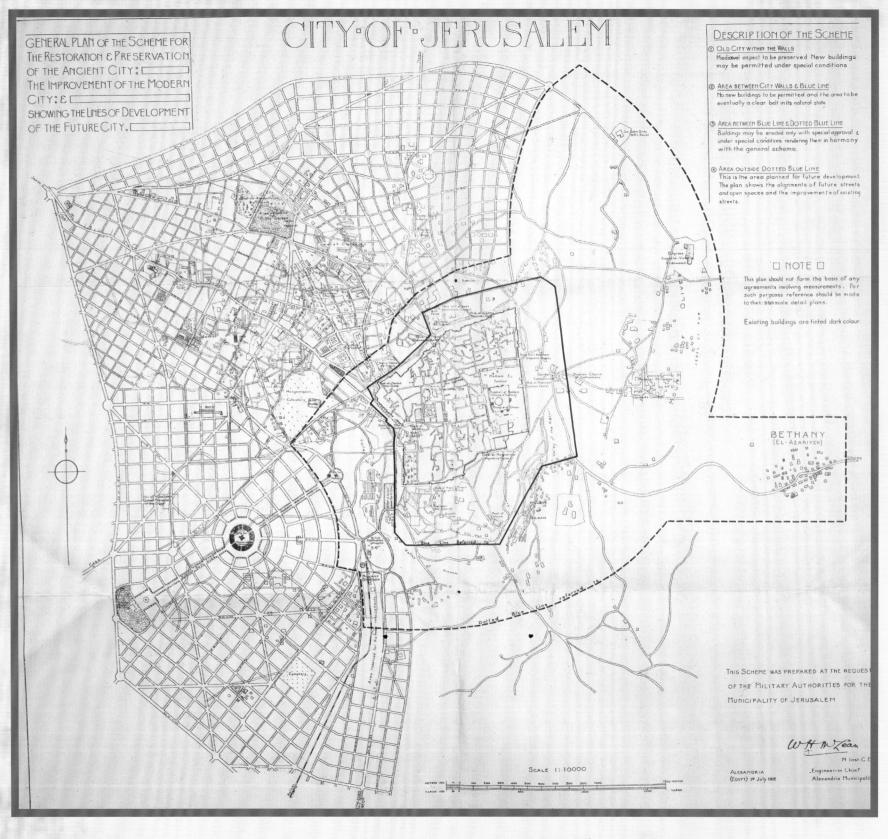

CITY·OF·JERUSALEM

GENERAL PLAN OF THE SCHEME FOR
THE RESTORATION & PRESERVATION
OF THE ANCIENT CITY:
THE IMPROVEMENT OF THE MODERN
CITY: &
SHOWING THE LINES OF DEVELOPMENT
OF THE FUTURE CITY.

DESCRIPTION OF THE SCHEME

① OLD CITY WITHIN THE WALLS
Medieval aspect to be preserved. New buildings
may be permitted under special conditions

② AREA BETWEEN CITY WALLS & BLUE LINE
No new buildings to be permitted and the area to be
eventually a clear belt in its natural state

③ AREA BETWEEN BLUE LINE & DOTTED BLUE LINE
Buildings may be erected only with special approval &
under special conditions rendering them in harmony
with the general scheme.

④ AREA OUTSIDE DOTTED BLUE LINE
This is the area planned for future development.
The plan shows the alignments of future streets
and open spaces and the improvements of existing
streets.

□ NOTE □

This plan should not form the basis of any
agreements involving measurements. For
such purposes reference should be made
to the 1:500 scale detail plans.

Existing buildings are tinted dark colour.

BETHANY
(EL·AZARIYEH)

THIS SCHEME WAS PREPARED AT THE REQUEST
OF THE MILITARY AUTHORITIES FOR THE
MUNICIPALITY OF JERUSALEM

W.H. McLean
M.Inst.C.E.

Scale 1:10000

ALEXANDRIA   Engineer-in-Chief
(EGYPT) 1st July 1918   Alexandria Municipality

LEFT: Although based on a map
produced on behalf of the British
based in Alexandria, in Egypt, in 1918
this map had been amended to
reflect the conservation of the
historic core of the city and the
plans for its future growth. At the
end of World War I, amidst the
destruction of the Ottoman Empire,
Britain had been granted control of
Palestine under the mandate of the
League of Nations and as a result
the British authorities produced this
view of the future development and
preservation of the city. Events,
however, were to overtake the
British authorities; following a period
of unrest, the British mandate
ceased on May 14, 1948 and the
independent state of Israel emerged.
At this time the city was divided
between Israel and Jordan, and this
division was to pertain until the war
of 1967, when Israel seized that part
of the city previously controlled by
Jordan in the east.

KOZHIKODE

INDIA

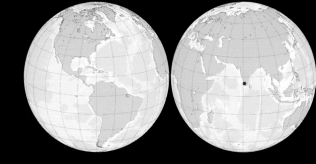

Kozhikode—previously known as Calicut—is the most important coastal city of Malabar in the state of Kerala with a contemporary population of some 436,000. It has been chosen for this book as it was historically a major trading post for spices and, in May 1498, was the first place in India to be visited by a European by ship when the Portuguese explorer Vasco da Gama landed at Kappad beach and was received at his palace by the ruler of the Samoothiripippadu—Anglicized to Zamorin (Lords of the Sea)—dynasty that ruled the area at the time.

Vasco da Gama arrived and initially obtained permission from Zamorin rulers to commence trading; however, the existing Arab traders opposed the arrival of the Europeans and this led to conflict between the Portuguese. In 1501 a Portuguese colony was destroyed and in 1510 Afonso de Albuquerque sacked the city. The subsequent wars were intense although victories by the Portuguese in 1528 and 1538, along with the construction of a Portuguese fort at Chaliyam, led to the weakening of Zamorin power and, in 1540, a treaty was signed which gave the Portuguese a monopoly of trade through Calicut. A short-lived peace ended in fighting, with the fort at Chaliyam being destroyed in 1571.

Other European powers, most notably the Dutch, English, and French, had also started to trade with India. The Zamorins allied themselves with the Dutch in the hope of expelling the Portuguese and gradually Portuguese influence and power waned. The English established a trading post in 1616, with the French following in 1722 and the Danes 30 years later. In 1695, Captain Kidd, the notorious pirate, sacked the city and, in 1766, when Haidar Ali attacked the city, the last Zamorin set fire to the palace, dying in the flames with the rest of his family

On March 22, 1792, as a result of the Treaty of Seringapatam with the defeated Tipu Sultan (the son of Haidar Ali), Calicut became a British possession, forming part of the Madras Presidency until Indian Independence in August 1947 and the creation of the state of Kerala nine years later. Today there is virtually no trace of the historic city despite its colorful past.

BELOW: Satellite image of Kozhikode, formerly known as Calicut, on the Malabar coast in the state of Kerala, south India. North is at the top. Forerested areas are in dark green; agricultural fields are lighter shades of green and brown; urban areas are grey and water is black. The image was created using data obtained from the Landsat-7 satellite.

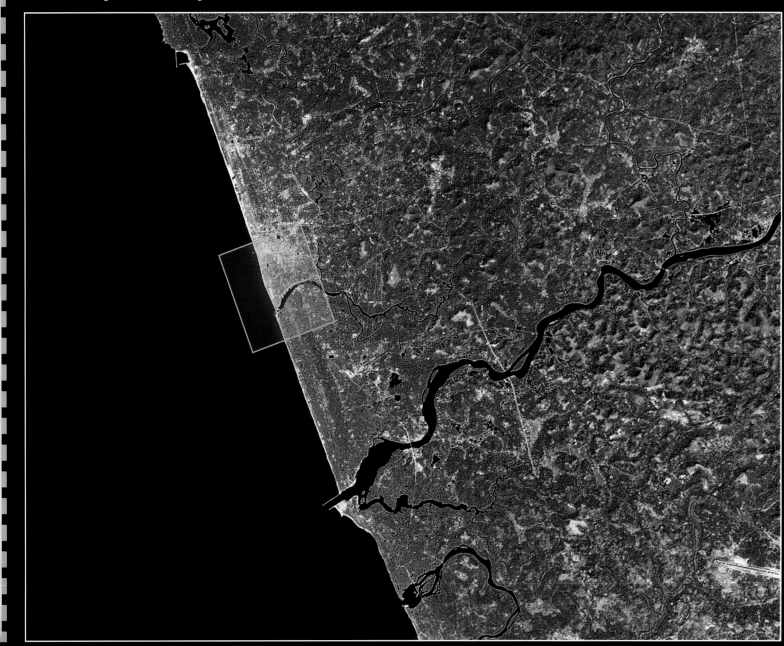

CALECHVT CELEBERRI:
MVM INDIÆ EMPORIVM.

ABOVE: Another map from the *Civitates*, with the Portuguese flag flying and with a soldier standing guard outside, the European presence in the city is clear. Trade was the primary purpose of the Portuguese settlement in places like Calicut but there was a constant threat to their presence and protection was essential if either European rivals or the local tribes were not to try and force them out. The area around the fort built at Velapuram in the fourteenth century became known as "Koli Kota" (or cock fort), which got converted into "Kalikat" by the Arabs, the first regular traders to reach the area by sea, and to "Kalifo" by the Chinese. It became known as "Calicut" to the Europeans and it was this name that was the origin of Calico cloth, a fine variety of hand-woven cotton cloth manufactured around the city.

Situated in the northwest of France at the estuary of the River Seine and located within the region of Haute-Normandie, Le Havre has a population of around 200,000 and is an important port—the second largest in France after Marseilles. The central area, much rebuilt as a result of severe damage during World War II, was declared a UNESCO World Heritage Site in 1995. Many of the buildings of note are the work of the architect Auguste Perret.

Le Havre was initially called Francisopolis in homage of the French king, Francis I (1494–1547), who founded it in 1517; work started on the city's cathedral in 1536. The name Le Havre simply refers to the harbor and was a shortened form of Le Havre de Grâce, the latter part of the name referring to the church of Notre Dame de Grâce, which existed on the site of the future city. In 1793, following the French revolution, the city changed its name to Hâvre-Marat in honor of the revolutionary leader Jean-Paul Marat (1743–93), who had been murdered in his bath by Charlotte Corday on July 13, 1793. The name change was to be brief, however; on January 14, 1793, the city became known simply as Le Havre.

The city was sited on the eastern side of the river; to the west was the ancient port of Honfleur and it was the silting up of this older port and a similar problem with the port at Harfleur that led to the establishment of the new port. The city grew in importance, particularly with the rise of the French overseas empire in the West Indies in the 18th century, and after the American Revolution. During the 19th century the city's economic base was expanded by industrialization.

Much of the historic city was destroyed during World War II when it was occupied by the Germans. It suffered major bombardment prior to the launching of the D-Day assaults on the beaches of Normandy on June 6, 1944, with some 5,000 people being killed and 12,000 homes destroyed. Following the successful Allied invasion of Normandy, the city was liberated and the port used to help reinforce and re-supply the advancing Allied forces.

LE HAVRE
FRANCE

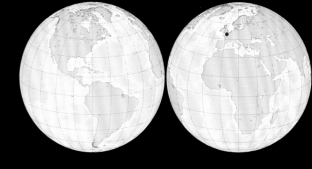

BELOW: Satellite image of the city of Le Havre (upper left) and its surrounding area on the northwestern coast of France. North is at top. Forested areas are dark green, agricultural fields are lighter shades of green and brown, urban areas are grey and water is black. The mouth of the river Seine is seen at centre and the city's ferry ports are the water channels at left. Image created using NaturalVue data obtained from the Landsat 7 satellite.

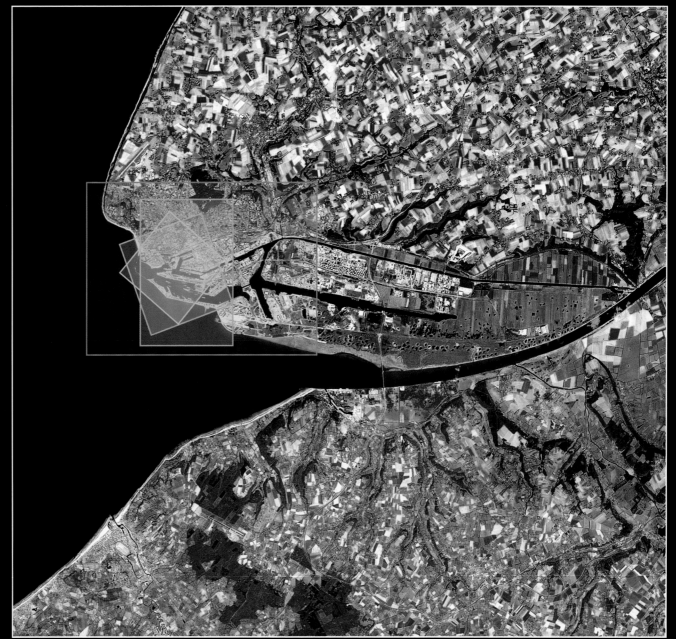

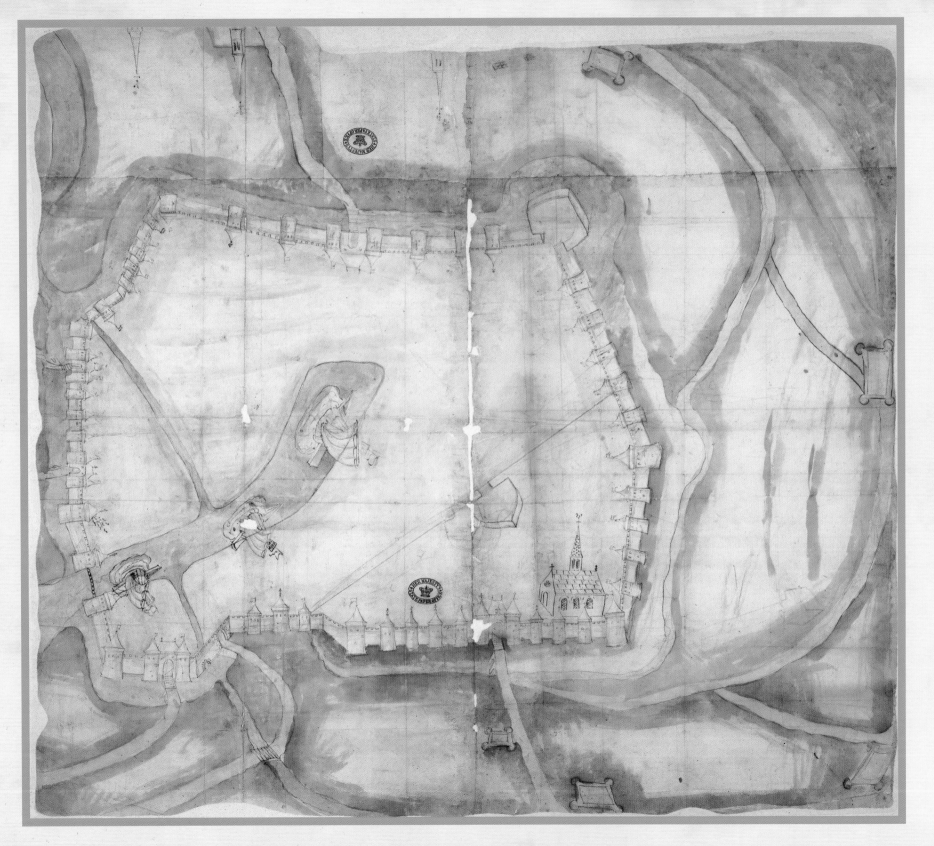

LEFT: This plan of Le Havre, believed to date from the early years of the reign of Queen Elizabeth I (ruled 1558–1603), shows a fortified harbor, shipping, towers, gates, churches, and a moat. No scale is shown. It is endorsed: "Platt of [...] sent by Sir Thomas Smythe," who may be the Sir Thomas Smith (1513–77) appointed Ambassador to France in September 1562. Sited just outside the city walls, to the north of the main city, is the Fort de Sainte-Adresse; in other contemporary maps this fort was known to the English as Fort Warwick.

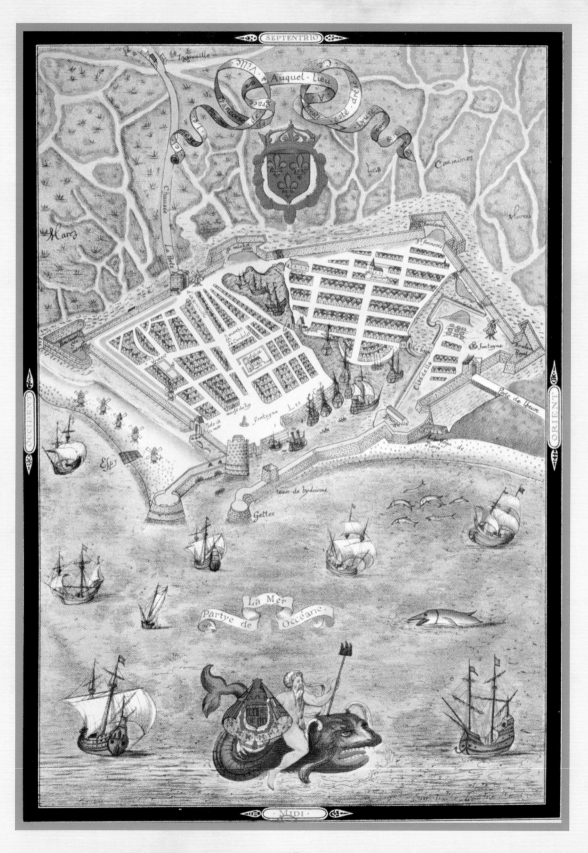

LEFT: This map, dating from the same time as those used in *Civitas Orbis Terrarum*, but not incorporated within Braun and Hogenberg's great work, was produced in France by Jacques Devaulx. At the time of the map's compilation, Le Havre was less than a century old, being founded in 1517 by King Francis I.

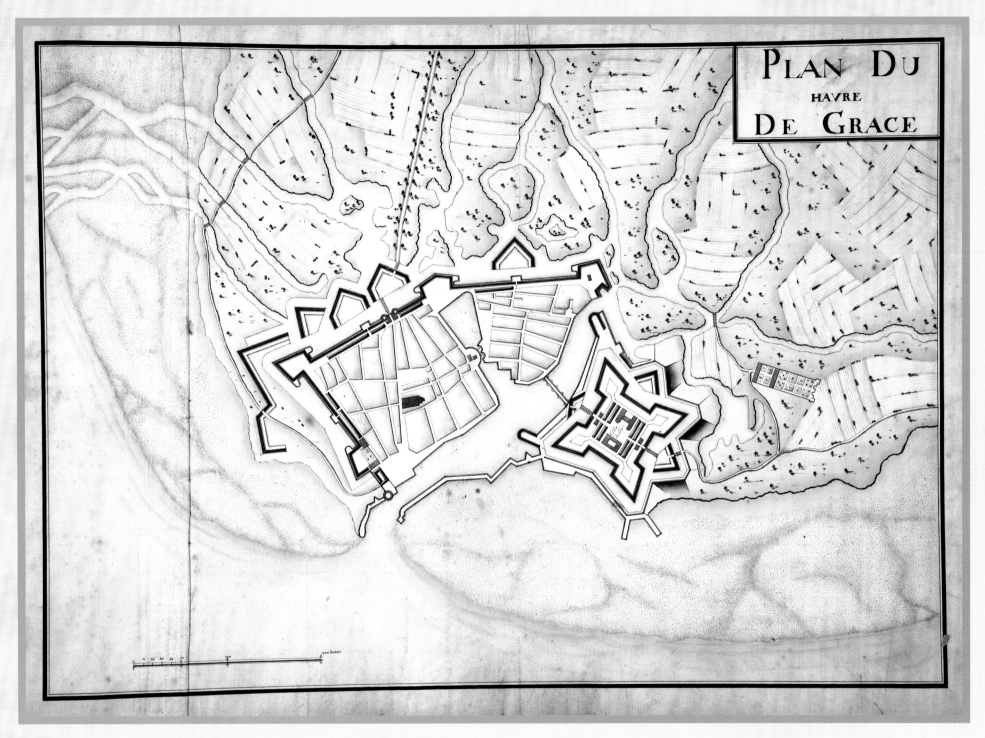

PLAN DU HAVRE DE GRACE

LEFT: One of a series of maps recording the fortified cities of France produced toward the end of the 17th century and now bound into a single volume, this plan of Le Havre records the city and its fortifications. Note that the city is given its full name of Havre de Grâce.

RIGHT: By the end of the 19th century, when this panoramic view of Le Havre was produced, the city and port had considerably expanded. By this date steam ships had begun to appear and the cross-channel trade with the ports of southern England was growing.

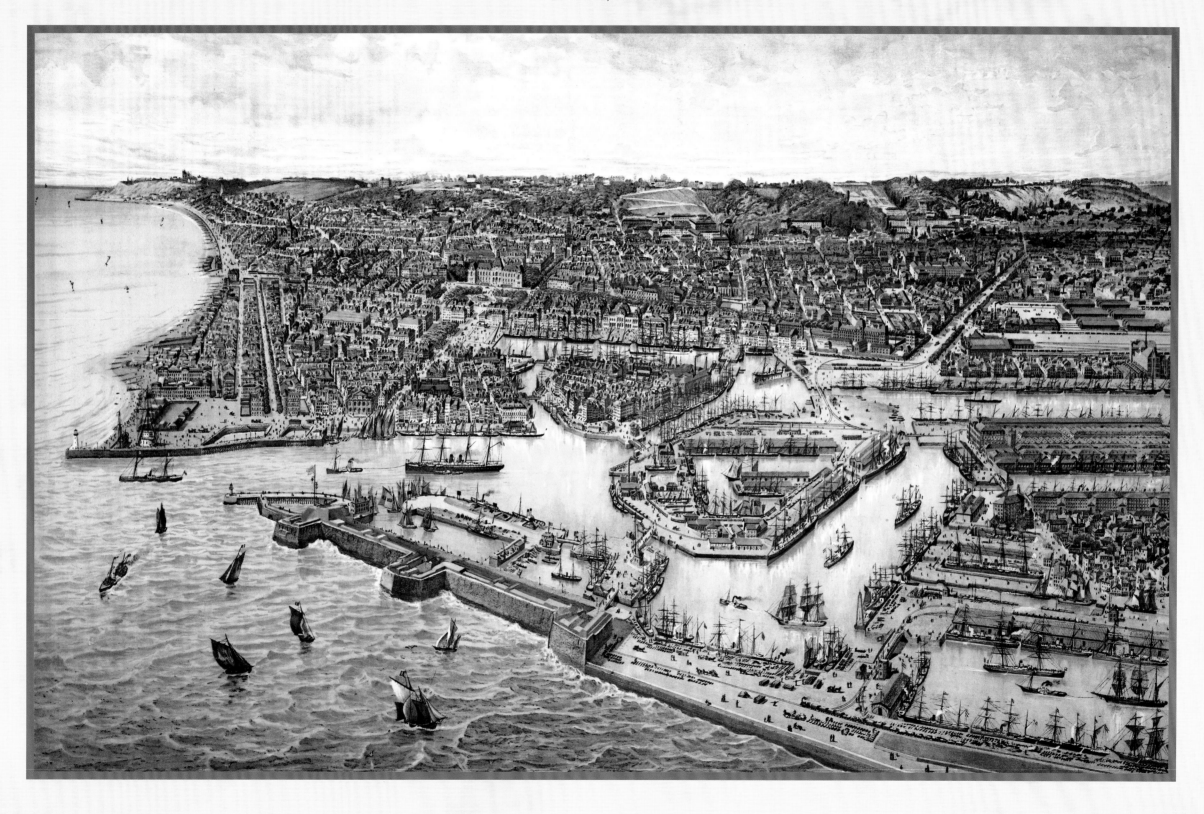

LISBON
PORTUGAL

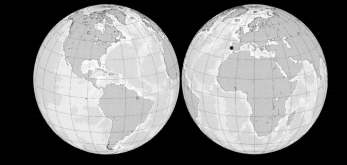

Lisbon (Lisboa), the westernmost capital in mainland Europe, sits beside the Atlantic Ocean at the mouth of the mighty River Tagus (Tejo), the largest river on the Iberian peninsula.

The city was probably founded by the Phoenicians, although local legend claims that the great hero Ulysses was responsible. From then on the Phoenicians, Greeks, Carthaginians, and Romans all fought for supremacy until, in 205B.C., the latter achieved dominance. Under the Romans, Lisbon became the most important city in western Iberia and was renamed Felicitas Julia by Julius Caesar in the 1st century B.C.

Lisbon was one of the most important points in early European trade and thrived during the late 15th and 16th centuries when Portuguese explorers opened up much of the world and brought back exotic treasures from far-flung lands. It was from Lisbon in 1497 that Vasco de Gama set sail on his voyage that would ultimately open up the sea route to India and the Far East. By the 1470s Lisbon had become the country's main slaving port.

Portugal possessed a complex marine economy based largely upon the ports of Lisbon and Oporto. Lisbon led Europe in the exploration of sea routes to Africa, the Atlantic Islands, Asia, and South America over the course of the 16th century. As a result of this activity, Portugal acquired a major worldwide empire that ultimately included Macau in the Far East, Goa in India, Mozambique and Angola in Africa, and Brazil in South America.

The country was a monarchy until October 1910 when, following a three-day insurrection, the Portuguese Republic was declared as a result of the abdication of King Manuel II. The republic was to survive until 1926 when a military dictatorship was established, with Antonio de Oliviera Salazar becoming leader in 1932. The following year a fascist constitution was adopted although, like neighboring Spain, Portugal managed to avoid direct involvement in World War II.

By the 1970s the parlous state of the country's finances resulted in its effective withdrawal from its remaining colonies—with the exception of Macau (not returned to China until 1999)—although Brazil had become independent much earlier and India had seized Goa in the 1960s. In 1974 a military coup started the process by which the country returned to democracy, but it was not until 1982 that full civilian rule was restored. Portugal became a member of the European Union four years later.

BELOW: Spot-5 satellite image of Lisbon and the mouth of the River Tagus.

LEFT: Lisbon has suffered severely from the consequences of earthquakes and, as illustrated here, had been rebuilt following a quake in 1531 that killed thousands and destroyed much of the city. Another catastrophic quake in 1755 killed between 60,000 and 90,000, and destroyed some 85 percent of the new buildings. The only district to escape significant destruction in both quakes was the Alfama area to the south of the Castle of St George (Castelo de São Jorge) and to the north of the Sé Patriarchal (cathedral)—both of which can be prominently seen in this late 16th century map. At this time this was the grandest part of the city, occupied by Moorish merchants and other traders. The area to the west of the cathedral, Baixa (or Lower Town), was the most severely damaged in the 1755 earthquake.

A View of LISBON before the Earthquake in 1755.

LEFT: Although produced by Captain Joseph Smith Seer in the early 1770s, this panoramic view of the city of Lisbon records the city, immediately prior to the devastating earthquake and flood of 1755. On the eastern side, on top of the hill, is the Castle of St George (Castelo de São Jorge). Virtually the whole of the area to the west of the castle was destroyed by the earthquake and flood, and was subject to wholesale redevelopment following the plans of the Marquês de Pombal. Such was the destruction that large sums of money were raised to assist the Portuguese in the reconstruction, with much coming from the City of London, reflecting the fact that Portugal was England's oldest ally.

ABOVE: Described as "Carta topographica da Cidade de Lisboa" (Topographical Map of the City of Lisbon), this Portuguese map was originally produced in the late 1850s and shows the north bank of the River Tagus from the Tower of Belem in the extreme west through the city to the hinterland to the east. The regular pattern of the redeveloped area following the 1755 earthquake can be clearly seen. The map has been annotated in 1871 with information about the military facilities in and around the city.

LONDON

ENGLAND

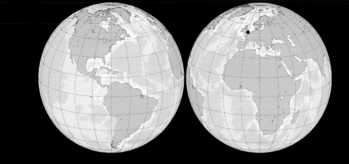

Effectively the sole capital of England for more than 1,000 years, and the capital of the United Kingdom since 1707, contemporary London straddles the River Thames. The historic city of London, however, developed on the north bank of the river.

Following the successful invasion of Britain under the Emperor Claudius in 43A.D., four legions converted southeast England into a Roman province and first established a fort on the north bank of the Thames. Called londinium by the Romans, after the invasion of the Anglo-Saxons "Lundenwic," as the city was known, became the capital of the Saxon kingdom of Essex.

With the Norman Conquest, in order to exercise control over London, William constructed a number of fortifications, including the first phase of the Tower of London. Under William's son, William II, work commenced on Westminster Hall; this was to become part of the future Palace of Westminster, which became the political and administrative center of the realm, with the original City of London becoming the mercantile center. In the late 12th century guilds elected the first Lord Mayor and these rights were enshrined in the Magna Carta, signed by King John in 1215.

During the Middle Ages London continued to expand in size, population, and wealth. However, as with the rest of the country, it was ravaged by the Black Death in the middle of the 14th century and about one-third of the population died. Despite this loss, London continued to grow in importance. By the end of the 16th century the population had expanded to some 300,000, and the city had evolved into the most important trading center in the world.

The next century, however, was to witness treason—as in 1605 when Catholic recusants attempted to blow up the Palace of Westminster and murder King James I in the Gunpowder Plot—and civil war in the 1640s. Shortly after the monarch was restored in 1660, two natural disasters were to strike. In 1665, the Great Plague devastated the population, whilst in September the following year the Great Fire destroyed some 80 percent of the historic city, including St Paul's Cathedral. After the fire, regulations were brought in to prevent such disaster in the future; however, a more radical scheme, favored by the architect Sir Christopher Wren, for the complete redesign of the city with wider roads and dramatic architecture, was rejected.

BELOW: London taken by Landsat in 2005. North is to the top.

RIGHT: The original City of London was situated on the north side of the River Thames and surrounded by its walls. By the date of this late 16th centurry map, settlement had extended across the river to Southwark, which was linked to the city by London Bridge, and along the north bank of the river toward the palaces of Westminster and Whitehall. Across the river from these buildings was Lambeth Palace, the London home of the Archbishop of Canterbury. The London portrayed in this map, including the numerous city churches and the medieval St Paul's Cathedral, would soon be swept away as a result of the Great Fire of London in 1666. Although Sir Christopher Wren had grandiose plans for the radical realignment of the city after the fire, the urgent need for rebuilding and existing property rights ensured that the city was rebuilt according to the street plans inherited from the medieval city.

AN EXACT SVRVEIGH OF THE STREETS LANES AND CHVRCHES CONTAINED WITHIN THE RVINES OF THE CITY OF LONDON FIRST DESCRIBED IN SIX PLATS, BY IOHN LEAKE, IOHN IENNINGS, WILLIAM MARR, WILL. LEYBVRN, THOMAS STREETE & RICHARD SHORTGRAVE in Decr Aͦ 1666. BY THE ORDER OF THE LORD MAYOR ALDERMEN, AND COMMON COVNCELL OF THE SAID CITY

Reduced here into one intire plat, by Iohn Leake, the Citty Wall being added alsoͦ. The places where the Balls stood, are exprest by Orbs of Armes, & all the Wards divided by pricks & Alphabet, &c

The Prospect of this City, as it appeared from the opposite Southwarke side, in the fire time.

The Right Honourable Sͬ William Turner the Lord Maior. Aͦ 1669

THE RIVER THAMES

Part of Southwarke

a Scale of Feet.

Published with the description of the Wards by the care Industrie and Charge of Nathanael Brooke Stationer, and are to be Sould at his shop at the Angel, in the second Yard of Gresham Colledge leading from Bishopsgate street.

Wenceslaus Hollar fecit, 1667.

Reproduced and printed by Edward Stanford Ltd.

HOLLAR'S "EXACT SURVEIGH" OF THE CITY OF LONDON, 1667

(from the 1669 copy in the British Museum)

PUBLICATION NO. 104 (replacing Nos. 22 & 26)
London Topographical Society · 9 Rivercourt Road · London W6

LEFT: The Great Fire of London, which burnt from Sunday September 2 to Wednesday September 5, 1666, was to see the destruction of virtually the entire historic center of the City of London. In all, the fire destroyed some 13,000 houses, 87 churches, St Paul's Cathedral, and most of the city's public buildings before it finally burnt itself out. Published in 1669 in London by N. Brooke, this map was surveyed by John Leake, Jonas Moore, and Ralph Graterix before being drawn by Wenceslaus Hollar, and records the area of the destruction caused by the fire.

RIGHT: Although dated 1732 and published in that year by Thomas Jeffery, this map—which was produced to a scale of 1 inch to 300 feet—owes its origins to work undertaken in the late 17th century by Robert Morden, Philip Lea, and William Morgan. The map portrays the City of London after the Great Fire, with the new St Paul's Cathedral prominently presented. The top of the map shows a panoramic view of the city from the south, with the old London Bridge and its ramshackle buildings, along with the large number of warehouses along the north bank of the River Thames, reflecting the growing importance of trade to London. Although the city walls can still be identified, the growth of the city was such that large areas outside the walls had already been developed and expansion was also to be seen south of the river—with Southwark expanding—and along the river to the east. Inset around the main map are illustrations of a number of notable buildings, whilst the dedication to King William and Queen Mary confirms the late 17th-century origin of the map.

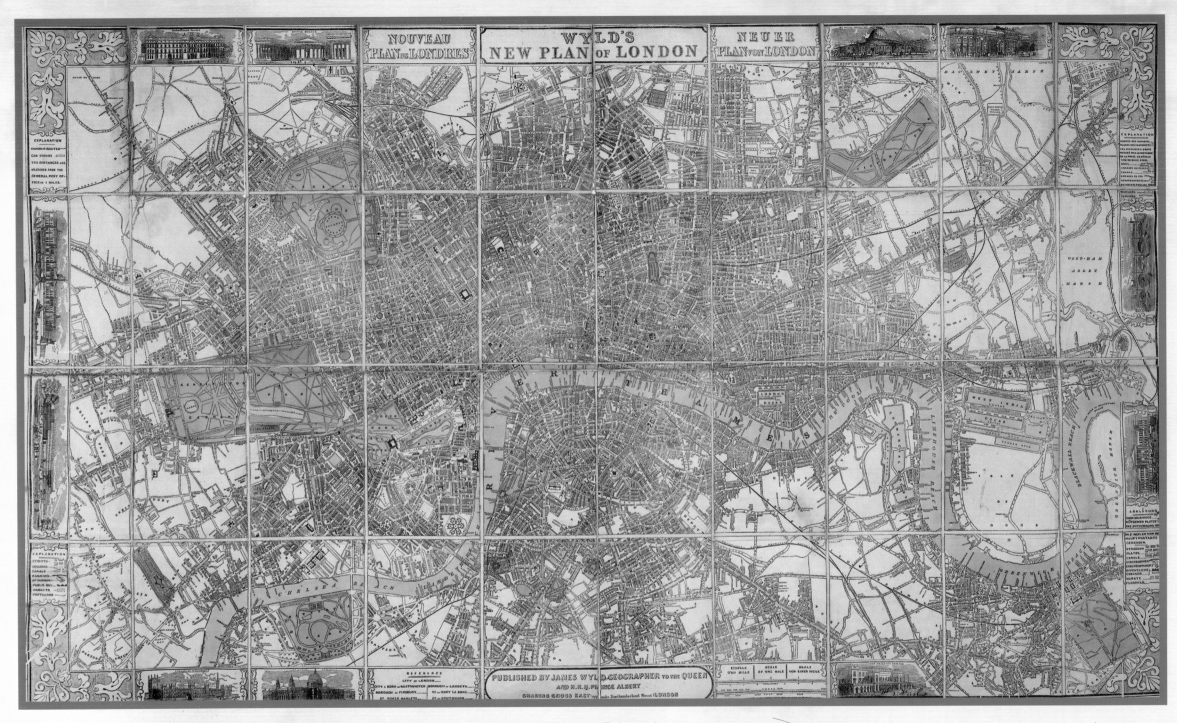

NOUVEAU PLAN DE LONDRES — **WYLD'S NEW PLAN OF LONDON** — **NEUER PLAN VON LONDON**

ABOVE: Between May 1 and October 15, 1851, London hosted the Great Exhibition of the Works of Industry of all Nations. To house the exhibition, a temporary hall—the famous Crystal Palace—was erected in Hyde Park. During the year some six million people visited the exhibition. At the time, this represented about a third of Britain's population. Published by James Wyld of Charing Cross in 1851, this map of London was also a guide to the Great Exhibition. The Crystal Palace itself, identified in red, can be seen located in Hyde Park; after the exhibition closed the building was dismantled and re-erected in south London where it was to survive until destroyed by fire in the 1930s. Inset around the frame of the map are illustrations of a number of notable buildings in London; these include the Houses of Parliament. This building was relatively new at this date, having been built on the site of the original palace, which had been destroyed by fire in 1834.

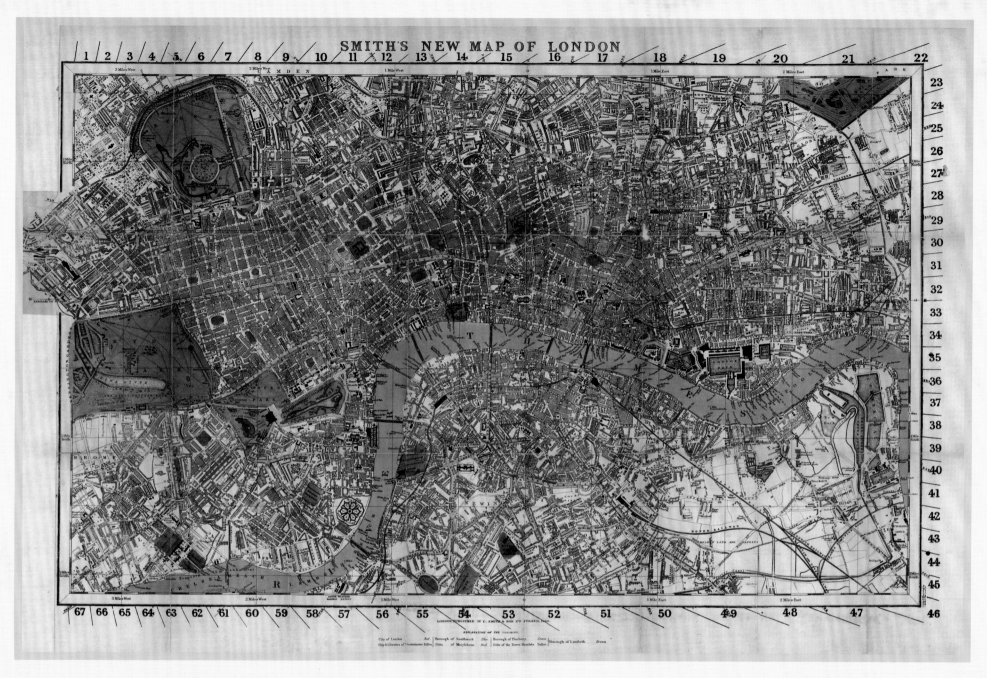

SMITH'S NEW MAP OF LONDON

LEFT: Drawn to a scale of 1:17,760, Smith's New Map of London records the dramatic growth of the city by the middle of the 19th century, when London was becoming a leading world power as British rule extended to all corners of the globe. The Industrial Revolution had seen Britain become the "Workshop of the World," and vast amounts of trade were to pass through the rapidly developing London Docks. As the city expanded, so the villages that had once been outside the metropolitan area were being swallowed up and the arrival of the railway age further encouraged the growth of the city's suburbs. South of the river, the network of railway lines that headed south from the city toward Kent, Sussex, and Hampshire were already well developed by this date and it was the presence of these railways that determined the routes of the later roads. Reflecting the development of the city, the number of river crossings had also significantly increased, although arguably the most famous bridge—Tower Bridge—was not to be completed until 1894.

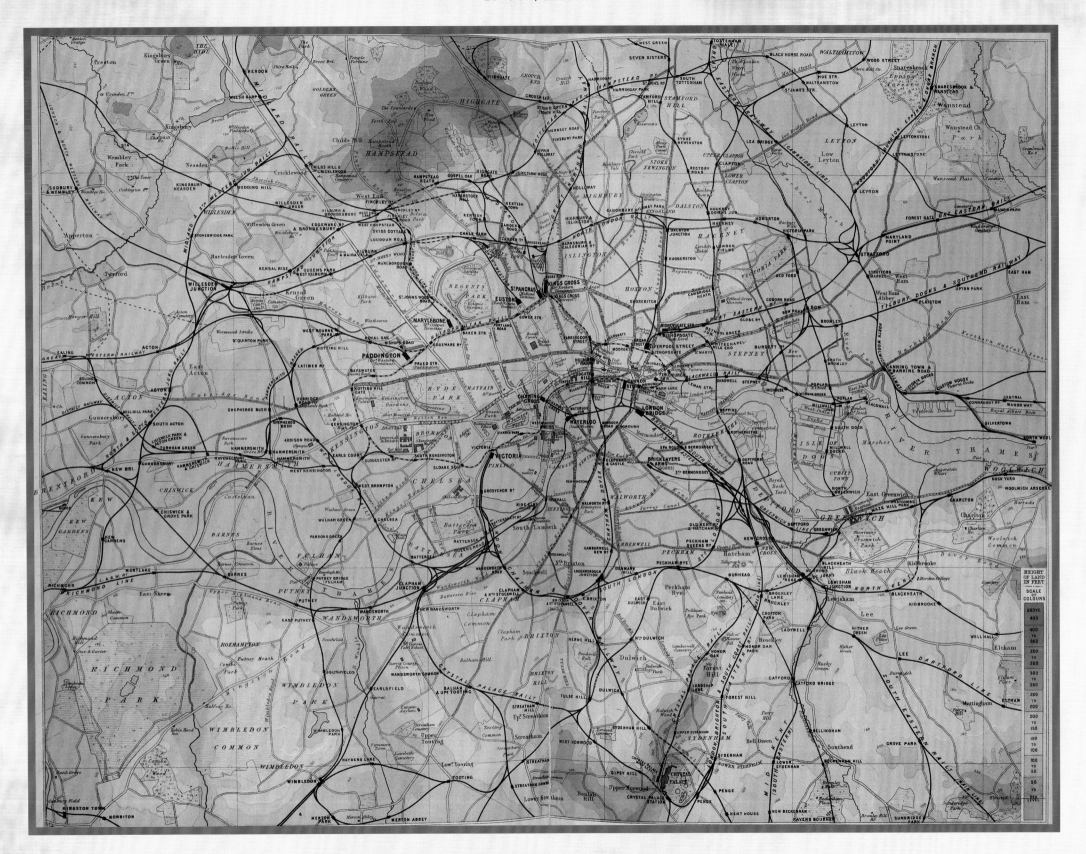

LEFT: Published by John Bartholemew & Co in 1898 as plate 65 in the company's *Royal Atlas of England and Wales*, this map records the extensive railway development in the London area over the previous 60 years. The first main-line railways, with termini at stations such as Paddington and Euston, had arrived in the 1830s, and by the date of this map the development of surface lines within the London area was largely complete. However, none of the main lines penetrated into the historic center of the traditional City of London and Westminster, and the main line termini were constructed at then end of the main built up areas, so the expansion of the railway system into the central area could only be achieved through the construction of the underground network. South of the river, the railways were to act as the precursor of massive urbanization during the course of the late 19th and 20th centuries.

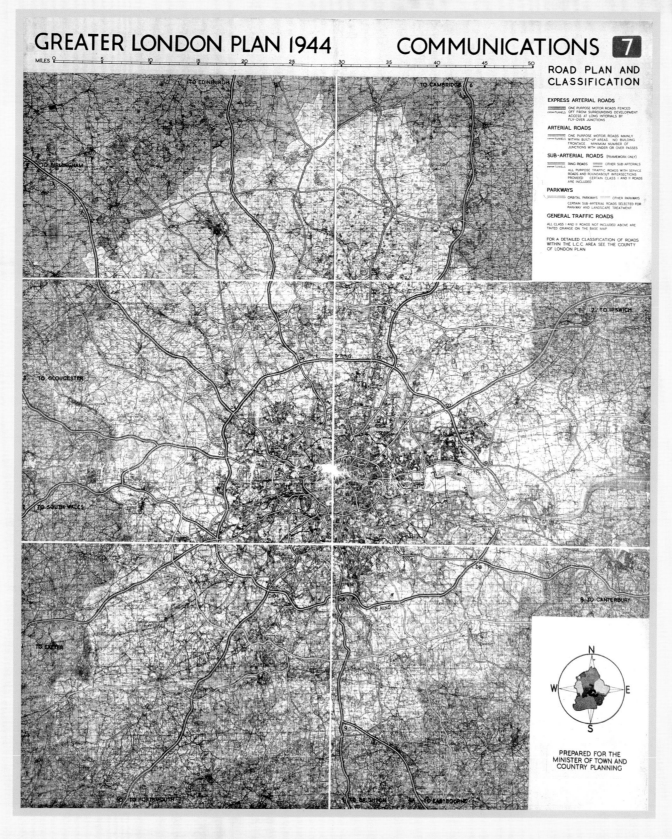

LEFT: Prepared for the Ministry of Town and Country Planning, this overview of Greater London shows the extent to which London had expanded as it gradually swallowed up towns and villages in outlying areas. The growth of the suburbs, aided by the massive development of the railway network of both the main-line railway companies and the London Passenger Transport Board, resulted in ever-increasing numbers of commuters heading into and out of the city. This map records the Ministry's plans for the improvement of the main road network in and around the London area; the express arterial roads represent effectively the motorway network that was ultimately to be completed with, for example, the circular M25 largely following the course of the D Ring. Although planned toward the end of World War II, it was some 40 years before the last links in the motorway network in the London area were finally completed.

LOS ANGELES

UNITED STATES

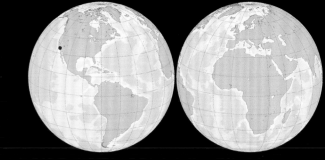

With a population now approaching four million, the city of Los Angeles is the second largest today in the US. Its name is an abbreviation of El Pueblo de Nuestre Señora la Reina de los Angeles de Porciúncula (The Village of Our Lady, the Queen of the Angels on the Porciuncula River), the title given to the location in 1781 following the establishment of the settlement by Spanish missionaries from the San Gabriel Mission some eight miles northeast of the modern city center.

Growth of the new settlement was relatively slow, with the population reaching just 650 by 1820; the following year, however, New Spain achieved independence from the Spanish Empire and the region became part of Mexico. Under Mexican rule the city grew considerably, becoming the capital of the country's Alta California province. During the Mexican-American War of 1846 the area was occupied by US soldiers, and under the treaties of Cahuenga (1847) and Guadalupe Hidalgo (1848) Alta California and other territory was ceded by Mexico to the US. At this time gold was discovered in the Sierra Nevada and this gave a further impetus to the city's growth. The years immediately following the US annexation of the territory were not always peaceful, however, as simmering resentment over loss of land caused banditry amongst the disposed Mexicans and, in 1871, a massacre occurred amongst the growing Chinese community as a result of gang warfare.

The next wave of mass migration to the region came in 1876 with the opening of the Southern Pacific railroad, the first transcontinental line to be completed and, by the early 1890s, the city's population had increased to more than 50,000. The discovery of oil in the region in 1892 was a further stimulus to growth and by the start of the 20th century the population had reached more than 100,000. The city continued to grow as a result of the construction of artificial harbors at Long Beach and San Pedro and had reached more than 300,000 by 1910.

Until the 1890s the city remained within its original 28 square mile land grant, but from the early years of the 20th century the city expanded by absorbing neighboring communities. A further factor in the city's growth at this time was the rise of the film industry, with Los Angeles—most notably within the district of Hollywood—becoming the world center for the business. Manufacturing, such as the automobile and aviation industries, were also drawn to Los Angeles during the 20th century, but many of these have largely disappeared over the past 20 years.

BELOW: Los Angeles with mountains behind, as taken by Landsat.

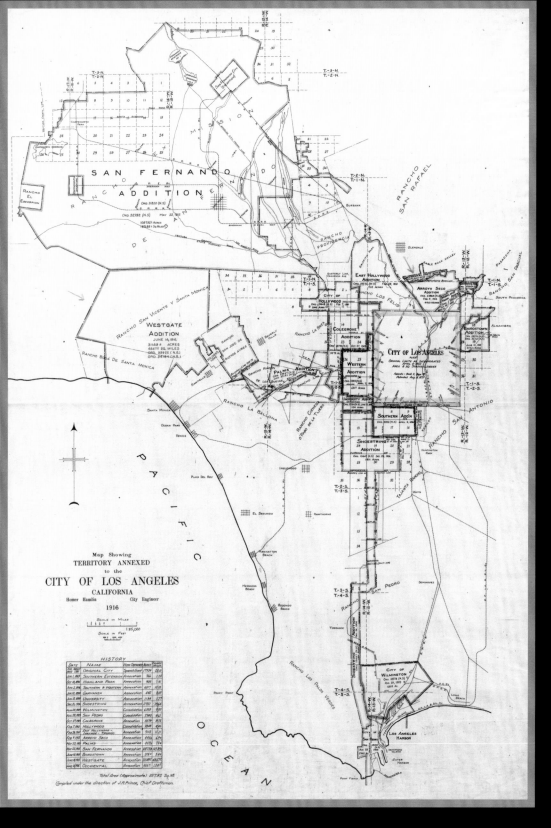

Map Showing
TERRITORY ANNEXED
to the
CITY OF LOS ANGELES
CALIFORNIA
Homer Hamlin   City Engineer
1916

SCALE IN MILES

SCALE IN FEET
1:85,000

LEFT: Compiled under the direction of J. R. Prince, Chief Draughtsman, and Homer Hamlin, the City Engineer, this map records the growth of Los Angeles from the late 18th century through to the first years of the 20th. Drawn to a scale of 1:85,000, it also includes a table giving details of those areas incorporated within the city, recording the date, how the land was obtained, and the size acquired.

FOLLOWING PAGE: Los Angeles 1932 Published by Metropolitan Surveys and designed by K. M. Leuschner, this map records the city of Los Angeles during the Great Depression.

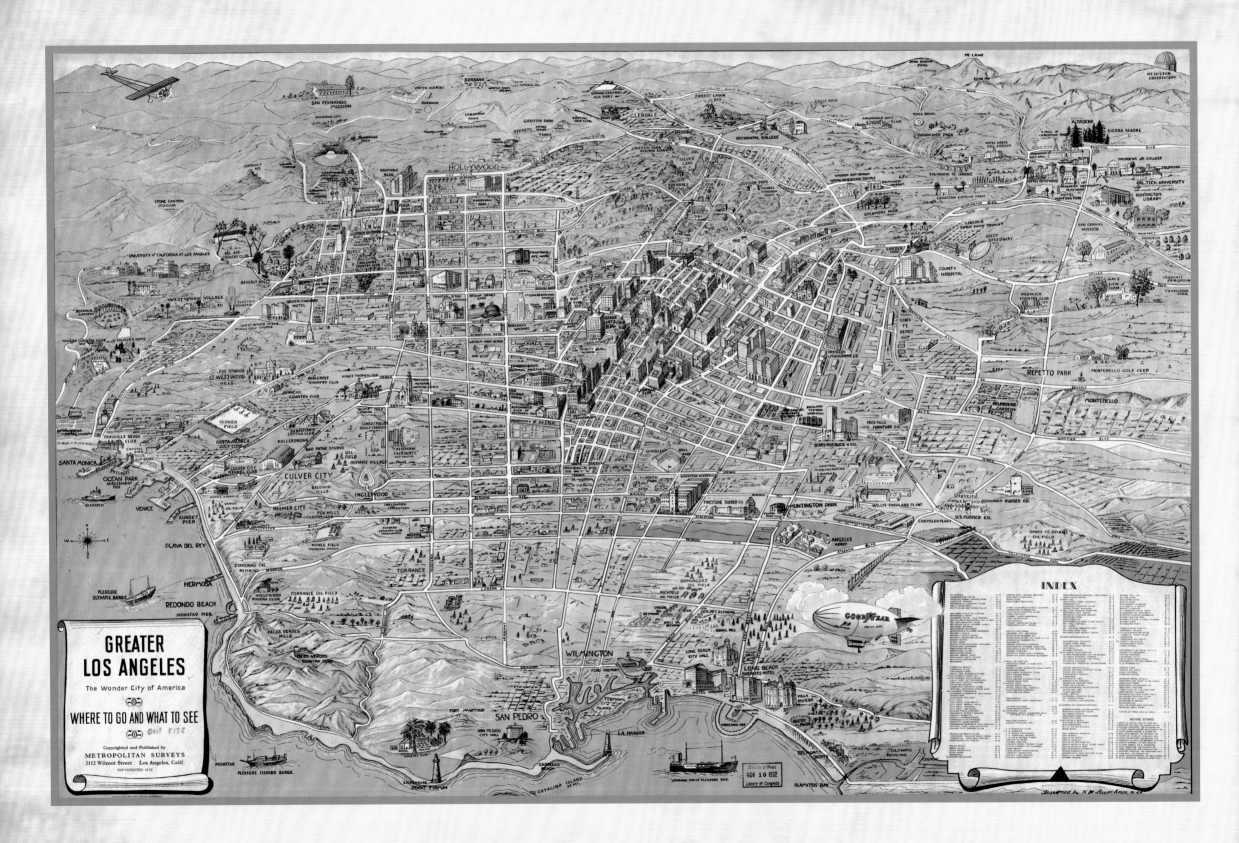

GREATER
LOS ANGELES

The Wonder City of America

WHERE TO GO AND WHAT TO SEE

Copyrighted and Published by
METROPOLITAN SURVEYS
2112 Wilmot Street   Los Angeles, Calif.
COPYRIGHTED 1932

INDEX

LYONS
FRANCE

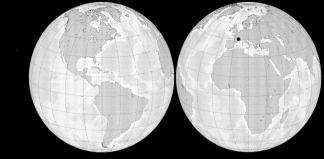

With a population of more than 400,000, Lyons—Lyon in French—is the main city of the French *département* of Rhône and the country's second-largest commercial and industrial center. It is sited at the confluence of the navigable rivers Rhône and Saône, and was historically known as the silk capital of the world. More recently, it has become the headquarters of Interpol.

The history of the city dates back to the pre-Roman era when a Celtic hill-fort existed. It was known as Lugdunon, the name being derived from "Lugus" (the name of the Celtic god of sun) and "dunon" (hill-fort). This evolved into Lugdunum and a Roman colony was established on Fourvière Hill. By the start of the 1st century A.D. the city had become the capital of the province of Gallia Lugdunensis, with its own mint, and during Roman occupation two future emperors—Claudius (10B.C.–54A.D.) and Caracalla (Antoninus Aurelius; 188–217A.D.)—were born in the city.

With the decline of the Roman Empire, Lyons became a refuge for those forced to flee from the advancing barbarian tribes, but by the 5th century the surrounding area was occupied by the Germanic Bugundii tribe. Lyons became part of the German Empire and it was to remain under the control of the Duchy of Burgundy, subject to the ultimate control of the Holy Roman Empire, until the late 15th century. In 1477, Charles I, Duke of Burgundy, was killed whilst attempting to conquer Lorraine. Both the French king, Louis XI, and Maximilian of Habsburg claimed the title.

After the French gained control of the city, its prosperity increased as both a commercial and a banking center. It was also during these years that the silk trade first developed. After the Napoleonic era, Lyons continued to grow as an industrial center although the silk workers were involved in two major rebellions in the early years of the 1830s.

During World War II the city was a base for both the occupying German forces and resistance activity. It was in Lyons that one of the more notorious war criminals in France—Klaus Barbie (1914–91), known as the "Butcher of Lyons"—operated as a Gestapo officer following the German occupation of Vichy France in 1942.

BELOW: Lyons, satellite image. North is at top. Vegetation is green, bare ground is shades of brown, water is blue and urbanised areas are pink and grey. Lyon is the second largest metropolitan area in France. The river running north to south is the Sâone and the river running west to south is the Rhone.

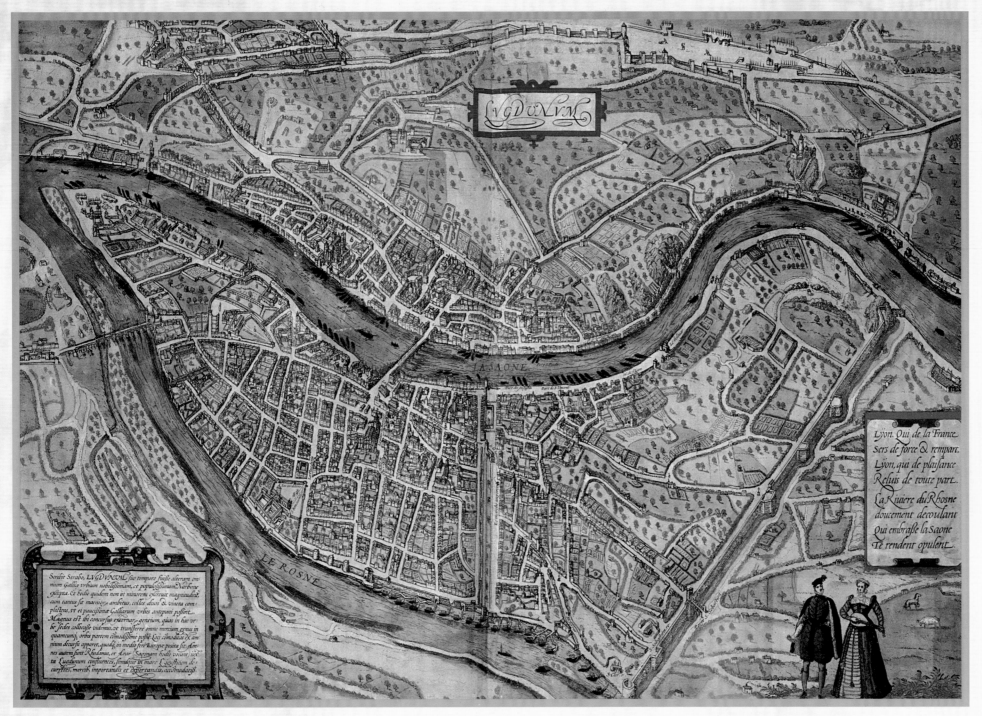

LVGDVNVM

RIGHT: Produced by Bradshaw & Blacklock of Manchester, England, this map, aligned with west toward the top of the page, records the city of Lyons in the mid-19th century. The growth of the city and the development of the railway network are clearly evident. The key details places of interest

ABOVE: Drawn originally by Joris Hoefnagel (1542–c.1600) and reproduced in *Civitates Orbis Terrarum*, this map of Lyon shows the city aligned with south to the left and north to the right. The city's position, on the peninsula known as the Presqu'île, at the confluence of the rivers Saône and Rhône, is clearly indicated. As the city expanded in the 18th and 19th centuries so the peninsula was gradually developed from south to north.

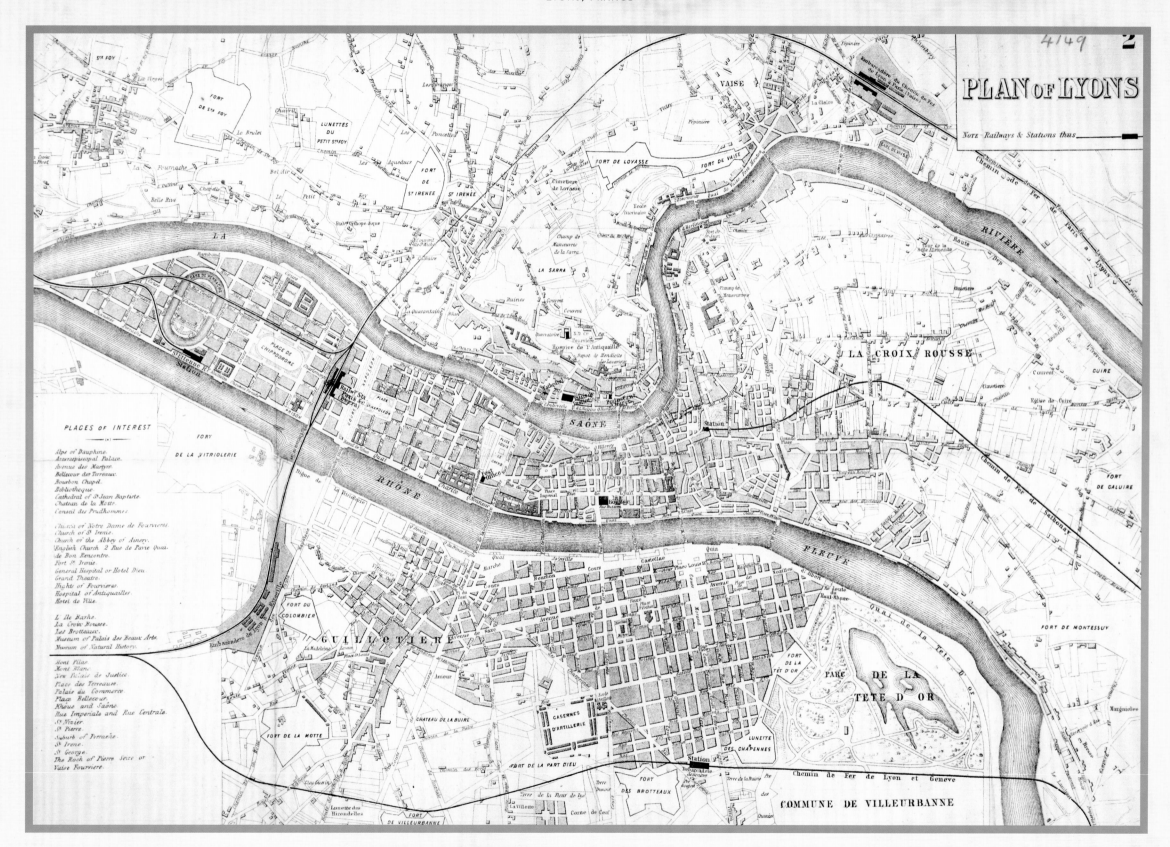

PLAN OF LYONS

Note.—Railways & Stations thus ____

PLACES OF INTEREST

Alps or Dauphine.
Archiepiscopal Palace.
Avenue des Martyrs.
Belleour des Terreaux.
Bourbon Chapel.
Bibliotheque.
Cathedral of St Jean Baptiste.
Chateau de la Motte.
Conseil des Prudhommes.

Church of Notre Dame de Fourvieres.
Church of St Irene.
Church of the Abbey of Ainory.
English Church. 2 Rue de Pavie Quai.
de Bon Rencontre.
Fort St. Irene.
General Hospital or Hotel Dieu.
Grand Theatre.
Hights of Fourvieres.
Hospital of Antiquailles.
Hotel de Ville.

L'Ile Barbe.
La Croix Rousse.
Les Brotteaux.
Museum or Palais des Beaux Arts.
Museum of Natural History.

Mont Pilas.
Mont Blanc.
New Palais de Justice.
Place des Terreaux.
Palais du Commerce.
Place Bellecour.
Rhone and Saône.
Rue Imperiale and Rue Centrale.
St Nizier.
St Pierre.
Suburb of Perrache.
St Irene.
St George.
The Rock of Pierre Seze or
Vaise Fourviere.

MADRID

SPAIN

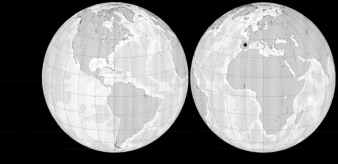

The largest city in Spain with a population approaching 3.5 million, Madrid is the capital of Spain. It is sited on the River Manzanares in the center of the country.

In the 2nd century B.C. the Romans established a settlement on the banks of the Manzanares, but with the decline of Roman power in the west, the Iberian peninsula was overrun by the Germanic tribes. In the 7th century the region was occupied by Islamic forces and Madrid remained under Moorish rule until 1085, when the area was captured by Alfonso VI of Castile during his advance on Toledo. The city remained under Castilian rule until the middle of the 15th century.

In 1479 the kingdoms of Aragon and Castile were united through the marriage of Ferdinand V, king of Aragon, and Isabella, Queen of Castile. The court was moved to Madrid during the reign of Philip II (1527–98).

It was during the reigns of Philip V (1683–1746), the first Bourbon king of Spain and nephew of Louis XIV of France, and Charles III (1716–1788) that many of the city's most impressive structures were completed. These included the Palacio Real (Royal Palace) and the Villahermosa Palace (which now houses the museum formed of the collection of Baron Heinrich Thyssen-Bornemisza).

Charles IV (1748–1819) acceded to the throne in 1788 but his reign was cut short when, in 1807, following Spain's alliance with France and the defeat at Trafalgar, he was forced to abdicate. His successor, Ferdinand VII, was sent into exile in 1808 when French troops entered Madrid, and Napoleon's brother, Joseph, was named as the new Spanish king.

Following the Peninsular War, in which British troops allied with the Portuguese, Ferdinand VII returned to the throne in 1814. A constitutional monarchy was imposed, but this was not wholly successful. In 1923 a virtual dictatorship was established under General Miguel Primo de Rivera (1870–1930). In 1931 Alfonso XIII (1886–1941) held elections; the electorate voted overwhelmingly for the creation of a republic and the king went into exile. The scene was then set for the Spanish Civil War (1936–9), which pitched the forces of the Republic against the Nationalist forces led by Francisco Franco (1892–1975).

Madrid remained loyal to the Republic and, from October 1936 through to its final surrender on March 28, 1939, the city was under siege. Franco managed to keep Spain neutral during World War II and his dictatorship was to survive until his death in 1975. Subsequently, the monarchy, in the guise of King Juan Carlos I, was restored.

BELOW: Map of central Madrid taken by taken by the Spot-1 satellite in 2002. At left is the River Manzanares and the green lawns of the Real or Eastern Palace; at right El Retiro, the "Lungs of Madrid," onto which Madrid's Prado Museum backs.

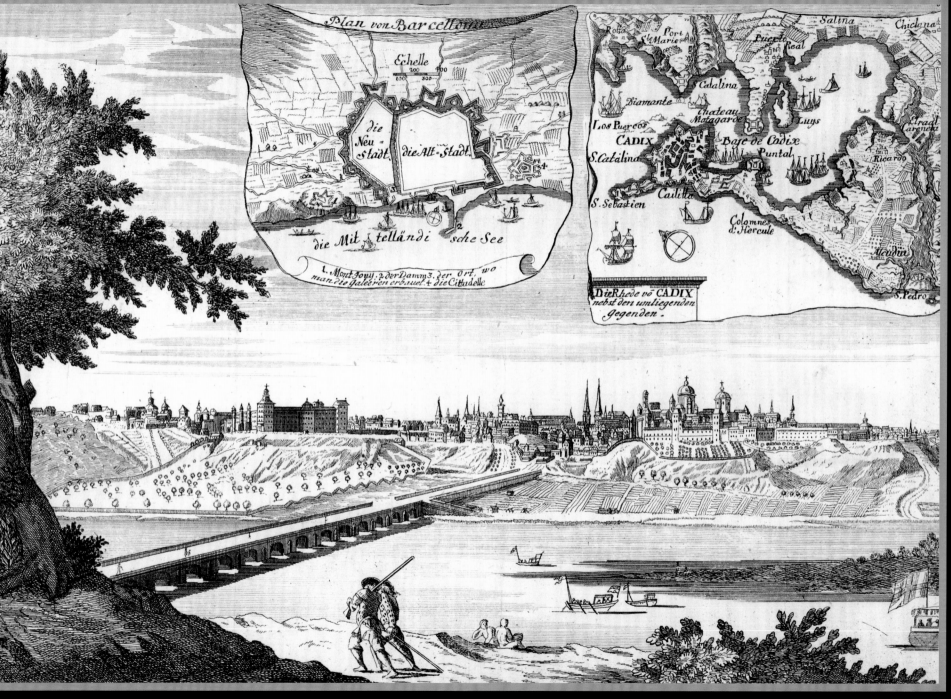

LEFT: Etched panorama of Madrid by
Georg-Paul Busch (d.1756) with plan
of Barcelona and map of Cadiz.

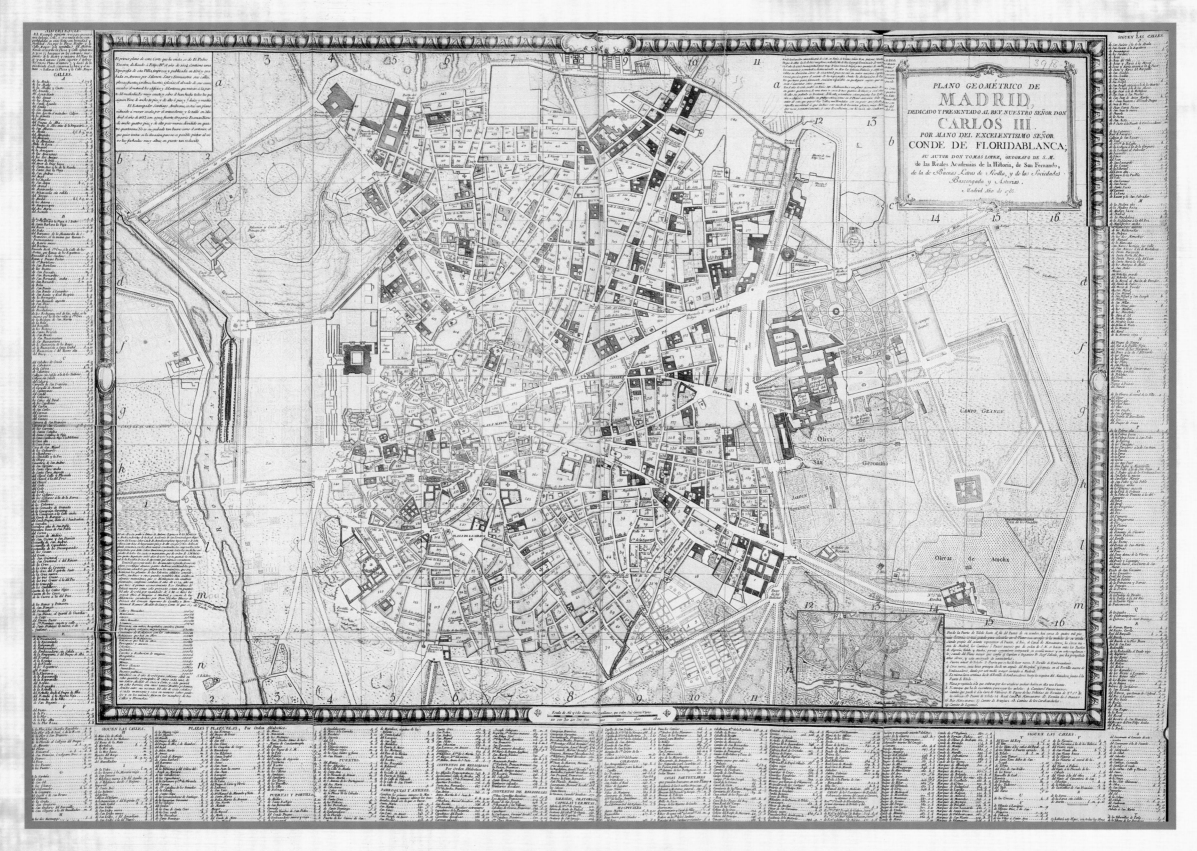

LEFT: Drawn to a scale of one inch to 455 yards by Tomas Lopez of Madrid, this late 18th-century map of the Spanish capital is dedicated to the then King of Spain Carlos (Charles) III. It is aligned with north toward the top of the map. On the western side of the city can be seen the Palacio Real (Royal Palace); until the 18th century the ruling Bourbon family had elected to live outside the city but, in 1734, Philip V moved into a new palace built on the site of the old Arab alcázar. The palace, which was extended on several occasions through to the 20th century, now includes 2,800 rooms.

RIGHT: This Spanish map, published to a scale of 1:5,000, records the city of Madrid as it existed in the middle of the 19th century.

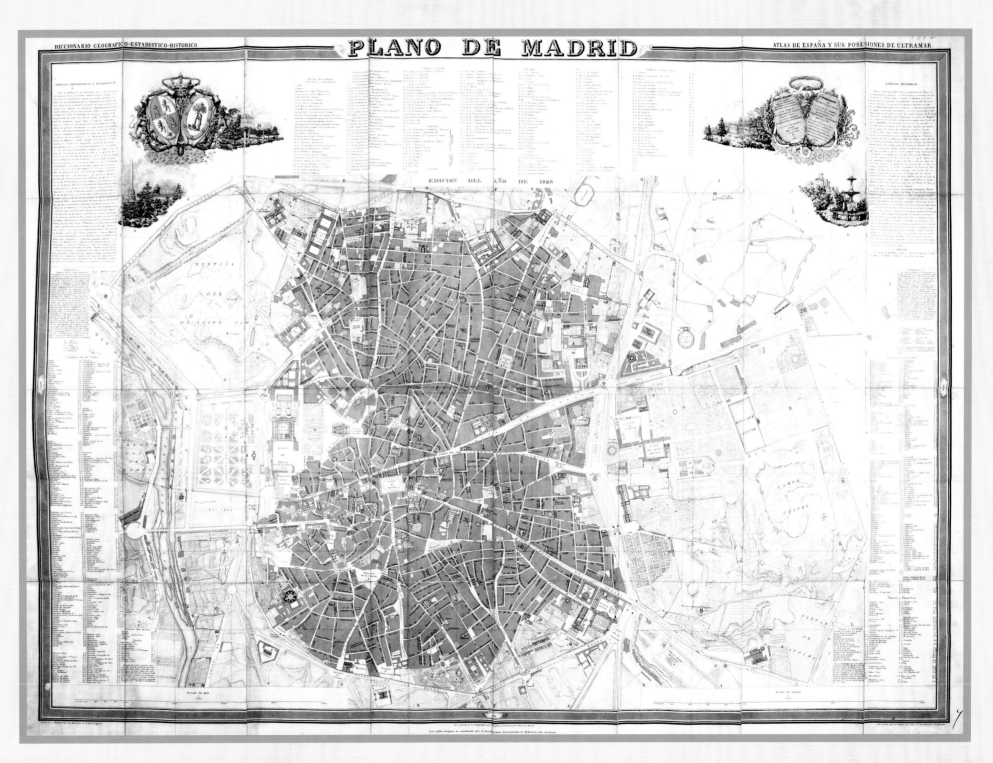

MANTUA
ITALY

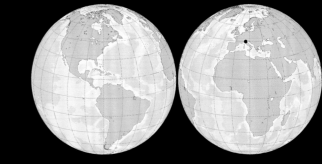

BELOW: Image of Mantua created using NaturalVue data obtained from the Landsat 7 satellite.

The city of Mantua (Màntova) is the capital of the province of Lombardy in northern Italy. Sited on the River Mincio, its strategic location was strengthened in 1198 when four artificial lakes were created around it. The name comes from the Etruscan deity Mantus, the God of the Underworld.

After a period of occupation by the Gallic Cenomani tribe, the settlement was conquered by the Romans in the 3rd century B.C. Virgil, whose *Aeneid* narrated the flight of Aeneas from Troy and the establishment of the city of Rome, was born near by in 70B.C.

With the collapse of the Roman Empire, Mantua was held by the Byzantines, Longobards, and Franks before becoming part of the territories held by the Canossa dynasty, which ruled the city until 1115, when it became a free city.

For the next two centuries Mantua sought to defend itself against the Holy Roman Empire. In 1273, following a period of strife between the Guelphs and the Ghibellines, Pinamonte Bonacolsi seized power. His family ruled the city until 1328, when the Gonzaga family headed a revolt and took over. Under the Gonzagas, the city's defenses were strengthened and much new construction took place. The new city walls were provided with five gates, each of which led across a causeway over the artificial lakes.

The Gonzaga family ruled Mantua until 1627, when the original line died out; they were succeeded by a cadet branch of the family from France, the Gonzaga-Nevers, but, in 1630, the War of the Mantuan Succession broke out and the city was besieged by an army from the Holy Roman Empire. The last Gonzaga-Nevers duke was Ferdinand Carlo IV; having backed the French during the War of Spanish Succession, he was forced to flee the city. Following his death in 1708, the family was deposed and power passed to the Habsburgs.

Under Austrian rule the city prospered; numerous palaces were built and in 1770 a new theater was completed—13-year-old Wolfgang Amadeus Mozart (1756–91) played in its inaugural concert. However, at the end of the 18th century, with Europe wracked by war, Mantua was besieged by the army of Napoleon until it surrendered. In 1799 the city was recaptured by the Austrians before again falling to Napoleon. It reverted to Austrian rule in 1814, becoming one of the Quadrilateral fortresses that helped to maintain Austrian power in northern Italy. In 1866, following years of anti-Austrian agitation, Mantua was incorporated within the new united Italy.

MANTVA.

Mantua, Lombardie Transpada-
ne vrbs clarissima et antiquissima,
venustissimum, in medio paludium,
situm obtinet Anno salutis CIↃ.
IↃ. LXXV. ad viuum delineata.

LEFT: The four artificial lakes surrounding Mantua are evident in this late Renaissance view. Lago Superiore (top right) is separated from Lago di Mezzo (bottom right) by the Ponte de Molin, defended at its landward end by a small fortress Lago di Mezzo is separated from Lago Inferiore (bottom left) by the Ponte de San Giorgio. The smallest of the four lakes was Lago Pajolo (top left); this was drained in the 18th century and this area has now been built over.

MARSEILLES

FRANCE

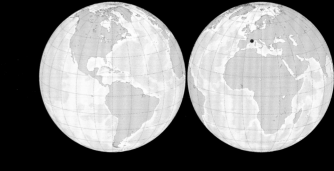

France's oldest city and, with a population of around 900,000, the third largest in the country, Marseilles (Marseille) is situated on an inlet of the Mediterranean just to the east of the Rhône delta.

The city's origins date back to the middle of the 1st millennium B.C., when traders from Greece established a settlement here. It was one of the first trading ports to be established by the Greeks in the western Mediterranean, and had become a fully-fledged city by the 3rd century B.C. The Greek colony, faced by the threat of the Celts, Carthaginians, and Etruscans, chose to ally itself with the emerging Rome and acted as a conduit for trade to and from the Roman Republic. Under Roman rule the city became one of the largest trading ports of the western Mediterranean and was linked with Rome by the Via Aurelia.

During the era of the Crusades Marseilles was an important port for the embarkation of soldiers heading to the Holy Land, and its fortifications were significantly improved to reflect the city's strategic importance. As a major trading port, Marseilles was hard hit by the onset of the Black Death in the 1340s. More than half of the population of some 25,000 died and the city's fortunes took time to recover.

The city was besieged twice by the forces of the Holy Roman Empire in the 16th century but it was often the residents of the city that posed the greater threat. The population rebelled on several occasions; toward the end of the 17th century, for example, Louis XIV had to lead his army against a rebellion against the city's governor. Following this, Louis further strengthened the city's defenses and enhanced the military presence in the city. The city's support for the French Revolution in 1789 saw a number of citizens march from Marseilles to Paris, and their marching song—the *Marseillaise*—became the French national anthem.

After the traumas of the Revolution and the succeeding wars, Marseilles continued to develop both as a port and as an industrial city. Although at the start of World War II it was situated within Vichy France (an area not initially occupied by the Germans), it nevertheless suffered bomb damage and was occupied by the Germans from November 1942 to August 1944. During the occupation much of the historic center of the city was destroyed as a means of countering the French resistance. It was rebuilt in the 1950s.

BELOW: Satellite image of Marseilles, the capital city of the Bouches-du-Rhône department in southeast France. It is the oldest town and second largest city in France. Marseilles is a major port and heavily industrialized. Image taken on December 6, 2002, by Space Imaging's Ikonos satellite.

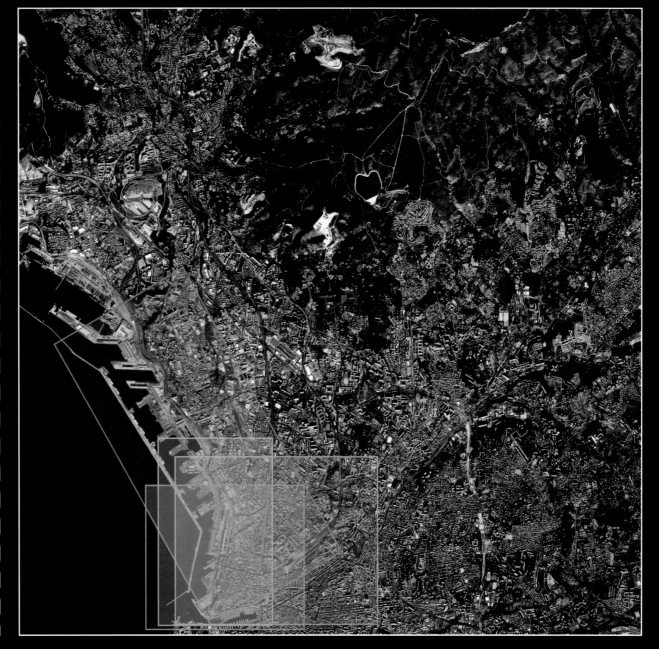

MARSEILLE.

LEFT: The strategic importance of Marseilles and its role as a naval dockyard is clearly shown in this late Renaissance view of the city. In the right foreground is the Vieux Port (Old Harbor), along with the Arsenal, which provided facilities and stores for much of the French fleet at the time, and the governor's residence. North of this area was the fish market and an Augustine monastery. In the left foreground, on an island, is the Chateau d'If; this was built between 1524 and 1531 on the orders of King François I to improve the city's defenses. The city walls were constructed between 1447 and 1453 and designed by Jean Pardo following orders given by King René. The city was further protected by forts built on the hills to the east of the city; Fort St Nicholas and Fort Notre Dame de la Garde can be seen in the middle foreground.

PLAN ROUTIER
DE LA VILLE ET FAUBOURG
DE MARSEILLE.
LEVÉ PAR CAMPEN en 1791
Et Gravé par Denis Laurent en 1792

MER MEDITERRANÉE

COMMENCEMENT DE LA RADE

PORT

Nouvelles Infirmeries
ou
Lazaret

Echelle de deux pouces pour Cent Toise

LEFT: Described as a "Plan Routier de la Ville et Fanbourg de Marseille," this plan of Marseilles was drawn by Camden in 1791 and engraved by Denis Laurent of Marseilles the following year. The original scale was 1 inch to 50 toises (about 300 feet). The date is significant in that it was produced just two years after the French Revolution, an event in which the citizens of Marseilles were to play a prominent role.

RIGHT: Produced by Bradshaw & Blacklock of Manchester, England, this map records Marseilles in the mid-19th century. Aligned with north toward the top of the page, it shows the growth of the city and the arrival of the railway; the railway was subsequently extended south from Gare Maritime toward Fort St Jean. The extensive defenses still protecting the harbor are also still evident.

FOLLOWING PAGE: By the end of the 19th century when this panoramic view of the city was produced, the city and port had considerably expanded.

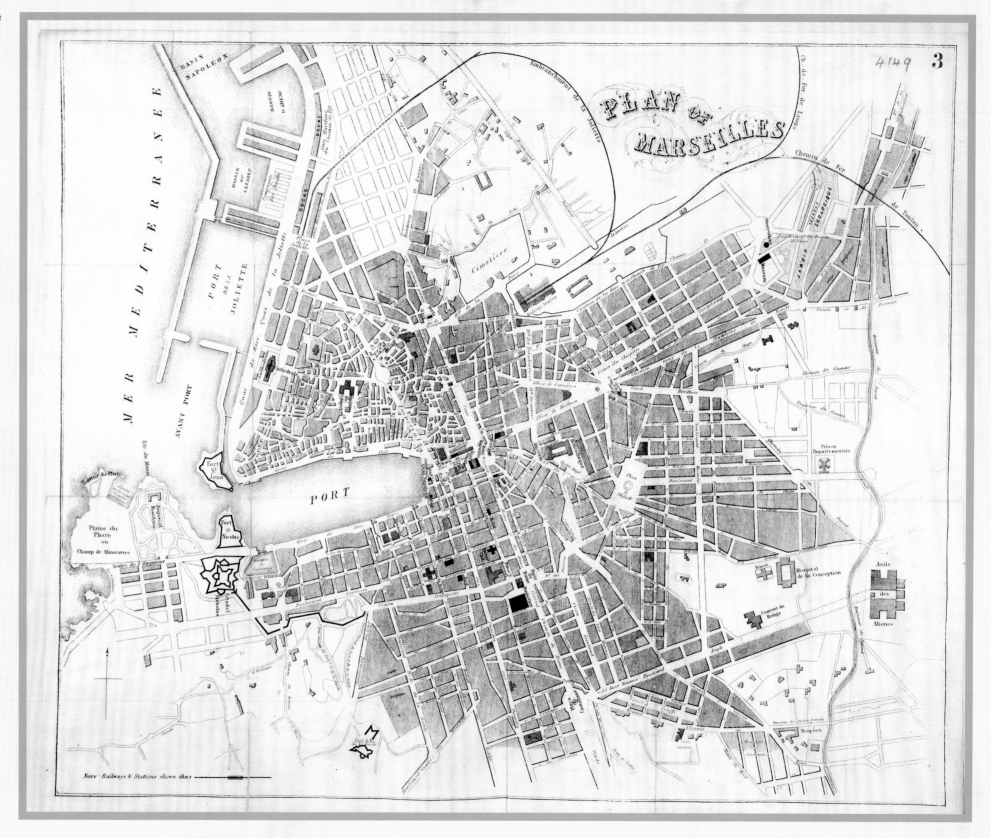

METZ

FRANCE

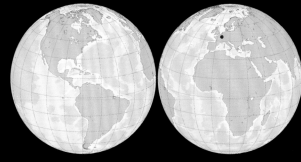

etz is the chief city of the French *département* of Moselle in the province of Lorraine and has a population of just over 100,000. It stands at the confluence of the rivers Seille and Moselle.

Known to the Romans as Divodorum, Metz was a strategically important settlement and one of the principal towns of the Roman province of Gallia. Strongly defended, it was one of the last Roman cities to surrender to the barbarians in the west, not being captured by Attila until 451A.D.

By the end of the 5th century Metz and the surrounding area was under the control of the Franks. In 843A.D. the city became the capital of the kingdom of Lotharingia, ultimately becoming part of the eastern Frankish kingdom and thus of the Holy Roman Empire.

Until the 12th century the town was administered by the Bishop of Metz but this clerical dominance ended in 1180 when the city's burgesses wrested day-to-day control of the city from the bishop. During the 13th century the resulting commune—a form of municipal government—was reinforced by an alliance with the local nobility, creating a balance between the church, nobility, and local artisans, who were all seeking to increase their power. During the late Middle Ages a number of attempts by the local artisans to overthrow the commune were bloodily suppressed.

As a border city Metz was often threatened by the competing forces of the great dynastic armies, but it remained an Imperial Free City until the middle of the 16th century, when war broke out between the Emperor, Charles V, and a number of rebellious princes who had allied themselves to Henry II (1519–59), king of France. On April 10, 1552 the gates of Metz were formally opened to the French and the new French commander in the city, the Duke of Guise, restored and expanded the city's old fortifications. The city was besieged twice during the Napoleonic Wars but on neither occasion did it fall.

However, the city was not to be so lucky the next time that war broke out along the Franco-German border. Following the Prussian advance, it was besieged in August 1870 and forced to surrender in the October. As a result of the peace treaty that settled the Franco-Prussian War, Alsace and Lorraine, including Metz, were ceded to Germany; France did not regain the region until the Treaty of Versailles following World War I.

LEFT: Satellite image of the city of Metz (center) and its surrounding area in northeastern France. North is at top. Forested areas are dark green, agricultural fields are lighter shades of green and brown, urban areas are grey and water is black. Image created using NaturalVue data obtained from the Landsat 7 satellite.

LEFT: A frontier settlement for much of its life, Metz had been occupied by France in 1552 shortly before the date of this map. Evidence of the French occupation can be seen in the citadel, which was constructed almost immediately after the capture of the city from the Holy Roman Empire. It had been fortified during the period of Roman occupation but the walls illustrated here dated from the 13th to 15th centuries.

RIGHT: One of a series of maps recording the fortified cities of France produced toward the end of the 17th century, and now bound into a single volume, this plan of Metz records the city and its fortifications. This map is oriented 180 degrees deifferently, with north facing down the page to the left.

FOLLOWING PAGE: Described as a "Plan de la Ville, Forts et Citadelle de Metz" (Map of the City, Forts and Citadel of Metz), this 18th-century map includes a key detailing the principal buildings of the city. It is aligned with north toward the left of the page.

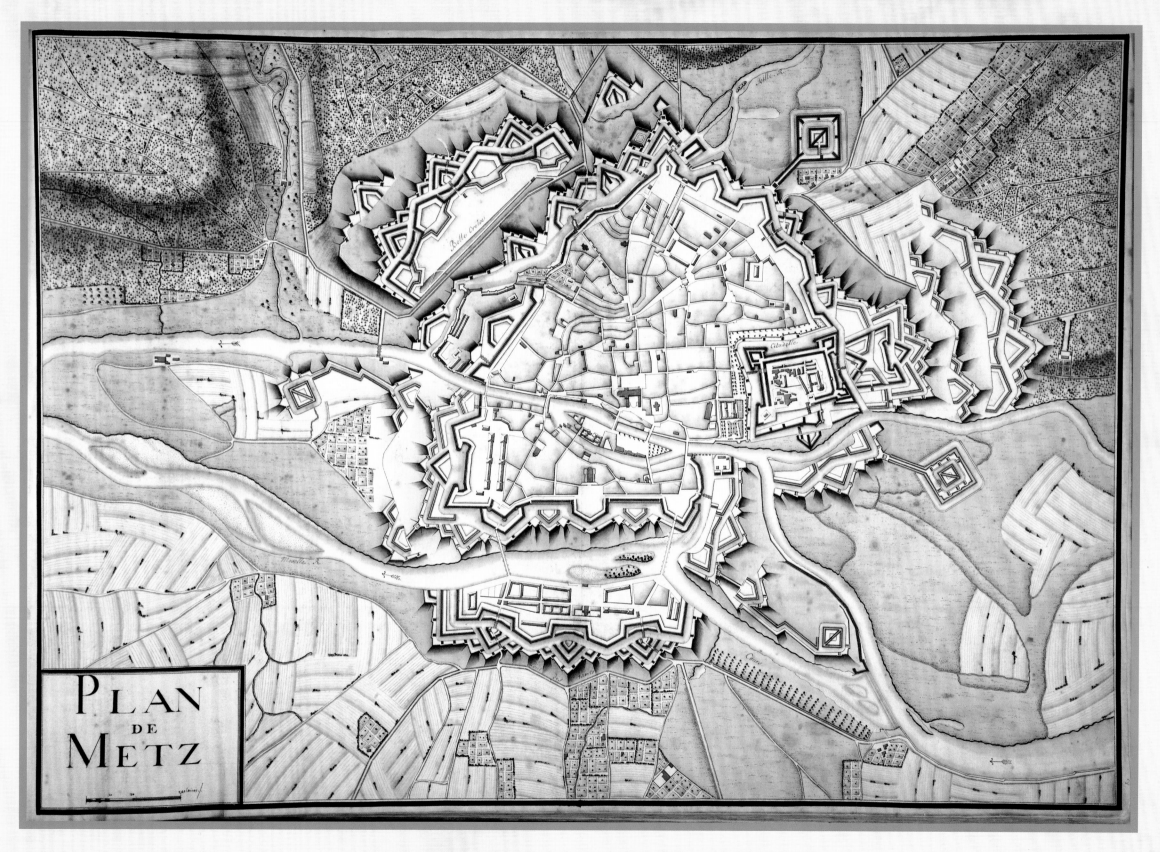

PLAN
DE
METZ

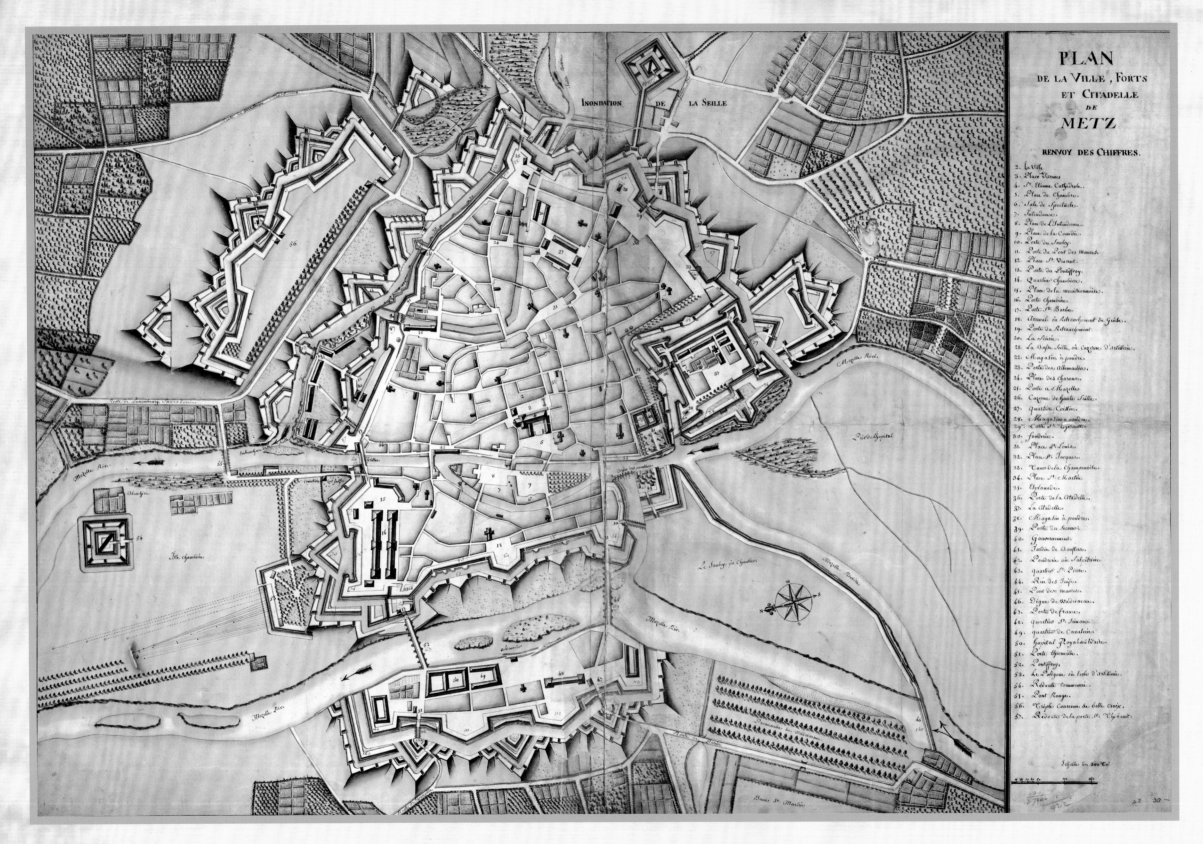

MEXICO CITY
MEXICO

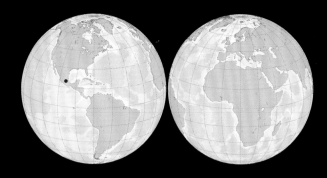

M exico City or, in Spanish, Ciudad de México, is the capital of Mexico. With a population approaching nine million, the city is also the largest in the country with a further 14 million people living within the Greater Mexico area. The total of some 23 million makes it the largest metropolitan area in the western hemisphere. The city is situated in the Valley of Mexico, 7,349 feet above sea level.

The city's origins date back to its foundation on an island in Lake Texcoco by the Aztec Indians in 1325. The island was connected to the shore by a number of causeways and the alignment of these remains the line of the principal roads of contemporary Mexico City. For the next two centuries Mexico-Tenichtitlan, as the city was then known, was the capital of the Aztec Empire. However, all this was to change in the early 16th century with the arrival of Hernán Cortés (c.1485–1547), a Spanish Conquistador, who became Governor and Captain-General of New Mexico in October 1522.

Mexico served as the capital of the Spanish possessions in Central and North America until the early 19th century. In 1810 the Mexican War of Independence started, but it was not until 1821 that Agustin de Iturbide was finally able to declare that the country was a constitutional monarchy separate from Spain. In 1824, following De Iturbide's abdication, the new country was declared a republic. Its area was, however, to be severely reduced when, following the war with the US in the mid-1840s, the Treaty of Hidalgo ceded sovereignty to a vast stretch of territory—the provinces of Santa Fe de Nuevo México and Alta California—to the US and recognized the independence of Texas.

The late 19th century witnessed considerable French influence in Mexico, most notably during the ill-fated reign of the Emperor Maximilian I (1864–67). During this period and under the subsequent dictatorship of Porfirio Díaz, parts of the city were redesigned and a number of major building projects completed.

By the middle of the 20th century Mexico City had a population of around three million; in the 50 or so years since then, the population has grown massively, largely as the result of inward migration from the rural areas of the country. Today, it is one of the most important commercial and cultural centers of the Americas.

LEFT: Satellite image of the city of Mexico showing the older section of the city. It is difficult to pinpoint the exact location of the island city today. The two later maps (pages 154–155) include the capture of Chapultepec Castle, off the image to the bottom left. Image taken by the Ikonos satellite on February 18, 2002

RIGHT: The city portrayed here represents the city of Mexico as rebuilt by the Spaniards after 1521. The city's location in the middle of Lake Texcoco and its links to the surrounding land by a series of causeways are clearly demonstrated. Also illustrated are the Chinampas, a series of man-made islands built by the Aztecs. As the lake was gradually drained, so these ceased to be separate. Of the surviving Aztec structures, the most conspicuous is the Dike of Nezehualcoyot. This 10-mile long structure, completed in the mid-15th century, was designed to keep to the east the salty water of the lake while allowing spring-fed fresh water to surround the city itself.

RIGHT: Drawn to a scale of about 1:15,000, this map was compiled by Manuel Ignacio de Jesus del Aguila and records the city as it existed toward the end of the 18th century.

RIGHT: In April 1846, following a gradual deterioration in relations between the US and Mexico, war broke out following an attack upon US forces to the east of the Rio Grande. As part of the land war, US forces invaded Mexico and marched upon the country's capital, Mexico City, which was captured and occupied in September 1847. This sketch map, produced to a scale of 1:16,000, records the operations of General Scott's army in and around Mexico City on September 8, 12 and 13, and was compiled by Joseph Goldsborough Bruff (1804–89), one of the army's Officers of Engineers. Following the Treaty of Guadalupe Hidalgo, 1848, the Mexicans recognized the independence of Texas and ceded a swathe of land from California to New Mexico to the victorious US.

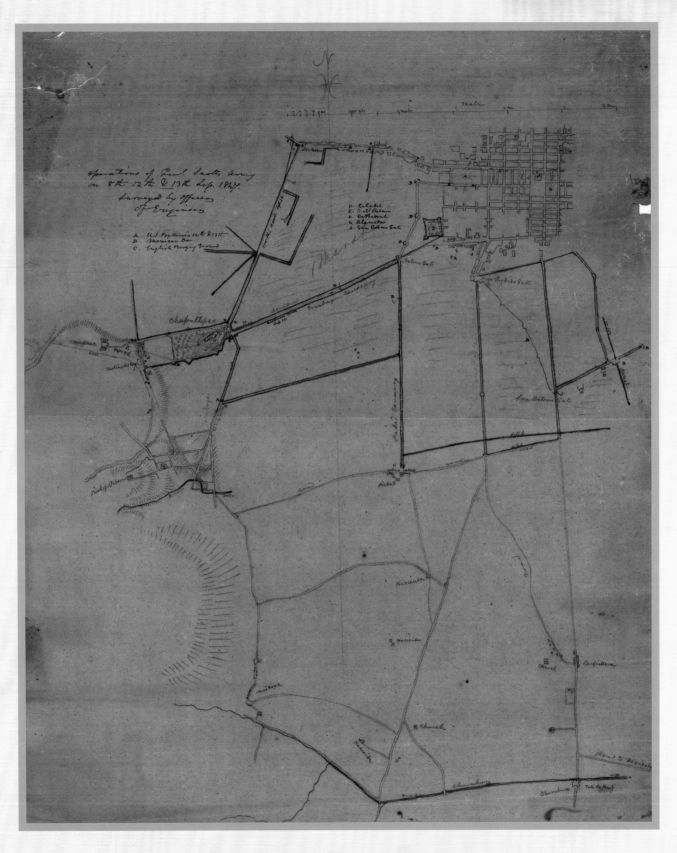

RIGHT: A companion to the preceding map, this records the attack by US forces on Mexico City on September 13 and 14, 1847, by the US army under General Scott.

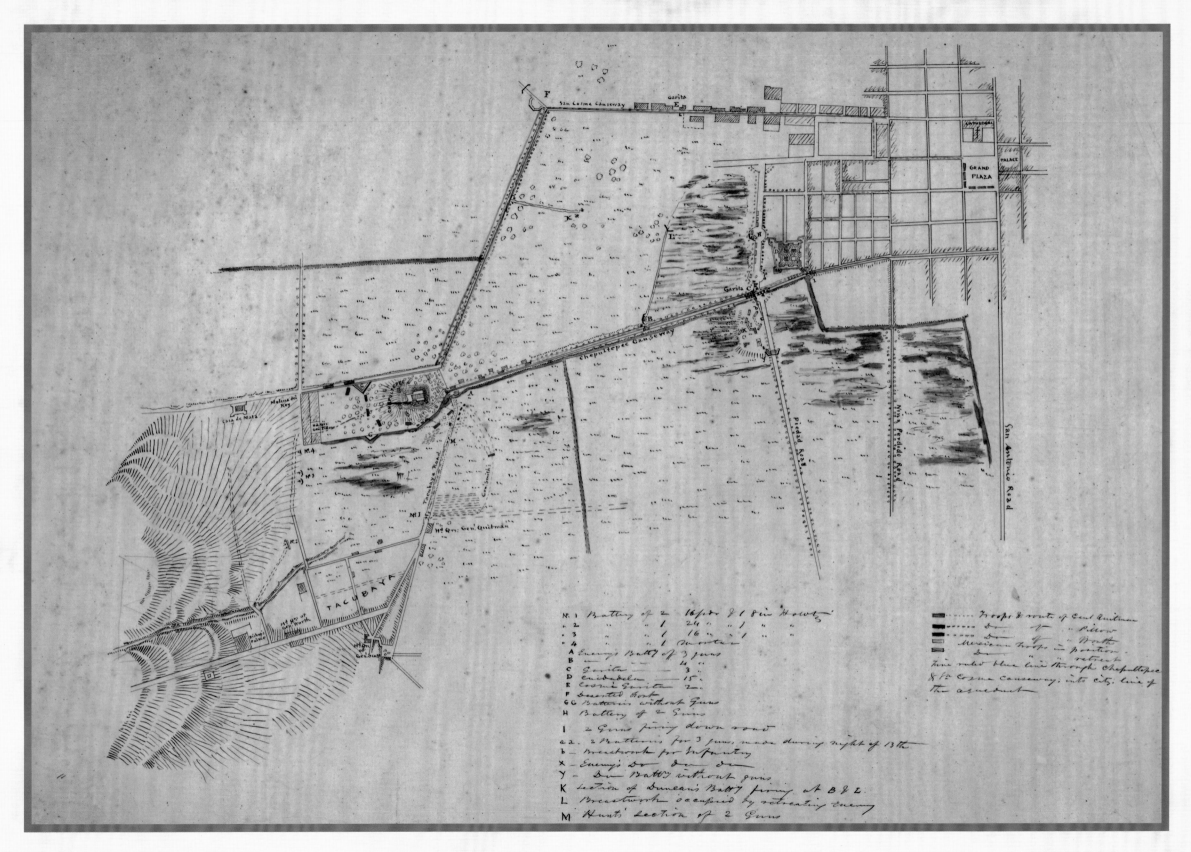

MILAN

ITALY

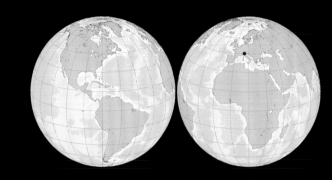

Milan, in northern Italy, is one of the country's most important urban centers. The settlement was known by the Romans as "Mediolanum"—"in the midst of a plain." Situated at the center of a network of roads linking this rich agricultural region, the city prospered.

Milan's importance rose significantly during the late 3rd century A.D. as a result of the Emperor Diocletian's decision to split the empire into two. Emperor Alexander Severus selected Milan as the capital of the western empire, and Maximian was made its first emperor. Under him, the city was to see a number of new public buildings, including a circus, baths, and an imperial palace, reflecting its new status.

Milan remained the capital of the western empire until 402A.D., when it was captured and sacked by the Visigoths; thereafter, the capital was transferred to Ravenna. As the western Roman Empire continued its inexorable decline, Milan was to suffer two further barbarian assaults—from the Huns in 452 and from the Ostrogoths in 539. In 774 the city became part of the Frankish Empire and then of the Holy Roman Empire.

In 1450 control of the Duchy of Milan passed to the House of Sforza, who were to rule the city until 1535. Under the new ducal family, Milan beaome one of the most important centers of the Italian Renaissance. However, the rise of the Sforzas coincided with renewed French claims to the territory of the duchy. Following the French victory at the Battle of Marginano in September 1515, fought near Milan, the Peace of Noyon (1516) transferred ultimate sovereignty to France. However, French defeat at the Battle of Pavia, on February 24, 1525, resulted in the Treaty of Madrid, under which the duchy passed to Spanish Habsburg rule.

For the next 200 years, until 1701 and the War of Spanish Succession when northern Italy was occupied by the French, Milan was ruled by the Habsburgs. In 1713, under the Treaty of Utrecht, sovereignty passed to Austria. Milan was to remain Austrian until 1796 when the territory was captured by Napoleon, who made the city the capital of the Cisalpine Republic. However, the Congress of Vienna, following Napoleon's fall, returned Milan to Austrian rule; it was not until 1859, following the Austrian defeat at the Battle of Solferino, that Milan was incorporated into the kingdom of Sardinia as part of the process of Italian reunification.

BELOW: Milan seen from space by the Ikonos satellite. North is at top. Castello Sforzesco lies at the southeastern end of the Parco Sempione (top left). Launched in 1999, Ikonos was the first commercial satellite to collect data at one-metre resolution. The satellite is owned by Space Imaging, Colorado.

LEFT: By the date of this late 16th century map, Milan had been ceded as a result of the Treaty of Madrid to the rule of the Holy Roman Empire. As with Florence, Milan was one of the centers of the Renaissance, with artists such as Leonardo da Vinci receiving the patronage of the Sfroza family in the late 15th century. The Castello Sforzesco (Sforza Castle) had been rebuilt between 1450 and 1466, and again partially after a fire in 1521. At the center of the city is the Duomo (cathedral), one of the largest churches in the world and one of the greatest of all Gothic structures: work on the existing building started in 1386. Such was the scale of construction that the completed building was not consecrated until 1577. Although the city was some 31 miles away from the River Ticino, it was linked to the river by a canal and a harbor area—known as the Darsena—grew up to serve the city.

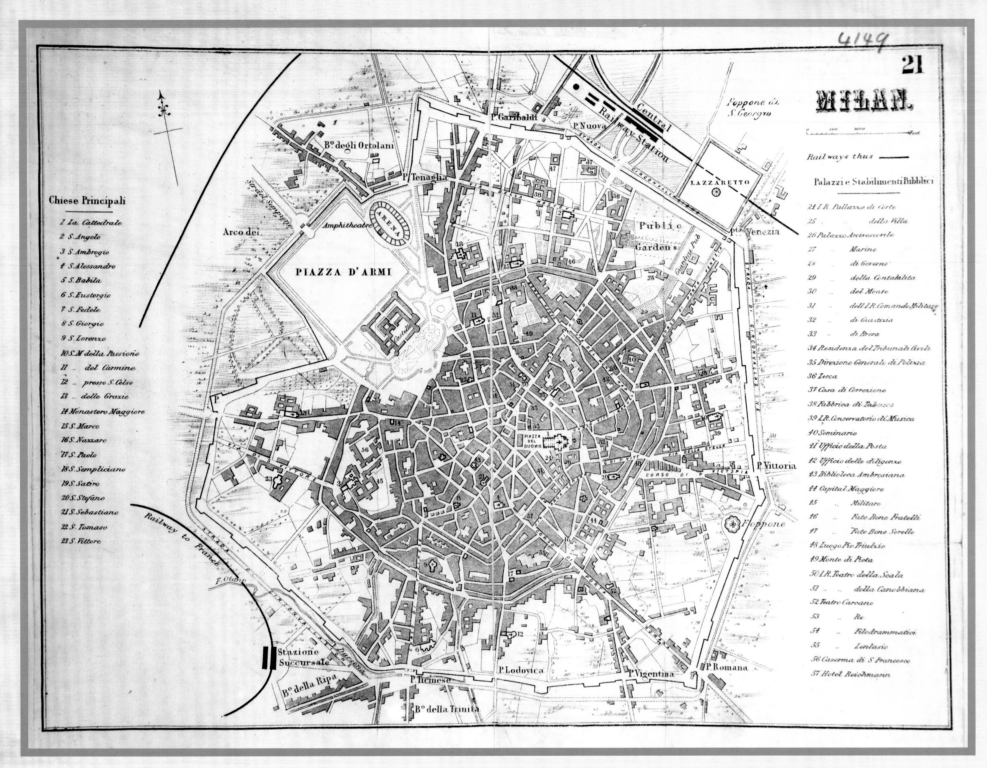

4149

21

MILAN.

LEFT: Produced by Bradshaw & Blacklock of Manchester, England, this map records the city of Milan in the mid-19th century. It is aligned with north toward the top of the page. By this date the city was still largely confined within is walls, although the arrival of the railway saw development starting to occur outside. The key gives the city's principal buildings.

Chiese Principali

1 La Cattedrale
2 S. Angelo
3 S. Ambrogio
4 S. Alessandro
5 S. Babila
6 S. Eustorgio
7 S. Fedele
8 S. Giorgio
9 S. Lorenzo
10 S. M della Passione
11 .. del Carmine
12 .. presso S. Celso
13 .. delle Grazie
14 Monastero Maggiore
15 S. Marco
16 S. Nazzaro
17 S. Paolo
18 S. Sempliciano
19 S. Satiro
20 S. Stefano
21 S. Sebastiano
22 S. Tomaso
23 S. Vittore

Railways thus ——

Palazzi e Stabilimenti Pubblici

24 I. R. Pallazzo di Corte
25 .. della Villa
26 Palazzo Arcivescovile
27 .. Marino
28 .. di Governo
29 .. della Contabilita
30 .. del Monte
31 .. dell I R Comando Militare
32 .. di Giustizia
33 .. di Brera
34 Residenza del Tribunale Civile
35 Direzione Generale di Polizia
36 Zecca
37 Casa di Correzione
38 Fabbrica di Tabacco
39 I. R. Conservatorio di Musica
40 Seminario
41 Ufficio della Posta
42 Ufficio delle diligenze
43 Biblioteca Ambrosiana
44 Ospital Maggiore
45 .. Militare
46 .. Fate Bene Fratelli
47 .. Fate Bene Sorelle
48 Luogo Pio Triulzio
49 Monte di Pieta
50 I. R. Teatro della Scala
51 .. della Canobbiana
52 Teatro Carcano
53 .. Re
54 .. Filodrammatici
55 .. Lentasio
56 Caserma di S Francesco
57 Hotel Reichmann

MONTREAL
CANADA

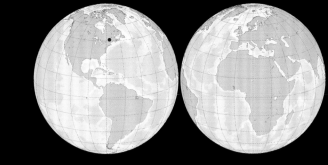

Situated on the largest of 234 islands that form the Hochelaga archipelago at the confluence of the Ottaway River and the St Lawrence in the southwest corner of the province of Québec in Canada, Montréal, with a population of just over one million, is one of the country's most important urban centers. The name is derived from the French words for royal hill—"Mont" and "Réal"—and this emphasizes the Francophonic origins of the settlement. The hill from which the city's name is drawn is the remnant of a long-extinct volcano and rises some 780 feet: it is one of eight such peaks in and around the city.

The French retained control of Montréal until the Seven Year's War. In 1760, the British captured the city with little opposition and the Treaty of Paris, signed in 1763, confirmed British control of the former French territories in Canada. During the American War of Independence, Montréal and the rest of Canada stayed loyal to Britain, although the city itself was besieged by rebels in 1775 in the hope of persuading the citizens to join the fight against the colonial masters. Following the British defeat, the Anglophonic population of Montréal was boosted by the large number of loyalists who chose to move north rather than remain in the newly independent Thirteen Colonies.

In the first half of the 19th century, the growth of the city was rapid, stimulated by the development of the St Lawrence as a route for commercial shipping and the completion, in 1825, of the Lachine Canal. This waterway opened up the route to the Great Lakes for commercial shipping. Population growth was also the result of the active promotion of emigration from Britain, particularly amongst the poor of Ireland and Scotland, from 1823 onward.

During the second half of the 19th century the city continued to grow as a result of industrialization and immigration from eastern Europe; by 1922, the population had reached almost half a million. Following the Depression of the 1930s and World War II, the city's fortunes were improved by the construction of the St Lawrence Seaway, which opened up the route through to the Great Lakes for larger vessels. However, this development was countered by the growing movement for independence for Québec, which encouraged businesses to relocate offices and facilities into the predominantly Anglophonic city of Toronto and province of Ontario.

BELOW: Montreal taken from Ikonos in 2002 with inset the same are during winter: note ice on the River Laurence.

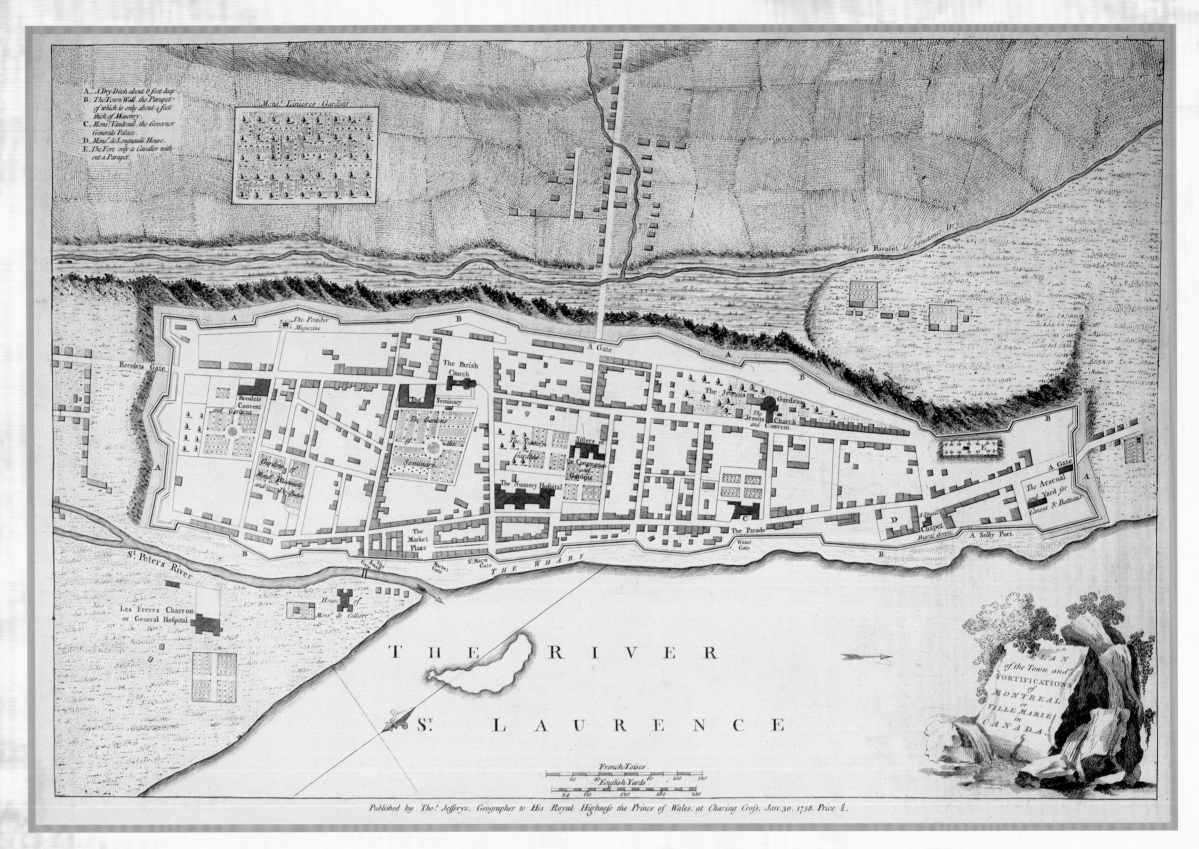

A. A Dry Ditch about 8 foot deep
B. The Town Wall, the Parapet of which is only about 2 feet thick of Masonry.
C. Mons. Vaudreuil, the Governor Generals Palace.
D. Mons. de Longueuils House.
E. The Fort only a Cavalier with out a Parapet

Mons. Lunieres Garden

This Rivulet is sometimes Dry

The Powder Magazine

Recolets Gate

A Gate

The Parish Church

The Seminary

Recolets Convent and Gardens

The Gardens of the Seminary

Gardens of Mons. Bradmore and De Quin.

The Jesuits

The Jesuits Church and Convent

Gardens

The Nuns Garden

Sisters of Congregation and Gardens

The Nunnery Hospital

The Market Place

The Parade

A Small Chapel Burnt down

The Arsenal and Yard for Canoes & Batteaux

A Gate

A Sally Port

Water Gate

The Market Gate

St. Marys Gate

THE WHARF

St. Peters River

Les Freres Charron or General Hospital

House of Mons. de Calliere

THE RIVER St. LAURENCE

PLAN of the Town and FORTIFICATIONS of MONTREAL or VILLE MARIE in CANADA

French Toises.
English Yards.

Published by Tho. Jefferys, Geographer to His Royal Highness the Prince of Wales, at Charing Cross. Jan. 30. 1758. Price 2.

LEFT: This is a "Plan of the Town and Fortifications of Montreal or Ville Marie in Canada. Published by Thos. Jefferys, Geographer to…the Prince of Wales at Charing Cross, Jan 30 1758." Drawn to a scale of about 1 inch to 48 yards, the map includes a reference table to buildings and defenses. The origins of Montreal stretch back to the first European explorers of the area. It was Jacques Cartier who found an Indian settlement—called Hochelage—on the shore of Lake Huron. He christened the site Mont Real (Royal Mount) in honor of the French king. The next European expedition was led by Samuel de Champlain in 1603. By this date the Indian settlement had disappeared and Champlain established a new—short-lived—settlement called Place Royale in 1611. In 1642 Paul de Chomeday, Sieur de Maisonneuve, founded Ville Marie de Mont-Réal as a mission station. As well as a religious center, Montreal also became an important center of the fur trade. At the time that this map was drawn the city was still in French hands, but with the renewal of British-French hostilities, resulting from the Seven Years' War, it was captured by the British in 1760 and formed part of the territory ceded to Britain by the Treaty of Paris in 1763.

LEFT: Originally surveyed in 1858 by Captain H. W. Hayfield and Commander J. Orlebar, and corrected and updated in 1906 by John Kennedy, chief engineer of the Montreal Harbor Commissioners, this map records Montreal Harbor at the start of the 20th century. The Victoria Bridge seen spanning the St Lawrence was first opened in 1859, having taken five years to complete. It was the first bridge to span the river and, at 2 miles, the longest bridge in the world at the time. It included 24 ice-breaking piers. The bridge was formally opened by the Prince of Wales, the future King Edward VII, in 1860 and was rebuilt in the late 1890s. The bridge, now modified to allow road traffic, remains in use.

MOSCOW
RUSSIA

The city of Moscow is now the capital of the Russian Federation, with the imposing Kremlin at its heart. The derivation of the city's name is uncertain, other than it comes from the old Russian for "the city on the Moskva River."

Founded by Yury Dolgoruky in 1147, the city was threatened in the early 13th century by the westward advance of the Mongols under Genghis Khan, when it was razed to the ground and all its inhabitants massacred. However, Moscow was to recover, and by the early years of the 14th century had become the capital of a small principality, albeit under ultimate Mongol control.

In 1331 most of Moscow, then largely built of wood, was destroyed by fire, but reconstruction work on the city, including the Kremlin, was completed by the end of the decade. From the middle of the 14th century internal dissension within the Mongol Empire started to weaken its control. In 1380 Grand Prince Dmitri Donskoi (Dmitri of the Don) defeated the Mongol army and Moscow became the focus of the war against the occupying Mongols. In revenge for their defeat, the Mongols besieged the city in 1382 and destroyed it once again.

In 1460, Ivan III the Great became Grand Prince. He summoned Italian architects to Moscow and work started on the reconstruction of the Kremlin Walls, the rebuilding of the Cathedral of the Dormition, the construction of the Palace of Facets, and on other major projects.

Ivan III's grandson, Ivan the Terrible, was the first ruler to adopt the title "Tsar," in 1547. In conflict with Poland and Sweden in the Livonian War, he ultimately lost Moscow's access to the Baltic. Ivan the Terrible died in 1584 leaving a weakened state and the succession in dispute, leading to civil war. In 1610, following an alliance with the Romanov family, the Polish army captured Moscow; the Poles held the city for two years until the city and the Kremlin were recaptured. Mikhail Romanov was elected Tsar in 1613. The male Romanov line survived until 1762, when Catherine the Great acceded to the throne.

In 1712, under Peter the Great, Moscow lost its status as capital city and the role transferred to St Petersburg until the October Revolution in 1918.

BELOW: Moscow taken by the Spot-1 satellite. Only two identification squares are shown here as the other two maps of Moscow (pages 166 and 168) go beyond the borders of the satellite image.

MOSCOVIA VRBS METROPOLIS TO:
tius Rufsiæ Albæ.

MOSCVÆ VRBS
LOCA INSIGNIORA.

1. Magni Ducis arx, dicta Czargorod.
2. Magni Ducis conclaue no.
3. Ecclesia S. Michaelis.
4. Aula, siue atrium vel P. latium Patriarchæ.
5. Conclaue, seu cænaculum latere exstructum, ... a. magnus Dux populo s...spiciendum præbet...unde Principis Ed...pulo proclamantur.
6. Tabernæ siue pergula... quibus diuersi generis... nimalium pelles, aliceequ... merces diuenduntur.
7. Curia ciuium, et Canc... laria prope quas Vngar... torum officinæ seu Ph... macopoliæ.
8. Legatorum externorum... Aula siue Hospitium.
9. Carceres seu Custdiæ reor.
10. Tabernæ pictorum.
11. Externorum Mercator. Aula siue Hospitium.
12. Forum in quo fœnum... diuersi generis tentoria... seu domunculæ vendunt.
13. Aquæ calidæ seu Thern.
14. Magni Ducis hortus.
15. Poganiski tesoro seu lac.
16. Equile M. Ducis.
17. Armamentarium.
18. Forum equarium.
19. Domus Fusoria.
20. Glinski aula.

Intima pars vrbis dicta Kitaigorod

Secunda pars vrbis, suo circumdata muro, dicta Bielgorod

Tertia pars vrbis versus Septentrionem vocata Skorodum.

LEFT: The impressive defenses of late 16th-century Moscow are clearly evident in this map of the city. Dominating the center is the massive fortress of the Kremlin, which is sited on a hill 131 feet above the River Moskva. The stronghold extends over 69 acres and is surrounded by walls some 1.4 miles in length. These walls are themselves supported by 20 towers and gatehouses, many of which were significantly rebuilt or strengthened in the late 15th century. The earliest record of a fortified structure on the site was in 1156 and the word "Kremlin," derived from the Greek word kremnos, was originally used to describe any stronghold. Following a fire of 1445, many of the buildings within the Kremlin's walls were rebuilt between 1475 and 1530. In front of the Kremlin is Red Square, which became the city's main ceremonial center in the mid-16th century when properties on the site were cleared, and St Basil's Cathedral. This was commissioned by Ivan the Terrible in 1552 to commemorate the capture of the Khanate of Kazan.

ПЛАНЪ
Императорскаго
Столичнаго города
МОСКВЫ
сочиненной
подъ смотренiемъ
Архитектора Ивана
Мичурина
въ 1739 году.

Москва река.

LEFT: Published in the Academy of Sciences' Atlas russicus and compiled by Ivan Fedorovich Michurin (1700–63), this map shows the city of Moscow as it existed in the middle of the 18th century. It is drawn to a scale of about 1:25,000.

RIGHT: This map, produced to a scale of 4.8 inches to 700 feet, records the destruction wrought to the Kremlin after the French retreat of 1812. The original sketch accompanied a letter sent to London on January 29, 1813.

FOLLOWING PAGE: This is a plan showing the streets, buildings, and gardens of the city of Moscow, produced to an original scale of 2.5 inches to 600 sazhens (about 4,2900 feet). The map, engraved by Frolov, Military Topographical Depôt, is surrounded by lists of monasteries, churches, buildings, streets etc.

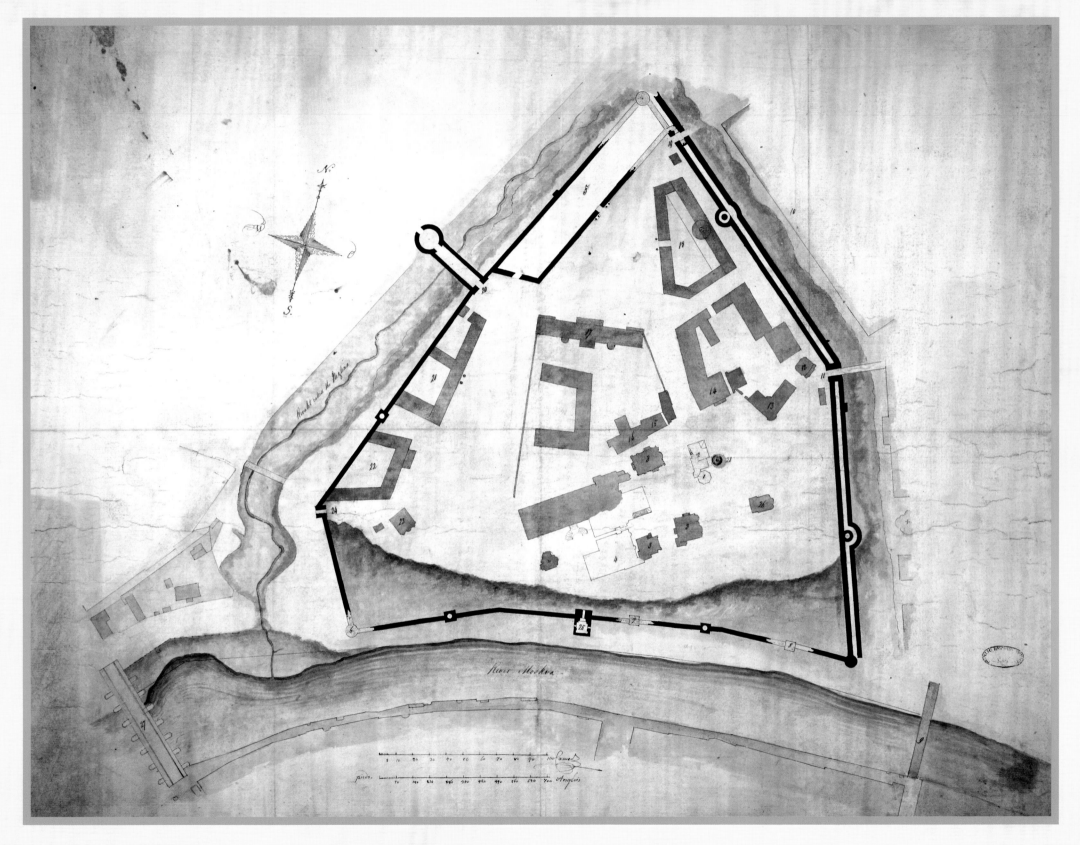

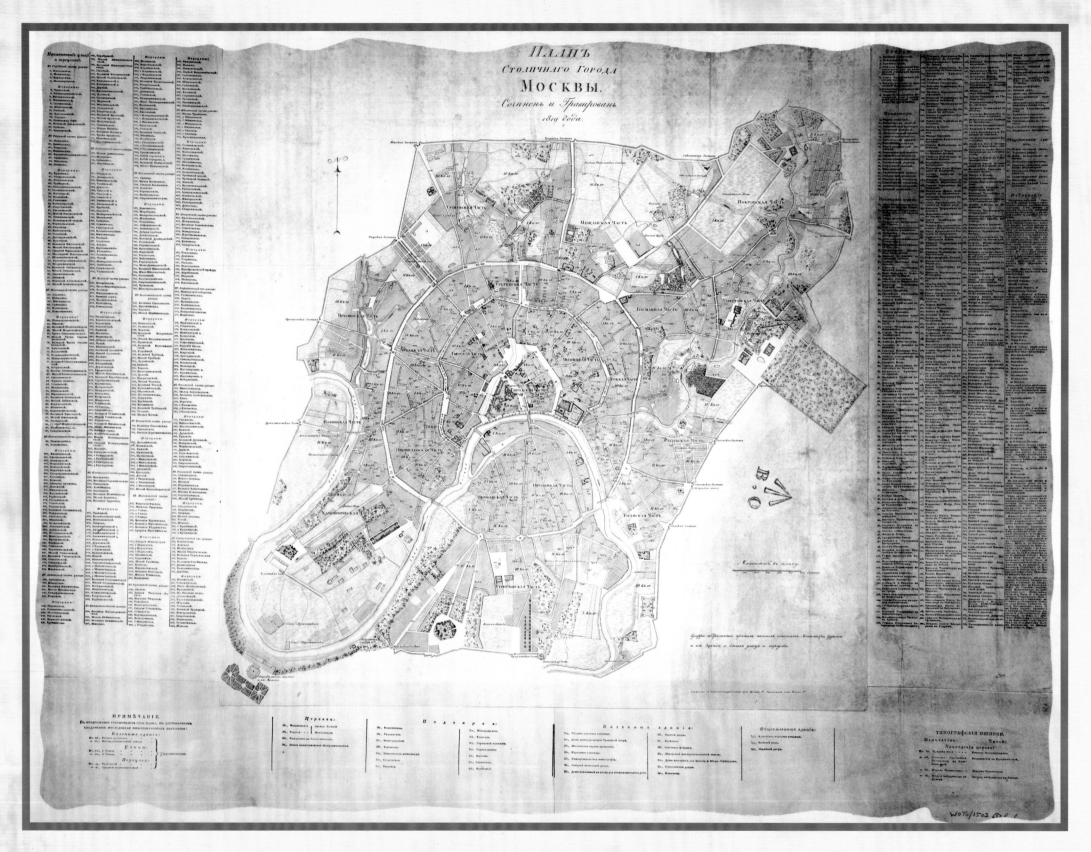

NAPLES
ITALY

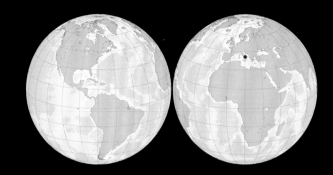

Sited at the eastern end of the Bay of Naples in southern Italy, and overshadowed by the volcano Vesuvius, Naples is one of the most important cities in modern Italy. From the 11th century B.C. onward the area was colonized by settlers from Greece and the city became one of the centers of Hellenic culture in Italy.

After being conquered by Rome, the area became a favored location for the development of coastal towns and villas, many of which were occupied by wealthy Romans seeking escape from the heat of summer. Naples itself retained a distinctly Greek character, with Greek as an official language, and the city became famous for study and culture. However, Vesuvius presented a persistent threat and on August 24, 79A.D. the eruption occurred that led to the destruction of Pompeii and Herculaneum.

During the final years of the Roman Empire Naples suffered at the hands of invading barbarian tribes, although none were able to retain control for any length of time. As an independent duchy, Naples prospered. However, in 1030, Sergius of Naples offered territory in lieu of payment to Ranulf, the Norman leader, and this gave the Normans a foothold in southern Italy. Over the next century they established the kingdom of Sicily, with its capital at Palermo, to cover Campania and Sicily, relegating Naples to the status of a provincial city.

Following the death of the heir to the throne, Conrad, the crown of Sicily eventually passed to Charles of Anjou by papal grant in 1262 and by actual conquest in 1266. To mark the arrival of a new regime, Charles I transferred the kingdom's capital city to Naples, although control over Sicily was lost in 1282. Under the Angevin monarchs, Naples again prospered but by the end of the 15th century the country was torn by factionalism and civil war as French and Spanish interests sought control. In the event Spain proved victorious and the kingdom was captured in 1503 by Gonzalo de Cordoba, who became the first Spanish viceroy.

For the next 200 years Naples was under the control of Spanish viceroys; this continued until 1707, when it was relinquished to Austria following the War of Spanish Succession. This, however, was short-lived as in 1734 Charles of Bourbon seized Sicily and then Naples, creating a new kingdom, centered on Naples, that survived until the unification of Italy under Guiseppe Garibaldi in 1860.

BELOW: Naples, Italy, seen from space by the Ikonos satellite in 2006.

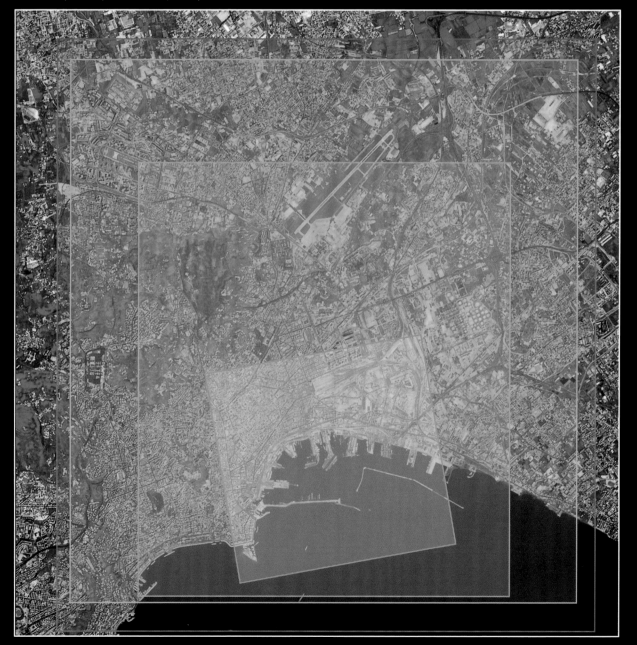

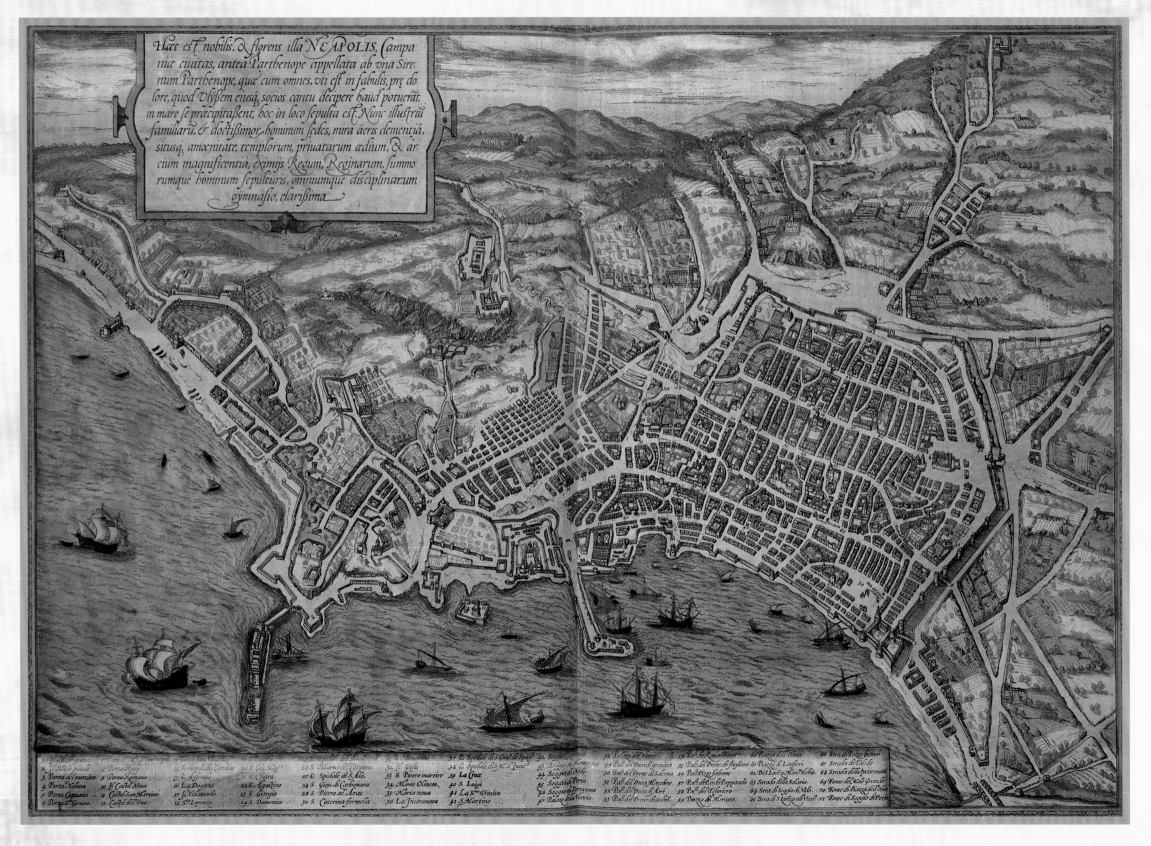

LEFT: Viewed looking toward the northwest, this late 16th-century map shows the extent of the city of Naples, situated between the Bay of Naples and Mount Vesuvius. Adjacent to the harbor is Castel Nuovo (New Castle); this was the royal residence of the Angevin kings and was first constructed for Charles I between 1279 and 1282, although not occupied until 1285. Extended in 1347, the castle was sacked in 1347 by the army of Louis I of Hungary before being restored. Rebuilt in the 15th century, the castle's role was reduced from royal palace to stronghold following the Spanish occupation of Naples in the late 15th century. Further to the west, and sited on a small island linked to the mainland, is Castle dell'Ovo (Egg Castle); this was initially constructed in the 12th century although on the site of earlier structures. The first colonists in the 6th century B.C. had settled on this island and, in 476A.D., the last emperor of the Western Roman Empire, Romulus Augustulus, was exiled here. On a hill to the northwest of the city can be seen Castel San Martino (now known as the Castel Sant'Elmo). It was built between 1329 and 1343 by Robert of Anjou, then rebuilt between 1537 and 1546 by Pedro Alvarez de Toledo, the Spanish viceroy. Adjacent to this castle is Certosa di San Martino (the Monastery of St Martin). This Carthusian monastery, dedicated to St Martin of Tours, was founded in the early 16th century.

RIGHT: Again aligned to the northwest, this street map of Naples was produced in Italy in the early 17th century. The main road bisecting the city from left to right is the road now known as Corso Umberto I.

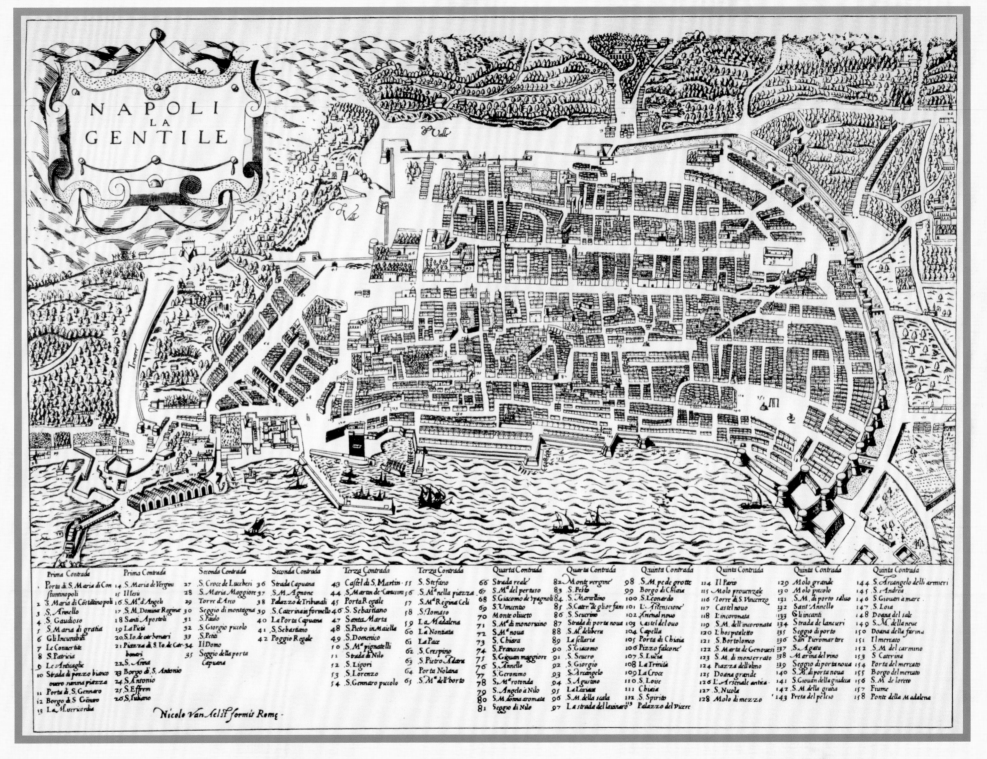

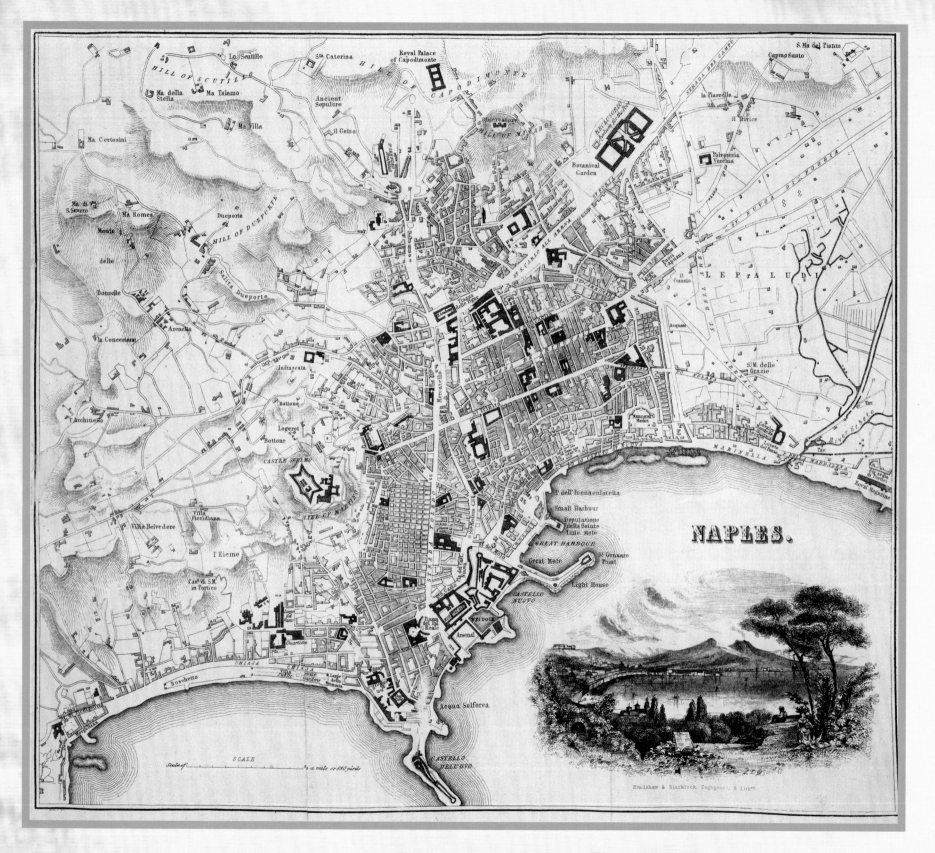

NAPLES.

LEFT: Produced by Bradshaw & Blacklock of Manchester in the middle of the 19th century, this map records Naples immediately prior to the arrival of the first railways. At this date the city was the capital of the kingdom of the Two Sicilies and the Royal Palace (Palzzo Reale) can be seen at the landward end of the Mole of St Vincent (Molo San Vincenzo). The palace, originally constructed by the Spanish viceroys in the early 17th century, was expanded and altered by the succeeding royal dynasties. Today the building houses the National Library (Biblioteca Nazionale). The inset shows how Mount Vesuvius dominates the Bay of Naples to the east of the city.

RIGHT: Produced by Bradshaw & Blacklock of Manchester, England, this map records Naples a decade after the previous map. The major change is the arrival of the railway in the city. Although it was the first in Italy to have a railway line with the opening of the line to Portici in 1839, this was not recorded in the map published in c.1850. In 1861 Garibaldi entered the city by train during the process of Italian Unification; the square in front of the station was subsequently renamed Piazza Garibaldi in his honor.

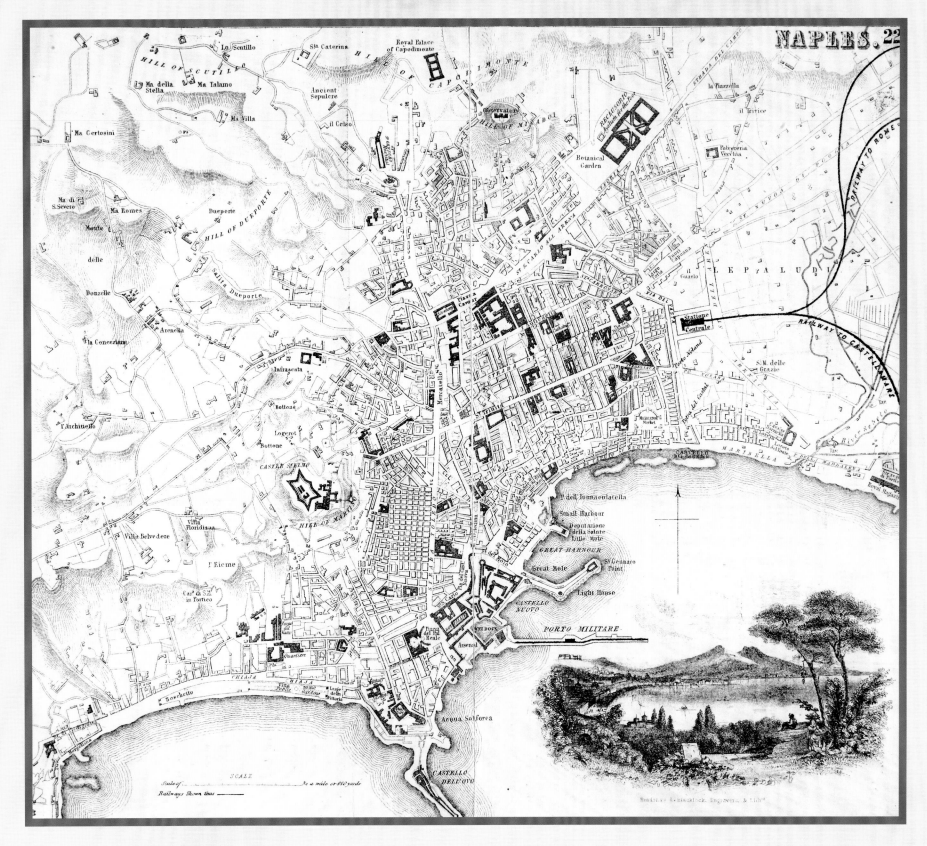

NEW YORK
UNITED STATES

With a population today of around 7.5 million, New York—or the Big Apple as it's popularly known—is the largest city in the US, although it's not the state capital of New York State (that honor belongs to Albany). The city is located at the confluence of the Hudson and East rivers as they enter Long Island Sound, and consists of five boroughs: the Bronx, Brooklyn, Manhattan, Queens, and Staten Island.

European settlement commenced at the start of the 17th century when the Dutch first arrived at the southern end of Manhattan Island to establish a fur trading post. The new settlement was named Nieuew Amsterdam (New Amsterdam) and expanded rapidly over the next few decades, particularly during 1647 and 1664 when the autocratic Peter Stuyvesant was governor of the area.

During the 17th century there was considerable rivalry between the English and Dutch as both sought to extend their overseas trading empires and, in 1664, Nieuw Amsterdam was captured by the English. It was renamed New York after the Duke of York a decade later. Under English rule the city grew to become one of the most significant within the original Thirteen Colonies.

In the American War of Independence, following victories in the autumn of 1776, Britain secured New York and the city remained a center for British military and political operations until final British withdrawal in 1783.

By 1898, with the union of Brooklyn and Manhattan and the other districts, the population had reached 3.5 million; by 1913 it had passed 5 million. In 1904 the first section of subway was built, and in 1913 work was completed on the first skyscraper, the Woolworth Building.

New York was to dominate the country's financial life, through Wall Street, and its culture, through the theaters of Broadway and the numerous museums. The population continued to grow, but the Wall Street Crash of 1929 and the consequent Great Depression caused serious economic problems; despite this, the 1930s witnessed the completion of some of the city's iconic structures, such the Empire State Building, the Chrysler Building, and the RCA Building.

Post World War II the city again boomed, and its global importance was emphasized when the headquarters of the United Nations were sited on 42nd Street in 1953.

BELOW: This is a 2004 satellite image of Manhattan and the other four boroughs of New York City—The Bronx (at bottom right of image; Brooklyn, center left; Queens in the lower center; and Staten Island above left. Today, some eight million live in these boroughs. No outline is given for later maps for clarity.

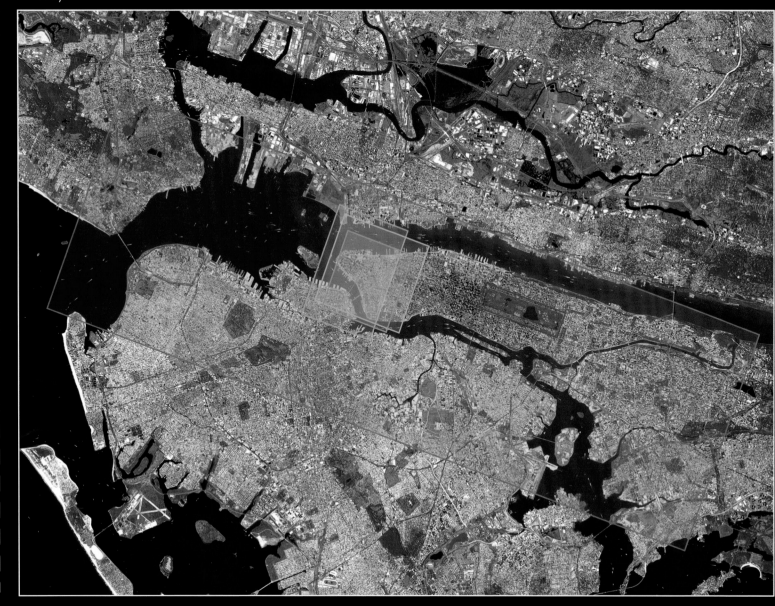

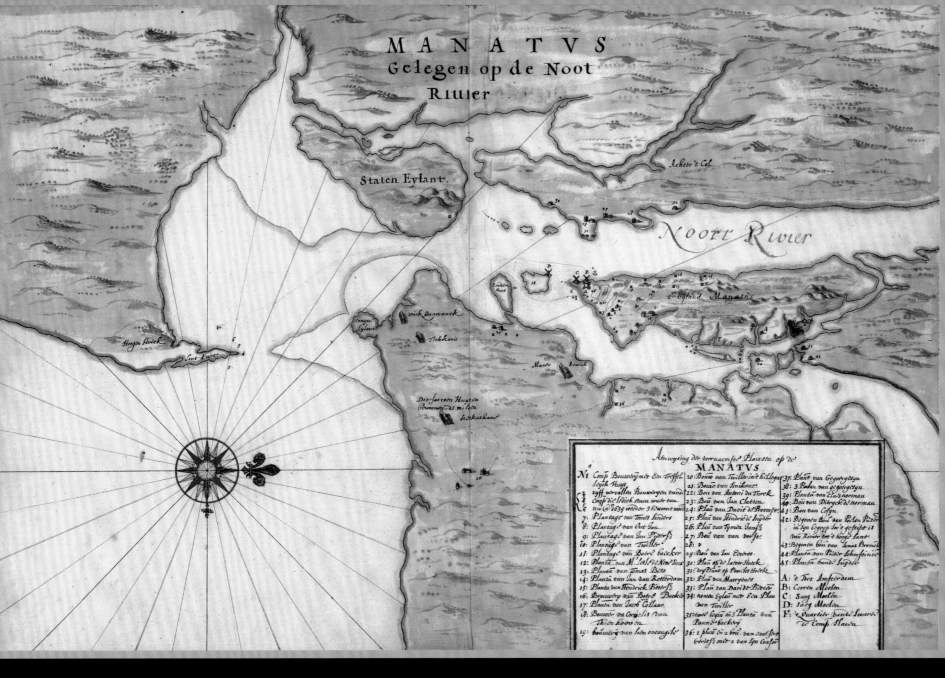

MANATVS
Gelegen op de Noot
Riuier

Staten Eylant.

Achter 't Col

Noort Rivier

't Eyland Manatus

LEFT: One of the earliest maps of the New World to be included in this volume, this map of the estuary of the Hudson River was compiled in the early 17th century by Joan Vinckeboons. It was only in 1626 that the Dutchman Peter Minnewit (or Minuit) acquired the island now known as Manhattan from the Manna-Hatta Indians and founded the settlement of Nieuw Amsterdam. Drawn to a scale of around 1:170,000, the map is oriented with north toward the right. Under Minnewit's successor, Peter Stuyvesant, Nieuw Amsterdam grew rapidly, but was to be seized by the British in 1664 and renamed New York.

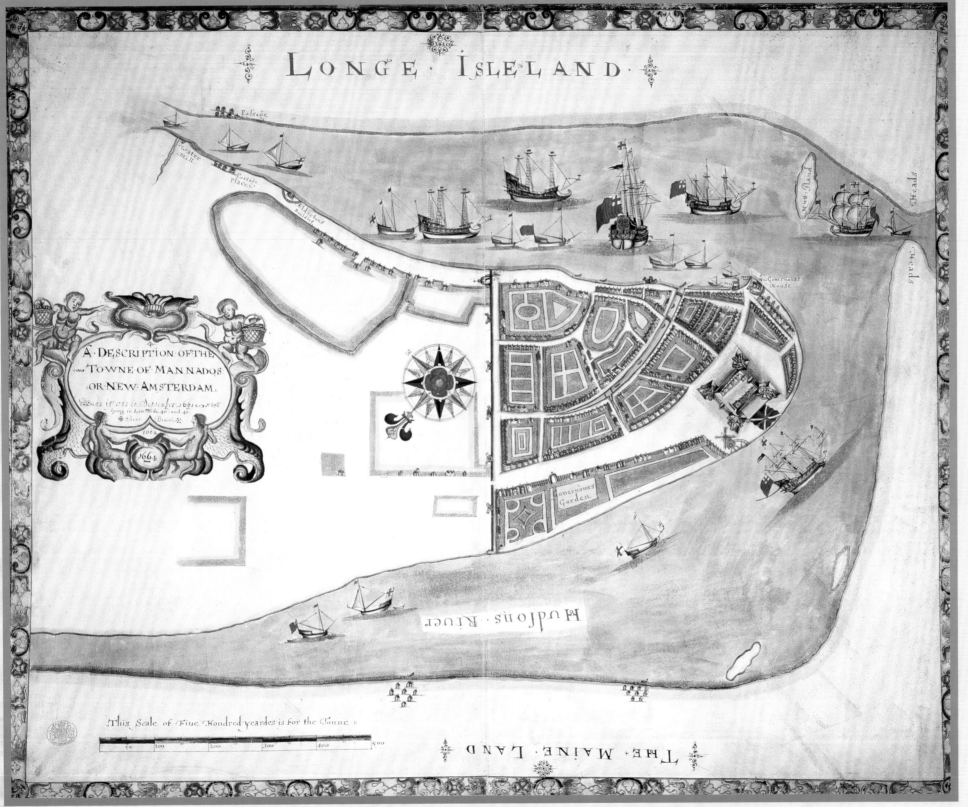

LONGE · ISLE·LAND ·

A DESCRIPTION OF THE
TOWNE OF MANNADOS
OR NEW AMSTERDAM

1664

This Scale of Fiue Hundred yeardes is for the Towne

Hudsons River

The · Maine · Land ·

LEFT: Produced on an alignment with north toward the bottom left, this map of New York was produced shortly after the British had seized Nieuw Amsterdam from Dutch control and shows the development of the settlement of Manhattan Island by this date.

RIGHT: This is a perspective of the city of New York across the North River, showing the position of King George III's fleet on November 1, 1765. An endorsement notes that this deployment was in connection with the riots of the Sons of Liberty following the Stamp Act Congress. The illustration was drawn by W. Cockburn. The Stamp Act was passed by Parliament in London, becoming law on March 22, 1765; it was an immensely unpopular act in the American colonies—"No Taxation without Representation"—and, ultimately, was the fuse which ignited the American Revolution. The Stamp Act Congress met in New York on October 7, 1765; representatives of nine of the Thirteen Colonies were present, and of these nine not all were official. The Congress did demonstrate, however, for the first time a sense of unity of purpose amongst the colonies, although at this stage it was reform rather than revolution that was the intention. The Sons of Liberty became increasingly important in the local administration of the states, often effectively supplanting the colonial administration, with the effect that the act was virtually unworkable. Although the Stamp Act was repealed the following year, it had fundamentally altered the relationship between Britain and its North American empire.

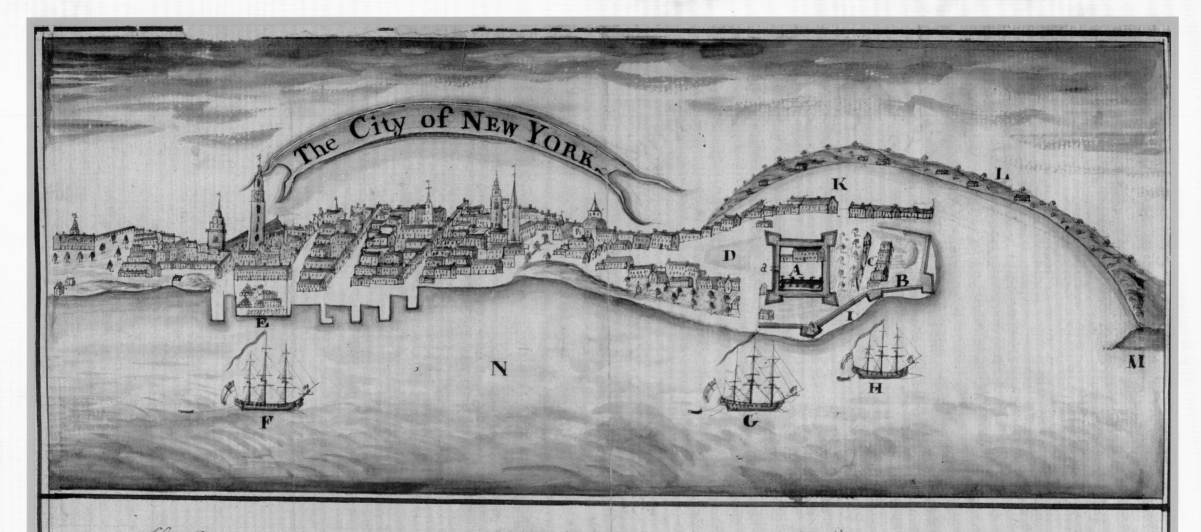

The City of NEW YORK.

W Cockburn fecit

The Position of his Majesty's ships as they where stationed on the 1st day of November 1765.

A. Fort George. a The Fort gate. B. The Battery. C. The Barracks. D. The Bowling green. and Broad way. E. The Kings Wharf. and Arsenal. F. His Majesty's Ship COVENTRY. to protect d.º G. The Guarland. to scour the street and defend the Fort gate. H. The Hawke. to preserve a Communication between his Majesty's Ships & the Fort by covering the landing of boats at i. The flat Rock. K. The East River L. Long Island M. Governors Island. N. The North River.

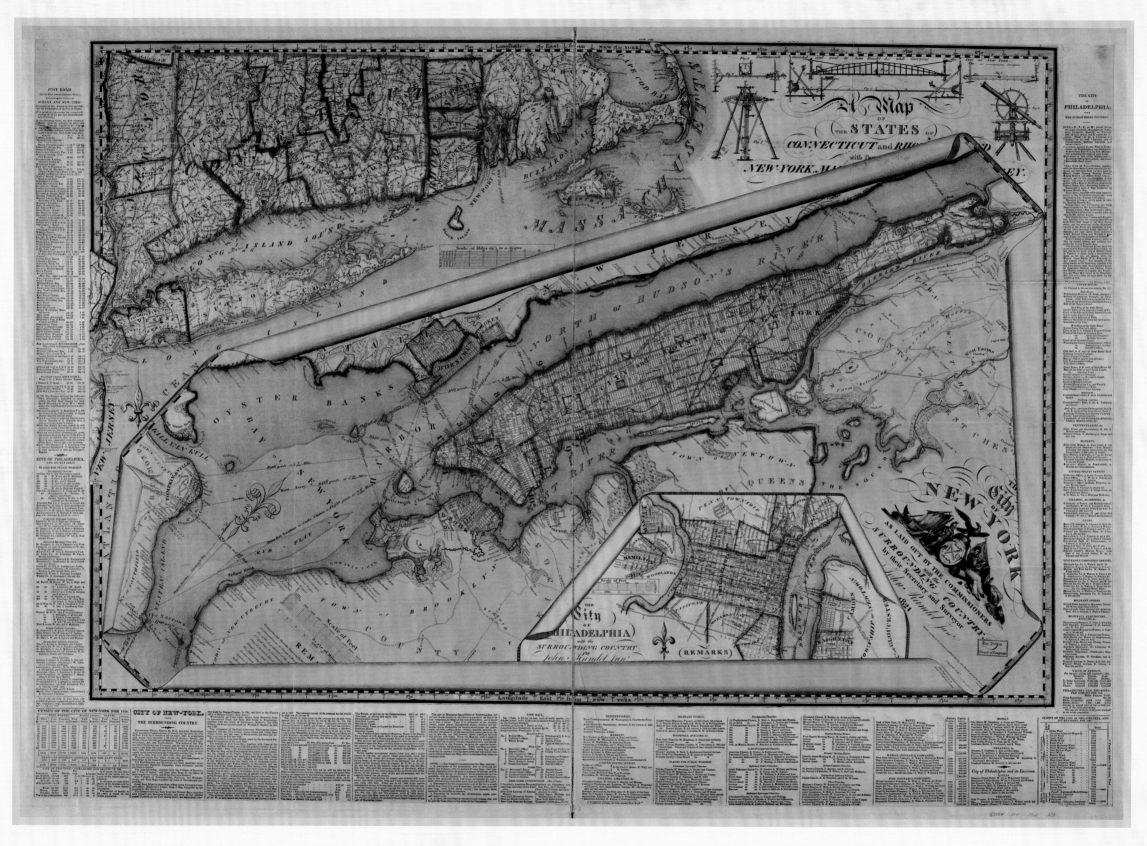

PAGE 178: This map, described as a "Plan of the City of New York Survey'd by Bernd. Ratzen, Lieut. in the 60th Regt. F. Walden Fecit.," records the city contemporaneously with the British occupation at the start of the War of Independence. Drawn to a scale of 400 feet to 1 inch, the map includes a reference table to churches and other principal buildings as well as an additional table detailing forts, batteries, entrenchments, and other military installations. On September 21 part of the city was destroyed by fire and this section is highlighted on the map with red shading, although this is now much faded.

PAGE 179: This is the city of New York and surrounding country as laid out by the commissioners and surveyor John Randel, Junior, and drawn by P. Maverik to a scale of around 1:42,000. It is a street-planning map and covers all of Manhattan Island and substantial parts of adjacent counties in New York and New Jersey. Existing and proposed streets are shown, as well as buildings and other structures, streams and wetlands, and political boundaries. Also included are illustrations of the equipment used by the surveyor and two ancillary maps showing the states of Connecticut and Rhode Island and the city of Philadelphia.

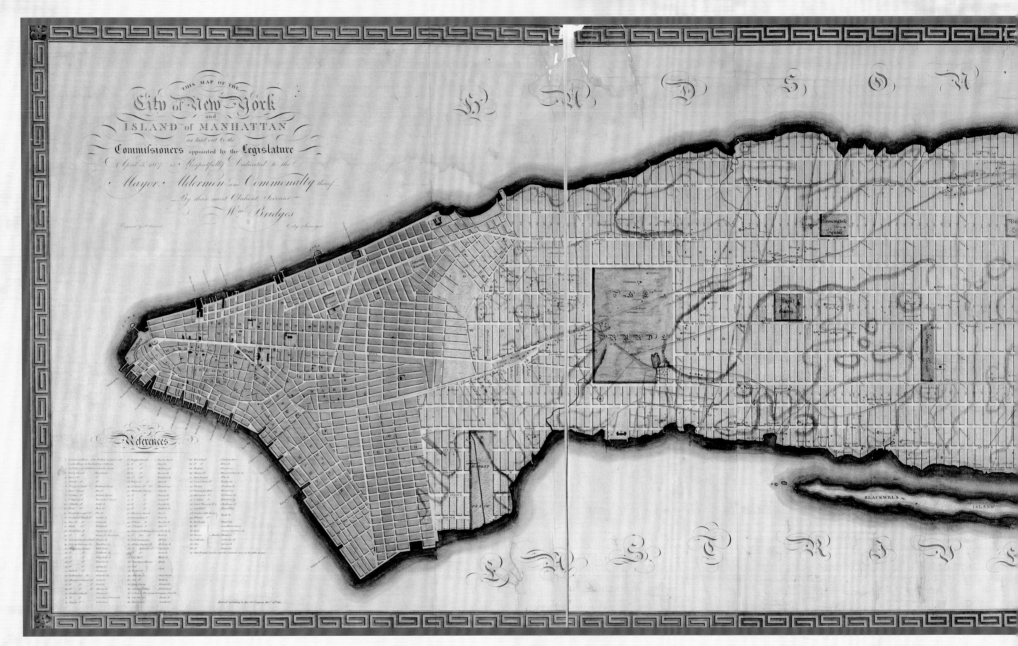

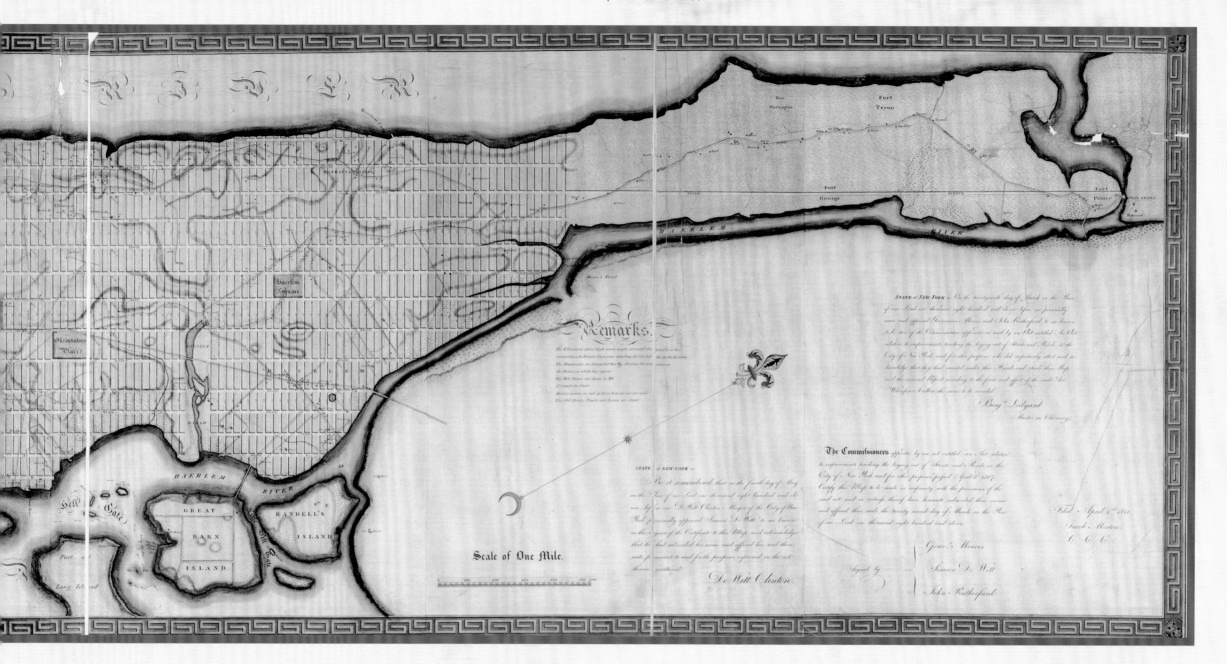

ABOVE: This 1811 map of the city of New York and island of Manhattan, as laid out by the commissioners appointed by the legislature, April 3, 1807, was respectfully dedicated to the mayor, aldermen, and commonalty of the city by their most obedient servant William Bridges (died 1814), city surveyor, and engraved by P. Maverick. Compiled to a scale of 1:10,000, the map is oriented with north toward the upper right. The map records ward boundaries, selected buildings and landowners' names, as well an index of points of interest. Note that Clinton Castle and Battery Park, at the southernmost point of the island, have yet to be constructed.

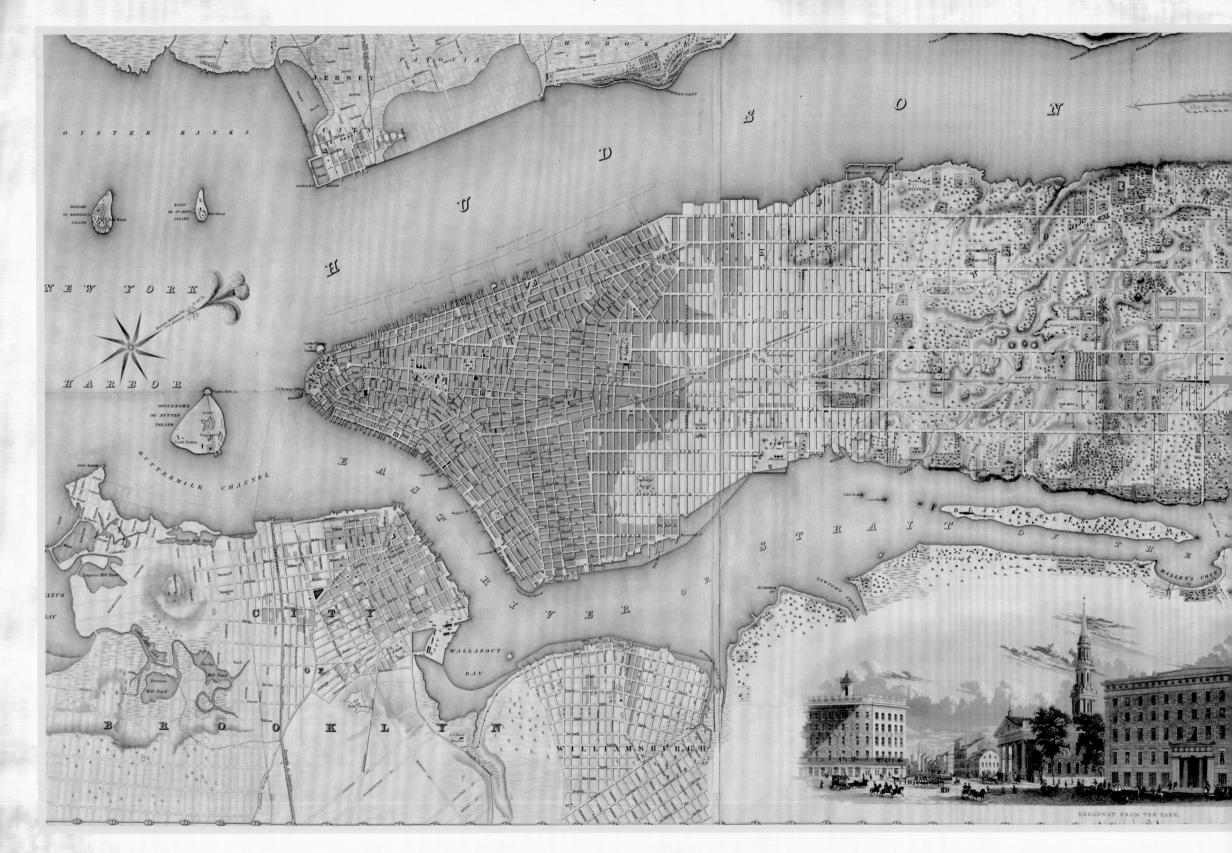

BROADWAY FROM THE PARK.

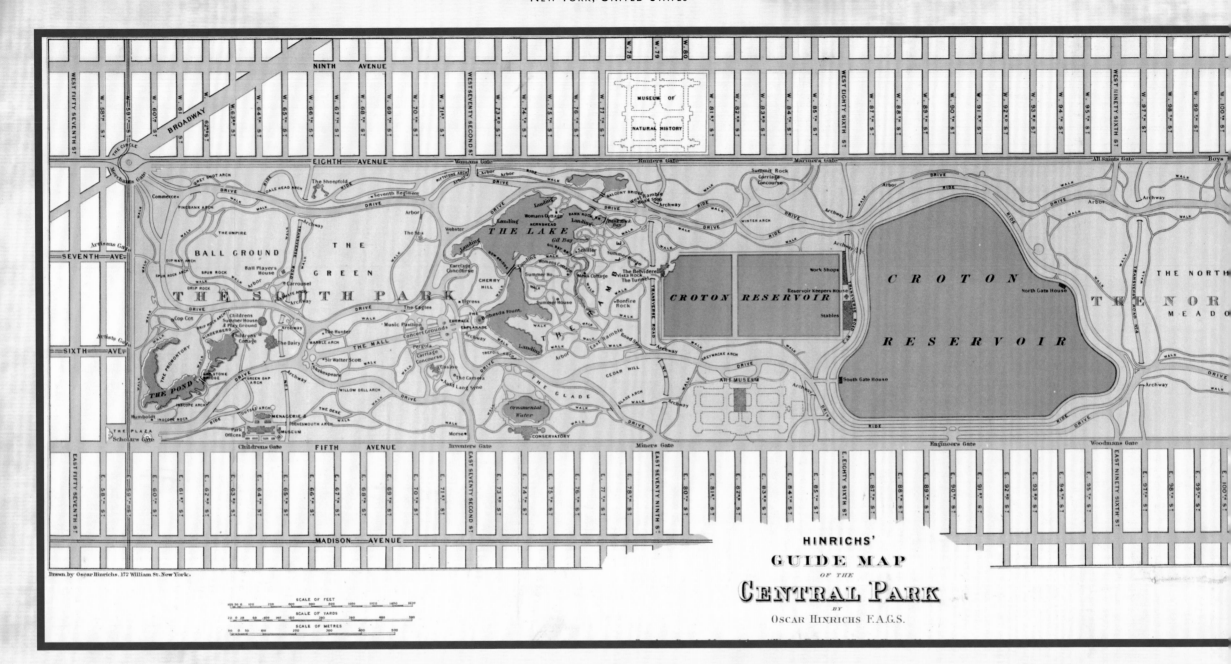

HINRICHS'
GUIDE MAP
OF THE
CENTRAL PARK
BY
OSCAR HINRICHS F.A.G.S.

Drawn by Oscar Hinrichs, 172 William St. New York.

SCALE OF FEET

SCALE OF YARDS

SCALE OF METRES

ABOVE: Oscar Hinrichs' map of Central Park was drawn in 1875 to a scale of 1:7,500 and published in *Hinrichs' Guide to the Central Park*. Bordered to the north by West 110th Street (Central Park North), the south by West 59th Street (Central Park South), the west by Eighth Avenue (Central Park West), and Fifth Avenue on the east, Central Park was designed by Frederick Law Olmsted and English architect Calvert Vaux. Completed in 1873, there have been many changes to the park since it was landscaped—such as the creation of the Great Lawn in place of the Croton Lower Reservoir.

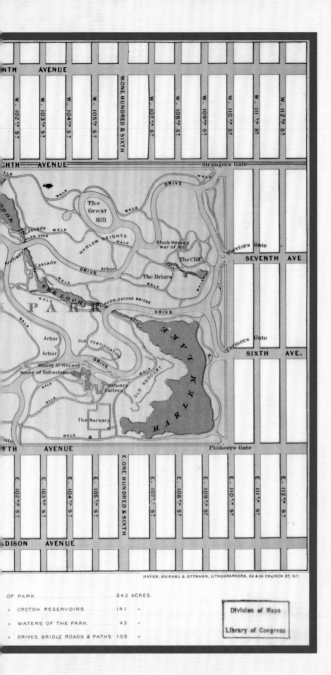

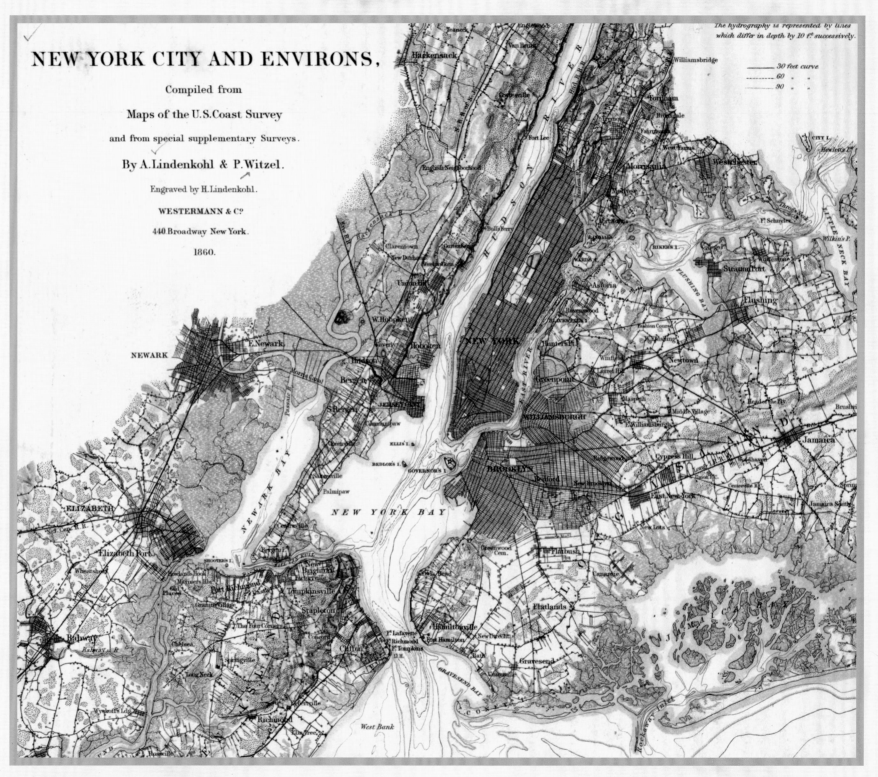

NEW YORK CITY AND ENVIRONS,

Compiled from

Maps of the U.S. Coast Survey

and from special supplementary Surveys.

By A. Lindenkohl & P. Witzel.

Engraved by H. Lindenkohl.

WESTERMANN & C?

440 Broadway New York.

1860.

RIGHT: Drawn to a scale of 1:200,000 and compiled by A. Lindenkohl from maps originally produced by the US Coast Survey and by special supplementary surveys, this map records the city of New York and the surrounding countryside on the eve of the civil war.

BELOW: This panoramic view of Manhattan Island from the south shows the extent of development by the late 19th century, both on the island itself as well as across the East and Hudson rivers. Prominent at the western end of the island are Castle Clinton and Battery Park; the former was completed in 1811. The building was used for concerts and entertainment before becoming an immigration station. It was subsequently used, until 1941, as an aquarium, before restoration. Crossing the East River is Brooklyn Bridge, this 1,150-yard long structure was constructed between 1867 and 1883 and was the first bridge across the East River, as well as being the first to be suspended with steel cables. Bisecting the island from Battery Park to the northeast is Broadway, with Trinity Church prominent.

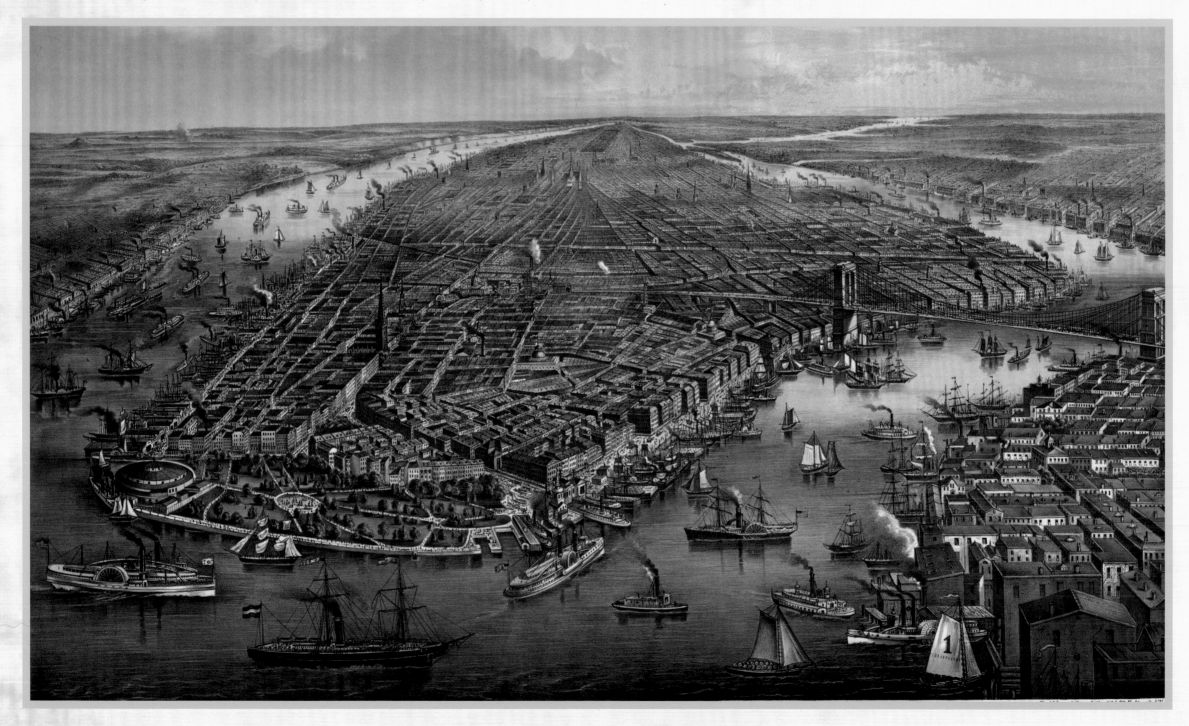

PALERMO
SICILY

Sited on the Gulf of Palermo, the city of Palermo is the capital of Sicily with a population approaching 700,000. It was initially founded in the 8th century B.C. by Phoenician tradesmen and remained under their control until the First Punic War (264–241B.C.), when it and the rest of Sicily fell under Roman control. With the split of the Roman Empire in the early 4th century A.D., Sicily eventually passed to the Byzantine (eastern) Empire.

In the 9th century, the Byzantine Empire divided control of the island into two prefectures, which led to civil war. Euphimius, the triumphant prefect, sought to strengthen his power by inviting an Arab army from North Africa to act as mercenaries, but this backfired and the Arabs gradually conquered the entire island. It was during their rule that the island's capital was moved to Palermo. The city prospered, and some 300 mosques were constructed.

The Arabs remained in control of the island until 1060, when the Normans invaded. Palermo was captured in 1072 but it was not until the final decade of the 11th century that Arab power was finally eliminated. Although the Normans had proved victorious, there remained a significant Arab and Muslim presence on the island and this was reflected in the art and architecture produced during Norman rule.

In 1194 Sicily fell to the rule of the Holy Roman Empire, initially through the Hohenstaufen line. The empire controlled the island until the 13th century when, after a brief period of Angevin rule (from 1266 to 1282), control passed to Aragon. This was one of the dominant kingdoms in Spain, and with the uniting of Aragon and Castile in 1479, Sicily became part of the kingdom of Spain.

Spanish rule was to last until 1713 when, under the Treaty of Utrecht, Sicily passed to the House of Savoy. Their rule, however, was to be short-lived as in 1734 the island was united with Naples to form the kingdom of the Two Sicilies, although Palermo's importance was reduced given that the new state capital was Naples. Sicily became part of the kingdom of Italy in 1860 following the process of Italian Reunification. Palermo suffered severe damage during the Allied invasion of the island in 1943, and it has been the victim of many earthquakes, most recently in the early 21st century.

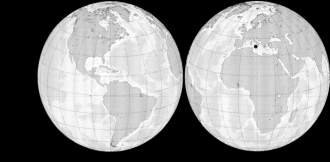

BELOW: Satellite image of the city of Palermo (center) and its surrounding area on the northern coast of Sicily. North is at top. Forested areas are dark green, agricultural fields are lighter shades of green, mountains are brown, urban areas are grey and water is black. Image created using NaturalVue data obtained from the Landsat 7 satellite.

LEFT: This late 16th-century map of the city of Palermo, which is aligned with the south toward the top, shows the city whilst it was under Spanish rule. At the top can be seen the Castello della Zisa, a castle built in the late 12th century for the Norman kings of Sicily. Linking the castle with the harbor is a road—known today as the Corso Vittorio Emanuele—which by 1600 had become one of the city's most impressive thoroughfares. It included two city gates—the Porta Felice (built in 1582) and the Porta Nuovo (built as a triumphal arch in 1535).

RIGHT: Published by the Hydrographical Office of the Admiralty in London in July 1823, this map was originally prepared by Captain William Henry Smith, Royal Navy, as part of his survey of Sicily, Malta and adjacent islands compiled between 1814 and 1816. The key identifies buildings of interest.

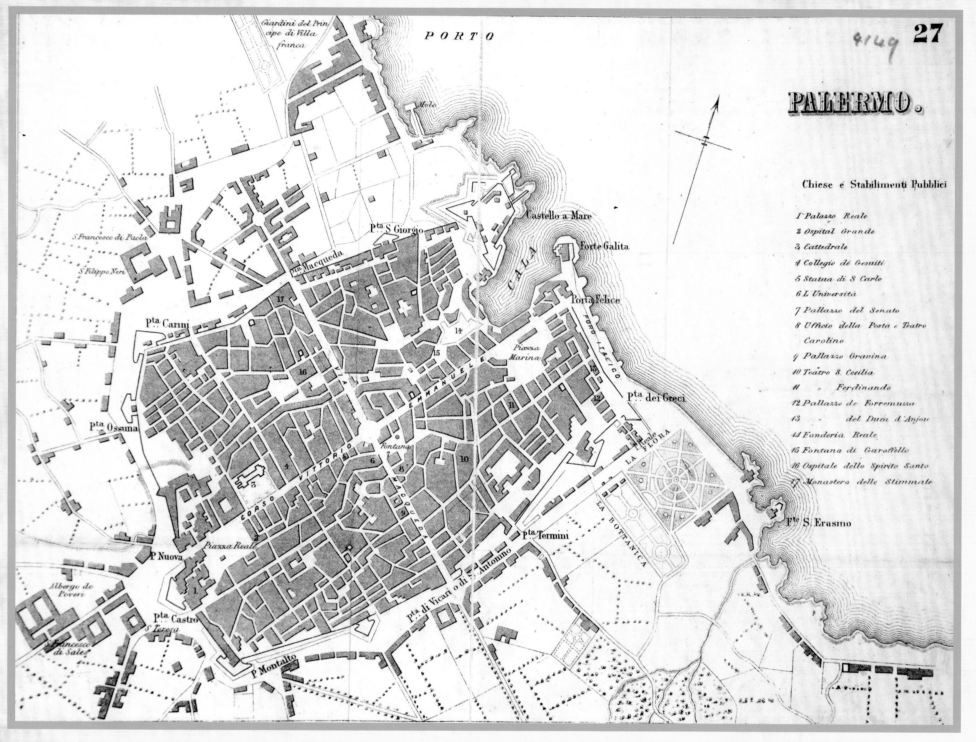

PORTO

Gardini del Principe di Villa franca

4149 **27**

PALERMO.

Mola

Castello a Mare

Pta S Giorgio

Forte Galita

S Francesco di Paola

pta Macqueda

CALA

S Filippo Neri

Porta Felice

Pta Carini

17

14

FORO ITALICO

15

16

Piazza Marina

13

Pta dei Greci

pta Ossuna

Fontana

11

12

Pta Reale FLORA

4

6   7

8

10

LA BOTANICA

Piazza Reale

P Nuova

Pta Termini

Albergo de Poveri

1

Pta di Vicari o di S Antonino

Pta Castro

S Teresa

Francesco di Sales

P Montalto

LEFT: Produced by Bradshaw & Blacklock of Manchester, England, this map records the city of Palermo in the mid-19th century. Although by this date most of the cities featured in this book had already seen the arrival of the railway, Palermo was still to be connected. It was not until 1863 that the line from the city to Bagheria was opened.

Chiese e Stabilimenti Pubblici

1 Palazzo Reale
2 Ospital Grande
3 Cattedrale
4 Collegio de Gesuiti
5 Statua di S Carlo
6 L Università
7 Pallazzo del Senato
8 Ufficio della Posta e Teatro Carolino
9 Pallazzo Gravina
10 Teatro S. Cecilia
11   Ferdinando
12 Pallazzo de Forremuxa
13   del Duca d'Anjou
14 Fonderia Reale
15 Fontana di Garoffello
16 Ospitale dello Spirito Santo
17 Monastero delle Stimmate

F.te S. Erasmo

PARIS
FRANCE

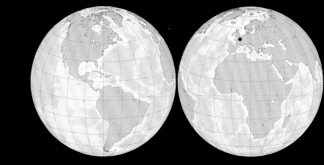

Few other capital cities are as integral to the workings of their country as is Paris. This hegemony started in medieval times, but was consolidated during the autocratic reign of King Louis XIV (1638–1715). He centralized all administration and culture in Paris, poured the vast wealth of his conquests into the city, and embellished the cityscape with monuments to his and France's magnificence. As if this was not enough, any prevailing provincial attempts to reassert independence were squashed by Napoleon Bonaparte.

Paris is more than 2,000 years old. Gauls of the Parisii tribe settled there between 250 and 200 B.C. and founded a fishing village on an island in the middle of the River Seine, now known as the Ile de la Cité. In 987 A.D. Hugh Capet, Count of Paris, became king of France, and under his Capetian successors the city's position as the nation's capital became established.

During the Middle Ages the city continued to develop. In 1163 construction began on the Gothic choir of Notre Dame Cathedral. In 1200 King Philippe II started work on the fortress of the Louvre. During the 13th century Louis IX (1214–70), who was later canonized, established the royal court of justice. In 1200, the future Sorbonne Institute was founded by one of the cathedral's canons, Robert de Sorbon.

Although the English had been largely forced from their French territories in the early 13th century, English monarchs maintained a claim to the French throne and there was regular warfare between the two countries as the English sought to regain their lost lands. The Hundred Years' War was fought between 1337 and 1453 and saw Paris twice occupied by English forces; it was not finally recaptured by the French until 1436.

During the 18th century, Paris was increasingly at the epicenter of the forces that led to the storming of the Bastille on July 14, 1789 and the start of the French Revolution. This caused the death of many, including Louis XVI and his wife Marie Antoinette, on the guillotine and to two decades of pan-European war, which culminated in the defeat of Napoleon at the Battle of Waterloo in 1815. In 1853 Baron Georges Eugéne Haussmann (1809–91) started the wholesale rebuilding of the city, which included elegant boulevards, parks, and bridges. The Eiffel Tower—then the tallest man-made structure in the world, was completed in 1889, and the first Metro line was opened 11 years later.

BELOW: False color image of Paris from 2000.

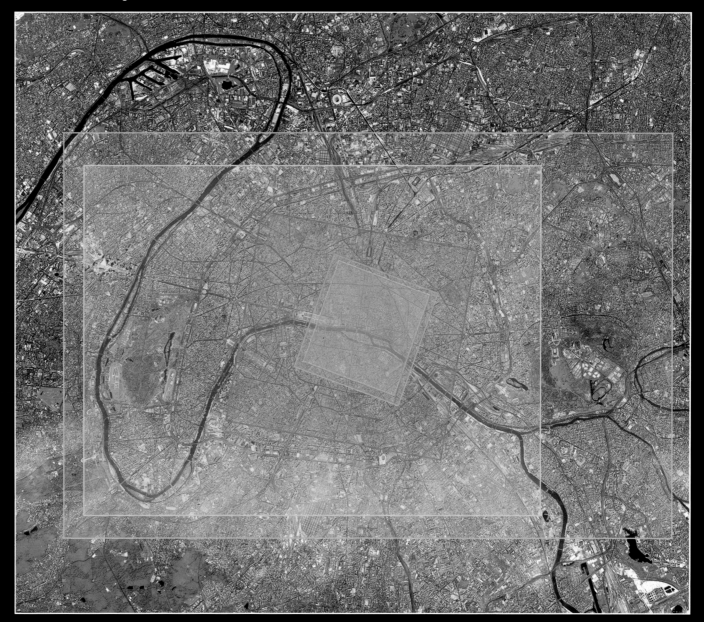

LEFT: Described as Lutetia—the city's Roman name—this late 16th century map portrays how the city of Paris had grown up around the historic core formed by the Île de la Cité in the center of the River Seine. Toward the top of the island can be seen the great cathedral of Notre Dame. Also visible toward the top of the map is the Bastille; this great prison was originally built in the late 14th century as part of the city's expanded defenses but was to become a prison in the 17th century. It was the storming of the Bastille in July 1789 that launched the French Revolution.

RIGHT: Labelled the Huitieme (eighth) plan de Paris, this was published around 1700 by Nicolas de Fer to a scale of 1:9,250,000. It shows Paris struggling to be contained by the old city walls. The king no longer lived here: King Louis XIV had moved the royal court to Versailles in 1682.

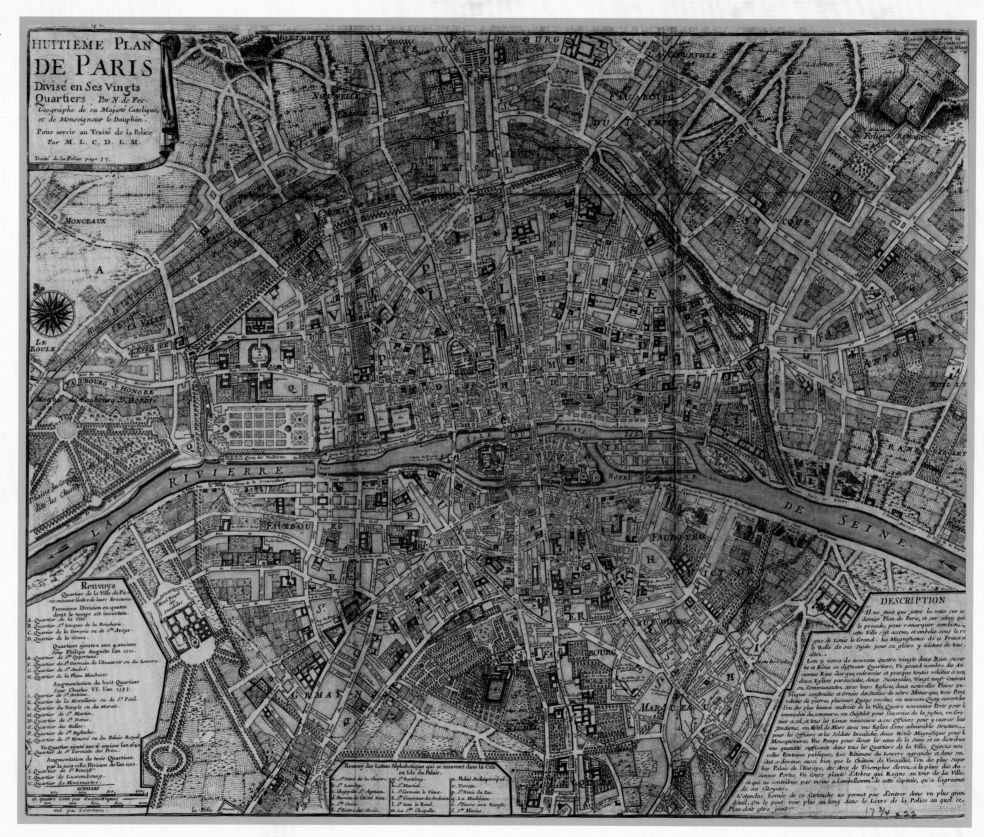

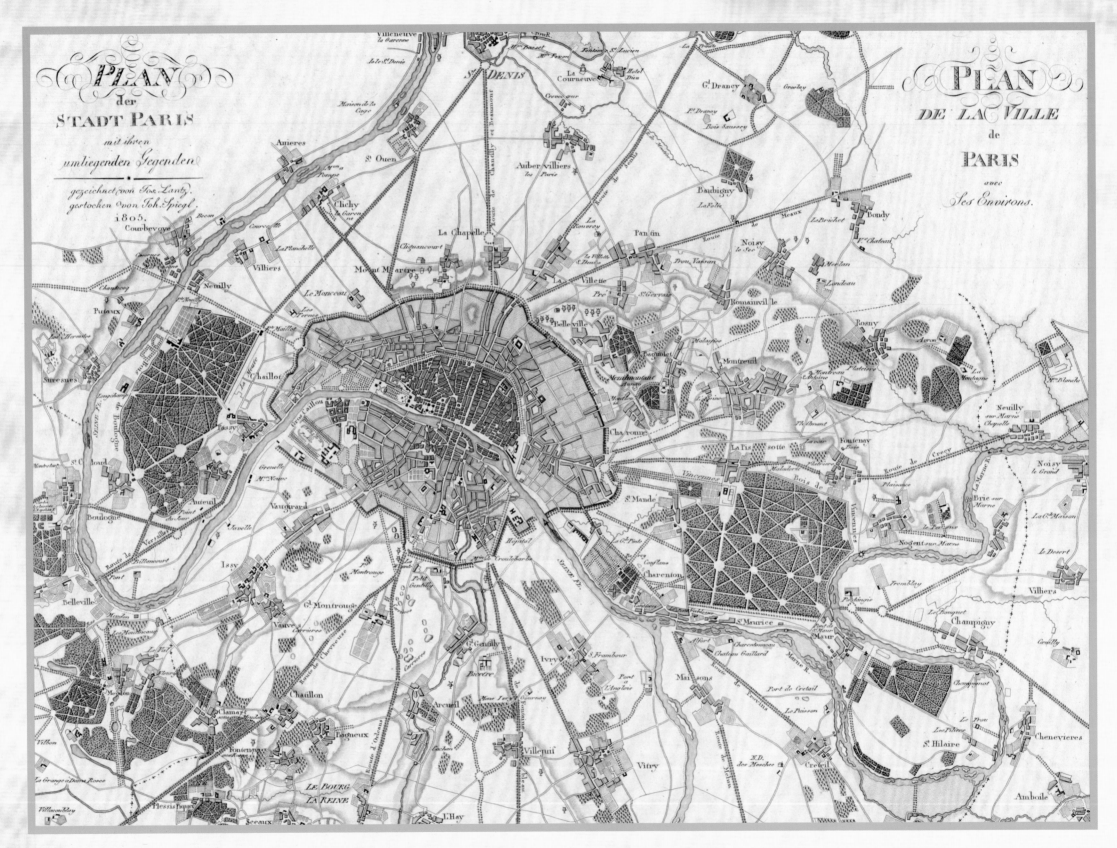

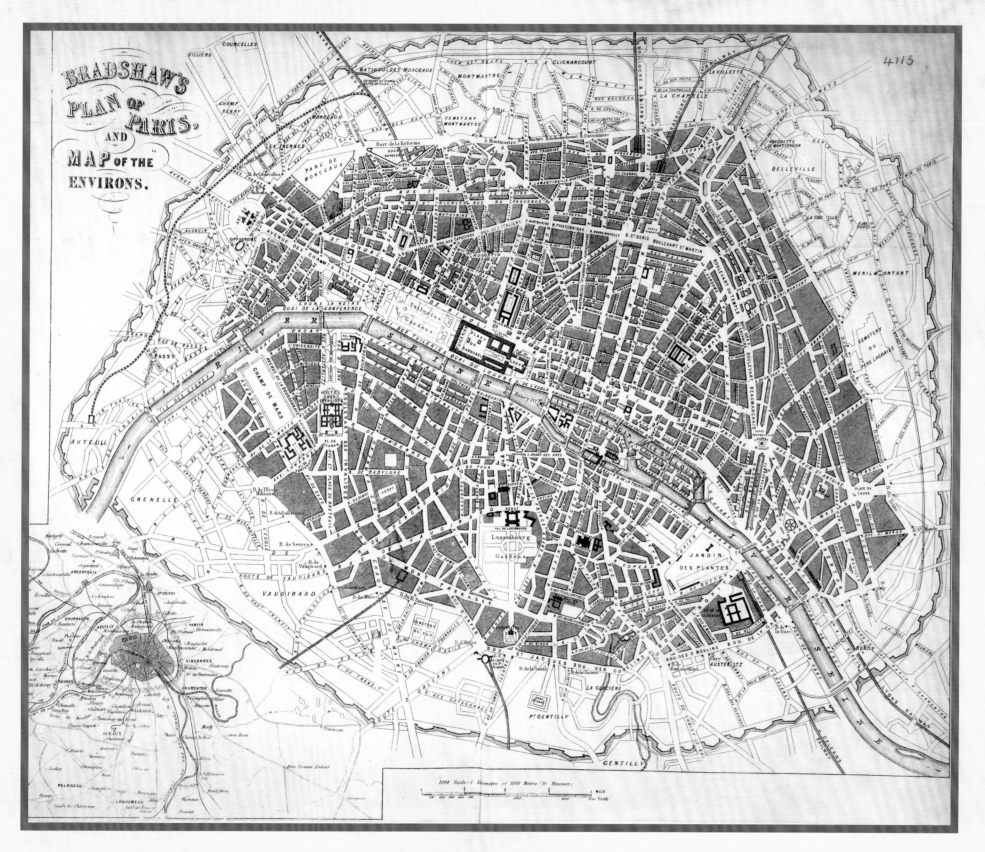

4113

FAR LEFT: This plan of Paris was produced in the middle of the Napoleonic period, in 1805. Note the woods of the Bois de Boulogne to the west (left) and Bois de Vincennes to the east (right). The latter was originally a royal hunting ground but was used for military exercises after the revolution. It was made into a public park by Napoleon III in 1860.

LEFT: Produced by Bradshaw & Blacklock of Manchester, England, this map records the city of Paris in the mid-19th century immediately prior to the start of Baron Haussmann's redevelopment of the city. By this date the presence of the railways was already beginning to become clear, with a number of stations extant on the fringes of the old city area. Railway development in France was relatively late; it was not until 1842 that an act legalizing railways was passed and, unlike many other countries, French railway development was much more state encouraged. The first main lines to be completed were those that radiated out from Paris. Amongst the lines to be built from Paris and recorded in this map is the Chemin de Fer du Nord; this opened from Gare du Nord in 1846 as part of a link between the city and the English Channel. This station is still in use today and is now, much expanded, the French terminus of the Eurostar services from London.

FOLLOWING PAGE: Produced by Bradshaw & Blacklock of Manchester, England, this updated version of the previous map records the city of Paris some seven years into Baron Haussmann's work. The expansion of the city's railway network over the preceding 10 years is also evident.

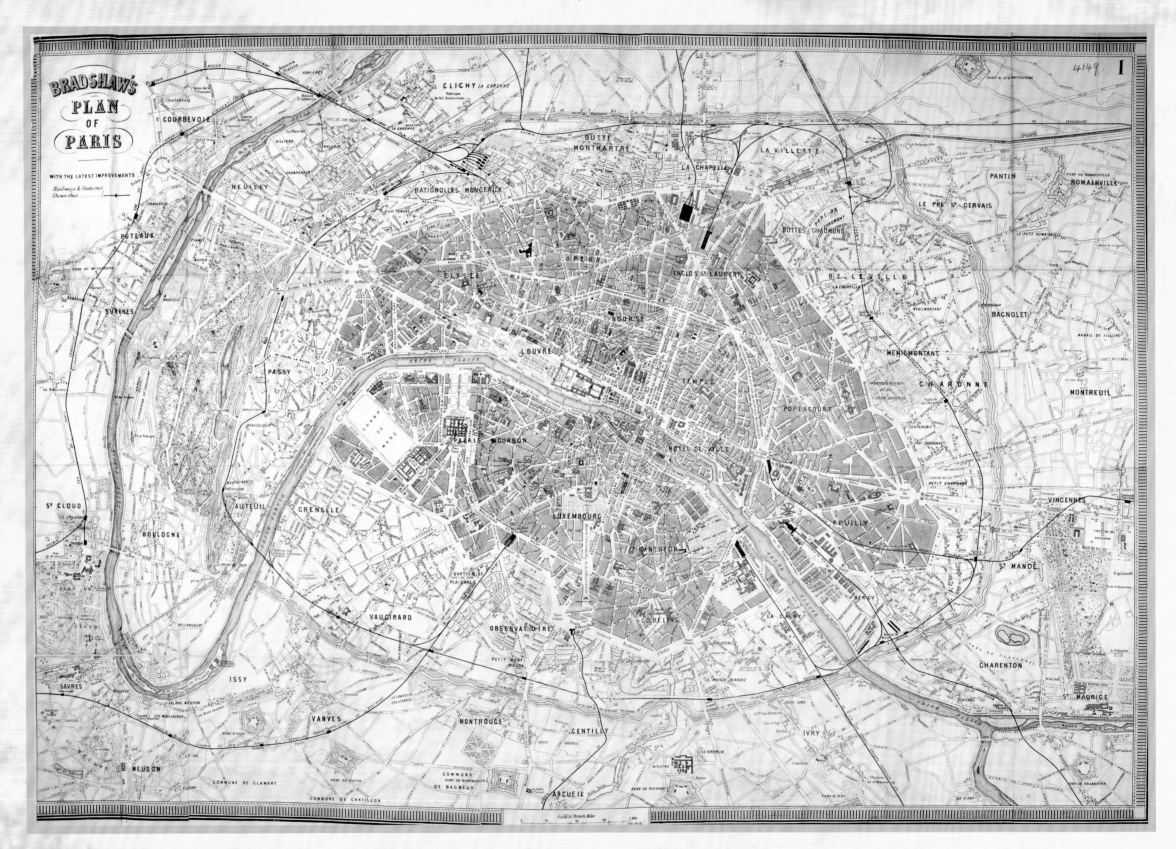

PHILADELPHIA

UNITED STATES

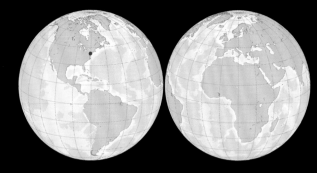

The state capital of Pennsylvania, Philadelphia has been the second city of the British Empire, the fulcrum of the American Revolution, and the capital of the early United States of America.

In 1681 William Penn was granted a charter by the British monarch King Charles II in lieu of a debt owed by the crown to Penn's father. William Penn was a Quaker, and his vision was to create a state free from the religious persecution that had afflicted other non-conformists in Britain and Europe. Penn began work on the new colony and on the design of its capital, Philadelphia—the city of brotherly love.

By 1699, the city had made considerable progress as a commercial center and already possessed a population of around 2,000, and this growth continued rapidly during the first half of the 18th century. However, there was increasing tension between the various religious and ethnic groups. The city developed a reputation for lawlessness and became a hub of the slave trade, yet it was also a center for culture, and drew notable traders and intellects to the city.

In 1756 the Seven Years' War between Britain and France broke out, and European strife extended to North America, where British and colonist forces sought to eliminate French control. Following the Treaty of Paris of 1763, which recognized the significant territorial gains made by the British in North America, the crown was forced to pay both the costs of the war as well as the increased burden of defending its extended empire. The subsequent taxes were received with considerable hostility in North America and over the next decade tension between colonists and Britain grew.

On July 4, 1776 the Declaration of Independence was issued from the Pennsylvania State House. For the next five years, until the final British defeat at Yorktown on October 19, 1781, the Thirteen Colonies were riven by civil war. The independence of the Thirteen Colonies was confirmed by the Treaty of Versailles on September 3, 1783. In May 1787, a Constitutional Convention, held in the Pennsylvania State House, established the constitution of the United States of America.

By 1800 Philadelphia had a population of 65,000 and was the largest city in North America, and the largest English-speaking community outside the United Kingdom. Further growth was fostered by rapid industrialization. In the 20th century, as traditional heavy industries declined, the city's economy diversified, with tourism, finance, and insurance replacing coal and iron.

BELOW: This satellite image of the city of Philadelphia, PA was created in 2006 using NaturalVue data obtained from the Landsat 7 satellite.

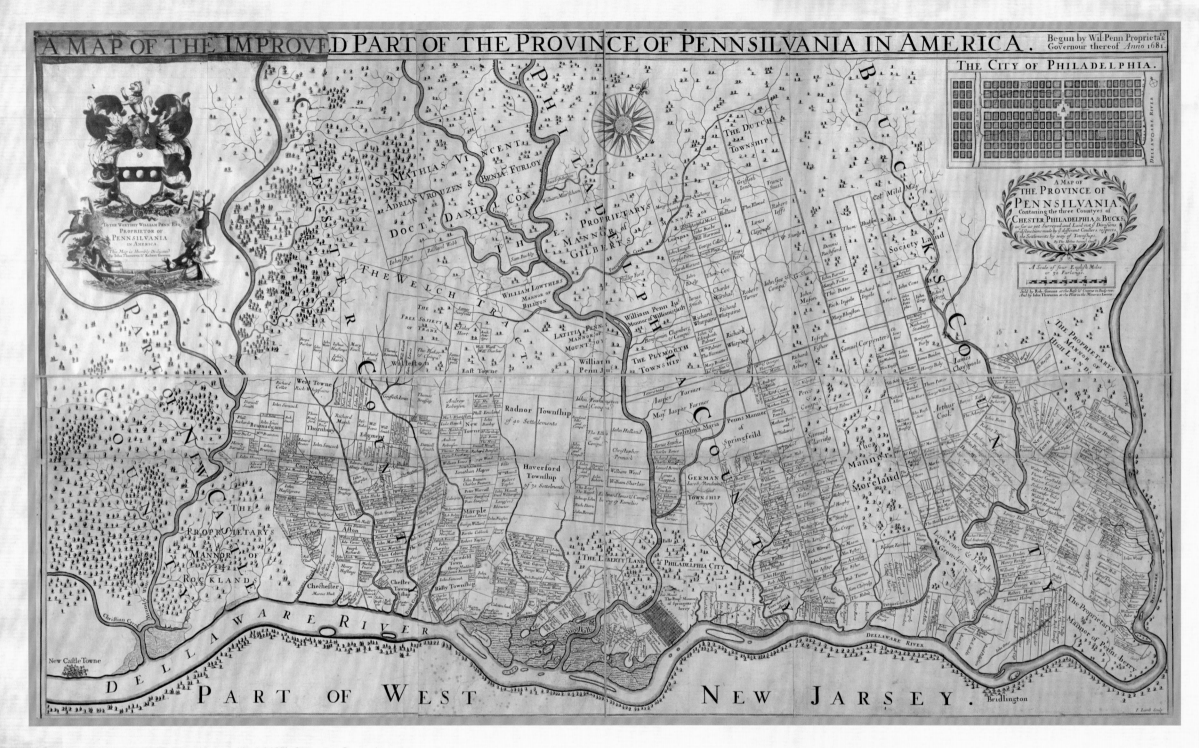

A MAP OF THE IMPROVED PART OF THE PROVINCE OF PENNSILVANIA IN AMERICA. Begun by Wil. Penn Proprietary Governour thereof Anno 1681

THE CITY OF PHILADELPHIA.

A MAP OF THE PROVINCE OF PENNSILVANIA Containing the three Countyes of CHESTER PHILADELPHIA, & BUCKS,

PART OF WEST   NEW JARSEY.

ABOVE: Originally drawn by Thomas Holme (died 1695), Surveyor General, in 1681 and published in London by Robert Greene and John Thornton in 1705, this map shows the counties of Chester, Philadelphia, and Bucks, as marked when the territory was granted to William Penn (to whom the map is dedicated) by King Charles II. European settlement in the region had first occurred in 1643 with the arrival of Swedish settlers, and the territory was ceded to England in 1664.

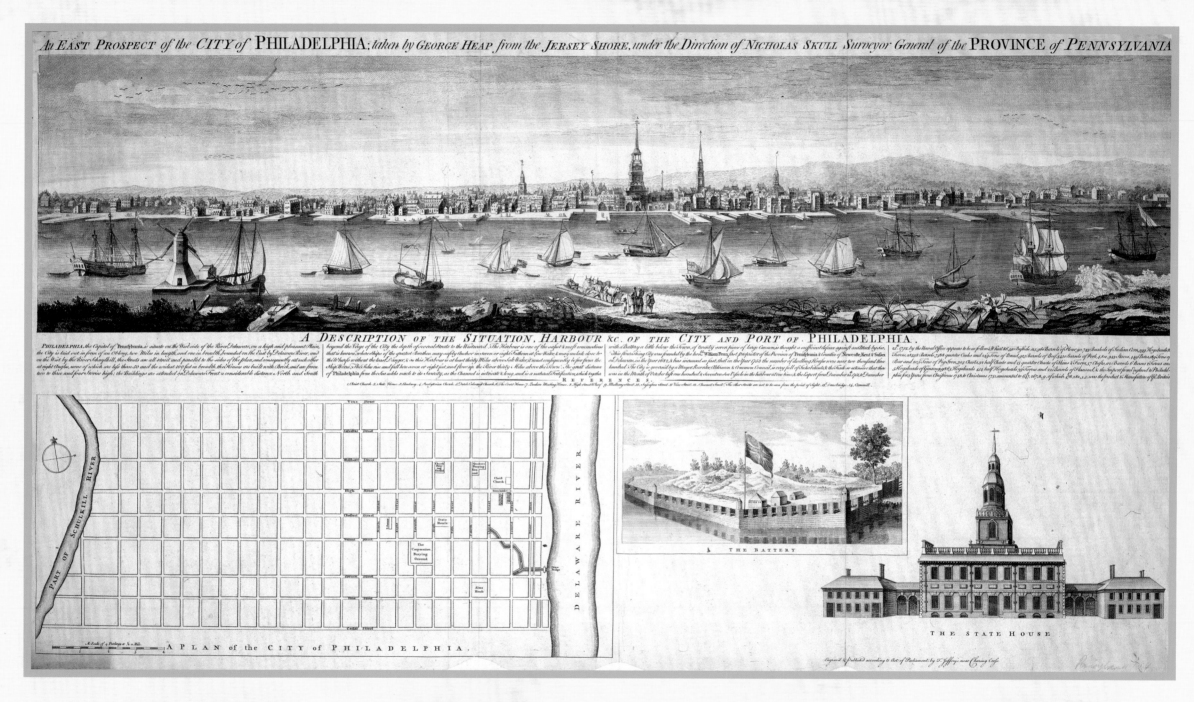

An EAST PROSPECT of the CITY of PHILADELPHIA; taken by GEORGE HEAP from the JERSEY SHORE, under the Direction of NICHOLAS SKULL Surveyor General of the PROVINCE of PENNSYLVANIA

A DESCRIPTION of the SITUATION, HARBOUR &c. OF THE CITY AND PORT OF PHILADELPHIA.

A PLAN of the CITY of PHILADELPHIA.

THE BATTERY

THE STATE HOUSE

ABOVE: This dramatic perspective shows the east prospect of the city of Philadelphia. It was drawn by George Heap under the direction of Nicholas Skull, who was the Surveyor General of the province of Pennsylvania. The map also shows a street layout, plus a view of the state house and the battery with the union flag. The primary view has a key to identify certain major buildings. The map was published by T. Jefferys of Charing Cross in London. Philadelphia was founded in 1682, and by the start of the 18th century had become a flourishing commercial center. Not only did the trade to and from Pennsylvania pass through the city, but the city also served Delaware, the lower part of New Jersey and Maryland. By 1760, shortly after the date of this drawing, Philadelphia had a population in excess of 23,000, and by the eve of the revolution this figure exceeded 40,000. This made the city the largest in the North American colonies and one of the largest in the empire; it was probably only exceeded by London, Edinburgh, and Dublin.

FOLLOWING PAGE: This plan of the city of Philadelphia and its environs (showing the improved parts) was dedicated to the mayor, aldermen, and citizens thereof by their most obedient servant, John Hills, surveyor and draughtsman, May 30, 1796, and published by him in Philadelphia the following year. The map was engraved by John Cooke of Hendon, Middlesex, near London. Pennsylvania had become the second state to adopt the US constitution, on December 12, 1787. The city was the capital of the US, a position it held from 1790 through to 1800, as well as capital of the state of Pennsylvania, a role it fulfilled until 1799. Drawn to a scale of about 1 inch to 600 feet, the map records all the buildings, the names of the wharves along the Delaware River, wooded areas, and land beyond the city's boundaries.

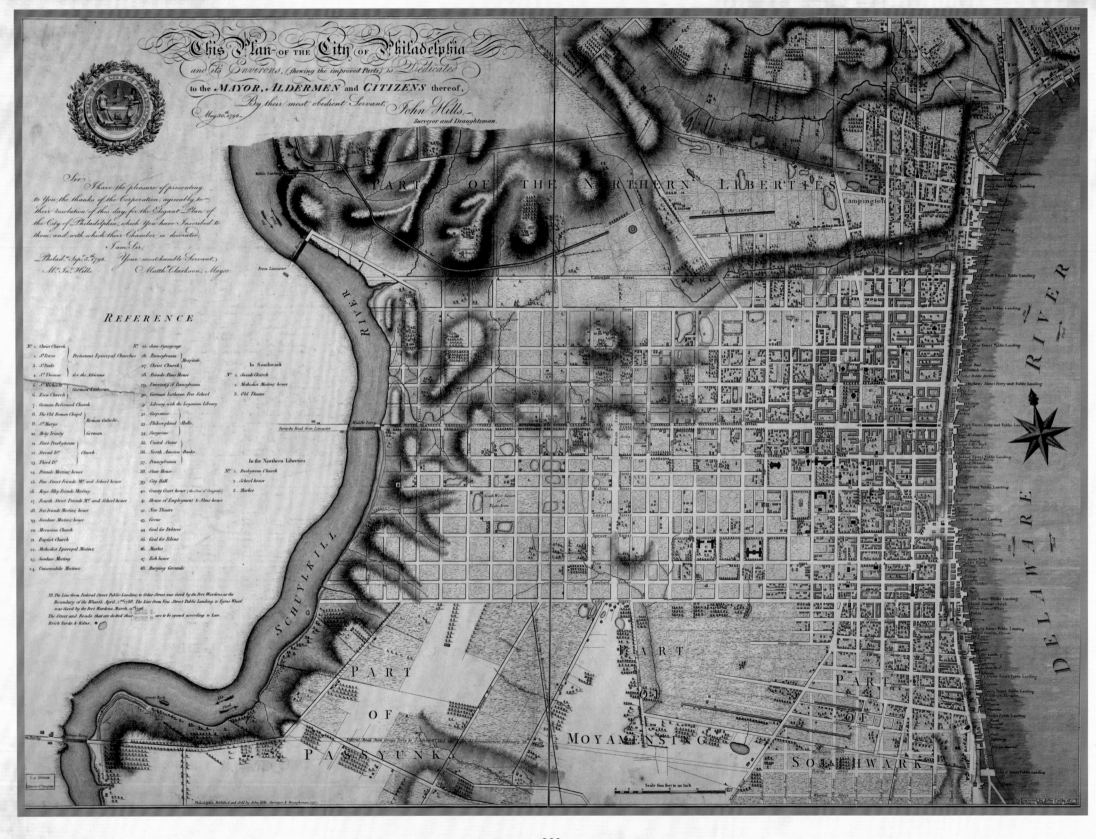

Today, Prague—or Praha in Czech—is the capital of the Czech Republic, with a population of over 1.2 million. It is situated on the River Vltava in historic Bohemia and the city center has been on Unesco's list of World Heritage Sites since 1992.

There is evidence of settlement in the area stretching back to the Palaeolithic Age, with the course of the river being used as a trade route. Celtic, Germanic, and various Slavic tribes followed and occupied the area before the Slavic Premyslids came to prominence in the early 8th century.

In 1306 this dynasty came to an end and the title passed to John of Luxembourg, who had married Eliska, the sister of the last Premyslid ruler. It was during the 14th century that Prague had its first golden age, with Emperor Charles IV making it his home. In 1338, John of Luxembourg gave permission for the Old Town to erect a town hall; in 1344, Prague was elevated to the status of an archbishopric; in 1348, both the New Town and Charles University—the first such establishment in central Europe—were founded; and, in 1357, the new Charles Bridge was started.

However, the next century was to witness controversy, inspired by the teachings of the reformer Jan Hus. Hus advocated considerable change within the Catholic church and as a result he was excommunicated by the Pope and burnt at the stake in 1410. Four years later, on July 30, 1419, supporters of Hus stormed the town hall to release Hussite prisoners.

The period of Habsburg rule in the 16th century was a further golden age for Prague. In 1583 it again became the center of the Holy Roman Empire, and the court of Rudolph II was based there. With a passionate interest in art and science, Rudolph drew many of the great thinkers of the age. However, religious and political tensions were never far from the surface and these exploded again early in the 17th century.

Prague remained part of the Holy Roman Empire until it was dissolved in 1806, becoming part of Austro-Hungary until after World War I. Between 1919 and 1939 Prague was capital of an independent Czechoslovakia, and after the defeat of Nazi Germany it was restored to this role—albeit as a client state of the Soviet Union. Following the Velvet Revolution of 1989 democracy was restored to Czechoslovakia, although in 1993 the two parts of the state divided into the Czech Republic and Slovakia.

PRAGUE
CZECH REPUBLIC

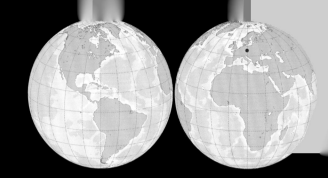

BELOW: Prague taken by the Ikonos satellite in 2004. The 1740 map on page 203 is not outlined as it covers a larger area than this. Note the upper image of page 202 shows Prague Castle—the largest in the world.

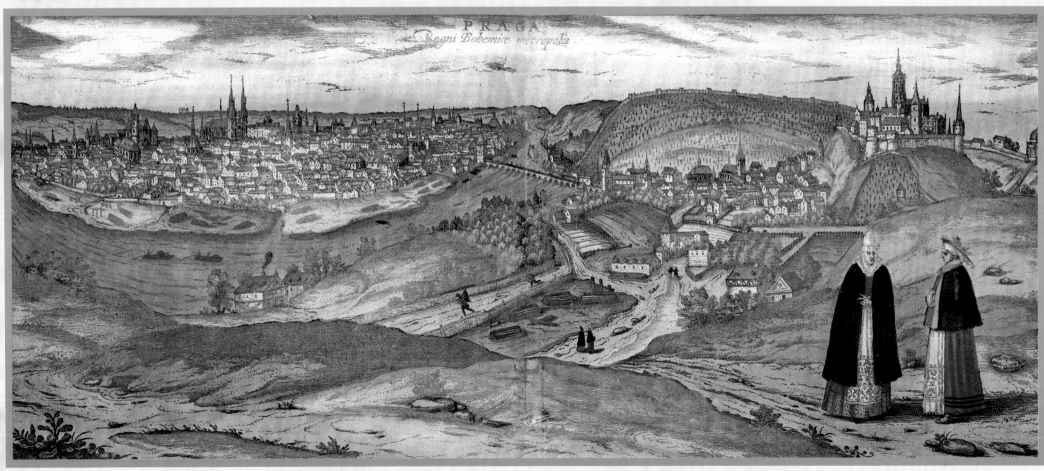

LEFT: Prague expanded rapidly during the 16th century as it was one of the most important cities in the Holy Roman Empire and hosted the imperial court from 1583. This pair of illustrations shows Prazsky Hrad (Prague Castle) in detail, with the Katedrále Sv Vita, Václava a Vojtecha (Cathedral of St Vitus), at its core. Prague Castle, with its origins in the 9th century A.D., is the largest castle in the world. The lower of the two illustrations shows the relationship between the castle and the city; between the castle and the Charles Bridge— the only river crossing in the city until the mid-18th century—were the districts of Staré Mesto (or Old Town) and Malé Strena (the lesser quarter occupied by merchants and craftsmen). Across the river were the districts of Nové Mesto (New Town), founded in 1348 by Charles IV, which was the newest of the four communities that ultimately formed the city, and Josefov, the Jewish quarter of the city that had its origins in the 10th century.

RIGHT: Produced in France and dedicated to the Prince of Soubise, this map records the French and Austrian forces around the city of Prague during the War of Austrian Succession. On October 20, 1740, Emperor Charles VI died; under the empire's constitution only a male could inherit the throne and Charles had died without male issue. Recognizing this, he had sought to obtain recognition that his eldest daughter, Marie Theresa, could succeed, but in this endeavor he was thwarted. His death, therefore, led to a power struggle with the great European powers seeking to gain advantage. In 1741 the French army under François-Marie de Broglie (1671–1745) advanced and captured the city of Prague on November 26, 1741. In June 1742, however, superior Austrian forces led by Prince Charles Alexander of Lorraine (1712–80) reached the city in June 1742 and effectively surrounded the French force and besieged the city. The siege was raised on September 14, 1742 as French reinforcements advanced, but the bulk of the French army withdrew from the city on December 16, 1742, leaving a small force under François de Chevert (1695–1769) to defend it; this too was soon to withdraw. This map shows the situation following the arrival of the Austrian force to the south of the city, with de Broglie's force located to the north.

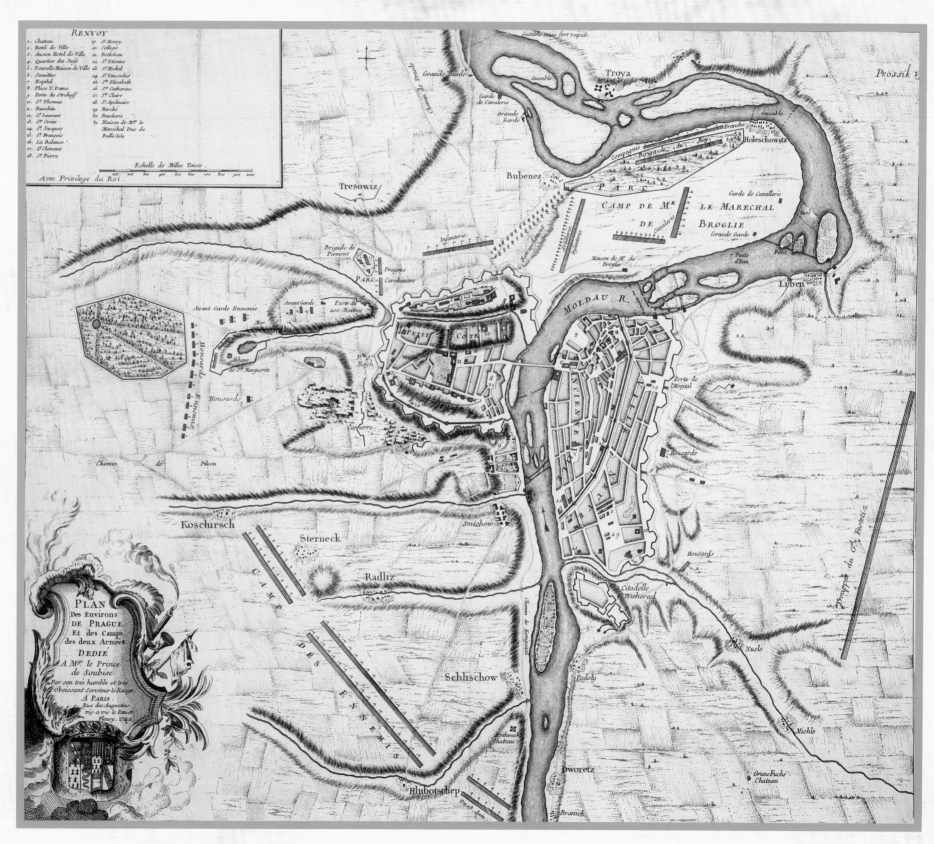

QUEBEC

CANADA

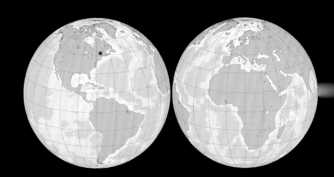

Québec City—known as such to differentiate it from the province of Québec, of which it is the capital—has a population of around half a million. Its city ramparts are the only surviving fortified city walls in North America and were declared a UNESCO World Heritage Site in 1985. The city is located on the St Lawrence at a point where the river narrows considerably, a geographical feature that helped give the city its name (Kébec being the Algonquin word for "where the river narrows").

The city was founded on July 3, 1608 by the French explorer Samuel de Champlain. As with other French settlements established in North America in the 17th century, it was primarily a trading post, with furs in particular being much sought after by the native tribes.

Although the peninsula offered a considerable defensive advantage, the settlement was first captured by the English in 1629, and another assault was attempted in 1690.

Recognizing the potential threat to the city, the French constructed defensive walls and the city was widely regarded as impregnable. However, in 1759 the British, under General Wolfe, launched a new attack supported by 40 ships and an army of 10,000, finally capturing the city. The British occupation and possession of New France was formally recognized by the Treaty of Paris in 1763.

In 1774 the British government passed the Quebec Act, guaranteeing the rights of the Québécois to religious freedom. This was undoubtedly instrumental in ensuring the city remained loyal to King George III when relations with the original Thirteen Colonies soured in the early 1770s.

In 1791 further legislation in London, the Constitutional Act, created the colonies of Upper (English-speaking) Canada and Lower (French-speaking) Canada; the latter had Québec as its capital. This was to remain the constitutional position until 1841 when the two were united into a single colony and then, in 1867, the self-governing Dominion of Canada was established.

In the 19th century the city grew as a port—becoming the third most important in North America for a period—and as a location for emigration from Europe. Today, it is an important commercial and cultural center, and the focal point for French culture in the country.

BELOW: Quebec as photographed by Landsat 7 in 2008.

LA GRANDE RIVIERE ou DE St LAURENS.

Coste de la Pointe de L'Isle d'Orleans

POINTE DE LEVY

Les 34 Vaisseaux Anglois

Bon Mouillage a 17. Brasses.

Village de Beauport

Maison Seigneur

Cap aux Diamants

Cul de sac oules petits Batime. as hiver

QUEBEC

Les 42 Chaloupes qui debarquerent les Anglois la Canardiere

Chemin de

Coteau de Ster Genevieve

ND. des Anges

QUBBEC, Ville de l'Amerique Septentrionale dans la Nouvelle France avec Titre d'Eveché, Situeé sur le Fleuve de St. Laurens a 310 Degrez 17 Minutes de Longitude, et 46 Degrez 55 Minutes de Latitude. Elle fut Assiegée par les Anglois, sur les Francois, par qui elle est encore possedée l'an 1670 depuis le 16e Octobre Jusqu'au 22e du meme. Mois. Monst de Frontenac etant pour lors Gouverneur du Pays qui leur fit honteusement lever le Siege.

Renvoy des Chifres qui se trouvent dans la Ville de Quebec

1. Le Fort Louis ou Loge Mr. le Comte de Frontenac.
2. N.D. et le Seminaire
3. Hospice des Recolets
4. les Peres Jesuites
5. le Urselines
6. l'Hospital
7. les Filles de la Congregation
8. Batterie de huit Cannons
9. Platte Forme, ou il y a une Batterie de 3 Cannons
10. Place ou en eleva en 1685 le Buste du Roy
11. Batterie de 3 Cannons
12. Do.
13. le Palais
14. l'Eveché
15. Moulin ou il y a une Batterie de trois Cannons
16. Batterie de 3 Cannons
17. Canots pour découvrir pandant la Nuit

Abr. Daubant delin

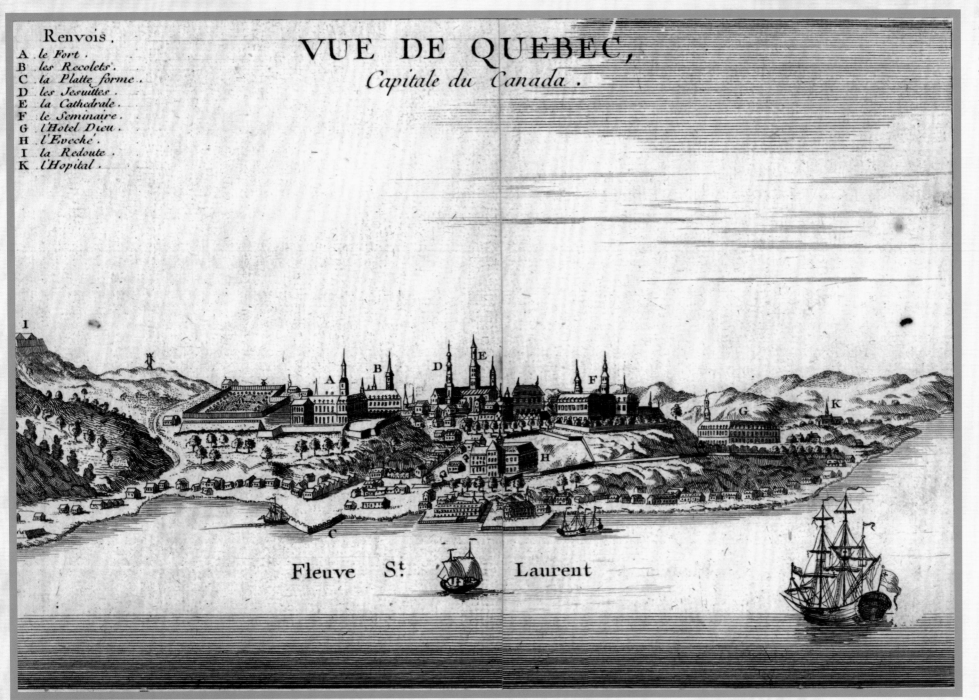

Renvois.

A. le Fort.
B. les Recolets.
C. la Platte forme.
D. les Jesuittes.
E. la Cathedrale.
F. le Seminaire.
G. l'Hotel Dieu.
H. l'Eveché.
I. la Redoute.
K. l'Hopital.

VUE DE QUEBEC,
Capitale du Canada.

Fleuve St. Laurent

RIGHT: This is described as "A Plan of Quebec The Capital of New France or Canada." The inset shows the course of the St Lau[w]rence River from Chaudiere Fall to Orleans Island, with the dispositions made by the English under the command of Sir W. Phipps to besiege the city in 1690. Engraved by Thomas Jefferys at Charing Cross, the map was published on October 9, 1758. The scale is about 96 yards to 1 inch, with the inset at 2.75 miles to 1 inch. With British-French tension rising, it was inevitable that attention would again turn to the possible acquisition of the remaining French territory in North America. The legend to the right of the map gives a succinct account, from contemporary knowledge, of the history of Quebec up to 1758. The city's strong defensive position is self-evident from the map, and the difficulties faced by the British General, James Wolfe, in attempting to capture it during the Seven Years' War are also clear. In the event, despite being fatally wounded himself, Wolfe's forces were to successfully breach the French defenses and capture the city in September 1759. The French commander, Montcalm, also lost his life during the battle.

ABOVE: This panoramic view of Quebec shows the city, described as the capital of (French) Canada, from the east in the period immediately prior to the British capture. Produced by Georges-Louis Le Rouge, the illustration portrays a number of the city's most prominent buildings.

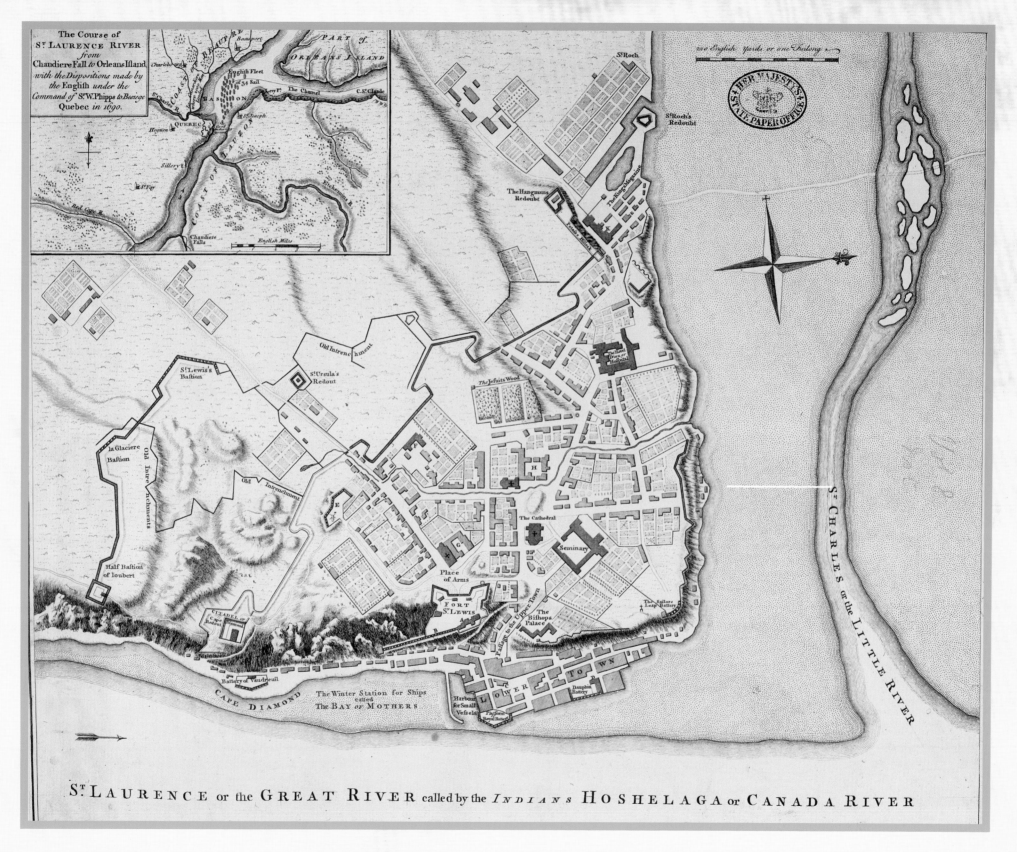

The Course of
ST. LAURENCE RIVER
from
Chaudiere Fall to Orleans Island,
with the Dispositions made by
the English under the
Command of Sr. W. Phipps to Besiege
Quebec in 1690.

220 English Yards or one Furlong

ST. LAURENCE or the GREAT RIVER called by the INDIANS HOSHELAGA or CANADA RIVER

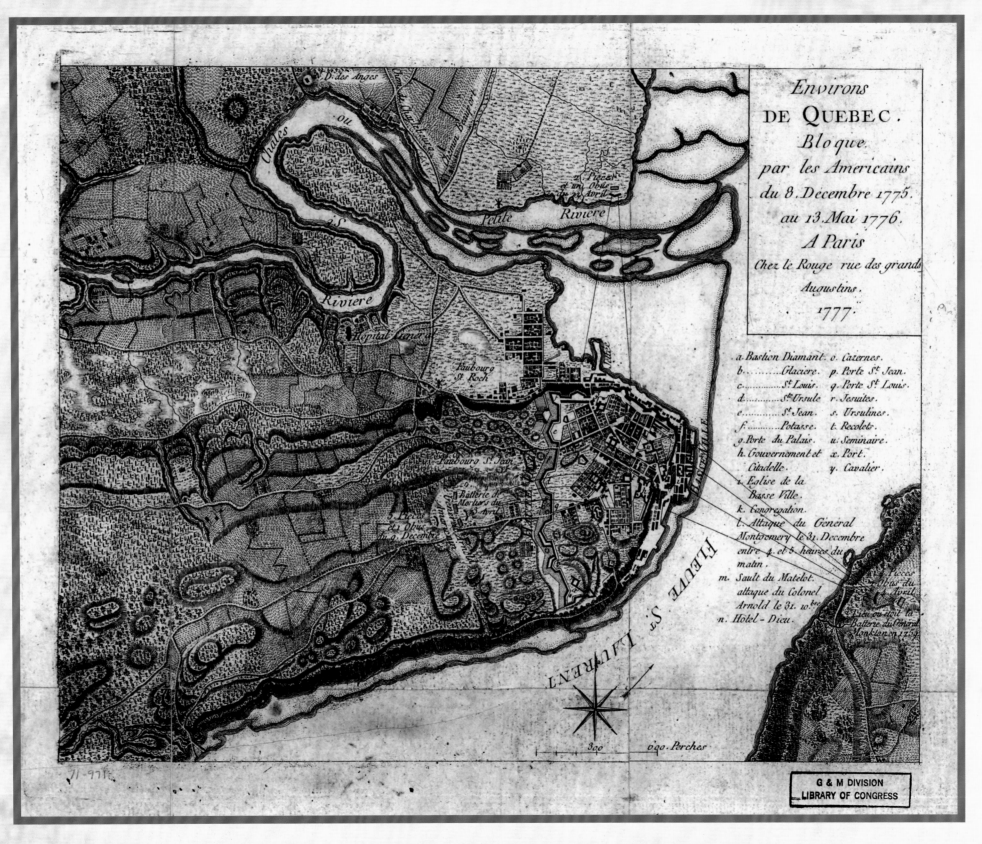

Environs
DE QUEBEC.
Bloque
par les Americains
du 8. Decembre 1775.
au 13. Mai 1776.
A Paris
Chez le Rouge rue des grands
Augustins.
1777.

a. Bastion Diamant.   o. Casernes.
b. .... Glaciere.   p. Porte St Jean.
c. .... St Louis.   q. Porte St Louis.
d. .... St Ursule.   r. Jesuites.
e. .... St Jean.   s. Ursulines.
f. .... Potasse.   t. Recolets.
g. Porte du Palais.   u. Seminaire.
h. Gouvernement et   x. Port.
   Citadelle.   y. Cavalier.
i. Eglise de la
   Basse Ville.
k. Congregation.
l. Attaque du Général
   Montgomery le 31. Decembre
   entre 4. et 5. heures du
   matin.
m. Sault du Matelot.
   attaque du Colonel
   Arnold le 31. 10bre.
n. Hotel - Dieu.

FLEUVE St LAURENT

300   600 Perches

LEFT: Even after control of Quebec was ceded to Britain from France, there remained a military threat, particularly as relations between Britain and the future United States deteriorated. This map, recorded as a "Plan of the City and Environs of Quebec, with its Siege and Blockade by the Americans from the 8th of December 1775 to the 13th of May 1776," was published by William Faden, successor to Thomas Jefferys, St Martin's Lane, London. The Americans had laid siege to the city in the hope of persuading the French-Canadians to come out in support of them in their struggle against the British. In the spring of 1776 a British frigate, HMS Surprise, sailed to Quebec, forcing the Americans to retreat. In the event, subsequent French-Canadian support of the British ensured that Canada remained British after the Thirteen Colonies gained their independence.

RIO DE JANEIRO

BRAZIL

The second largest city in Brazil, Rio de Janeiro—River of January—is the capital of the state of the same name and was the capital of the country from 1763 through to 1960. With a population of over six million, it is situated slightly north of the Tropic of Capricorn to the east of São Paulo.

The first permanent European settlement was established in 1555 when two ships and 600 soldiers under the command of a Frenchman, Nicolas Durand de Villegaignon, landed. The new settlement was called France Antarctique, although de Villegaignon was to leave two years later. The city of São Sebastião do Rio de Janeiro was founded on March 1, 1565 by Estácio de Sá, a Portuguese officer, as a base from which to expel the French settlers. In 1567 the French were defeated but the area remained vulnerable to attack from the enemies of Portugal thereafter. The division of South America between Spain and Portugal had been settled by the Treaty of Tordesillas of 1494, in which Pope Alexander VI fixed a line of demarcation 370 miles west of the Azores; anything to the east of that line was Portuguese and to the west Spanish.

The 16th century was the apogee of the Portuguese maritime and trading empire and Rio became one of the most important transit ports for ships trading through this empire. As a result, its defenses were strengthened and treaties were negotiated with the local native tribes. In 1720 gold was discovered inland and the city became important as a transhipment point for the metal trade to Europe. The city became the capital of all of Portugal's colonies in South America in 1763; in 1808, following the French conquest of the Iberian peninsula, the Portuguese king, John VI, and his government fled from Lisbon and made Rio the national capital.

In 1821 John VI returned to Portugal, leaving his son Pedro I (1798–1834) as Prince Regent. Pedro I was succeeded in turn by his son, Pedro II (1825–91; crowned 1841), who reigned until the revolution in 1889 that established the Brazilian republic. Throughout the period of the monarchy Rio remained the country's capital, a role it continued to hold until the new city of Brasilia was officially declared the new capital on April 21, 1960.

BELOW: Satellite image of the city of Rio de Janeiro and its surrounding area taken by Landsat 5 in 2006 and Spot-5 in 2005. The map on page 210 is not identified as it covers a larger area than the satellite image. Note the large amount of land reclmation that has led to significant differences between the coastal outline in the last century.

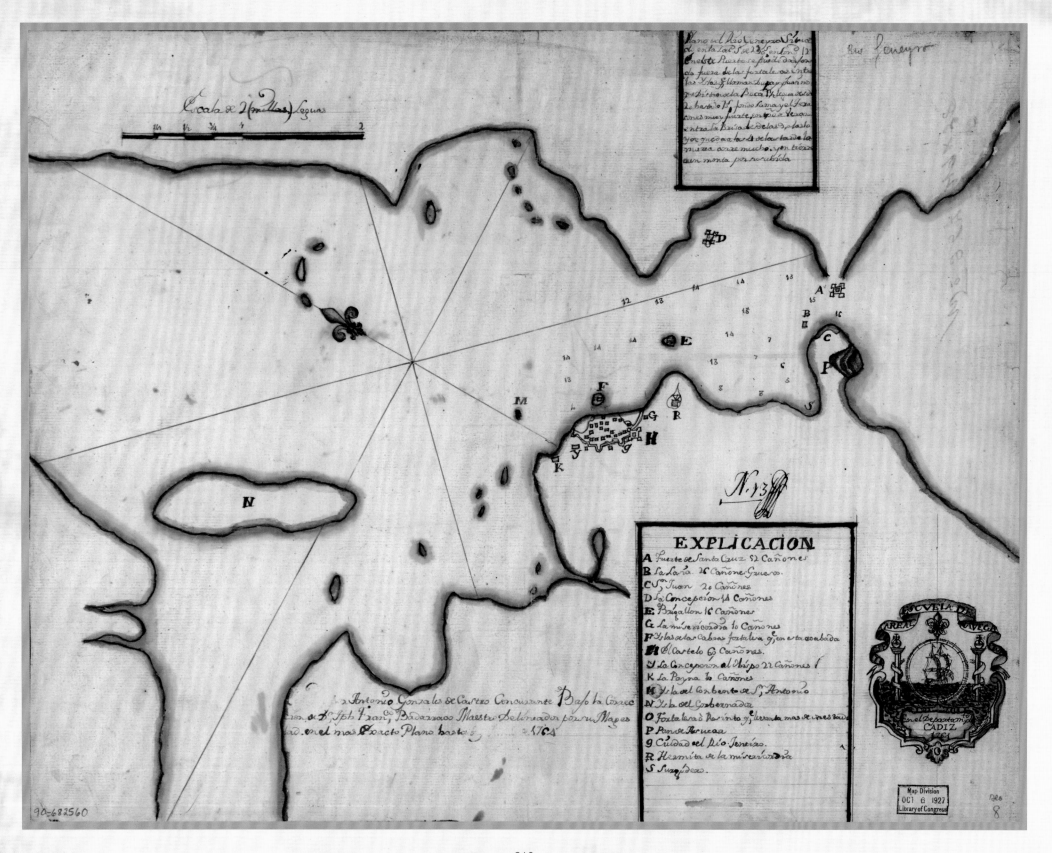

LEFT: Produced to a scale of around 1:91,500, this map records Guanabara Bay and the Rio de Janeiro harbor area. It was compiled by Antonio Gonzales de Castro, and is oriented with north toward the upper left.

RIGHT: Compiled by E. de la Michellerie, this map records the church parishes that formed the city of Rio de Janeiro at this time. Each parish is delineated in a different colour: Candelaria—yellow; San José—pink; Sacramento—blue; Santa Anna—green; and Santa Rita—peach.

FOLLOWING PAGE: Described as a new plan of the city of Rio de Janeiro, this map records the growth of the city by the middle of the 19th century. It was compiled by E. & H. Laemmert.

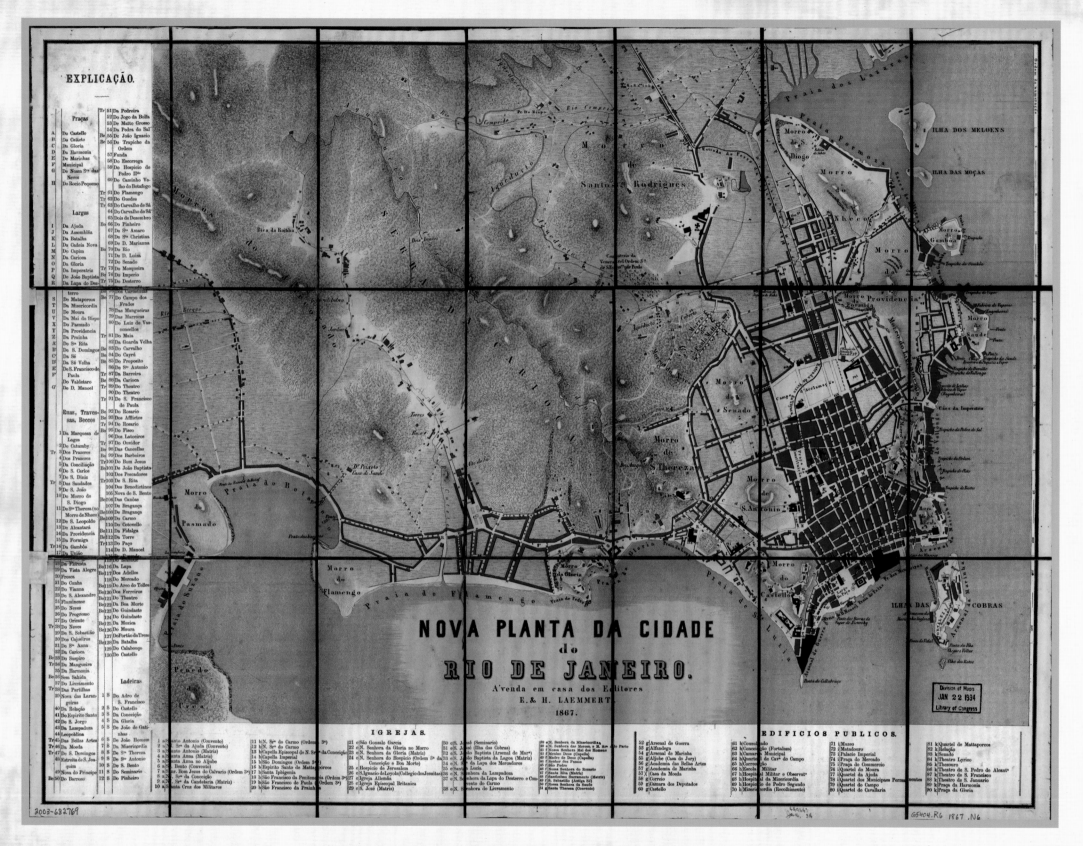

NOVA PLANTA DA CIDADE
do
RIO DE JANEIRO.
A venda em casa dos Editores
E. & H. LAEMMERT.
1867.

ROME

ITALY

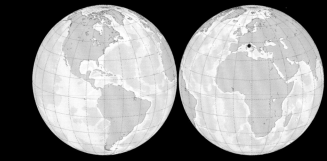

One of the most historically important cities in the world, Rome (Roma) has a continuous history stretching back almost three millennia. Now the capital city of Italy with an urban population approaching three million, it is also the center of the Roman Catholic faith worldwide. The historic core is a UNESCO World Heritage Site and one of the world's most popular tourist destinations.

The city stands on the River Tiber some 15 miles inland from its estuary. It was built upon seven hills—Aventine, Caelian, Capitoline, Esquiline, Palatine, Quirinal, and Viminal—which surrounded a ford across the river.

According to legend, Rome was founded by the twins Romulus—from whom the city derives its name—and Remus in the middle of the 8th century B.C. From the late 5th century B.C. onward the power of Rome expanded, and the empire was to reach its apogee in the early 2nd century A.D., when it stretched from the British Isles to Asia Minor and from the River Rhine to North Africa.

In the early 7th century Pope Gregory took control of the city, establishing it as the capital of a new papal state. On Christmas Day in 800A.D. the Frankish ruler Charlemagne was crowned as the new Holy Roman Emperor—defender of the Church. However, hopes for secular protection soon faded and, instead, there was a long-running struggle for supremacy between pope and emperor.

The 15th century saw the Italian Renaissance, and a succession of popes embraced the cultural movement as a means of strengthening their authority. Artists such as Bramante, Raphael, Cellini, and Michalangelo were hired to create the buildings, statues, and works of art that transformed the city.

By and large Rome remained under papal rule until the mid-19th century, when Italian nationalism grew significant and Rome was again briefly declared a republic. In 1861 Rome was declared the capital of Italy even though it was still under the control of the pope. During the 1860s the last vestiges of the papal states were under French protection. Not until this protection was lifted in 1870, owing to the outbreak of the Franco-Prussian War, were Italian troops able to capture Rome. The Italian conquest resulted in the creation of a new state—the Vatican City—over which the pope still retains control However, it was not until the Concordat with Mussolini in 1929 that the papacy recognized the Italian state and its sovereignty over Rome outside this enclave.

BELOW: Satellite image of the city of Rome on the meandering River Tiber as obtained from the Landsat 5 satellite in 2006.

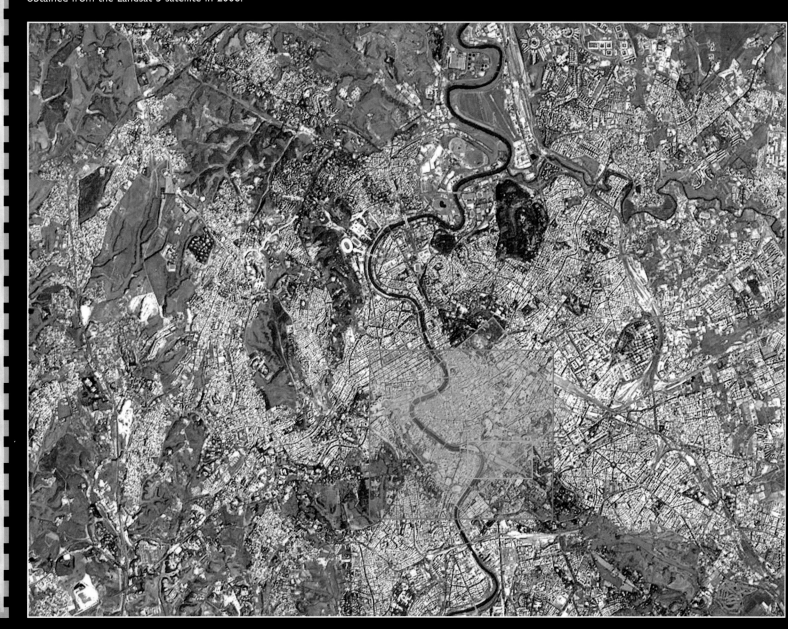

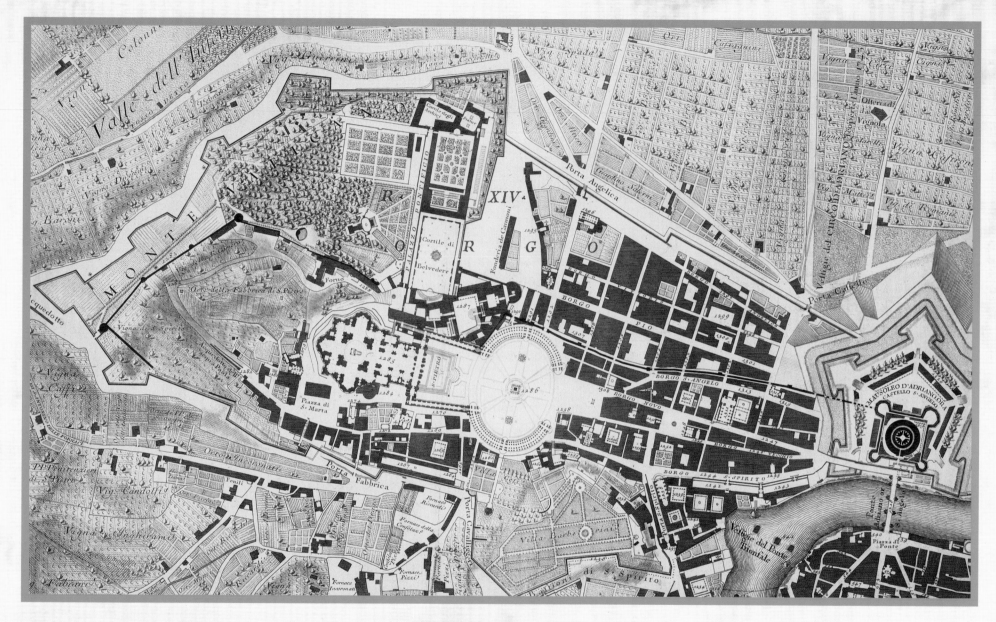

LEFT: This and the next map show two sections of a large-scale map of the city of Rome in the mid-18th century. Engraved by Rocco and Stefano Pozzi, Pietro Campana, and Carlo Nolli, the map is dedicated to Pope Benedict XIV. This section shows the area of the Vatican; at this date Rome and the papal states were ruled by the pope from Rome, and the concept of the Vatican City as a sovereign enclave within Rome did not exist. It was not until the Concordat with Mussolini in 1929 that the Papacy recognized the Italian state and its sovereignty over Rome outside the enclave. The map illustrated here shows the future Vatican City as it existed in 1748. It was in 1610 that the cupola over St Peter's was completed, and the familiar colonnade in St Peter's Square was completed to the designs of Bellini in 1665.

LEFT: This view toward the northeast illustrates how the city of Rome straddles the River Tiber. On the left-hand side of the map—on the west bank of the river—can be seen the complex that today forms the enclave of the Vatican City; at this time, however, all of Rome was controlled by the papacy. Construction work on the great basilica of St Peter's would not be completed until the early 17th century. Between the Vatican and the river is the Castel sant'Angelo; this fortification was erected in the 15th century on the site of Emperor Hadrian's mausoleum. When threatened by revolt or enemy armies, the pope and his entourage were able to take refuge in the castle. In 1527, for example, when the city of Rome was successfully besieged and sacked, Pope Clement VII withstood the marauding Germans by retreating here. Apart from its defensive use, the castle was also used as a papal prison. Rome was built originally on seven hills; on this map they are numbered according to the key. In the center of the city on the east bank of the river can be seen the Pantheon; originally built during the reign of the Emperor Hadrian, the building was subsequently used as a Christian church and as a mausoleum. It is one of the few buildings from the Roman era to survive in reasonably good order; the map portrays the ruins of others within the city walls in varying degrees of decay and neglect.

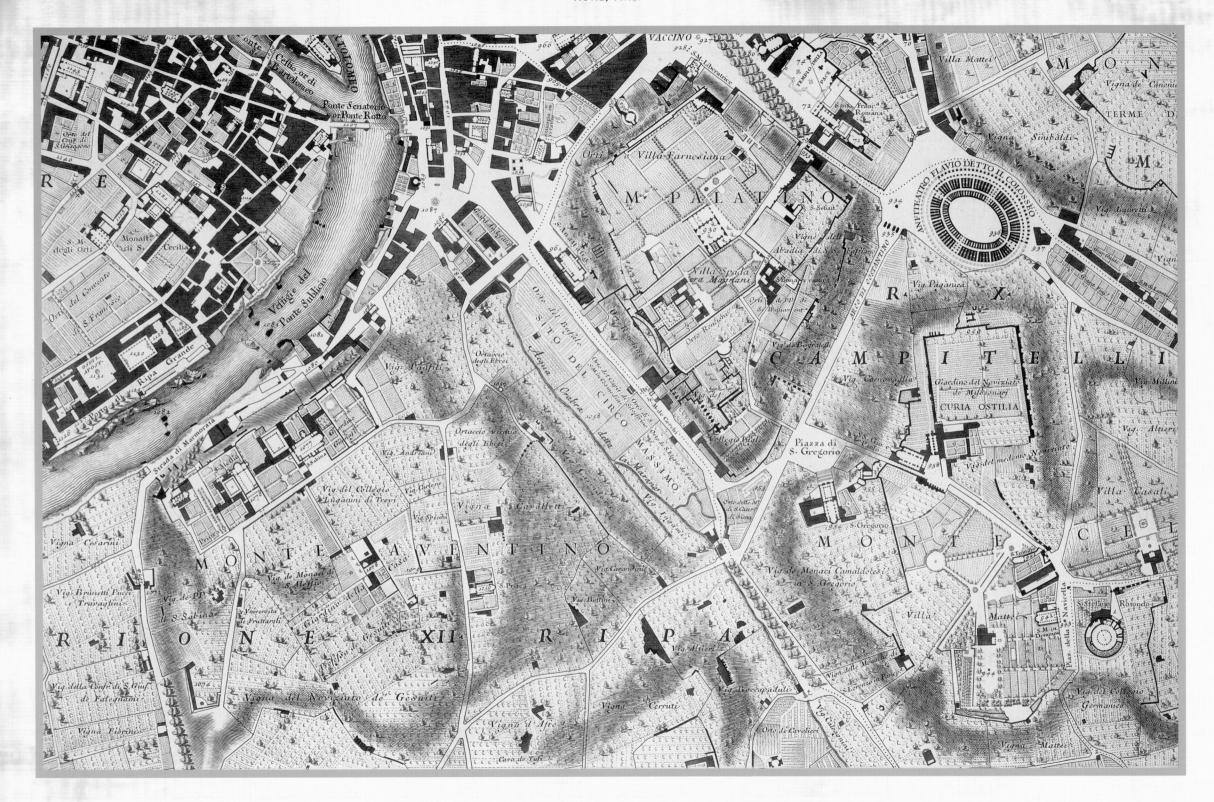

LEFT: This second extract of the 1748 map shows part of the erstwhile imperial Rome in ruin, concentrating on the area around the Coliseum. Following the collapse of the Roman Empire and the relentless assaults upon the city of Rome by the various barbarian tribes, the population rapidly diminished and the space occupied by the inhabited part of the city also declined. As a result, large tracts of the historic city were left largely derelict, but they were often plundered for the buildings of the new city. It was only as increasing awareness of the importance of these historical structures became greater that this destruction was largely to cease and preservation undertaken. See also the map of Imperial Rome from *Civitates* on page 7.

RIGHT: Produced by Bradshaw & Blacklock of Manchester, England, this map records the city of Rome in the mid-19th century. The map is aligned with north to the left. Clearly visible is the Vatican City and the Castello sant'Angelo to the west of the Tiber. To the east—ie toward the top of the page—is the city's main railway station—now known as Stazione Termini. At this stage in Rome's history the city was still ruled by the papacy, although the pope's power was largely maintained as a result of support of French troops who had occupied the city following the short-lived Roman republic of 1848–9.

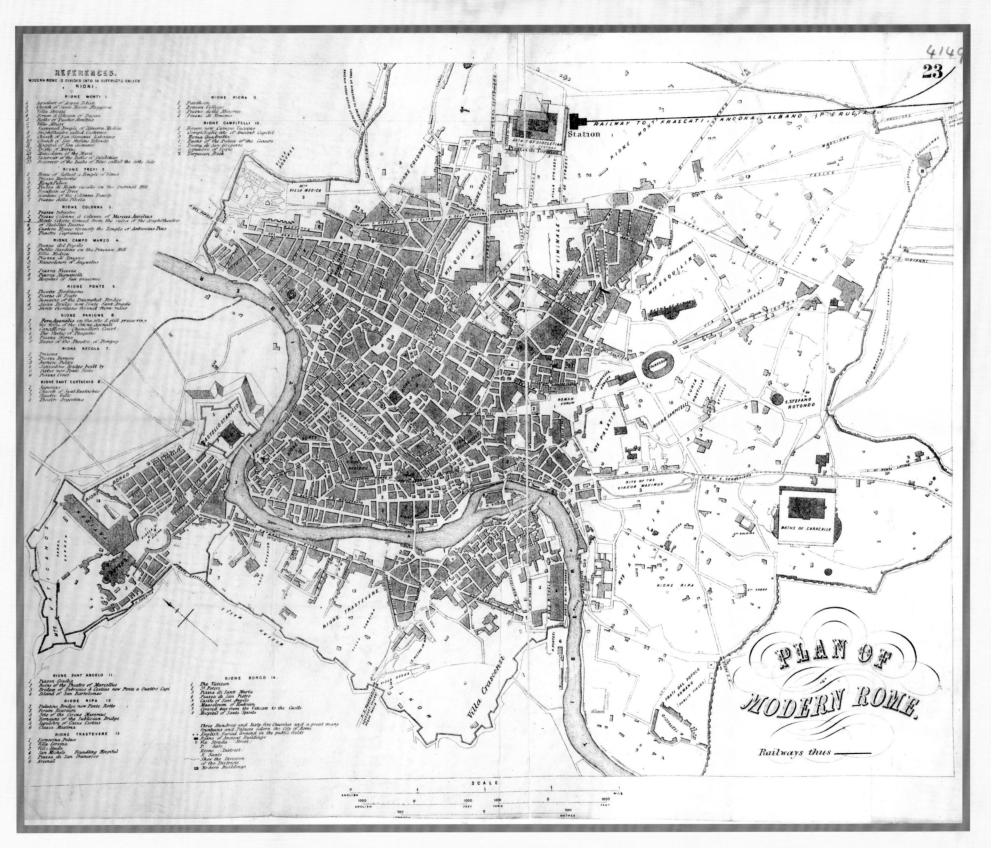

SAN FRANCISCO
UNITED STATES

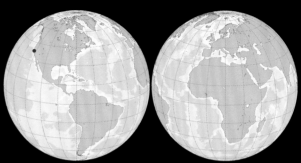

With a population of some 750, 000, San Francisco is the fourth largest city in the state of California. It is built on 40 or so hills situated on the 7.5 mile-long peninsula that separates San Francisco Bay from the Pacific Ocean.

The first European settlement was established in 1776 with a Spanish fort, along with a mission about 4 miles inland. However, in 1821 the region achieved independence from Spain and a new country—Mexico—was born. William Richardson, an Englishmen, established a settlement—Yerba Buena—outside the mission in 1835, which attracted new settlers. War broke out in 1845 between Mexico and the US, and on July 7, 1846, Commodore John D. Sloat claimed California for the US. Yerba Buena's name was changed to San Francisco the following year.

With the discovery of gold in the Sierra Nevada, the population rose from 1,000 in 1848 to 25,000 by the end of the following year. The city became the largest in the western US, until it was overtaken by Los Angeles after World War I. Transport connections with the rest of the country were improved in 1869 with the opening of the Central Pacific Railroad.

Not all was positive, however; in late 1855 refugees from the Far East brought cholera to the city. With the rapid expansion of the city in the preceding decade, sanitation was poor and a cholera epidemic ensued. This was followed in October 1865 by a major earthquake, and in July 1877 antagonism against the migrant Chinese population led to rioting.

The earthquake of 1865 was, however, just a foretaste of the city's defining disaster—the great earthquake and fire of 1906. The fire raged for three days, destroying some 80 percent of the city. At the time it was estimated that almost 500 people lost their lives, but this estimate has in recent years been substantially increased. The city was quickly rebuilt, although grandiose plans for redevelopment along the lines of the 19th-century redevelopment of Paris by Haussmann proved impractical.

The city continued to grow during the first decades of the 20th century. During World War II it was one of the main bases for the war in the Pacific, and it was in the War Memorial Opera House, opened in 1932, that the conference that established the United Nations in 1945 was held.

Since the war, the city has undergone further growth and economic transformation; however, the continuing threat posed by the San Andreas Fault remains.

BELOW: Spot satellite image of San Francisco, Golden Gate Bridge at top; Alcatraz the small island center right; and Treasure Island bottom right.

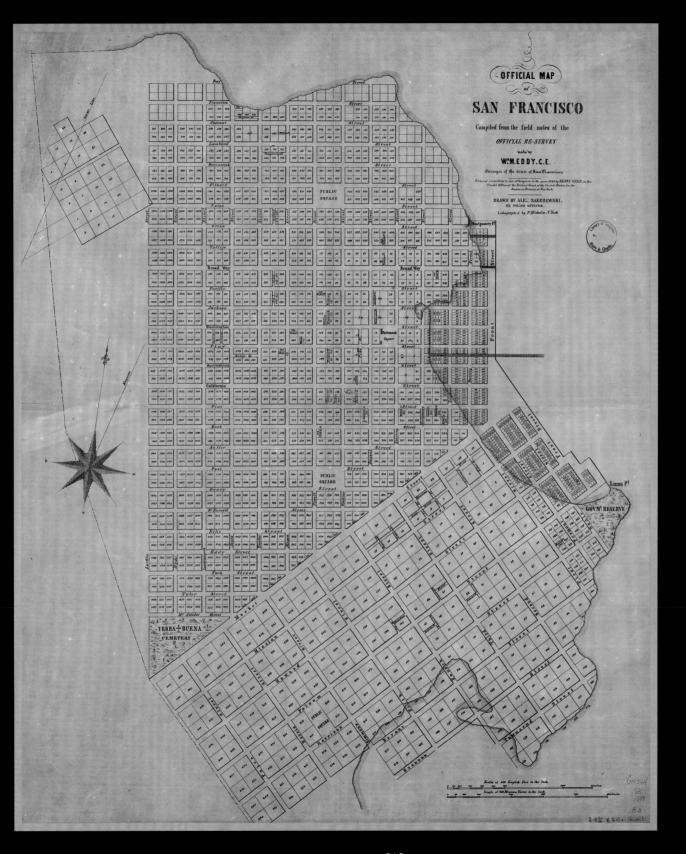

LEFT: This is an official map of San Francisco drawn to a scale of 1:6,600. It was compiled from the field notes of the official re-survey made by William. M. Eddy, surveyor of the town of San Francisco; drawn by Alexander Zakrzewski; and lithographed by F. Michelin. Yerba Buena was renamed San Francisco in 1847 and US possession of California was confirmed in 1848 as a result of the Treaty of Guadalupe Hidalgo, which settled the Mexican-US war and saw California and other territory ceded by Mexico to the US. In the same year, gold was discovered and a gold rush ensued. This resulted in the massive growth of the city, with the population rising from 2,000 in 1848 to 35,000 the following year.

FOLLOWING PAGE: On April 18, 1906 the city of San Francisco was hit by a massive earthquake measuring 8.3 on the Richter Scale. More destructive, however, was the fire that broke out shortly afterward. The earthquake had destroyed much of the city's infrastructure, including its water mains, which made fighting the fire all the more difficult. With the aid of finance from the Federal Government, the city was rebuilt and this map, produced by the California Promotion Committee, records the buildings either built or under construction since the fire. The map records the area of destruction as 4 square miles, and is oriented with north toward the lower right. An inset at the bottom left records the relative size and location of the destroyed area within the whole city.

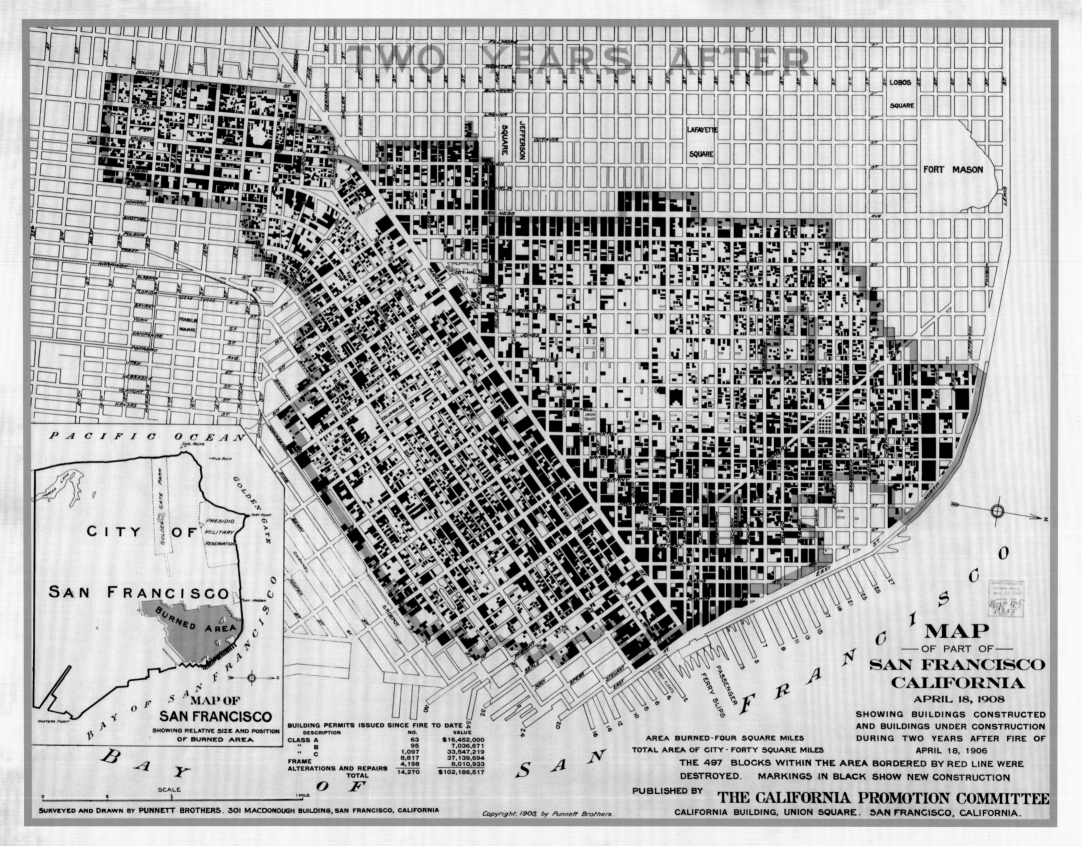

TWO YEARS AFTER

MAP OF SAN FRANCISCO

SHOWING RELATIVE SIZE AND POSITION OF BURNED AREA

BUILDING PERMITS ISSUED SINCE FIRE TO DATE		
DESCRIPTION	NO.	VALUE
CLASS A	63	$16,452,000
" B	95	7,036,671
" C	1,097	33,547,219
FRAME	8,817	37,139,694
ALTERATIONS AND REPAIRS	4,198	8,010,933
TOTAL	14,270	$102,186,517

AREA BURNED - FOUR SQUARE MILES
TOTAL AREA OF CITY - FORTY SQUARE MILES

MAP
— OF PART OF —
SAN FRANCISCO
CALIFORNIA
APRIL 18, 1908

SHOWING BUILDINGS CONSTRUCTED AND BUILDINGS UNDER CONSTRUCTION DURING TWO YEARS AFTER FIRE OF APRIL 18, 1906

THE 497 BLOCKS WITHIN THE AREA BORDERED BY RED LINE WERE DESTROYED.   MARKINGS IN BLACK SHOW NEW CONSTRUCTION

PUBLISHED BY

THE CALIFORNIA PROMOTION COMMITTEE
CALIFORNIA BUILDING, UNION SQUARE.   SAN FRANCISCO, CALIFORNIA.

SURVEYED AND DRAWN BY PUNNETT BROTHERS. 301 MACDONOUGH BUILDING, SAN FRANCISCO, CALIFORNIA

Copyright, 1908, by Punnett Brothers.

SCALE

TANGIER

MOROCCO

ith a population approaching 700,000 Tangier, lies on the North African coast slightly to the west of the Strait of Gibraltar. Now part of the kingdom of Morocco, the city has belonged to Portugal, Britain, and Spain over the past 500 years. It is known as Tanja in Berber, Tánger in Spanish, Tanger in French, and Tânger in Portuguese.

The city dates back to the 5th century B.C. and the establishment of a Carthaginian colony. This was to pass to Roman rule in the 1st century B.C., but with the collapse of the Roman Empire in the west, it was overrun by the Vandals before becoming part of the Byzantine Empire between 534 and 682. In the early 8th century the city fell to the Arabs, who used the area as a springboard for the invasion of the Iberian peninsula, setting the scene for some 500 years of Moorish domination of southern Spain and Portugal.

It was to be the Portuguese who wrested Tangier from the control of the Arabs in the 15th century, and it remained under Portuguese rule until, in 1661, it passed to British sovereignty as part of the dowry given with Catherine of Braganza on her marriage to King Charles II.

British rule was, however, destined to be short-lived. Much of the North African coast was ruled by Sultan Moulay Ismail (1672–1727) and the seas were full of his pirate ships. There was almost constant naval warfare between Britain, France and other powers—including later the US—for more than a century as efforts were made to suppress this piracy. In 1679 Moulay Ismail made his first attempt to seize Tangier from the British; he was initially unsuccessful but the British were to withdraw five years later as the defense of the city proved untenable.

Under the rule of Moulay Ismail and his successors, Tangier gradually declined in importance and population. In 1821, however, it became home to the US consulate—the first overseas property acquired by the US government. Morocco remained independent until the early 20th century, but, prior to the outbreak of World War I, it became the target for the international rivalry that ultimately led to war in 1914.

In 1923 Tangier was declared an international zone and placed under the joint administration of Britain, France, and Spain; Italy was to become the fourth partner in 1928. This status survived until 1956, when the city was formally reintegrated into the now-independent kingdom of Morocco as a result of the Tangier Protocol.

BELOW: The north coast of Africa and the city of Tangier as seen by Spot-5 in 2002.

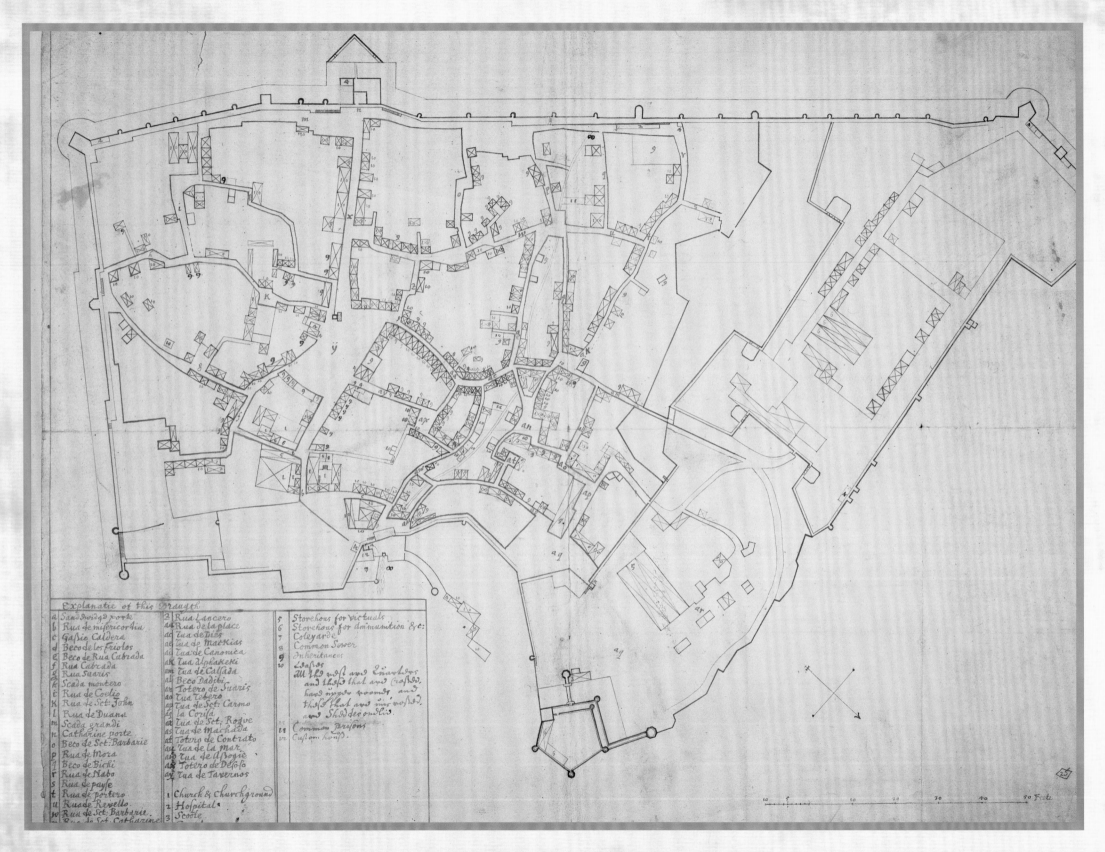

Explanatie of this Draught

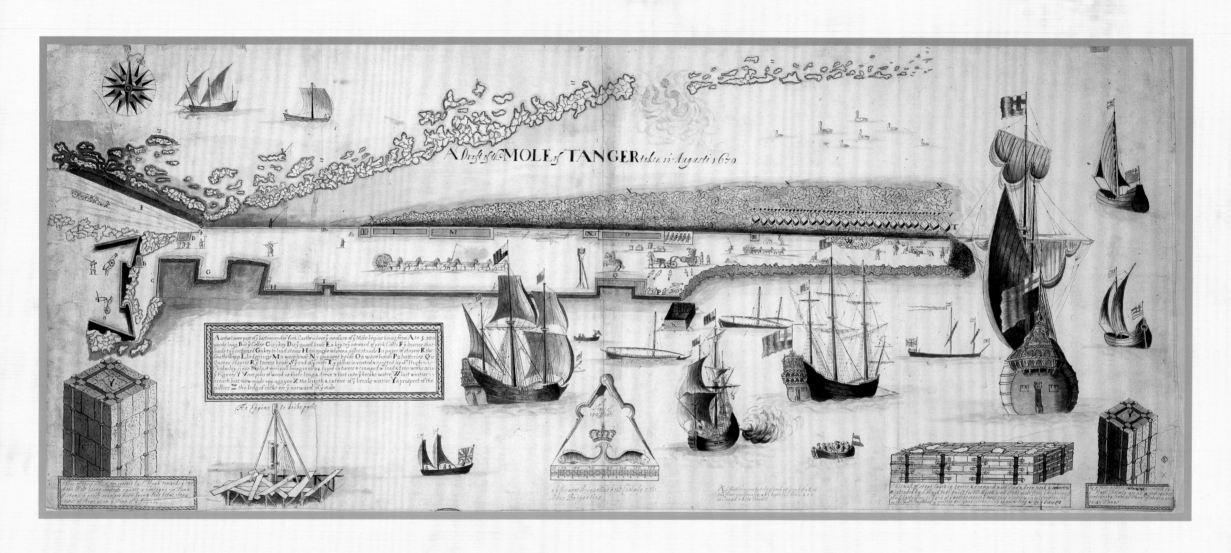

A Draft of the MOLE of TANGER taken in Augustis 670

LEFT: Tangier was under Portuguese rule from 1471, when the city was finally captured from the Arabs, through to 1661, when it was to briefly become British as a result of the marriage between King Charles II and Catherine of Braganza. This map dates to the brief period between 1661 and 1684, when the enclave was ruled as a British territory. The map is aligned with north toward the bottom right-hand corner.

ABOVE: In 1661 Britain acquired the sovereignty of Tangier, although from the outset the new territory was threatened by assault from the forces of Moulay Ismail, the Sultan who ruled most of the North African coast. In order to improve the city's defenses, as well as provide a better anchorage for the Royal Navy in an era before Britain had gained Gibraltar, the new colonial administrators undertook considerable defensive work. This included the construction of as a massive mole and this map, dated August 10, 1870, and drawn to a scale of 1 inch to 40 feet, shows work in progress upon this project. Prior to the British abandonment of Tangier in 1684, the mole was destroyed.

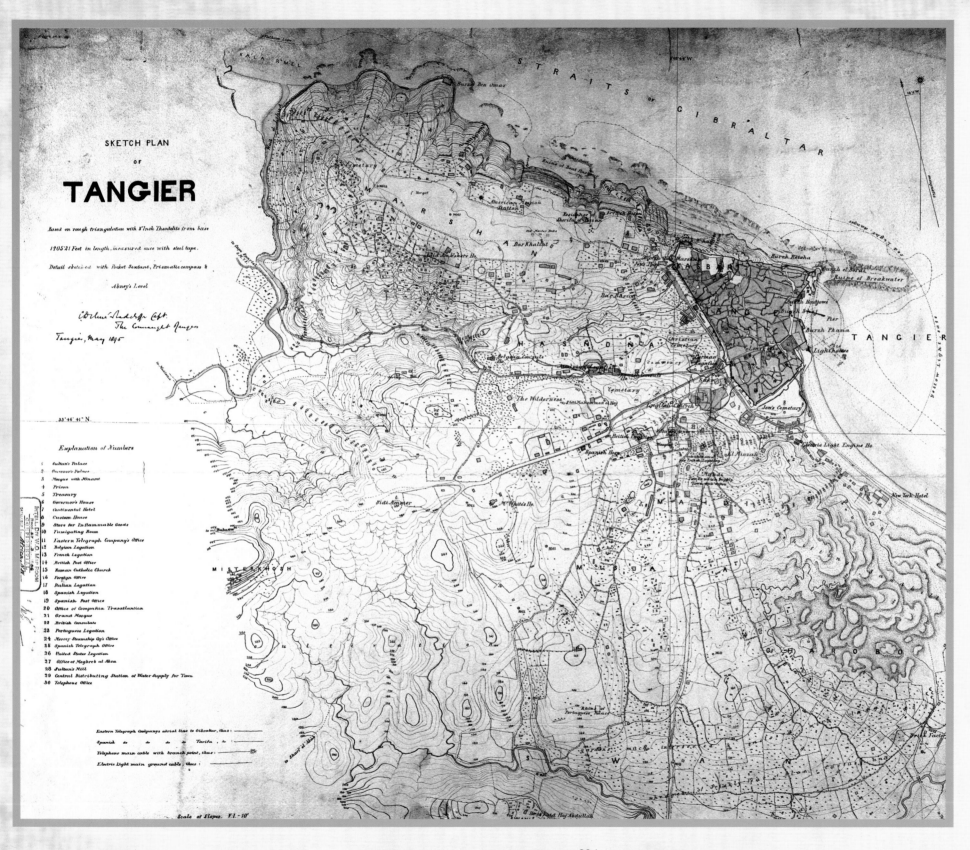

SKETCH PLAN
OF
TANGIER

Based on rough triangulation with 5 Inch Theodolite from base

1205.21 Feet in length, measured once with steel tape.

Detail sketched with Pocket Sextant, Prismatic compass &

Abney's Level

C. Delmé Radcliffe Capt.
The Connaught Rangers

Tangier, May 1895

35°46'41" N.

Explanation of Numbers

1   Sultan's Palace
2   Governor's Palace
3   Mosque with Minaret
4   Prison
5   Treasury
6   Governor's House
7   Continental Hotel
8   Custom House
9   Store for Inflammable Goods
10 Fumigating Room
11 Eastern Telegraph Company's Office
12 Belgian Legation
13 French Legation
14 British Post Office
15 Roman Catholic Church
16 Foreign Office
17 Italian Legation
18 Spanish Legation
19 Spanish Post Office
20 Office of Compañia Trasatlantica
21 Grand Mosque
22 British Consulate
23 Portuguese Legation
24 Mercy Steamship Co's Office
25 Spanish Telegraph Office
26 United States Legation
27 Office of Maghreb al Aksa
28 Sultan's Mill
29 Central Distributing Station of Water Supply for Town
30 Telephone Office

Eastern Telegraph Company's aerial line to Gibraltar, thus
Spanish   do   do   do Tarifa, do
Telephone main cable with branch point, thus
Electric Light main ground cable, thus

Scale at Slopes. V.I. = 10°

LEFT: This map records the city of Tangier and its environs toward the end of the 19th century, when it was part of an independent Morocco. This status was to survive until just prior to World War I, when the country was split between France and Spain. Northern Morocco passed to Spanish rule—indeed Spain still retains two outposts on the North African coast as a result (the final European colonies in Africa)—with Tangier being declared an international zone in 1923.

TOKYO

JAPAN

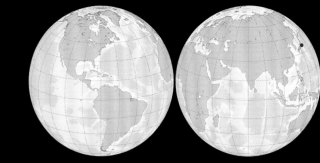

The capital city of Japan since 1868, Tokyo—the name means literally Eastern Capital—is one of 47 prefectures (districts) that make up the modern state and is situated on the eastern side of the country's largest island—Honshu. Apart from its administrative and political role, Tokyo is one of the most important financial centers in the world, rivaling London and New York.

Its origins date back to the 7th century A.D. and a small fishing village—Edo, but it was not until the 15th century that the rise to prominence began. In 1457 ta D kan (1432–86), a samurai warrior and poet, constructed Edo Castle, which is now part of the Imperial Palace in the city. Tokugawa Ieyasu (1543–1616) made Edo his base in 1590 and with his appointment as Shogun, the city became the effective capital of the country. Although titular power rested with the emperor, based at Kyoto, real power was held by the Shogun, and the Tokugawa Shogunate was to last until the late 1860s, when imperial power was restored under Emperor Meiji (1852–1912). On November 6, 1869, the city was officially renamed Tokyo. Following this transfer, the city underwent considerable expansion and development, and industrialization began.

The city suffered significant damage on September 1, 1923 when it was struck by the Great Kant earthquake, estimated to be between 7.9 and 8.4 on the Richter Scale. The Imperial Palace caught fire, landslides caused massive loss of life, and the port city of Yokohama was seriously damaged.

Although there were grand plans for the rebuilding of the city after the 1923 quake, the costs involved precluded this and the city was restored in a piecemeal fashion. Inevitably, following the Japanese expansion into China and its attack on Pear Harbor in December 1941, as the tide of World War II turned against Japan, the city of Tokyo was to become a military target. It was first raided on April 18, 1942 in the Doolittle Raid, although this was more of an exercise in boosting US morale than the start of a serious air offensive against Japan. More serious were the aerial assaults that started in 1945 as the Allies gradually turned the screw on the Japanese. Much of the city was destroyed, although Tokyo was to escape the fate of Hiroshima and Nagasaki, both of which were devastated by atomic bombs before the unconditional Japanese surrender in August 1945.

BELOW: Part of the huge metropolis of Tokyo as taken by the Spot–5 satellite in 2005—the largest metropolitan area in the world, the Greater Tokyo Area is home to 35 million people. The map on pages 226–227 isn't identified here as most of its coverage is off this photograph.

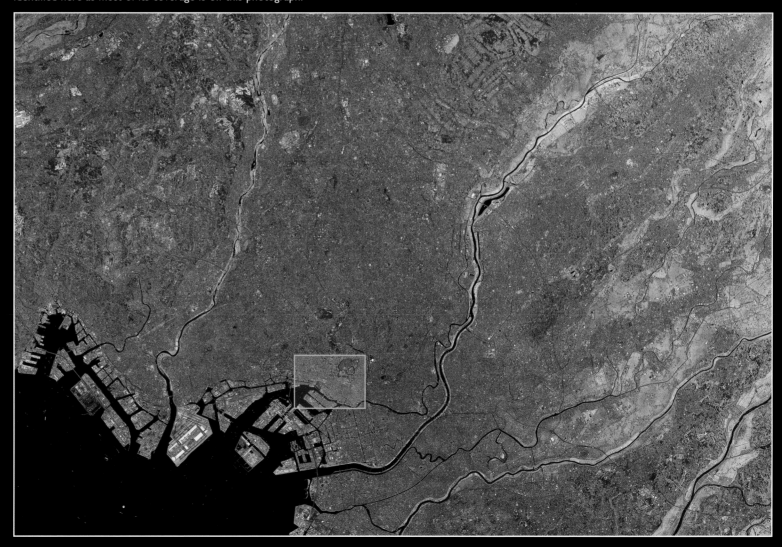

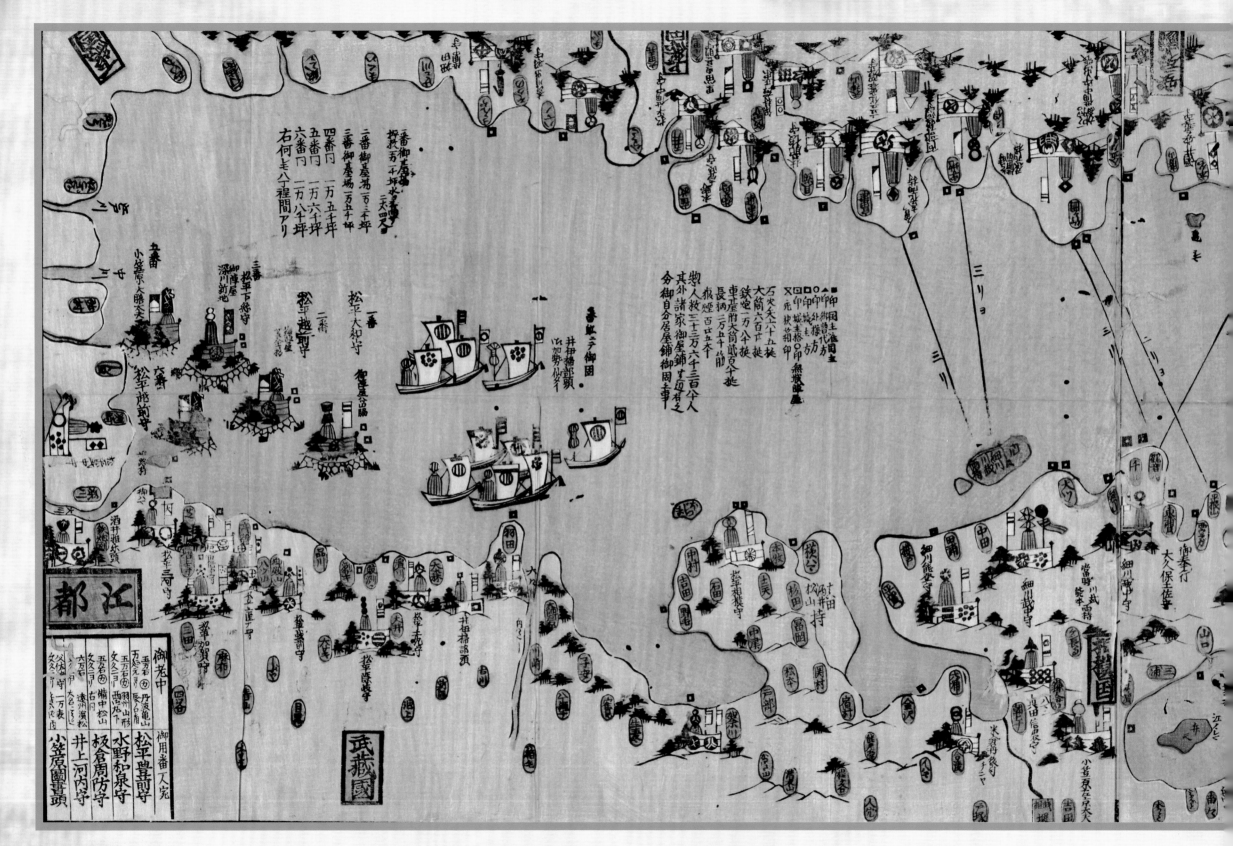

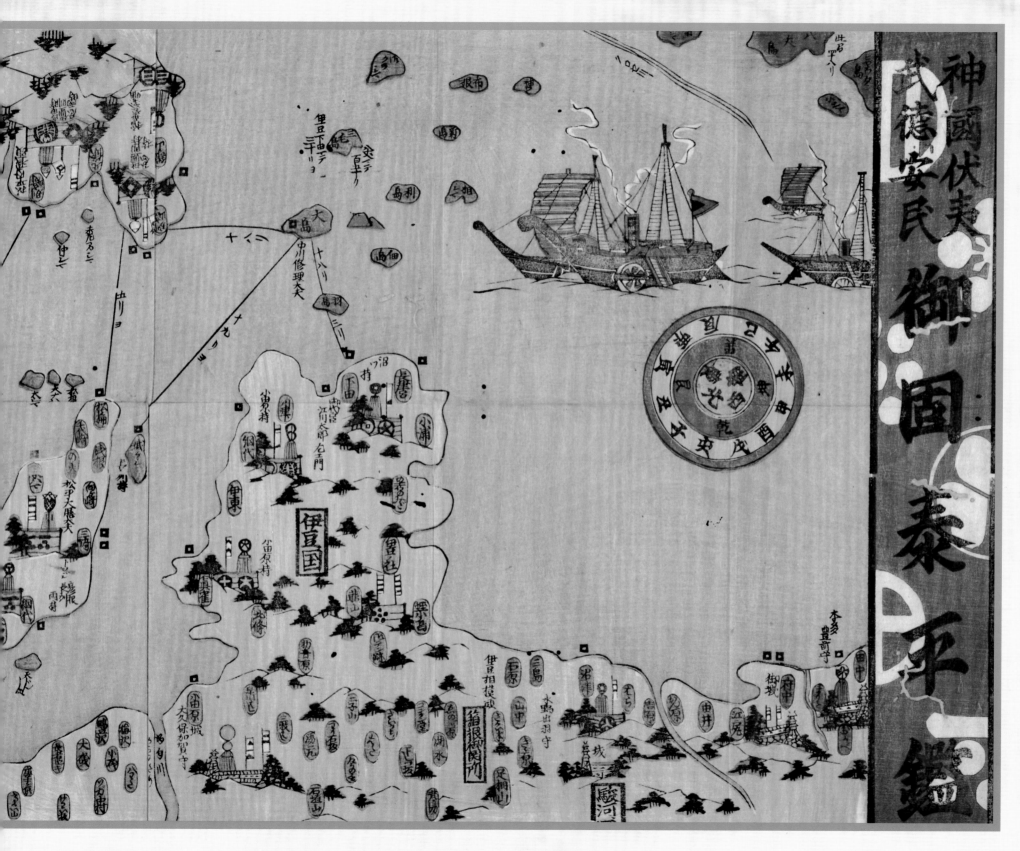

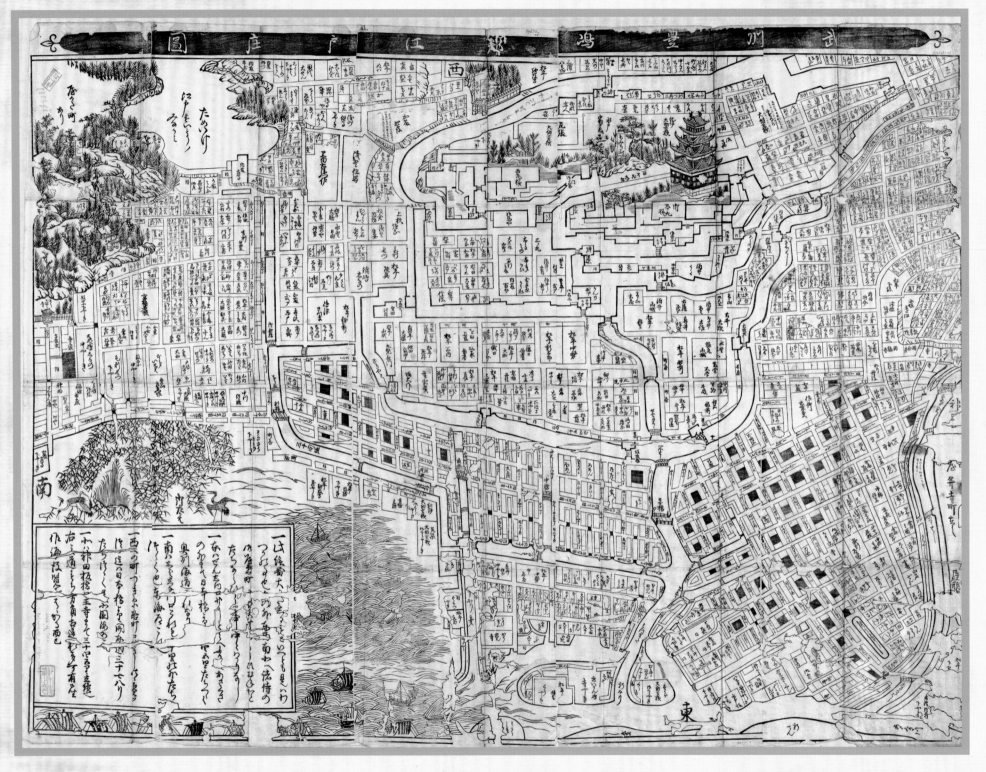

The original woodblock of this map of Tokyo was produced around 1630 during the Edo period, while Tokugawa Iemitsu was shogun. Built up by Tokugawa Ieyasu (who became shogun in 1603 and died in 1616), Edo was the effective capital of Japan because the power rested with the shogun rather than the emperor in Kyoto. Indeed, the emperor would only move there after the fall of the shugunate in 1863. Edo became Tokyo in 1868. Much of the city was destroyed by fire in the 1630s, and shortly after the date of this map a further disaster was to befall the city when ash from a major eruption of Mount Fuji caused serious damage. The map shows landholding in the city with what we call Tokyo Bay in the bottiom left corner and Edo Castle (that would become gthe Imperial Palace) top right.

VENICE
ITALY

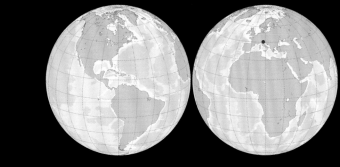

Known to the Italians as Venezia, Venice is widely regarded as one of the finest cities in the world. It is based around 118 islands that lie within the Venetian lagoon, a stretch of salt water situated between the estuaries of the Po and Piave rivers in northeast Italy on the Adriatic Sea. With its network of canals and buildings constructed on wooden piles sunk into the shallow waters of the lagoon, it is particularly susceptible to the rising sea levels and the historic center is increasingly threatened by regular flooding.

Between the 9th and the 12th centuries Venice became an increasingly powerful city-state. Its position at the head of the Adriatic made it strategically important, and it was from Venice that many of the ships carrying Crusaders to the Holy Land departed. Venice's maritime and commercial empire expanded with interests along much of the Dalmatian coast and most of the islands in the Aegean and eastern Mediterranean. Venice was still, in theory, subject to the ultimate overlordship of the Byzantine Empire, but this was to cease in the early 13th century when the participants in the Fourth Crusade attacked Constantinople rather than the Holy Land.

By the end of the 13th century Venice had become the most prosperous city in Europe and the the 14th and much of the 15th century saw it reach the height of its power; it was during these years that many of the city's finest buildings were built. However, a new force from the east was threatening, and the Turks declared war on Venice in the second half of the 15th century, resulting in the gradual decline of Venetian power.

Following the Treaty of Campo on October 12, 1797, Napoleon ceded control of Venice to the Austrians and the city remained under Austrian rule until 1848. This was to be short-lived though, as, following a year-long siege, the city was forced to surrender in 1849. In 1866, after the war between Austria and its one-time ally Prussia, Venice was annexed by the kingdom of Italy.

Although the suburbs of the city were severely damaged during World War II, the historic center escaped virtually unscathed. A more serious threat emerged after 1945 when the 3-mile long seawall, completed in 1782, proved insufficient to cope with the threat of flooding. In 1966 a combination of high tides and storms resulted in the city being flooded to a record level for some 20 hours.

BELOW: This image of Venice was taken from the taken from the International Space Station in March 2007. Note the rail link from the mainland to Venice.

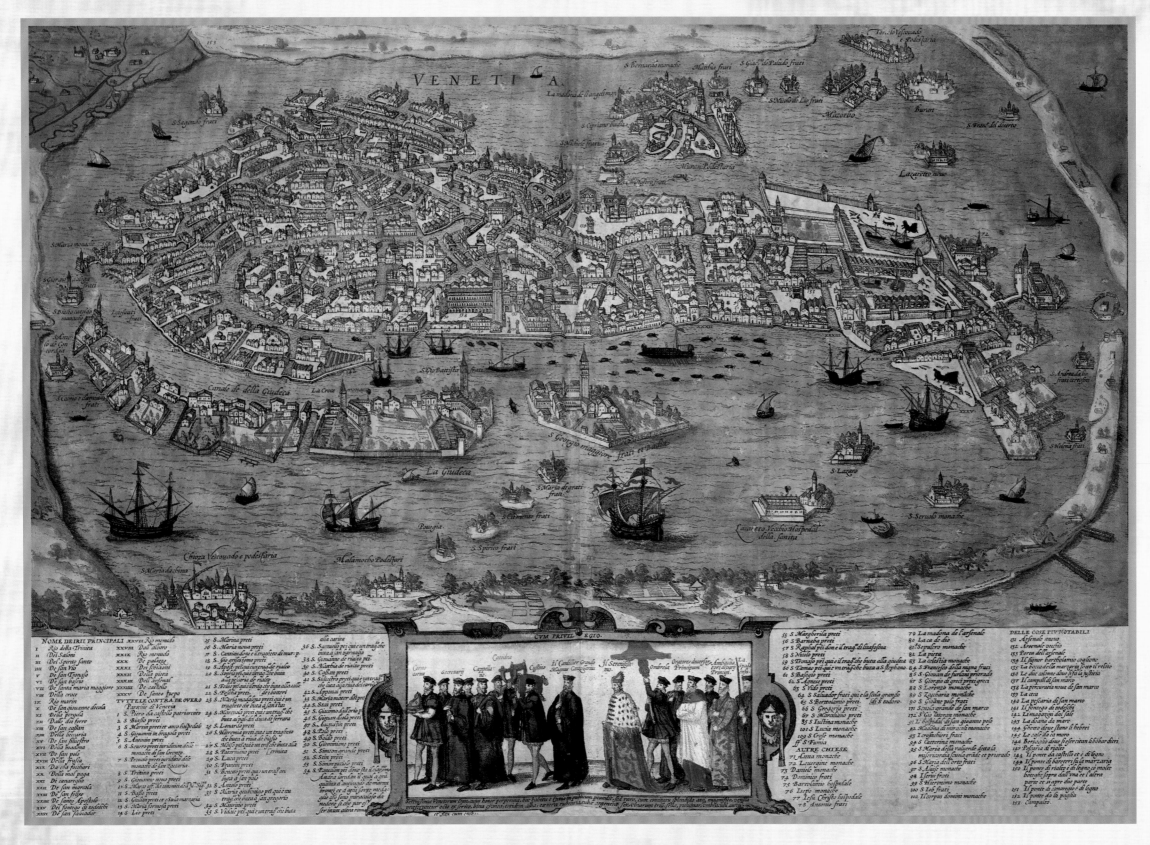

LEFT: By the date of this map the golden age of Venice had passed, with the loss of much of its maritime empire and the discovery of new shipping routes to India and the Far East. Dominating the border of the map is an illustration portraying the Doge in procession. Venice itself, surrounded by the lagoon that offered essential protection to the city, is dominated in the center by the Piazza San Marco (St Mark's Square), which is widely regarded as one of the greatest of all European urban spaces. On the square is the 1094 basilica, in which the remains of St Mark are housed, and the Doge's Palace, constructed between 1309 and 1424. At the extreme east of the city—the map is aligned with north toward the top—can be seen the Arsenal. Venice's power rested with its navy and army and the military power of the city was concentrated in and around the Castello district. The Arsenal Nuovo (New Arsenal) illustrated here was constructed from 1320, and by its peak in the early 16th century, some 16,000 were employed there. Alongside the Arsenal were shipyards employed in the mass production of warships and other military establishments.

RIGHT: This Italian map records the city around 1730. The years of the Venetian empire were long gone and, although its inhabitants did not know it, Venice was coming toward the end of its life as an independent republic as well. On May 12, 1797, the city was seized by the French army under Napoleon before falling under Austrian rule.

FOLLOWING PAGE: Produced by Bradshaw & Blacklock of Manchester, England, this map records Venice in the mid-19th century. It was in 1846 that the railroad link to the mainland was officially opened; prior to that date the only access between the city and the mainland had been via the water. Santa Lucia railroad station, built on the site of a church dedicated to the same saint, is situated at the end of a 3-mile causeway to the mainland; a road causeway was added on the western side of the railroad causeway in the 20th century.

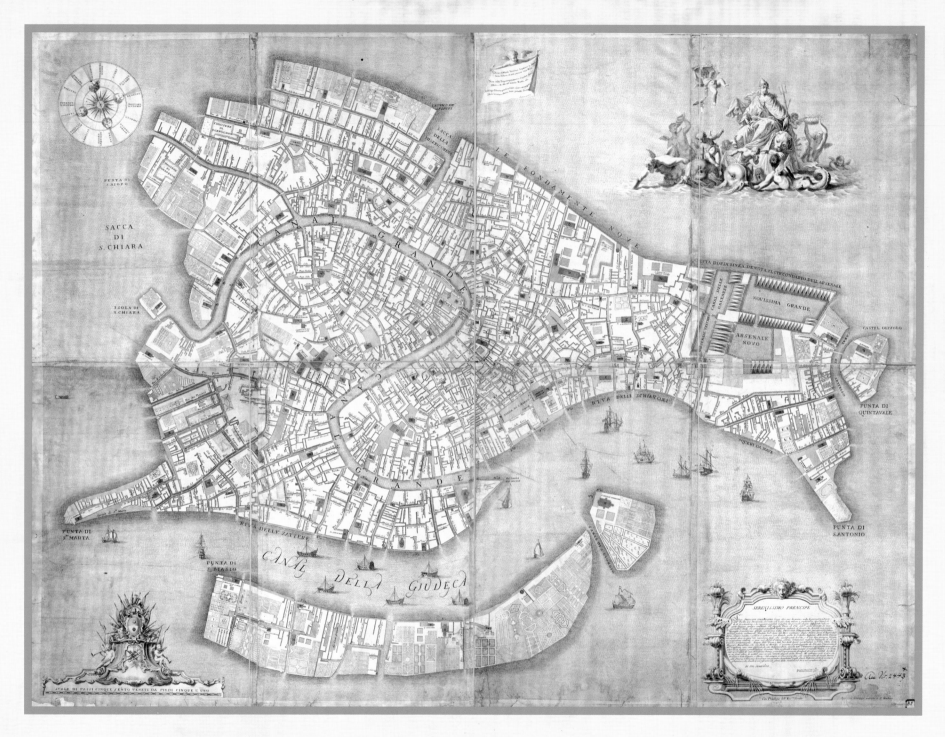

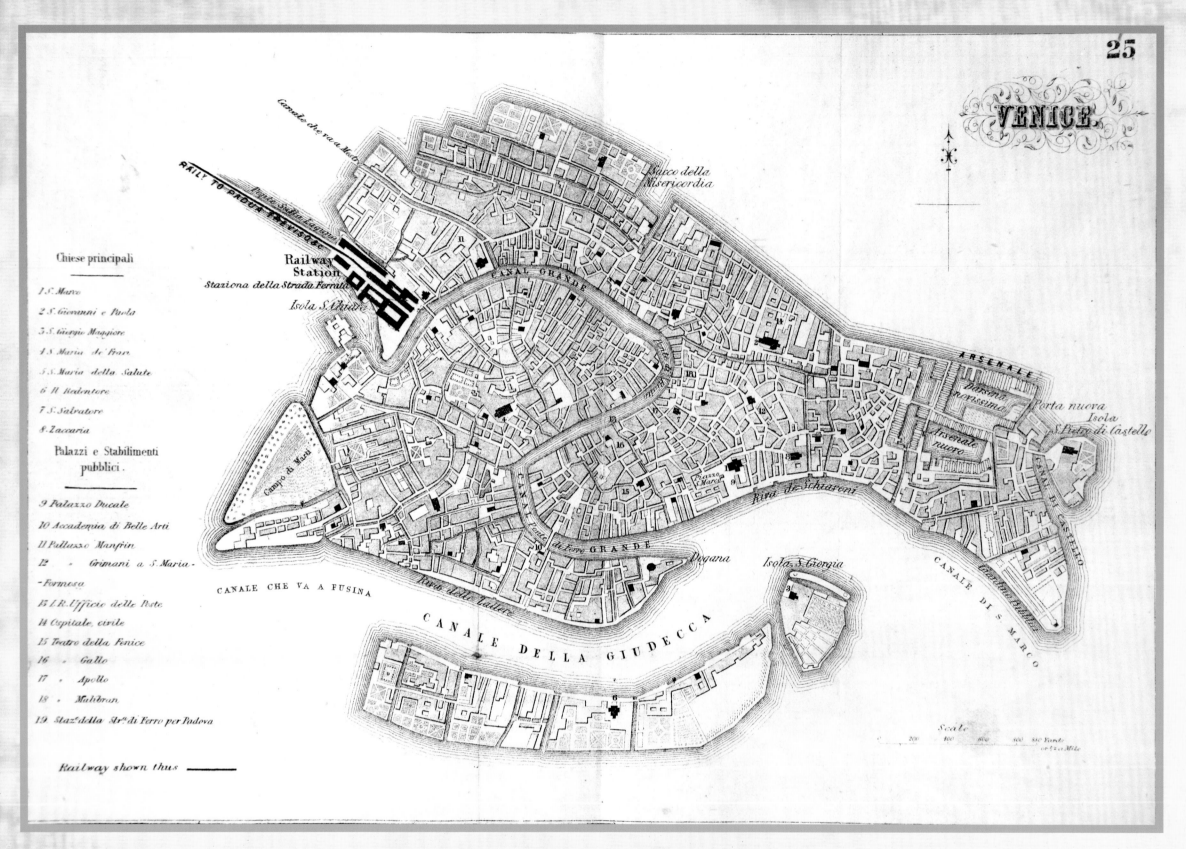

25

VENICE

Chiese principali

1 S. Marco
2 S. Giovanni e Paolo
3 S. Giorgio Maggiore
4 S. Maria de' Frari
5 S. Maria della Salute
6 Il Redentore
7 S. Salvatore
8 Zaccaria

Palazzi e Stabilimenti
pubblici.

9 Palazzo Ducale
10 Accademia di Belle Arti
11 Palazzo Manfrin
12 " Grimani a S. Maria -
- Formosa
13 I.R. Ufficio delle Poste
14 Ospitale civile
15 Teatro della Fenice
16 " Gallo
17 " Apollo
18 " Malibran
19 Staz.e della Str.a di Ferro per Padova

Railway shown thus ———————

Railway Station
Staziona della Strada Ferrata
Isola S. Chiara

Canale che va a Mestre
Ponte sulla Laguna
RAIL.Y TO PADUA TREVISO &c.

Sacco della Misericordia

CANAL GRANDE

ARSENALE
Darsena novissima
Arsenale nuovo
Porta nuova Isola
S. Pietro di Castello

Piazza S. Marco
Riva de Schiavoni

Campo di Marte

CANAL Ponte di Ferro GRANDE

CANALE CHE VA A FUSINA
Riva delle Zattere

Dogana
Isola S. Giorgio

CANALE DI S. MARCO

CANALE DELLA GIUDECCA

Scale
200   400   600   800   880 Yards
or ½ a Mile

VERONA

ITALY

F amous as the city in which William Shakespeare set both *Romeo and Juliet* and *The Two Gentlemen of Verona*, modern Verona is situated in northern Italy. With a population approaching 300,000, it is one of the principal centers of the province of Veneto. The city's historical and economic importance lay in its location on a loop of the River Adige, close to Lake Garda, and as an intersection for a number of important Roman roads. Until the mid-1950s, when flood alleviation schemes were completed, the district was prone to regular flooding.

After Roman occupation the city was successively occupied by the Byzantine Empire and the Lombards before it fell to the Carolingian Franks under Charlemagne in 774 A.D. As such it became part of the Holy Roman Empire. However, in 1100 the residents of the city formed themselves into an urban commune and overthrew their feudal rulers. As a leading member of the Lombard League, which the city was forced to join by Venice, the city helped to over throw imperial rule in several neighboring cities and so became involved in the political infighting between the papacy and the empire.

In 1259, Mastino della Scalla took control of the city and ruled as a dictator until his assassination 13 years later. Further members of the della Scalla family ruled Verona thereafter, and the city prospered, adding Brescia, Parma,and Lucca to its territory. However, an alliance of rival states, led by Milan, managed to recapture much of this territory and, following the Veronese defeat at the Battle of Castagnaro in 1387, the della Scalla dynasty was overthrown and the city fell briefly under Milanese rule until 1404 when the Veronese regained their independence. This was, however, to be short-lived as the city was conquered by Venice in 1405. Apart from a brief period between 1507 and 1517 when, following the Venetian defeat in the Wars of the Cambrai, the city was again occupied by the troops of the Emperor Maximilian, Verona was to remain part of Venice's domains until Italian unification in the 19th century.

In 1866 the kingdom of Lombardy-Venetia became part of the unified Italy, following the Six Weeks' War; at the time, Verona was the strongest Austrian-held fortress in the region. During World War II, when Italy initially sided with Germany, and following the Italian surrender, the city suffered some damage from bombing, but this was repaired after the war.

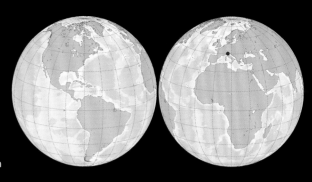

BELOW: Satellite image of Verona and its surrounding area in northern Italy. North is at top. Forested areas are dark green, agricultural fields are lighter shades of green and brown, urban areas are grey and water is black. The southern region of the Dolomites mountain range is seen at top right. Image created using NaturalVue data obtained from the Landsat 7 satellite.

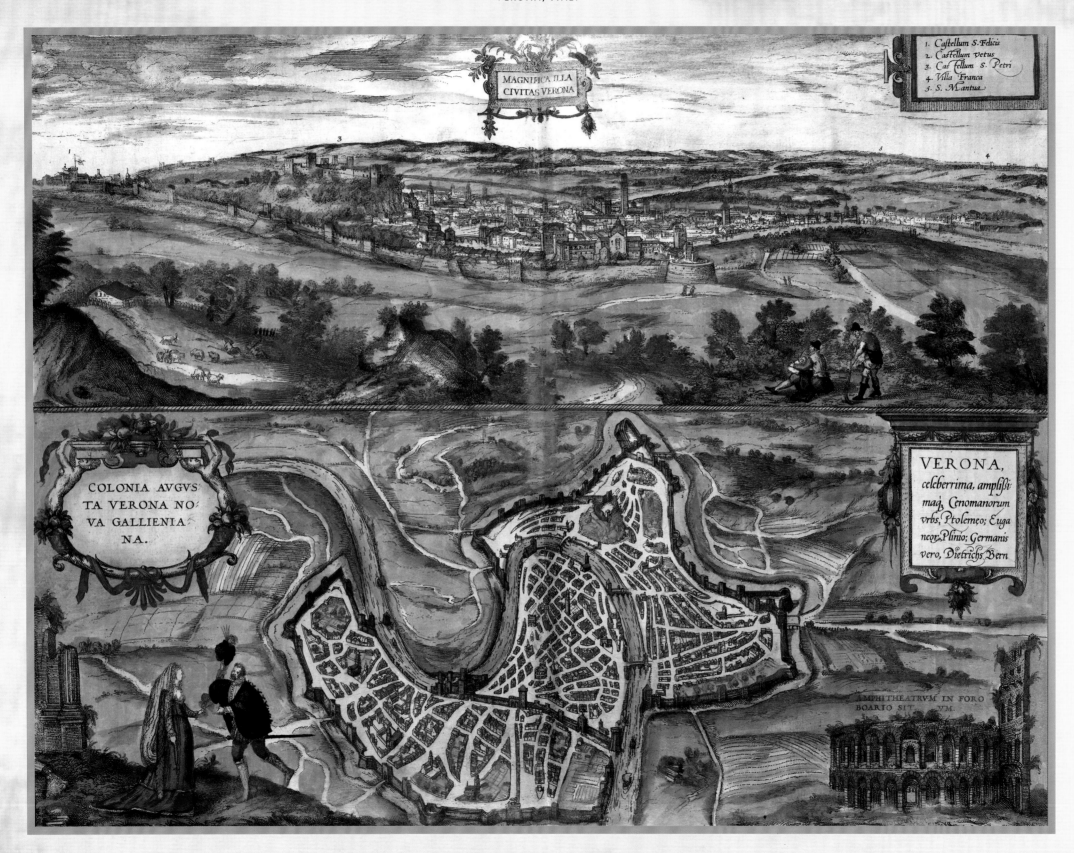

MAGNIFICA ILLA
CIVITAS VERONA

1. Castellum S. Felicis
2. Castellum Vetus
3. Castellum S. Petri
4. Villa Franca
5. S. Mantua

COLONIA AVGVS
TA VERONA NO
VA GALLIENIA
NA.

VERONA,
celeberrima, ampliſſi
maq̄, Cenomanorum
vrbs, Ptolemeo; Euga
neor, Plinio; Germanis
vero, Dietrichs Bern

AMPHITHEATRVM IN FORO
BOARIO SIT VM.

LEFT: Reproduced in *Civitates Orbis Terrarum* by Georg Braun and Franz Hogenberg, this map shows the city toward the end of the 16th century with aerial and panoramic views. In the bottom right an inset records the city's amphitheater; this great arena had been built around 30A.D. and is one of the best-preserved examples of its type to survive. Designed to accommodate 20,000 spectators, it fell into disuse but was renovated in the early 12th century, and from the 16th century was used as a site for plays and other events. Also illustrated are the Castelvecchio and the city's defenses; the former was the power-base of the Della Scalla family. The castle as seen here was rebuilt in the mid-14th century on the foundations of an older stronghold. The city's walls were rebuilt at the same time, incorporating parts of the earlier Roman structures.

RIGHT: Produced by Bradshaw & Blacklock of Manchester, England, this map records Verona in the mid-19th century.

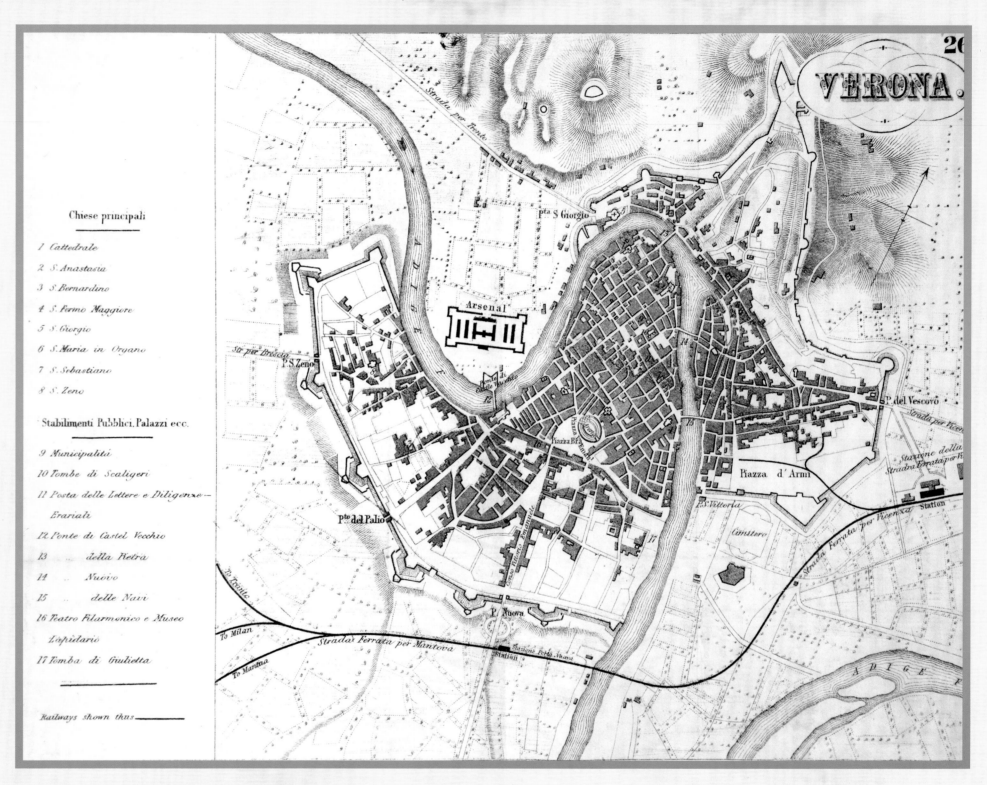

Chiese principali

1 *Cattedrale*
2 *S. Anastasia*
3 *S. Bernardino*
4 *S. Fermo Maggiore*
5 *S. Giorgio*
6 *S. Maria in Organo*
7 *S. Sebastiano*
8 *S. Zeno*

Stabilimenti Pubblici, Palazzi ecc.

9 *Municipalità*
10 *Tombe di Scaligeri*
11 *Posta delle Lettere e Diligenze—Erariali*
12 *Ponte di Castel Vecchio*
13 ,, *della Pietra*
14 ,, *Nuovo*
15 ,, *delle Navi*
16 *Teatro Filarmonico e Museo Lapidario*
17 *Tomba di Giulietta*

Railways shown thus _____

VIENNA

AUSTRIA

Known in German as Wien, Vienna is the capital of Austria and the largest city in the country. It lies toward the east, south of the River Danube. The core is the Innere Stadt—Inner Town—one of the 23 districts forming the modern city.

Up to the 10th century there is considerable evidence to show the importance of the area as a commercial and trading center. The patronage of the Babenberg family led to the founding of numerous churches and monasteries, and commercial growth was encouraged after 1221 when laws required all passing merchants to offer their goods for sale in the city.

The 16th century was to witness the Reformation. Initially, under the Emperor Maximilian, Vienna was tolerant of the cause. However, Maximilian's successors, Charles V and Ferdinand I, were more orthodox and, as a result, Vienna became one of the centers for the counter-Reformation. Although these developments resulted in the construction of a number of superb baroque churches and other buildings, religious controversy and the threat from the Turks had the effect of undermining the local economy.

For the next 400 years the history of Vienna was inextricably tied up with the aspirations and ambitions of the ruling Habsburg dynasty. By 1724 its population had increased to around 150,000, and by 1790 to around 200,000. During the Napoleonic Wars the city was captured twice by the French and it was at the Congress of Vienna, held between September 1814 and June 1815, that the post-Napoleonic settlement in Europe was determined.

During the early 19th century the city continued to grow; it was connected to the expanding railroad network in 1838, and, in 1858, the 16th-century defenses were demolished to construct the Ringstraße boulevard and its associated buildings.

During the 18th and 19th centuries the powers of the Habsburg Empire had been gradually eroded and, in 1867, following a compromise with moderate forces in Hungary, the state became known as Austro-Hungary. This was to persist until defeat in World War I when the remaining empire was dismembered and Vienna became capital of the new Austrian republic in 1920.

Although several historic buildings were damaged during World War II, many have been restored. The nature of post-war Vienna was graphically portrayed in the classic film *The Third Man*, with Orson Welles playing the black-market dealer Harry Lime.

The Allied forces of Britain, France, Russia, and the US occupied Vienna and Austria until 1955. Austria became a member of the European Union in 1995.

BELOW: This image shows the old city of Vienna as taken by the Spot-5 satellite in 2004. It is too tightly focussed to allow the first map—showing the 1529 siege of Vienna—to be highlighted.

SIEGE
de
VIENNE
par
Souleïman I.

Du 27 Septembre au 14 Octobre 1529.
(23 Moharrem au 10 Safer 935.)

I Porte du Château
II Porte de Carinthie
III Porte du Poêle
IV Porte de la Tourrouge
V Porte du Sel
VI Porte de Werder
VII Porte des Ecosais

A Bastion de Henri
B Bastion de Jacques
C Bastion des Predicateurs
D Bastion du Castor
E Bastion du Roi
F Bastion du Château
G Couvent des Augustins
H Couvent de Clara

Ottomans sous les ord.ᵉ de Souleïman I
(120,000 hommes, 20000 chameaux)

A Tente du Sultan, sous la garde de six escadrons de cavalerie regulière et de 12,000 Janissaires
B Troupes d'Asie sous les ord.ᵉ du Beglerbeg d'Anatolie, Behrampascha.
C Tentes du Defterdar et des employés du trésor
D Camp du Grand Vizir Ibrahim-Pascha.
E Parc d'Artillerie, 300 canons de divers calibre
F Camp sous les ord.ᵉ de Koutschouk Balibeg, Paschá de Servie
G Camp de Khosrewbeg, gouverneur de Bosnie
H Camp du Beglerbeg de Roumilie, commandant les troupes de Servie de Croatie et de Bulgarie
I Camp du Sandschak de Semendra
K Camp du Sandschak de Mostar
L Camp du Pascha de Roum (Amassia)
M Camp de Kasim Woiwoda, commandant en Chef de la flottille du Danube composée de 400 Nassades

Autrichiens sous les ord.ᵉ de Philippe Duc de Bavière et du Comte Eck de Salm
(16,000 hommes)

L'étendue de 1 à 2 est confiée à Philippe de Bavière 14 bannières de troupes imperiales
100 cavaliers
L'étendue de 2 à 3 est assignée au Colonel Eck de Reischach 3000 hommes de la
Basse Autriche)
L'étendue de 3 à 4 est défendue par les bannières de Styrie sous les
ord. d'Abel de Holneck et Jean de Purgstall
3 la défense du Château est confiée aux soins du Colonel commandant en chef de l'Artillerie Ulric Leisser
L'étendue de 5 à 6 est occupée par sept bannières d'Aut
riche et 500 cavaliers derrière lesquels est placée la
garde civique
L'étendue de 6 à 7 est confiée à Remprecht d'Ebersdorf
avec une bannière d'Archers de la ville
De 7 à 6 Lays de Avalos avec 200 Espagnols
De 8 à 9 et 2 Quatre bannières d'infanterie sous
les ord. d'Ernest de Landenstein et une bannière
de Cavalerie commandée par Jean de Hardeck

Jedlersee
Nussdorf
Heiligenstadt
Jedlersdorf am Spitz
Kagran
Döbling
VIENNE (Vindabona)
Penzing
St Veit
Schœnbrun
Simmering
Wiener B.
Kaiser Ebersdorf
Danube Fl. Ister
Schwegat

LEFT: Although produced in France in 1843 and included within a book covering the history of the Ottoman Empire published that year, this map records the pivotal moment in European history when the almost inexorable rise of the Ottoman Empire was finally halted. Between September 27 and October 14 in 1529, Vienna was besieged by the Ottoman army under the command of Sultan Suleiman I (1494–1566). The Sultan's campaign to seize Hungary and reduce the threat to his empire from the Holy Roman Empire was launched in May 1529 and, by the time his forces reached Vienna they had been much reduced. In particular he was short of both camels and heavy equipment, and his position was further weakened by exhaustion within his army and Suleiman was forced to withdraw in mid-October. The gates and fortifications of Vienna are described in a key toward the bottom left.

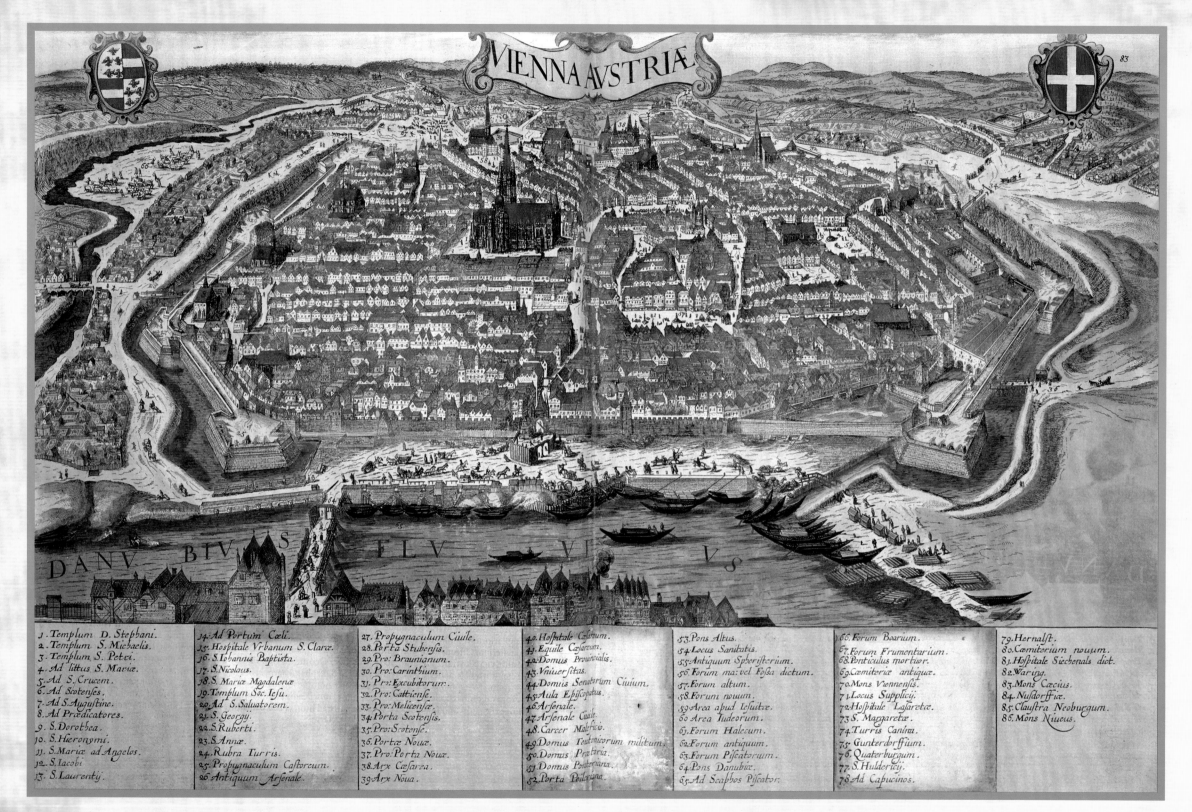

VIENNA AVSTRIAE

83

1. Templum D. Stephani.
2. Templum S. Michaelis.
3. Templum S. Petri.
4. Ad littus S. Mariæ.
5. Ad S. Crucem.
6. Ad Scotenses.
7. Ad S. Augustine.
8. Ad Prædicatores.
9. S. Dorothea.
10. S. Hieronymi.
11. S. Mariæ ad Angelos.
12. S. Iacobi.
13. S. Laurentij.

14. Ad Portum Cœli.
15. Hospitale Vrbanum S. Claræ.
16. S. Iobannis Baptista.
17. S. Nicolaus.
18. S. Mariæ Magdalenæ
19. Templum Soc. Iesu.
20. Ad S. Saluatorem.
21. S. Georgij.
22. S. Ruberti.
23. S. Annæ.
24. Rubra Turris.
25. Propugnaculum Castoreum.
26. Antiquum Arsenale

27. Propugnaculum Ciuile.
28. Porta Stubensis.
29. Pro: Braunianum.
30. Pro: Carinthium.
31. Pro: Excubitorum.
32. Pro: Catticense.
33. Pro: Melicense.
34. Porta Scotensis.
35. Pro: Scotense.
36. Portæ Nouæ.
37. Pro: Porta Noua.
38. Arx Cæsarea.
39. Arx Noua.

40. Hospitale Cæsareum.
41. Equile Cæsareum.
42. Domus Prouincialis.
43. Vniuersitas.
44. Domus Senatorum Ciuium.
45. Aula Episcopatus.
46. Arsenale.
47. Arsenale Ciuile.
48. Career Maleficij.
49. Domus Teutonicorum militum.
50. Domus Prætoria.
51. Domus Pontoriana.
52. Porta Peilriana.

53. Pons Altus.
54. Locus Sanitatis.
55. Antiquum Spheristerium.
56. Forum ma: vel Fossa dictum.
57. Forum altum.
58. Forum nouum.
59. Area apud Iesuitæ.
60. Area Iudeorum.
61. Forum Halecum.
62. Forum antiquum.
63. Forum Piscatorum.
64. Pons Danubij.
65. Ad Scaphos Piscator.

66. Forum Boarium.
67. Forum Frumentarium.
68. Ponticulus mortuor.
69. Cæmiteriæ antiquæ.
70. Mons Viennensis.
71. Locus Supplicij.
72. Hospitale Lasaretæ.
73. S. Margaretæ.
74. Turris Canina.
75. Gunterdorffium.
76. Quaterburgum.
77. S. Hulderici.
78. Ad Capucinos.

79. Hernalst.
80. Cæmiterium nouum.
81. Hospitale Siechenals dict.
82. Waring.
83. Mons Cæcius.
84. Nusdorffiæ.
85. Claustra Neoburgum.
86. Mons Niueus.

LEFT: During the late Middle Ages, Vienna and the rest of eastern Europe was under military threat from the expansion of the Ottoman Empire. The old medieval walls were swept away and replaced by more advanced defenses, deigned to maximize the potential of artillery. They incorporated 10 artillery bastions, which covered all but the river approaches to the city. Also visible in this view are the Stephensdom (St Stephen's Cathedral, which had been founded in 1147) and, outside the city walls, the Fort Boarium (pig market).

RIGHT: Described as a "Plan der Turckischen Attacquen voor Wien" (Plan of the Turkish Attack on Vienna), this shows the siege works and fortifications of the city under attack between July and September 1683. Although no scale is shown, the map does include a reference table. It was drawn on 10 August, 1683 by Daniël Wolff von Dopff (1655–1718), who was in the service of Field Marshal Prince Georg Friedrich Waldeck, the commander of the "Statish" contingent sent to help fight the Turks at Vienna.

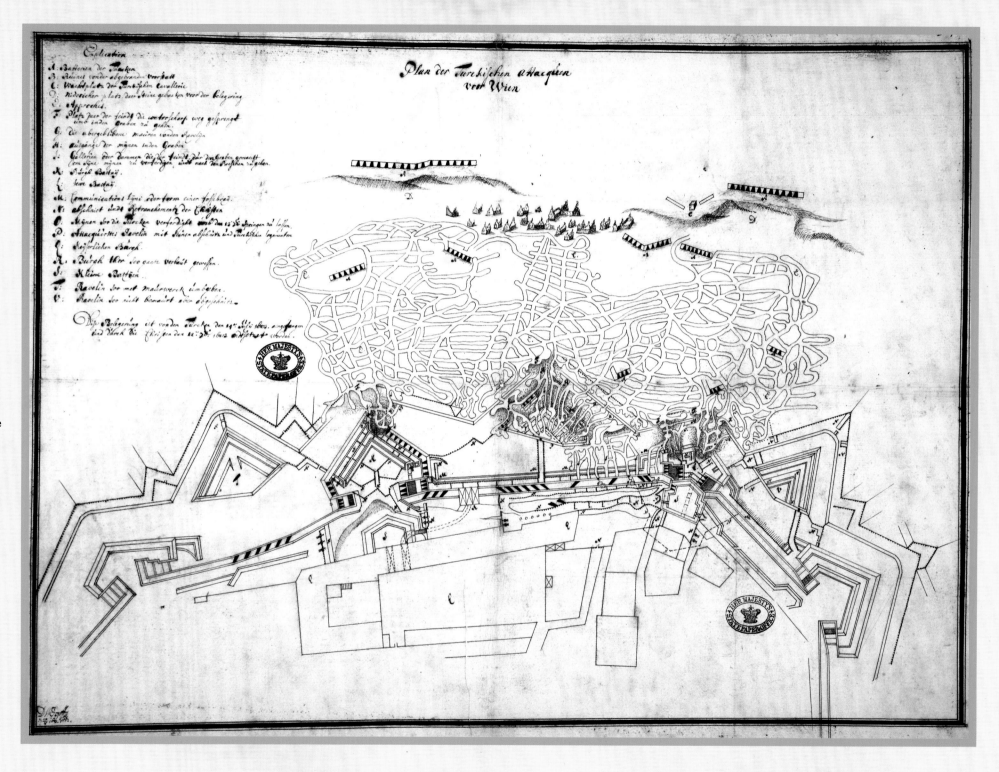

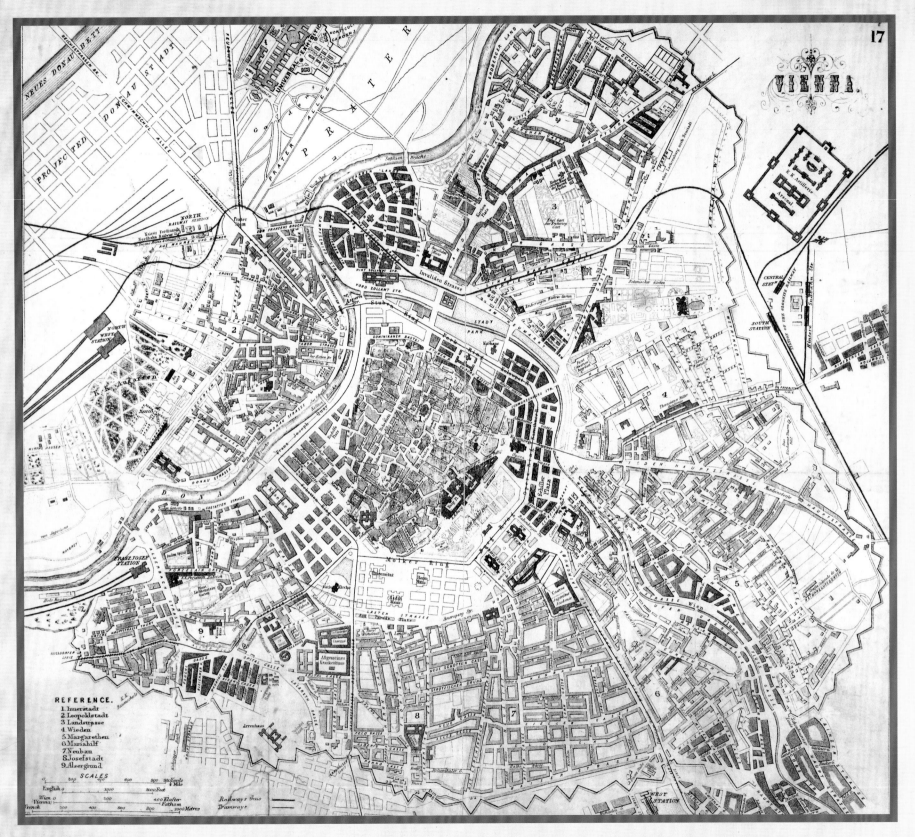

LEFT: Produced by Bradshaw & Blacklock of Manchester, England, this map records the city of Vienna in the mid-19th century. It shows the scale of the city when it was an imperial capital, as well as the arrival of the extensive railway network built to serve it. The map records the city's defensive walls, although in 1857 Emperor Francis Joseph decided to have the defenses razed. The Ringstraße, a splendid boulevard with many stately public buildings, was built to replace the fortification.

WARSAW

POLAND

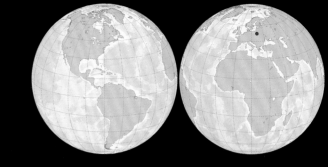

Now the capital of Poland, Warsaw (Warszawa) has a population of just under two million. It is located on the River Vistula (Wisla), in the heartland of the Masovian Plain 1,214 miles from the Baltic Sea. Although severely damaged during World War II, the historic core of the city was declared a World Heritage Site by UNESCO in 1981.

The first evidence of settlement in the area came in the 9th to 10th centuries, with the establishment of a fortified settlement at Bródno, and in the 12th to 13th centuries with a further fortified settlement at Jazdów. Following a raid on the latter site, a new settlement was established around a small fishing village called Warszowa.

In 1413 Warsaw became the capital of the Duchy of Masovia and the city started to grow rapidly as both an economic and cultural center. In 1526, following the extinction of the ducal line, the duchy was incorporated into the Polish crown and the castle became one of the royal residences as well as the seat of the national parliament.

Following the creation of the Polish-Lithuanian Commonwealth as a result of the Union of Lublin in 1569, Warsaw, situated between the two existing capitals of Cracow and Vilnius, became the de facto capital of the union. The Commonwealth survived until the late 18th century, but the threat from neighboring powers and internal instability led to the Partitions of Poland. With the Third Partition, in 1795, the Commonwealth ceased to exist and Warsaw became capital of New East Prussia, part of the kingdom of Prussia.

Following the German invasion in 1939, the city—and in particular the royal castle—suffered severe damage. As with other eastern cities, Warsaw possessed a large Jewish population and this was herded into a ghetto; a rising amongst the residents here in January 1943 led to massive destruction and loss of life. By the end of the war some 85 percent of the city had been destroyed.

Warsaw was liberated by the Russians in January 1945. After the war, Warsaw remained capital of the new Polish state, although now a client state of Russia. Since the demise of Russian influence in the former Warsaw Pacts states of eastern Europe, Poland has become a member of the European Union.

BELOW: Another tightly focussed satellite image taken by Spot-5 in 2005. It shows off the old town of Warsaw. Note at top right the 10th-Anniversary Stadium, which was demolished in 2008–2009 to make way for a new national stadium that will be ready to host games for the Euro 2012 soccer tournament.

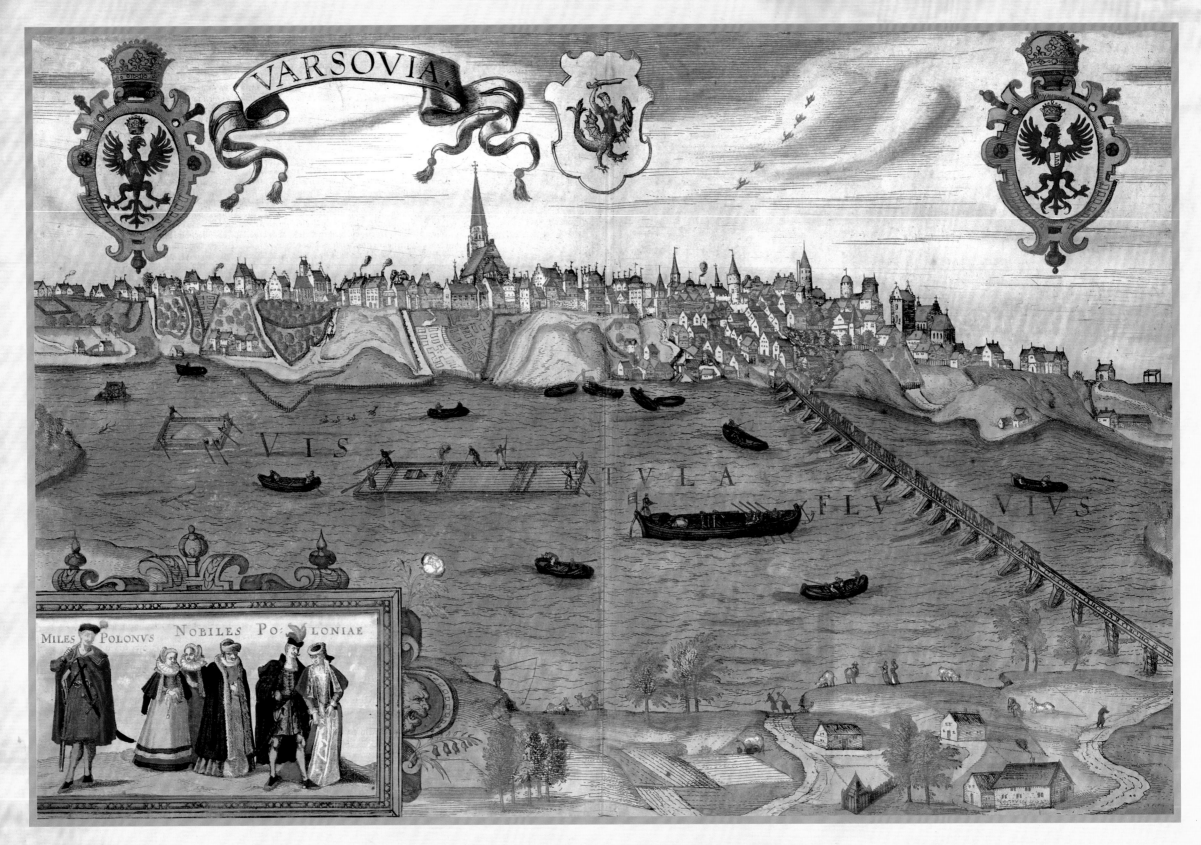

VARSOVIA.

VIS TVLA FLV VIVS

MILES POLONVS NOBILES PO LONIAE

LEFT: Viewed from across the River Vistula, this perspective of Warsaw shows the main districts—the Stare Miasto (Old Town) and Nowa Miasto (New Town)—that formed the core of the city at this period. Also illustrated are the Zamek Królewski (or royal castle, which originated in the 14th century) and the Katedra sw. Jana (St John's Cathedral, also dating back to the 14th century).

ABOVE: This is an extract of a French map, described as "Carte de la Pologne, divisee par provinces et palatinats, et subdivisee par districts" (Map of Poland divided into provinces and palatinates and subdivided into districts). It was produced J. A. B. Rizzi-Zannoni to an original scale of 1:700,000. The date of the map is significant as it is contemporary with the first partition of Poland in August 1772. One-third of the original state was annexed by Prussia, Austria, and Russia; subsequent partitions in 1793 and 1794 would see the elimination of Poland as an independent country.

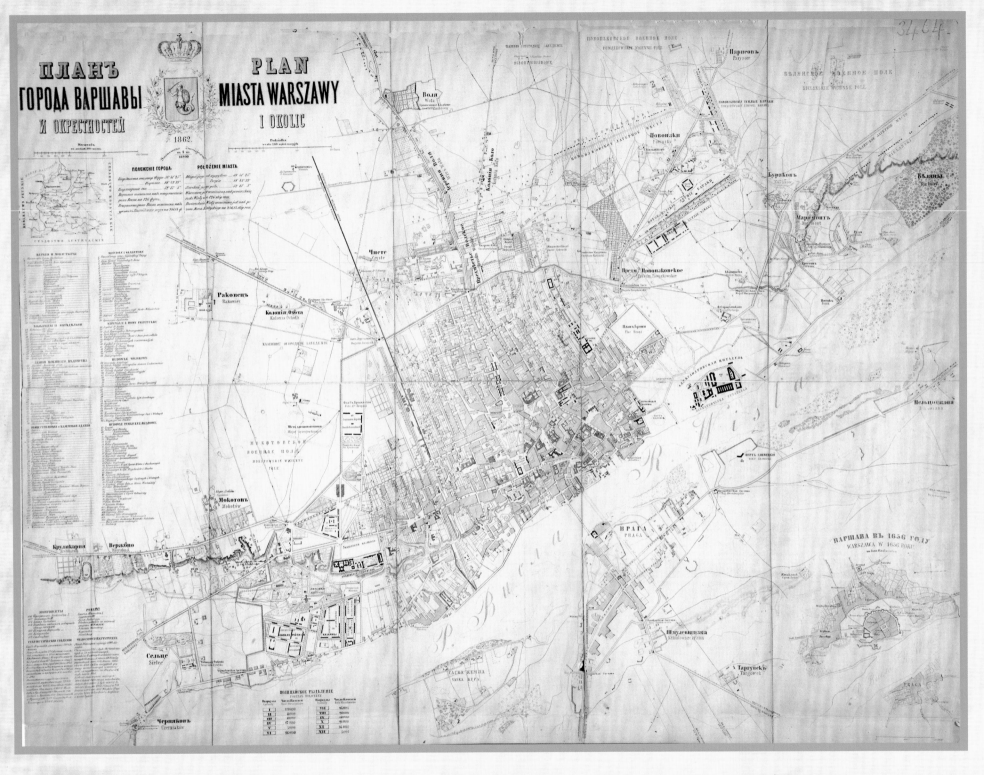

LEFT: This map, with its legend in both Russian and Polish, was produced to an original scale of 1:16,800 and records the city as it existed in the middle of the 19th century. The map is aligned with west toward the top of the page. At this date Warsaw was under Russian rule, although nominally remained an independent state. The Russian presence can be seen by the recently completed citadel (Alexadryjska Cytadella); this had been built in 1832 following an attempted insurrection against Russian control two years earlier. A further insurrection in January 1863 again emphasized how unpopular Russian rule was. The map shows how the city had grown during the first half of the 19th century, as well as the arrival of the railways. The first railway to serve the city, forming part of a line toward Vienna, opened in 1845.

WASHINGTON

UNITED STATES

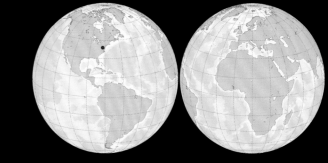

The federal capital of the United States of America, Washington DC (District of Columbia) did not exist until the late 18th century, although there was an earlier settlement—Georgetown—slightly to the northwest, which had been founded in 1751.

After the War of Independence, the US had no fixed capital until New York was selected in 1789, which was supplanted by Philadelphia, but in the same year the Congress passed the Residence Act, which empowered George Washington to select a site for a federal capital. He chose an area on the Potomac River close to Mount Vernon (his country house), and selected Pierre-Charles L'Enfant to produce designs for the new city. By 1800, both Congress and the President were able to occupy the Capitol and White House respectively, although L'Enfant had himself been dismissed in 1792 for insubordination.

It was not until the second half of the 19th century and the early years of the 20th that Washington, as we know it today, was more fully completed. In 1871 the District of Columbia Organic Act created a single municipality incorporating the districts of Georgetown, Washington County, and the City of Washington. In the late 19th century structures such as the Washington Monument were completed, whilst the architect Adolf Cuss, an émigré from Germany, designed the National Museum and the Agriculture Department, as well as some other 80 buildings in the city.

In 1900 Congress established the Senate Park Improvement Commission of the District of Columbia—better known as the MacMillan Commission—whose task it was to create a plan, produced the following year, for the redevelopment and renewal of the city. The result of this work was the elimination of slum housing and the construction of further monuments, such as that to Abraham Lincoln, completed in 1922.

Today Washington D.C. has an area of some 68.3 square miles and a resident population of almost 600,000; constitutionally, the United States Congress has supreme control over the district, although on a day-to-day basis it is run by a locally elected mayor. Although its residents can vote in federal elections, the district does not have a senator and has only one non-voting Congressional delegate.

BELOW: This 2005 view of Washington D.C. was taken by Landsat 7. Two of the subsequent maps extend beyond the right (eastern) edge of the satellite image.

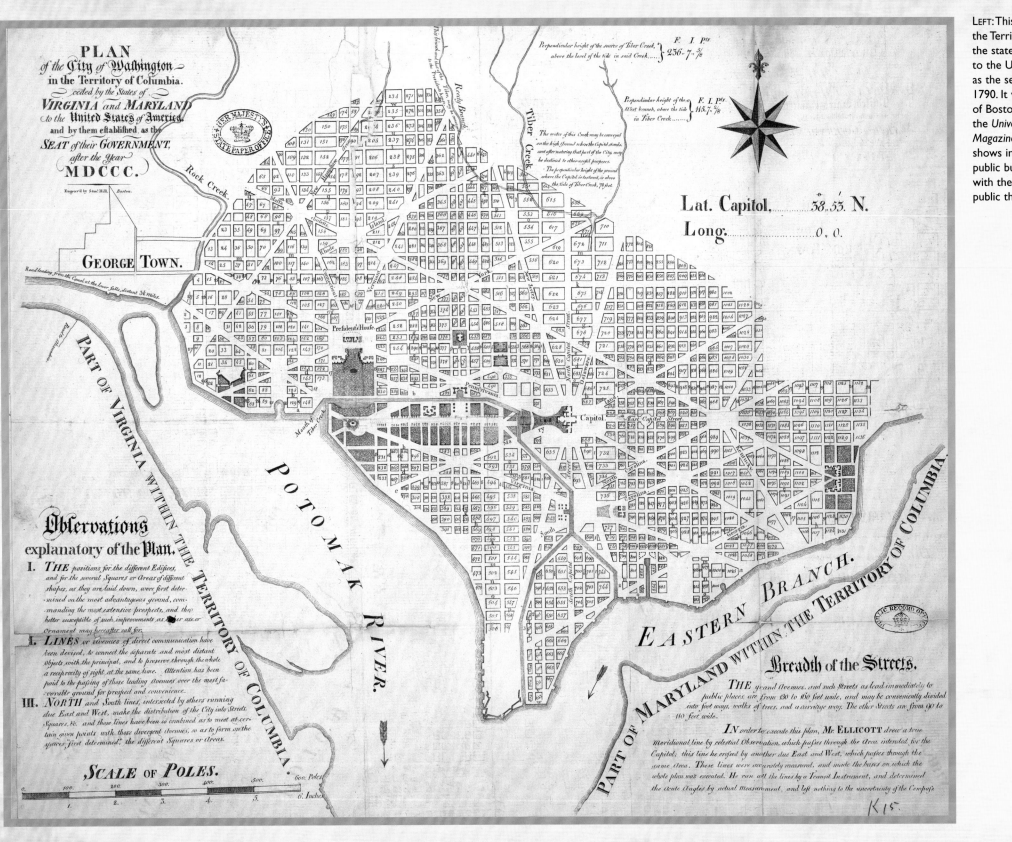

PLAN
of the City of Washington
in the Territory of Columbia.
ceded by the States of
VIRGINIA and MARYLAND
to the United States of America.
and by them established, as the
SEAT of their GOVERNMENT,
after the Year
MDCCC.

Engrav'd by Sam.l Hill, Boston.

GEORGE TOWN.

Observations
explanatory of the Plan.

I. THE positions for the different Edifices,
and for the several Squares or Areas of different
shapes, as they are laid down, were first determined on the most advantageous ground, com-
manding the most extensive prospects, and thee
better susceptible of such improvements as either use or
Ornament may hereafter call for.

II. LINES or avenues of direct communication have
been devised, to connect the separate and most distant
objects with the principal, and to preserve through the whole
a reciprocity of sight at the same time. Attention has been
paid to the passing of those leading Avenues over the most fa-
vorable ground for prospect and convenience.

III. NORTH and South lines, intersected by others running
due East and West, make the distribution of the City into Streets,
Squares, &c. and those lines have been so combined as to meet at certain given points with those divergent Avenues, so as to form on the
spaces first determined, the different Squares or Areas.

SCALE of POLES.

Breadth of the Streets.

THE grand Avenues, and such Streets as lead immediately to
public places, are from 130 to 160 feet wide, and may be conveniently divided
into foot ways, walks of trees, and a carriage way. The other Streets are from 90 to
110 feet wide.

IN order to execute this plan, Mr. ELLICOTT drew a true
Meridional line by celestial Observation, which passes through the Area, intended for the
Capitol; this line he crossed by another due East and West, which passes through the
same Area. These lines were accurately measured, and made the bases on which the
whole plan was executed. He ran all the lines by a Transit Instrument, and determined
the Acute Angles by actual Measurement, and left nothing to the uncertainty of the Compass.

Lat. Capitol,..............38.53. N.
Long.........................0, 0.

POTOMAK RIVER.

PART OF VIRGINIA WITHIN THE TERRITORY OF COLUMBIA.

EASTERN BRANCH.

PART OF MARYLAND WITHIN THE TERRITORY OF COLUMBIA.

LEFT: This is a plan of Washington in the Territory of Columbia, ceded by the states of Virginia and Maryland to the US and established by them as the seat of their government after 1790. It was engraved by Samuel Hill of Boston and appeared as part of the *Universal Asylum and Columbia Magazine* for March 1792. The map shows in detail the arrangement of public buildings and streets, along with the dimensions of the major public thoroughfares.

RIGHT: This is a map showing the property of the US in the vicinity of the Capitol, colored red. It was drawn by B. H. Latrobe, one of the surveyors of the city of Washington, and dated December 3, 1815. The area covered is bounded by 2nd Street East, D Street South, 6th Street West, and D Street North, and was drawn to a scale of about 1:2,400. The map is oriented with north to the left. At the center is the Capitol Building; the first building on the site was built between 1793 and 1812 by William Thornton, but the Senate was destroyed by the British in 1814. Today's building is largely the result of reconstruction work following this destruction; the familiar dome, based on St Peter's in Rome, was added between 1851 and 1865, along with the side wings. The main façade was completed between 1858 and 1862. Heading from the Capitol toward the White House are Pennsylvania Avenue and Maryland Avenue, separated by the National Mall.

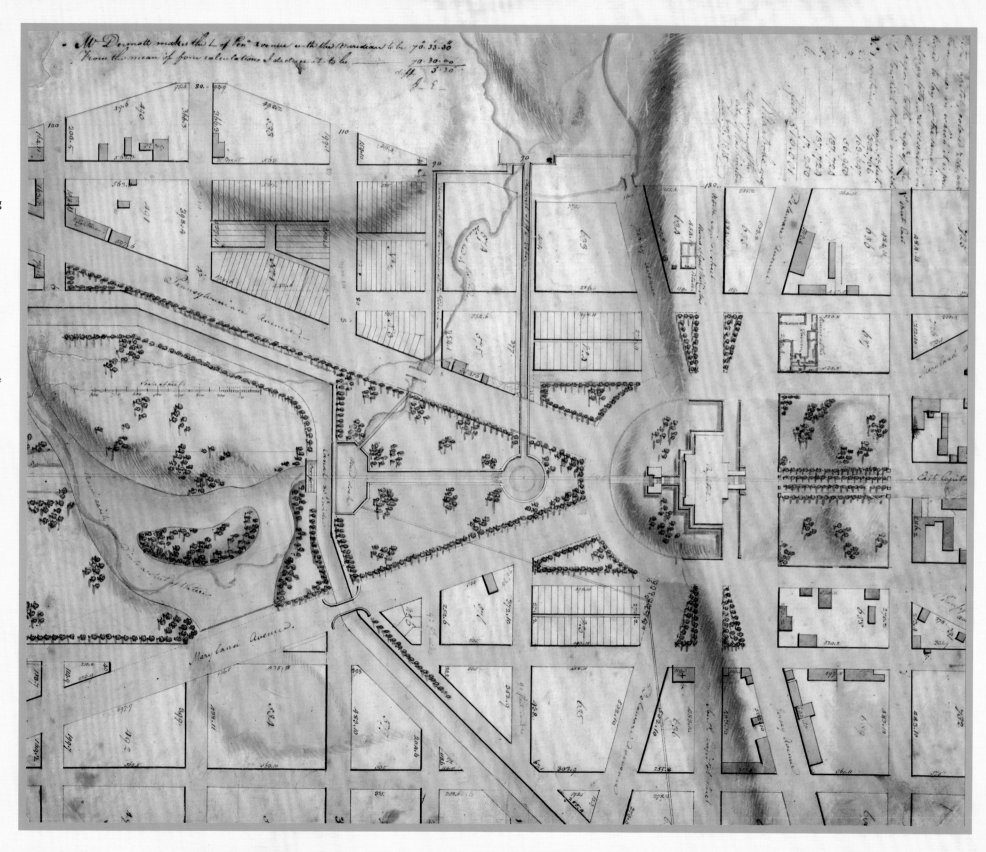

LEFT: "Panoramic view of Washington City: from the new dome of the Capitol, looking east/ drawn from nature and print. in colors by E. Sachse & Co." Published in 1857 it shows a very different city to that after the Civil War. The decade after the end of the war and the arrival of large numbers of former slaves saw the rapid enlargement of the city in fulfilment of L'Enfant's original plan.

ABOVE: This map records Washington—the Mall and vicinity—with the public buildings indicated in red. It was prepared by the Public Buildings Commission under the direction of Colonel W. W. Harts and Colonel C. S. Ridley, with James G. Langdon, city-planning designer, and drawn by K. Hilding Beij. It was produced to a scale of 1:4,800.

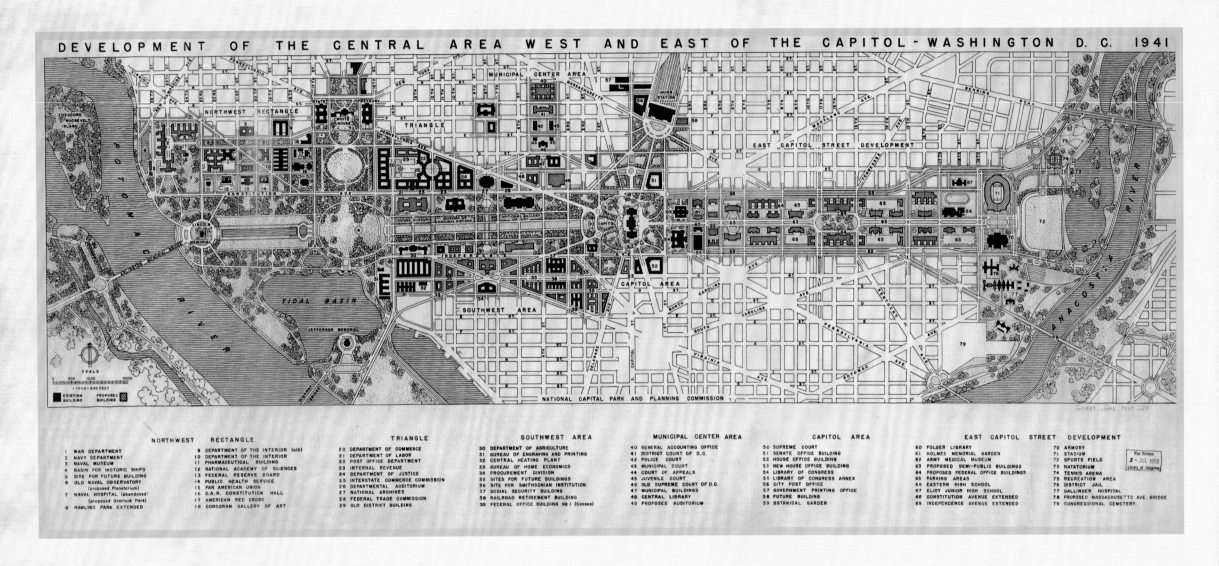

DEVELOPMENT OF THE CENTRAL AREA WEST AND EAST OF THE CAPITOL - WASHINGTON D. C. 1941

NATIONAL CAPITAL PARK AND PLANNING COMMISSION

NORTHWEST RECTANGLE		TRIANGLE	SOUTHWEST AREA	MUNICIPAL CENTER AREA	CAPITOL AREA	EAST CAPITOL STREET DEVELOPMENT
1 WAR DEPARTMENT	9 DEPARTMENT OF THE INTERIOR (old)	20 DEPARTMENT OF COMMERCE	30 DEPARTMENT OF AGRICULTURE	40 GENERAL ACCOUNTING OFFICE	50 SUPREME COURT	70 ARMORY
2 NAVY DEPARTMENT	10 DEPARTMENT OF THE INTERIOR	21 DEPARTMENT OF LABOR	31 BUREAU OF ENGRAVING AND PRINTING	41 DISTRICT COURT OF D.C.	51 SENATE OFFICE BUILDING	71 STADIUM
3 NAVAL MUSEUM	11 PHARMACEUTICAL BUILDING	22 POST OFFICE DEPARTMENT	32 CENTRAL HEATING PLANT	42 POLICE COURT	52 HOUSE OFFICE BUILDING	72 SPORTS FIELD
4 BASIN FOR HISTORIC SHIPS	12 NATIONAL ACADEMY OF SCIENCES	23 INTERNAL REVENUE	33 BUREAU OF HOME ECONOMICS	43 MUNICIPAL COURT	53 NEW HOUSE OFFICE BUILDING	73 NATATORIUM
5 SITE FOR FUTURE BUILDING	13 FEDERAL RESERVE BOARD	24 DEPARTMENT OF JUSTICE	34 PROCUREMENT DIVISION	44 COURT OF APPEALS	54 LIBRARY OF CONGRESS	74 TENNIS ARENA
6 OLD NAVAL OBSERVATORY	14 PUBLIC HEALTH SERVICE	25 INTERSTATE COMMERCE COMMISSION	35 SITES FOR FUTURE BUILDINGS	45 JUVENILE COURT	55 LIBRARY OF CONGRESS ANNEX	75 RECREATION AREA
(proposed Planetarium)	15 PAN AMERICAN UNION	26 DEPARTMENTAL AUDITORIUM	36 SITE FOR SMITHSONIAN INSTITUTION	46 OLD SUPREME COURT OF D.C.	56 CITY POST OFFICE	76 DISTRICT JAIL
7 NAVAL HOSPITAL (abandoned)	16 D.A.R. CONSTITUTION HALL	27 NATIONAL ARCHIVES	37 SOCIAL SECURITY BUILDING	47 MUNICIPAL BUILDINGS	57 GOVERNMENT PRINTING OFFICE	77 GALLINGER HOSPITAL
(proposed Overlook Park)	17 AMERICAN RED CROSS	28 FEDERAL TRADE COMMISSION	38 RAILROAD RETIREMENT BUILDING	48 CENTRAL LIBRARY	58 FUTURE BUILDING	78 PROPOSED MASSACHUSETTS AVE. BRIDGE
8 RAWLINS PARK EXTENDED	18 CORCORAN GALLERY OF ART	29 OLD DISTRICT BUILDING	39 FEDERAL OFFICE BUILDING No 1 (Census)	49 PROPOSED AUDITORIUM	59 BOTANICAL GARDEN	79 CONGRESSIONAL CEMETERY
					60 FOLGER LIBRARY	
					61 HOLMES MEMORIAL GARDEN	
					62 ARMY MEDICAL MUSEUM	
					63 PROPOSED SEMI-PUBLIC BUILDINGS	
					64 PROPOSED FEDERAL OFFICE BUILDINGS	
					65 PARKING AREAS	
					66 EASTERN HIGH SCHOOL	
					67 ELIOT JUNIOR HIGH SCHOOL	
					68 CONSTITUTION AVENUE EXTENDED	
					69 INDEPENDENCE AVENUE EXTENDED	

ABOVE: Produced by the National Capital Park and Planning Commission in September 1941, this map, drawn to a scale of 1 inch to 800 feet, records the development of the city's central area west and east of the Capitol.

YORK

UNITED KINGDOM

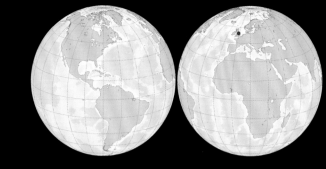

York lies in the Vale of York at the confluence of the rivers Ouse and Foss. The name York comes from the Viking name Jorvik (horse bay), but was known as Eoforwic (wild boar town) to the Anglo-Saxons and Eboracum to the Romans. The latter is derived from a Celtic phrase meaning "the place of the Yew Trees."

Archaeological evidence suggests that the first human occupation occurred some 10,000 years ago during the Mesolithic age. However, the later city was founded in 71A.D. following the Roman invasion of Britain, and it became England's largest Roman military base.

In 410 the Romans withdrew from Britain, leaving the province open to invasion from northern Germany and southern Scandinavia. The arrival of the Anglo-Saxons saw York ultimately become capital of the kingdom of Northumbria and it was here that the conversion of the Northumbrian Anglo-Saxons to Christianity began with the baptising of King Edwin in the early 7th century.

In the 9th century a new threat from the east came in the shape of the Vikings and they captured York in 866. From the middle of the following decade Jorvik became the capital of a Viking kingdom that dominated much of eastern England. Viking control of York was to last almost two centuries, until the resurgent Anglo-Saxons defeated the last Viking King, Eric Bloodaxe, in 954.

Following his successful invasion William of Normandy was faced by two rebellions in the north; this resulted in the "Harrying of the North," a series of military campaigns in 1069–70 that subjugated the northern counties. To defend the city and its environs, the Normans constructed two castles and restored the city's walls. s

During the Middle Ages York experienced considerable prosperity, attested to by the number of churches built within the city walls and the commercial buildings constructed at this time. The Minster is the largest medieval Gothic cathedral in northern Europe and the Council of the North, the administrative body that controlled northern England, was based in the city from 1537 until it was dissolved in 1641.

During the English Civil War York supported King Charles I and was besieged and captured by the Parliamentarian forces under Lord Fairfax in 1644. In 1660, following the restoration of the monarchy, York was the third most important city in England. Its relative prominence declined with the rise of the major industrial centers following the Industrial Revolution, but it remained an important commercial and transport hub—a role that it continues to play in the 21st century.

BELOW: North is at the top of this image of York and its surrounding area. The River Ouse is seen running through the city from upper left to bottom. Forested areas are dark green, agricultural fields are lighter shades of green and brown, urban areas are grey and water is black. Image created using NaturalVue data obtained from Landsat 7.

RIGHT: Sited on the low-lying land formed by the confluence of the rivers Foss and Ouse, York was an ideal defensive point and its role as a strategic and administrative center developed from the earliest years of the Roman occupation of Britain. This map records the city shortly after the Reformation and shows York Minster, the largest Gothic church in northern Europe, along with the city walls and Cliffords Tower, one of the two motte and bailey castles built to defend the city shortly after the Norman Conquest of England in 1066.

RIGHT: This plan of the city of York and its suburbs, with various buildings, field, and street names, was drawn to a scale of 1 inch to about 300 feet. It was published by John Rocque of Charing Cross, London, in 1750. In the top right-hand corner of the map is an inset showing the Roman roads in the county of Yorkshire known at the time. Also illustrated are a number of the city's most notable buildings. The prison buildings were built on part of the original castle and were designed for debtors; today they house the city's Castle Museum. The City House— now known as the Mansion House—was built between 1725 and 1727. The Assembly Rooms were designed in 1730 by the third Earl of Burlington; the façade that survives is, however, the result of a redesign in the early 19th century.

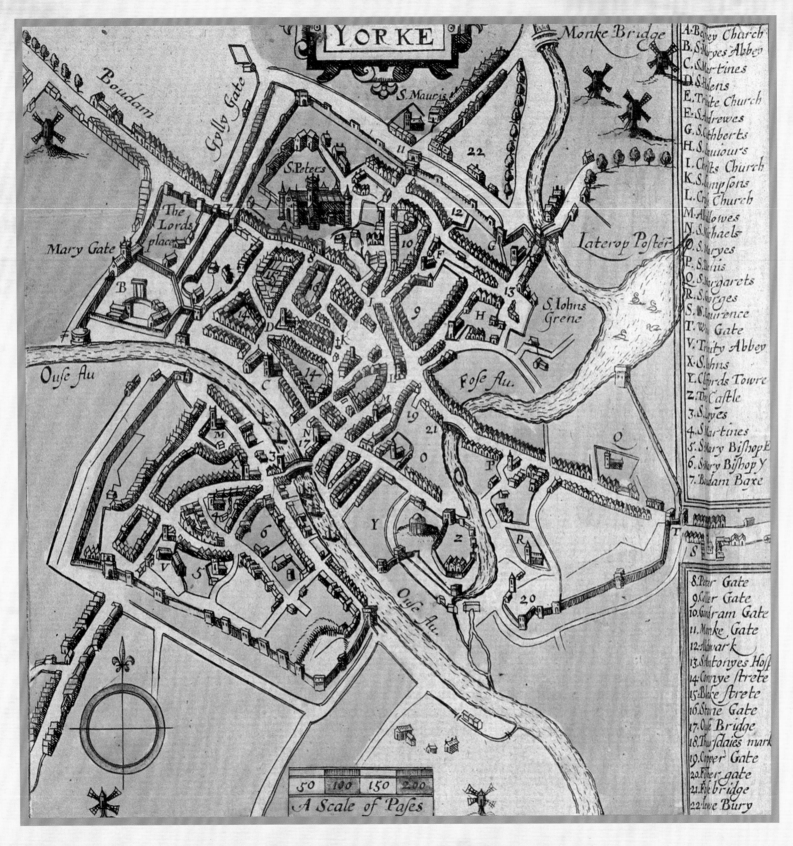

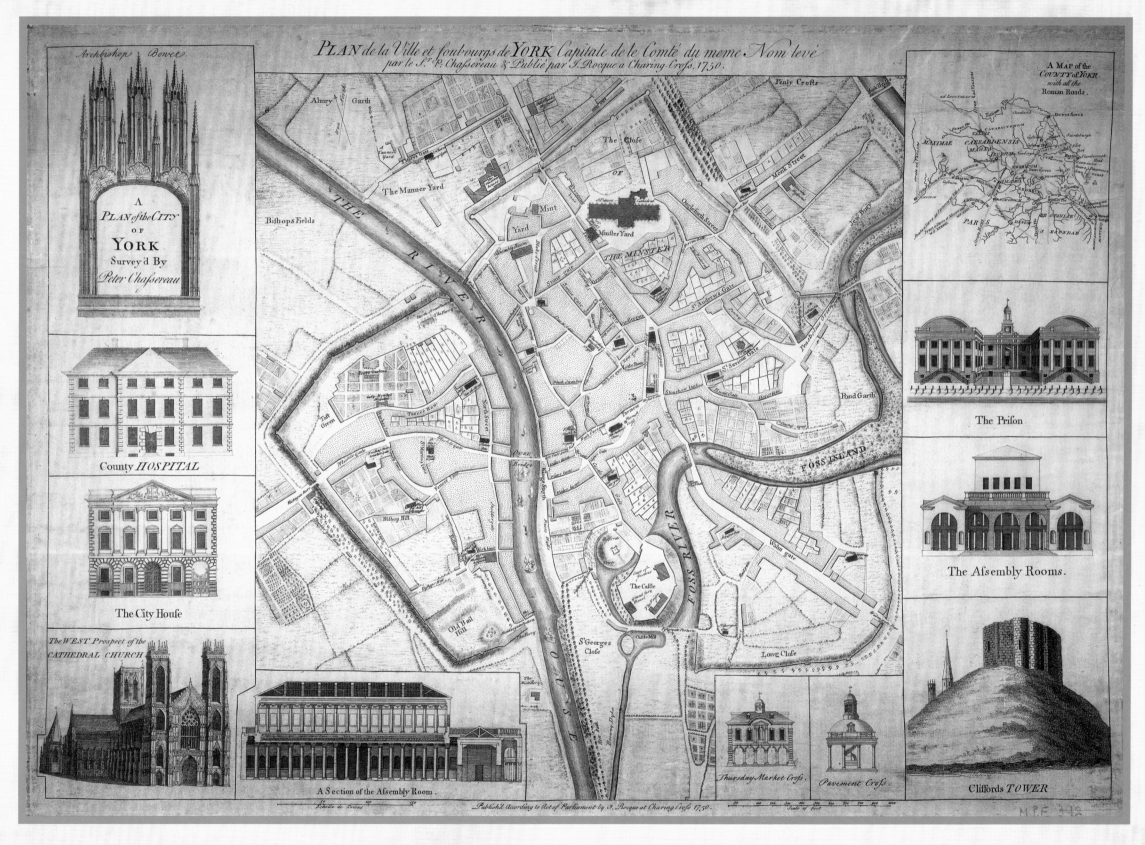

PLAN de la Ville et fauxbourgs de YORK Capitale de le Comté du meme Nom levé
par le Sr. P. Chassereau & Publié par I. Rocque a Charing-Cross, 1750.

Archbishop Bowet

A PLAN of the CITY OF YORK Survey'd By Peter Chassereau

County HOSPITAL

The City House

The WEST Prospect of the CATHEDRAL CHURCH

A Section of the Assembly Room.

A MAP of the COUNTY of YORK with all the Roman Roads.

The Prison

The Assembly Rooms.

Thursday Market Cross.

Pavement Cross.

Cliffords TOWER

Publish'd According to Act of Parliament by J. Rocque at Charing Cross 1750.

CREDITS

Thanks to Jo St. Mart who researched all the satellite views and to Ed Whitley of the Bridgeman Archive.

1   NASA
2–3 Private Collection/The Stapleton Collection/The Bridgeman Art Library (Stapleton/Bridgman)
4–5 National Archives, Kew WO 78-1078 (74)
7   Stapleton/Bridgeman
8L   Compendium Collection
8R   Stapleton Collection/Corbis AABR002091
10   NASA via Jo St. Mart
11   Stapleton/Bridgeman
12   National Archives, Kew MPH 1/459 (2)
13   National Archives, Kew MPH 1/543
14   National Archives, Kew FO 925/2946 (1)
15   NASA via Jo St. Mart
16   Stapleton/Bridgeman
17   Gemeente-Archief, Amsterdam, The Netherlands/Giraudon/The Bridgeman Art Library
18   National Archives, Kew ZMAP 1/1
19   Library of Congress (Library of Congress) hl000003
20   NASA/Science Photo Library
21   Stapleton/Bridgeman
22   The British Library
23   National Archives, Kew MPH 177
24   Private Collection/The Bridgeman Art Library
25   National Archives, Kew MPI 328 (14)
26   National Archives, Kew FO 925/4149 (7)
27   Earth Satellite Corporation/Science Photo Library
28   UCL Art Collections, University College London, UK /The Bridgeman Art Library
29   Stapleton/Bridgeman
30   UCL Art Collections, University College London, UK /The Bridgeman Art Library
31   UCL/NASA via Jo St. Mart
32   Stapleton/Bridgeman
33   National Archives, Kew MR 1/552 (2)
34   National Archives, Kew MR 1/552 (6)
35   National Archives, Kew WO 78/1017 (20)
36   Earth Satellite Corporation/Science Photo Library
37   Stapleton/Bridgeman
38   UCL/NASA via Jo St. Mart
39   The British Library
40   UCL/NASA via Jo St. Mart
41   Library of Congress ar302100
42L National Archives, Kew CO700 Massachusetts 14
42R and 43L Library of Congress ct002294

43R Library of Congress ct002280
44   Library of Congress pm002750
45   ESA/via Jo St. Mart
46   Stapleton/Bridgeman
47   National Archives, Kew MPHH 1/27 (4)
48   National Archives, Kew WO 78/5792 (XXI)
49   National Archives, Kew FO 925/4149 (6)
50   NASA via Jo St. Mart
51   Stapleton/Bridgeman
52   National Archives, Kew FO 9225/2946 (3)
53   UCL/NASA via Jo St. Mart
54   Stapleton/Bridgeman
55   National Archives, Kew MPF 1/14
56   National Archives, Kew MPH 1/138 (19)
57   National Archives, Kew MPI 1/215
58   NASA via Jo St. Mart
59   Library of Congress pm001460
60   Library of Congress pm001500
61   Library of Congress pm001523
62   Library of Congress pm001521
63   CNES, 1994 Distribution Spot Image/Science Photo Library
64   National Archives, Kew FO 925/4149 (9)
65   ESA/via Jo St. Mart
66   Bibliotheque Nationale, Paris, France/Giraudon/The Bridgeman Art Library
67   National Archives, Kew MPH 1/617 (51)
68   National Archives, Kew MPH 167
69   Planetobserver/Science Photo Library
70   Stapleton/Bridgeman
71   Earth Satellite Corporation/Science Photo Library
72   Stapleton/Bridgeman
73   National Archives, Kew MFQ 212 (2)
74   ESA/via Jo St. Mart
75   Stapleton/Bridgeman
76   Private Collection /The Bridgeman Art Library
77   National Archives, Kew MPH 202 (5)
78   National Archives, Kew MPD 148 (28)
79   NRSC Ltd/Science Photo Library
80   Stapleton/Bridgeman
81   Stapleton/Bridgeman
82   The British Library
83   Royal Geographical Society, London, UK /The Bridgeman Art Library
84   Earth Satellite Corporation/Science Photo Library
85   Stapleton/Bridgeman
86   The British Library
87   National Archives, Kew WO 78/5781
88   NASA/via Jo St. Mart
89   Stapleton/Bridgeman
90   National Archives, Kew FO 925/4149 (19)

91   Planetobserver/Science Photo Library
92   Stapleton/Bridgeman
93   National Archives, Kew MPHH 26
94   National Archives, Kew FO 925/4149 (11)
95   Earth Satellite Corporation/Science Photo Library
96   Stapleton/Bridgeman
97   The British Library
98   National Archives, Kew FO 925/4149 (20)
99   NASA/via Jo St. Mart
100 Stapleton/Bridgeman
101 National Archives, Kew FO 925/3753
102 National Archives, Kew FO 925/4149 (13)
103 NASA/via Jo St. Mart
104 Archivo Iconografico, SA/Corbis
105 National Archives, Kew FO 925/3254 (Pt 2 [39])
106 National Archives, Kew FO 925/4149 (28)
107 National Archives, Kew FO 925/41186
108 NASA/via Jo St. Mart
109 Roger Viollet Collection/Getty Images
110 National Archives, Kew MPK 1/39
111 National Archives, Kew FO 925/41043
112 National Archives, Kew CO 537/3881
113 Earth Satellite Corporation/Science Photo Library
114 Stapleton/Bridgeman
115 Earth Satellite Corporation/Science Photo Library
116 National Archives, Kew MPF 1/118
117 Bibliotheque Nationale, Paris, France/Lauros/Giraudon/The Bridgeman Art Library
118 National Archives, Kew MPH 1/138 (21)
119 National Archives, Kew WO 78/1078 (74)
120 NASA/via Jo St. Mart
121 Stapleton/Bridgeman
122 National Archives, Kew SP112/101
123 National Archives, Kew FO 925/3965
124 NASA/via Jo St. Mart
125 Glasgow University Library, Scotland /The Bridgeman Art Library
126 National Archives, Kew ZMAP 4/18
127 National Archives, Kew MR 1/694
128 National Archives, Kew ZLIB 19/125
129 Library of Congress ct000585
130 National Archives, Kew Royal Atlas of England and Wales Plate 65
131 National Archives, Kew MF 1/1 (11)
132 NASA/via Jo St. Mart
133 Library of Congress ct001800
134 Library of Congress ct001804
135 Planetobserver/Science Photo Library
136 Stapleton/Bridgeman
137 National Archives, Kew FO 925/4149 (2)
138 ESA/via Jo St. Mart
139 UCL Art Collections, University College London, UK /The Bridgeman Art Library
140 National Archives, Kew FO 925/3918
141 National Archives, Kew FO 925/3982
142 Earth Satellite Corporation/Science Photo Library

143 Stapleton/Bridgeman
144 Planetobserver/Science Photo Library
145 Stapleton/Bridgeman
146 National Archives, Kew FO 925/3853
147 National Archives, Kew FO 925/4149
148 National Archives, Kew W078/1078 (88)
149 Earth Satellite Corporation/Science Photo Library
150 Stapleton/Bridgeman
151 National Archives, Kew MPH 1/138 (2)
152 National Archives, Kew MPHH 6 (17)
153 Geoeye/Science Photo Library
154 Stapleton/Bridgeman
155 Library of Congress ct000338
156 Library of Congress ct000599
157 Library of Congress ct000598
158 Planetobserver/Science Photo Library
159 Stapleton/Bridgeman
160 National Archives, Kew FO 925/4149 (21)
161 both NASA/via Jo St. Mart
162 National Archives, Kew CO700 Canada 17
163 National Archives, Kew CO700 Canada 181
164 UCL/ESA/via Jo St. Mart
165 Stapleton/Bridgeman
166 Library of Congress hl000004
167 National Archives, Kew MPH 389
168 National Archives, Kew MPK 1/30
169 UCL/ESA/via Jo St. Mart
170 Stapleton/Bridgeman
171 Private Collection/Ken Welsh/The Bridgeman Art Library
172 National Archives, Kew FO 925/4113 (19)
173 National Archives, Kew FO 925/4149 (22)
174 NASA
175 Library of Congress ct000050
176 The British Library
177 National Archives, Kew MPI 1/168
178 National Archives, Kew MPH 1/225 New York
179 Library of Congress ct001389
180–181 Library of Congress ct000812
182–183 Library of Congress wd000155
184 Library of Congress ct001972
185 Library of Congress ct000245
186 Library of Congress pm005981
187 ESA, Eurimage/Science Photo Library
188 Stapleton/Bridgeman
189 National Archives, Kew FO 925/3643
190 National Archives, Kew FO 925/4149 (27)
191 NASA
192 Archivo Iconografico, SA/Corbis
193 Library of Congress ct000646
194 Library of Congress ct001516
195 National Archives, Kew FO 925/4113
196 National Archives, Kew FO 925/4149 (1)
197 UCL/NASA/via Jo St. Mart
198 Library of Congress ct001815
199 National Archives, Kew CO700 Pennsylvania 4
200 Library of Congress ct001369
201 UCL/NASA/via Jo St. Mart

202 Stapleton/Bridgeman
203 National Archives, Kew MPF 1/347
204 UCL/NASA/via Jo St. Mart
205 Library of Congress ct001307
206 Library of Congress pm010733
207 National Archives, Kew CO700 Canada 16
208 Library of Congress ar061000
209 UCL/NASA/via Jo St. Mart; inset NASA/via Jo St. Mart
210 Library of Congress ct000051
211 Library of Congress ct000633
212 Library of Congress br000055
213 UCL/NASA/via Jo St. Mart
214 Stapleton/Bridgeman
215 National Archives, Kew MPH 668 (6)
216 National Archives, Kew MPH 668 (11)
217 National Archives, Kew FO 925/4149 (23)
218 NASA/via Jo St. Mart
219 Library of Congress ct000187
220 Library of Congress ct001848
221 UCL/NASA/via Jo St. Mart
222 National Archives, Kew MPH1/1/25
223 National Archives, Kew MPH 1/1/9
224 National Archives, Kew MPH222
225 UCL/NASA/via Jo St. Mart
226–227 Library of Congress ct001482
228 Library of Congress ct002119
229 NASA/via Jo St. Mart
230 Stapleton/Bridgeman
231 Library of Congress ct001653
232 National Archives, Kew FO 925/4149 (25)
233 Earth Satellite Corporation/Science Photo Library
234 The British Library
235 National Archives, Kew FO 925/4149
236 Maps.com
237 National Archives, Kew FO925/3254 (pt 2; [37])
238 Stapleton/Bridgeman
239 National Archives, Kew MPF296
240 National Archives, Kew FO 925/4149 (17)
241 maps.com
242 Stapleton/Bridgeman
243 National Archives, Kew FO 925/3486 (7)
244 National Archives, Kew FO 925/3464
245 UCL/NASA/via Jo St. Mart
246 National Archives, Kew MPK 1/15 Washington DC
247 Library of Congress ct001112
248 Library of Congress pm104798
249 Library of Congress ct000616
250 Library of Congress ct001907
251 Earth Satellite Corporation/Science Photo Library
252 Stapleton/Bridgeman
253 National Archives, Kew MPE 1/392

INDEX